The Zondervan
DICTIONARY
of
CHRISTIAN
LITERACY

Key Concepts of the Faith

Dr. Larry Richards

Lamplighter Books
Grand Rapids, Michigan
Zondervan Publishing House

The Zondervan Dictionary of Christian Literacy
Copyright © 1987 by Larry Richards
All rights reserved

Previously published as *The Dictionary of Basic Bible Truths*

Lamplighter Books are published by the Zondervan Publishing House
1415 Lake Drive, S.E.
Grand Rapids, Michigan 49506

Richards, Larry, 1931 –
   [The Dictionary of basic Bible truths]
   The Zondervan dictionary of Christian literacy / Larry Richards.
      p.   cm.
   Originally published under title: The Dictionary of basic Bible
truths.
   ISBN 0-310-51981-0
   1. Theology — Dictionaries. 2. Bible — Dictionaries. I. Title
BR95.R46   1990
230'.03 – dc20   89 – 28923
                                                                      CIP

Edited by Lori J. Walburg, John Sloan

Printed in the United States of America

90   91   92   93 / AM / 6   5   4   3   2

Preface

This book has a simple format.

PART I—Credo

PART II—The Vocabulary of Faith

Index

This book also has a simple purpose. It is intended to help you better understand your own faith in the light of what untold generations of Christians have believed.

You and I want to understand our faith. Our desire to understand comes not because we want an intellectual mastery of religion. Rather, our goal is to know God better, to love him, and to live our lives to please him. The better we understand what the Bible teaches about God, about human beings, and about how we are to live out our lives on earth, the better we'll be able to make the choices that will bring us to this goal.

At first glance, we might think that Christians have believed a number of confusing and contradictory things. Christian groups differ in their emphases and their doctrines. History has shown even greater variations. But the more we look at the differences, the more we realize that there is a common core of shared conviction. Christian faith through the ages has been one faith. Despite the rich and varied emphases that have developed as human beings have struggled to encompass the wonder of God and fit him into our systems, that common core of shared conviction has remained. Out of our common understanding of God, you and I share a transforming vision of the nature and meaning of the universe we inhabit.

I begin this book by simply affirming those wonderful truths that Christians of all the ages hold in common. In the second and major part of the book, a series of alphabetical entries examines specific aspects of Christian faith. Where there are differences in perspective and understanding, I've tried to present these fairly, emphasizing the harmony of belief rather than the differences. And I've tried to point to the basic biblical passages that will let you study and come to your own conclusions about what God has revealed. Perhaps most importantly, I've tried to discuss these basic tenets of our faith in a way that will enrich your personal relationship to God. The more we learn of the Lord, the more our wonder grows and the more we are moved to praise. If you explore this book and find your heart moved to praise and your life shaped toward love, my purpose and the purpose of the publishers will have been achieved.

PART I

Credo

A creed is a confession or affirmation of faith. It is a statement, "This I believe."

The first part of this book is a summary statement affirming the basic convictions shared by Christians throughout the ages. It does not seek to argue or to explain; it simply affirms.

As you read it, confidently and joyfully affirm with me, "This I believe."

We believe in God

We believe God is the creative source of our universe. The material universe is no accident. The vast, empty reaches of space scattered with myriads of stars and the rich environment of planet earth is all the handiwork of the being we call "God." Everything that exists testifies to the complex mind and majestic power of the Creator. His inventiveness and infinite attention to detail are revealed in the design of living creatures, from the tiniest cell to the most complex systems that enable human beings to see, taste, smell, think, feel, and choose. No random mating of lifeless atoms in some ancient sea can adequately account for life as we know it in all its varied forms. No unexplained explosion billions of years ago can account for the order exhibited in the heavens or the friendly features of this planet. No, in all that is, we see the hand of God. And in reasoned faith, we understand with all God's people that "the universe was formed at God's command, so that what is seen was not made out of what was visible" (Heb. 11:3).

We believe God is a loving, personal being. God is a person, not some impersonal force. His personhood shines through his creation and is fully unveiled in Scripture. It is also reflected in our own personal attributes. We reason and we recognize the vast wisdom displayed in all that God has made. We see beauty and we wonder at the one who designed delight for every sense as he shaped this world to be a home for humankind. We love and, caught in wonder, we pause to realize that the one who gave us the capacity to care loves us supremely. Because God is a person, we can have a personal relationship to him on every level of our being. Our deepest yearnings to know and be known, to love and be loved, can be fully satisfied only in a personal relationship to the one who made us like himself. God is a person, and we are destined for endless fellowship with our God.

We believe God is a moral, responsible being. The pain and the ugliness that mar our lives are evidence of human failure, not of divine

7

indifference. Our own sense of justice is but a distorted echo of God's total commitment to all that is good. Because human beings, too, are moral beings, our consciences judge our thoughts and actions, and we condemn the wrong actions of others. But one greater than the human conscience is judge of the universe. God's judgments can be traced in the rise and fall of empires and in the consequences of our individual moral choices. However, the full revelation of God's moral nature awaits the judgment to come at history's end. Until then, judgment withheld demonstrates the richness of God's kindness, tolerance, and patience as he continues to hold open to all mankind the door of repentance and moral reform.

We believe God is active in our world. We affirm a hidden God, not directly accessible to the senses. But though God remains hidden, he has acted in this world of space and time, and God is at work among us today. Evidence of God's involvement is found in history past, culminating in the man, Christ Jesus, who bridged the gap between the invisible and the visible to reveal in human flesh the true nature of deity. And evidence of God's active involvement can be found, too, in life's present moments. His handiwork is recognized by the eyes of faith but is also visible to all human beings who trust themselves to Jesus. They, through his transforming touch, reflect Jesus' own love and compassion for others. We do believe in God. And the God we believe in is powerful, loving, personal, moral, and is at work in our world.

We believe that God has spoken

We believe God has spoken at many times and in many ways. God has spoken wordlessly in heavens that declare his glory, and he has established in human nature mute testimony to his existence. Through the ages nature's silent witness has been supplemented by special gracious acts of self-revelation. God whispered to the ancients in dreams and visions, thundered from cloudshrouded Sinai, uttered calls for holiness through Israel's bold prophets. God confounded disbelief with mighty acts of power, enriched the worship of Israel with symbolic ritual, and patterned life for his people with a law that speaks compellingly of his own concern for the poor, for the oppressed, and for healthy relationships in the community of faith. Ultimately God's self-disclosure culminated in the incarnation of his Son, who is the full and exact representation of his being. In Jesus, God made flesh, God speaks in unmistakable, human terms, inviting us to hear, see, and touch the Word of life. God has spoken at many times and in many ways; the ear of faith knows and acknowledges his voice.

We believe God has spoken in a reliable and relevant written word. The Scriptures, both Old and New Testament, are a unique treasure, filled with words breathed by God through writers he inspired. Reality, which no eye can see, no ear can hear, and no human mind conceive, has been revealed to us in words taught by the Spirit of God. The Bible alone of all books blends, as does the person of Jesus Christ, the human and divine, so that it is rightly called the Word of God. Relying fully on its trustworthy nature, we look to the Bible confidently, submitting to its teaching, rebuke, correction, and training in righteousness. Looking into Scripture, we hear and recognize God's contemporary voice; responding, we grow in our personal relationship to the Lord. We believe with the saints of all the ages that God has spoken to humankind. We recognize his voice, and we joyfully obey his living and his written Word, which speak together in fullest harmony.

We believe in God the Father

We believe in God the Father, who planned the ages. God, though one and indivisible, existing in three distinct persons, is the Father. From eternity past, before the first creative word was spoken, God the Father designed the ages, shaping all that is and will be to display his attributes and to express his love. In the outworking of God's great and multifaceted plan, his sovereignty, holiness, mercy, justice, grace, and every other quality that makes him so worthy of our worship will ultimately be known. All who look in faith to Jesus will experience the glorious fulfillment he has been pleased to plan for us. Because God the Father has brought the whole creation into full submission to his will, history moves inevitably toward his intended end, and human existence is infused with purpose.

We believe in God the Father, who guards the present. God, the Father of our Lord Jesus Christ, is Father to Jesus' people. Assured of the Father's constant love, we come to him freely, sharing every need. We rejoice in Jesus' reminder that we are truly valuable to our heavenly Father, and thus, released from anxiety, we seek first his kingdom and his righteousness, knowing that the Father will provide. Acknowledging God as Father, we take our place as obedient children, fully aware that we are to love our enemies and seek a perfection that mirrors his own.

We believe in God the Father, who guarantees the future. God the Father has committed himself to covenants that establish the shape of the future. His ancient covenants with Israel and the new covenant he has established in Jesus stand as his unbreakable oath. The details of the future God intends, although enriched by the prophets' visions of a dim tomorrow, may not be clear. But the bold outlines of God's plan for time and for eternity continue to provide a sure and certain hope. In God's good time, Jesus will return, hurts will be healed, and the sweet smell of justice and peace will fill the valleys and hover over every hill. Then, in that end which is a beginning, a worn universe will be replaced with one that is vital, holy, fresh, and new. With judgment past, God's people of every age and nation will join in endless celebration of eternal life in the presence of the Lord. We believe in God the Father, who planned the ages, guards the present, and guarantees the future that his covenants with us proclaim.

We believe in Jesus

We believe in Jesus, who existed from the beginning. We believe that God, though one and indivisible, existing in three distinct persons, is Jesus Christ the Son. With God, as God, God from the beginning, himself uncreated, the Son was the active agent in the Creation and even today sustains the existence of all things by the power of his being. All things visible and invisible owe their existence to the Son, and he is the one who is the source of all life. The unique person we meet in Jesus of Nazareth is truly God the Son.

We believe in Jesus, who lived and died on earth as a real human being. Jesus, though truly God, is also fully human. In history's ultimate miracle, God the Holy Spirit joined the human to the divine. And so the virgin Mary gave birth to her son, and in him, God the Son entered time and space to live as one of us. He never surrendered his nature as God but shrouded his splendor in flesh and submitted to the limitations that human nature imposed: So the eternal Son humbled himself. He became obedient to death, even the shameful death of the cross, that through his suffering Jesus might win for his human brothers and sisters a salvation that, apart from him, no one could earn. God the Son was made like us in every way that, stooping a little lower than the angels, he might taste death for every person and so bring us back with him to glory. The unique person we meet in Jesus of Nazareth is in the fullest sense a human being as well as truly God.

We believe in Jesus, who lives today in resurrection. Jesus of Nazareth hung on a criminal's cross, suffered death, and was buried in a rich man's tomb. Yet after three days, in a burst of divine power, the God/Man, Jesus, was raised to life again, his flesh transformed and energized by the Spirit. Jesus, forever liberated from bondage to decay, is seated today at the right hand of God the Father. There he intercedes for us and carries out his role as the living head of the church that is his body. In his resurrected body Jesus will come again. And in his resurrected form Jesus will exist eternally, the source and model of a resurrection that awaits all the saved.

We believe in Jesus, who lives within us. Today the living Jesus takes up residence in those who believe in him. Through a mystical but real union, our personalities are linked with his. As branches draw strength and life from the vine and so are enabled to bear fruit, you and I draw from Jesus. Living close to him, dependent on him, obedient to him, we experience the reality of Jesus' living presence within. Yes, we do believe in Jesus. We acknowledge him as the eternal God. We stand amazed before the cradle of his incarnation, kneel beneath his cross, rejoice at his resurrection, rely on his guidance and intercession, and depend on his living presence within us for strength to live our daily lives.

We believe in the Holy Spirit

We believe in the Holy Spirit, who strengthened Jesus. We believe that God, though one and indivisible, existing in three distinct persons, is the Holy Spirit. The Holy Spirit, eternally existing with the Father and the Son, supported and sustained Jesus in his mission to earth. From the moment of Jesus' conception to the unleashing of resurrection energy, the Spirit ministered to and through Jesus. The Spirit's breath accompanied each miracle and shared each whispered prayer, infusing Jesus' touch and teaching with added power. One with the Father as with the Son, the Spirit served Jesus, even as today the Spirit does not speak of himself but points the believing heart to Christ.

We believe in the Holy Spirit, who energizes us today. The Spirit continues to be active in our world today. He convicts those who do not yet believe, binds to Jesus those who trust in him, and by his presence serves as God's own seal and guarantee of our full redemption. That matchless power exhibited in the resurrection of Jesus flows from the Spirit into the believer, bringing life to mortal bodies and enabling us to live a life that pleases God. The Holy Spirit is the source of the fruit of divine transformation: love, joy, peace, patience, goodness, and all that marks us as Jesus' own. The Holy Spirit is the one who manifests himself in varied gifts that enable us to contribute to the common good, and who, as God, remains unlimited despite our theologies. Yes, we do believe in the Holy Spirit. We see him in all Jesus' words and works, and we are awed to realize that this same Spirit now infuses us.

We believe in a redeemable humanity

We believe humanity was created and loved by God. We believe human beings are unique in creation. Alone among the living creatures that share our planet, humankind has been endowed with the image and likeness of God. Crowned with that glory and honor by God's personal creative act, human beings are also entrusted with dominion over the works of God's hands. But mankind's special place in the Creation, evidenced by God's rich endowment of personhood and powers, is seen most clearly in the constant love God bears for us. Human beings were created for fellowship with God, and history is but the stage on which the Lord's unquenchable love for men and women has been dramatized. Because human beings are special to God, each individual is of ultimate worth and value, to be loved and cherished, to be aided in the fullest possible development of every potential — especially the potential for knowing and loving God.

We believe humanity is trapped in and twisted by sin. By an act of disobedience that took place in space and time, the original people, Adam and Eve, fell. The Fall drained them of innocence and wrenched their very nature so that the imprint of the eternal was distorted. In the Fall mankind's capacity for righteousness and for actual fellowship with God was destroyed. A distorted nature, not original sinlessness, has been passed on to all of Adam's children but one, and so the human family has found itself trapped in and twisted by sin. All our misery, all our failures, all our hateful and criminal acts can be traced directly or indirectly to the sin that now infects the race. All the injustices of society and all the oppression is symptomatic of the same disease institutionalized. Although endowed with a moral sense and still able to do limited good, human beings all fall short of the glory of God and even of the demands of their own consciences. We live with the reality of sin in personal and international relationships. No heartfelt desire or determined act of will can release us from our tragic bondage. Wars and fightings without, like selfish cravings within, bear constant testimony to the reality of the Fall and its tragic consequences. Similarly a sense of inescapable guilt and shame provide compelling evidence that sin has alienated us from God and has made us objects of his necessary wrath.

We believe humanity is redeemed by God's action in Jesus. A sinning humanity is both condemned and loved by God, the object of both his wrath and his mercy. The stern warnings of Scripture tell us that God must and surely will judge. But the dominant theme of God's message to us is this: Because of his great love for us, God, who is rich in mercy, has acted in Jesus to provide redemption and release. God in Jesus slipped into our race to bend his shoulders under the weight of our burdens and to hang lifeless on Calvary's cross, so that his own blood's bright flow might wash away our sins. God's action in Jesus dealt decisively with human sin, providing a basis on which we can be forgiven, offering to all who believe a life of renewed righteousness.

We believe humanity is invited to experience an abundant life of true goodness. With forgiveness God offers human beings an abundant life, rich in all those qualities that bring inner satisfaction even as they overflow in Christlike love to family and neighbor alike. Made alive in Christ, God's restored humanity leaves behind those desires and thoughts that mark the stunting grip of sin. We, his new creation, are renewed by Jesus' touch and reach toward those good works that God has prepared in advance for us to do. Human beings were created to know and love God and to express their relationship to him through caring acts. A dynamic righteousness is the mark of the redeemed, and through that righteousness, which mirrors the beauty of the Lord, God's people can be fulfilled.

We believe humanity will experience ultimate transformation. Every individual human being is destined for endless, conscious, personal existence. Physical death is a transition, not an end. In Christ, God has acted to make it possible for us to experience an ultimate transformation, a resurrection into Jesus' full likeness and full restoration of all that was lost in Adam's fall. Mankind's destiny is to be lifted up above the angels, swept into the most intimate fellowship with God. All who trust in Jesus and accept God's offer of eternal life will know that final transformation. Humanity will be redeemed. We acknowledge human beings as unique in our universe, shaped in God's own image and likeness. We admit that a tragic Fall has warped every person. Yet we live in hope because mankind is redeemed through Jesus. Accepting God's gift of life in Jesus, we stretch out toward the good we are now able to do, and we yearn for the ultimate transformation that we know will come.

We believe in salvation

We believe in a salvation illustrated in God's mighty acts in history. God visited his people as they lay helpless in Egypt. In majestic acts of power God reshaped his people's history, winning their release from bondage and leading them in triumph to the promised land. God stretched out his hand for individuals, too, working awesome wonders as he miraculously intervened in space and time on their behalf. In the signs and wonders God worked in history, we catch a glimpse of the meaning of salvation. God finds us helpless, and moved by love alone, he intervenes. What we could never do, God does, and those who are the recipients of his grace can only acknowledge his work and give him praise.

We believe in a salvation won for us by Jesus' self-sacrifice. History's wonders culminate in Jesus. In Jesus, God's greatest act of intervention for a helpless humanity was accomplished; Jesus' self-sacrificial death met humankind's greatest need. No physical peril can compare to the eternal peril that endangers every human being. All who share in physical life are spiritually dead in trespasses and sins, unwilling and unable to reach out to God. All human beings stand condemned before the bar of God's justice. Yet in Jesus, God stripped off his judicial robes, and taking on our nature, he took the penalty of our sins as well. Dying for us, raising us through his resurrection, Jesus won us a deliverance that discharges us from sin's penalty, frees us from its power, and ultimately will release us from the very presence of evil within. Salvation is found in no one else, for "there is no other name under heaven given to men by which we must be saved" (Acts 4:12).

We believe in a salvation that is experienced in forgiveness. Jesus stands as the focal point of history, the one by whom time itself is reckoned. We look to him as the focal point of our lives, the one by whom we reckon our passage from death to life. And the great invitation stands: Salvation, the free gift of God, is received by faith, and all who put their trust in Jesus are forgiven of all their sins. Thereafter we are at peace with God. The source of our guilt is removed, and God himself is satisfied. Forgiven, we know the meaning of grace and freely enter the presence of the Holy, knowing that in Jesus our welcome is guaranteed.

We believe in a salvation that is expressed in love and justice. We believe in a dynamic salvation. Forgiveness from past sins propels us into a life of active righteousness because God is intent on restoring human beings to his full likeness. The law's stern expression of righteousness is summed up in love, and salvation creates in human hearts a capacity to love the individual, the world, and God. Love must find expression both in simple acts of kindness to the needy neighbor and in commitment to that which is just and best for all of humanity. A zeal for good works that benefit people and bring glory to God is a natural and necessary expression of a salvation wrought by God.

We believe in a salvation to be enjoyed forever in God's presence. That salvation, experienced and expressed here and now, will be enjoyed forever. Long after this universe has been discarded and a new creation, vital and vibrant with holiness, has come, we who believe will experience the joy of our salvation in the presence of our Lord. In Jesus the threat of eternal condemnation is replaced by the promise of perfected life, and we are destined to worship God and enjoy him forever. Yes, we do believe in salvation, for we have a God who acts to aid the helpless. We see his power in history's mighty acts, and we discover his love in the self-sacrifice of Jesus, who through his death won us a salvation so great. That salvation becomes ours through faith, bringing with it forgiveness and a commitment to love and justice. That salvation will ultimately issue in an endless life of joy lived in the very presence of the Lord.

We believe in a redeemed community

We believe in a redeemed community, called to live together in love and in unity. God's people are not called to live alone. Instead God has always placed his people in community. Surrounded by love, we are to live together as family and body, supporting and encouraging each other in good works and growth in godliness. All who acknowledge Jesus are to be welcomed and accepted as brothers or sisters in one holy community. Our differences are of less concern than the fact that as children of one Father, we owe each other the debt of love. The redeemed community, affirming its mystical unity and acting ever in heartfelt love, gives compelling testimony to the reality and the presence of the Lord.

We believe in the redeemed community that celebrates its relationship to God in worship, baptism, and the Lord's Supper. The redeemed community shares not only in the life of its members but also in worship and remembrance. We come together as a people not only to hear God's Word but also to offer him our prayers, our praise, and our worship. In rituals long established, we act out the great realities of our faith: our union with Jesus in death and resurrection and our participation in his broken body and shed blood. In all we do together, we affirm him, confess him, and testify of him until Jesus comes.

We believe in the redeemed community that gives spiritual significance to each person. No person is unimportant in the body of Christ. Along with new spiritual life, each believer is given capacities that make him or her spiritually significant. Each person in the community of faith has the capacity to glorify God, reflecting the Lord in a transformed Christian character and in moral and loving daily choices. Each person in the community is given gifts by the Holy Spirit, special abilities that enable him or her to minister to others in ways that contribute to their good and to the vitality of the whole community. Although each individual has a different role to play, as God sovereignly determines, each person is a full participant in the ministry and mission of the church. The commitment of each to his or her calling is vital if the body of Christ is to function as Christ intends.

We believe in the redeemed community that recognizes and responds to servant leaders. Christ is the living head of his church. God has placed human leaders in the community of faith, not to lord it over his people, but to equip his people for ministry and to encourage their growth as believing persons. God's servant leaders live among his people, both demonstrating the Christian qualities Christ intends to work in every believer and sharing their understanding of his written Word as a guide to faith and life. Deserving of respect and material support, leaders of the community of faith are brothers and sisters who are among, not above, the other members of the body. Yes, we do believe in a redeemed community that works out a common faith in loving unity, celebrates its relationship to God in worship, affirms each person as a spiritually significant participant in the church's ministry, and responds to leaders who live among us as our servants for Jesus' sake.

We believe in the future

We believe in the future of life on earth as meaningful and worthwhile. God's kingdom is now as well as future, and life on earth has significance. The present time is of the utmost significance because our todays as well as our tomorrows give us the opportunity to glorify God. The sorrows that cause us to cry out to God and the joys that move our hearts to praise are woven into the tapestry of our lives, designed alike for good. By our touch, we can enrich others. By our responses to the challenges of life, we can offer others hope in God. Our involvement can better our society, relieve injustice, and offer hope to the helpless. Because all that we do shapes our own character, affects society, and reflects glory on God, this life we know on earth is both meaningful and worthwhile.

We believe in the future of Jesus' return. History moves beyond our individual tomorrows toward a grand culmination. In God's good time the Jesus of history will return to execute God's final judgment and to bring in his realm of eternal righteousness. We look forward, not to the cooling of our sun or the dissolution of all things, but to God's grand denouement. Then, visible to all, Christ will receive the voluntary or forced worship of every bended knee, and time will give way to eternity.

We believe in the endless existence of every person. The brief time we know in our life on earth is not the end of any human being's self-conscious existence. Each of us is stamped by God's gift of life with the mark of the eternal; we are destined forever to be and to be aware. For those who respond to God's invitation to life in Jesus, death is merely a transition to a new and fuller experience of joy. For those who failed to respond, physical death is a transition, too, but it is a transition from alienation to endless alienation — the unutterable tragedy of condemnation to what the believers have long called hell. Yes, we do believe in the future. We believe in the future of life here on earth, the future of Jesus' return, and the future that stretches on endlessly, long after what we call time has passed away.

We believe in the unseen universe

We believe in the unseen universe and in the personality of Satan and the angels. God's creative work is not summed up in the visible. Beyond the spectrum that our eyes can see lies a universe filled with spiritual beings who have an impact on our lives. The source of evil in our universe is rooted there in Satan, who rebelled against the divine order, carrying with him other spiritual beings who have arranged themselves against God and his beloved. The influence of the evil one, resonating in harmony with the sinful nature of humankind, warps our society and holds people captive. But other beings, faithful to their Creator, continue to obey his will and act as ministering spirits who serve his saints. Yes, we do affirm the supernatural, but we remain confident that Christ, exalted over every authority and power, is supreme in the seen and unseen realms. And so we worship him and are released from the superstitious fears that hold captive so much of humankind.

PART II

The Vocabulary of Faith

Throughout the centuries believers have struggled to express their understandings of Christian faith. Biblical words have been used, and other terms have been designed to explore the meaning of Bible words. The language of theology has developed as a technical language, one that examines what God has revealed about himself and his relationship to humanity.

At times the vocabulary of faith is confusing. Words used in one sense in the Bible have been used in different senses by theologians. The words invented to explore aspects of Christian belief have seemed too technical, too far removed from the daily life of God's people. And yet the vocabulary of Christian faith is vital and exciting. Each word pulses with life because the focus of each is God and our life with God.

In this second, largest section of *Dictionary of Basic Bible Truths*, we explore the vocabulary of faith, looking not so much at the technicalities as at the vital and life-changing realities that the words of Christian faith express. We discover, with the saints of every age, just how our faith reshapes our understanding of our world and how it enables us to live triumphantly in intimate relationship to God.

ADAM

Whenever we ask the question, "What is mankind?" the Bible points us back to Adam. The answers we find in the Bible's teaching about Adam are both wonderful and terrible.

The wonderful is sensed in the story of the Creation. In the first two chapters of Genesis, we see God's measured creation of the physical universe, comfortable in its regularity and stability and exciting in the rich variety of living beings that populate the earth. Then, as the culminating act in his creation, we see God stoop to intimate personal involvement in the shaping of a special being. The spoken word that caused the existence of all else was not intimate enough for God's climactic act. No, God took dust from his earth and gently breathed into the being the "breath of life." It was thus that humankind was formed, and God called the first person "Adam." Genesis then traces how lovingly God worked with Adam. In a garden designed by the Lord to permit Adam the discovery of his every potential, God guarded Adam's emerging personality. When Adam was ready, God gave him Eve, taken from his own body, sharing his own nature and identity, suitable to be a companion and friend as well as a wife and lover. Throughout this tender story we sense the special concern that God has for the first human beings. When you and I feel unloved or unimportant and wonder about our own role in God's grand plan, we can turn to the first chapters of Genesis and sense again just how significant human beings are to the Lord. As descendants of Adam and Eve, you and I are special to God and deeply loved by the Lord who took such care in their creation. Sensing the same wonder, the psalmist lifts his heart in praise: "When I consider your heavens, the work of your fingers, the moon and the stars, which you set in place, what is man that you are mindful of him, the son of man that you care for him?" (Ps. 8:3–4). And yet God does care for human beings, for you and me.

But the terrible is also found in what the Bible says about Adam. Those same early chapters of Genesis tell of a willful failure (1 Tim.

21

2:14). In a crisis Adam chose to disobey God and, as a result, experienced a tragic twisting of his nature. The Bible is clear that Adam's uniqueness as God's culminating and most special creation has been passed on to his descendants; and not only that, but the twisted nature that warps human personalities and distorts our experience has been passed on as well. In a central theological passage, the New Testament affirms the mystery of our participation in Adam's failure and of the damaging impact that first sin has had on all of us. "Just as sin entered the world through one man, and death through sin, and in this way death came to all men, because all sinned" (Rom. 5:12). "In Adam," Corinthians adds, "all die" (1 Cor. 15:22).

In telling the wonderful and terrible story of Adam, the Bible lays the foundation for our understanding of ourselves and others. Humanity, unutterably precious because we are the direct and special creation of God, is also flawed and subject to everything that "death" implies. Because this story is so central in our understanding of ourselves and our relationship to God and so basic to a grasp of biblical faith, many important biblical and theological terms look back to the Genesis story. Words like *Fall, impute, death, life, sin, image, likeness,* and *humanity* all direct our attention back to the story of God's creation of the first humans.

But when the Bible speaks of Adam, it calls us to look forward as well as backward. For Scripture knows two Adams. The first, the historic figure directly created by God, is the prototype of mankind as we know it. Rich in potential, yet terribly flawed, the first Adam speaks of all that we might have been. The second Adam is Jesus. Uncreated, he stepped into history to redeem us and to serve as the prototype of all that we will become. Scripture contains God's promise: "Just as we have borne the likeness of the earthly man, so shall we bear the likeness of the man from heaven (1 Cor. 15:49). (To explore what the Bible tells us about Adam, read Gen. 2:4–3:24; Rom. 5:12–19; and 1 Cor. 15:20–49.)

ADOPTION

We all sense the wonder of adoption. A couple decides to accept as their own someone not born into their family. The couple loves the child and shares with him or her the family name. No wonder, then, that the fact that God's choice to adopt human beings is deeply moving. And yet this is the Bible's testimony which affirms our adoption (using the basic Greek word, which is variously translated in Romans 8:15, 23; 9:4; Galatians 4:5; and Ephesians 1:5).

Freely and spontaneously God chose to adopt human beings who were his enemies, redeeming us that "we might receive the full rights of sons" (Gal. 4:5).

In Paul's day Roman law controlled adoption. A significant change of status took place upon adoption. All of a person's old ties, obligations, and debts were cancelled. The adopted child was placed under the authority of the father of the new family. That father owned all the child's possessions, but in exchange the child as an heir possessed all the resources of the father. The father was committed by adoption to support, discipline, and take responsibility for the child's actions, while the adopted child was committed to be responsive to a new father.

How rich the imagery is for Christians today. "You are all sons of God through faith in Christ Jesus," Paul writes in Galatians 3:26. In God's family now, we have been set free from the things that bound us before. We owe allegiance not to our old passions but to God. We have exchanged our weakness for his strength. We have exchanged our poverty for his riches. We have exchanged our sin for his righteousness, our guilt for his grace. And in it all we are heirs to all that God the Father possesses, including that quality of life that enriches us now and will merge one day into eternity.

ANGELS

Human beings are not the only intelligent beings in God's universe. Other intelligent creatures are found in what might be thought of as another, parallel dimension. Both testaments speak of these beings as powerful yet limited personalities who stand in contrast to humans in several significant ways. Angelic beings are the direct creation of God. They neither marry nor reproduce. Angelic beings can move between the physical universe and a parallel spiritual or supernatural realm, and although angels can appear in the material universe, their bodies are not composed of matter as we know it.

While a liberal branch of Christianity has questioned the supernatural and has denied the existence of spiritual beings, historic Christianity has affirmed with the Bible that angels do exist and do play a role in God's plan for humankind. Catholic theologians have speculated on that role, and the Council of Trent even encouraged the faithful to appeal to angels to pray for them. Protestants have tended to limit speculation and rely on specific passages of Scripture. These passages suggest the existence of an invisible realm that we cannot penetrate. Scripture describes beings that are involved, as we are, in God's titanic struggle against evil. The Bible unveils both a bright and a dark host in this invisible universe: angels who remained faithful to God, continuing to do his will; and angels who rebelled against God, now obstinately trying to distort the good God intends. The dark angels, familiar to us from the New Testament, are known as demons. ◗ DEMONS, SATAN

When we treat the words of Scripture with respect, refusing to explain away whatever fails to fit into modern scientific categories, we are able to make a number of statements about these unseen but very real beings. While these statements do not express everything that Christians have thought or imagined about angels, they do sum up a consistent tradition that finds its roots in Scripture's teaching.

Angels are an order of created spiritual beings. The invisible universe seems to be filled with hosts of these beings (Ps. 103:20–21). God's direct creations, who do not reproduce as humans do (Matt. 22:30), angels seem to have been gifted with individuality and a type of personhood. Angels can experience emotions (Luke 2:9–14; 15:10), exhibit intellectual curiosity (1 Peter 1:10–12), and, like Adam, were faced in history with the necessity of making a moral choice (2 Peter 2:4). Some have personal names. Two notable angels are identified in the Bible as Michael (Dan. 10:21; 12:1; Rev. 12:7) and Gabriel (Dan. 8:16; Luke 1:19, 26). The term *angel* seems to include several distinct types of spiritual beings. Cherubim are winged and powerful (Ezek. 1:5–8; 13–14) and are closely linked with upholding God's glory (Exod. 37:1–9; 1 Kings 6). Seraphim, linked with God's holiness, have yet another form (Isa. 6:2, 6). Other angels appear in Scripture in human form, always represented as males (Gen. 18:1–22; Dan. 10:5–6; Mark 16:5; Luke 24:4; Rev. 4:6–8). These spiritual beings seem to be organized in ranks and orders, much like military organizations. We find suggestions of this in Daniel 10 and quite possibly in Colossians 1:16. As created beings, angels are not all-powerful. But they do have great power, including the ability to drastically impact events on earth. It was angels who were God's agents of destruction at Sodom (Gen. 19:12–29) and angels who will take that role in the last days (Rev. 6).

At times believers have been so attracted by the idea of these spiritual beings that they have overemphasized their importance in Christian experience. Paul warns against "the worship of angels" along with other practices that are products of an "unspiritual mind." Such practices involve losing connection with the church's head (Col. 2:16–19). Paul's point is that Jesus himself is the focus of the Christian's faith and the source of all our spiritual growth. Jesus is the creator of the invisible as well as the visible universe, "head over every power and authority," including the angelic. Angels are his messengers and servants, and whatever their powers, angels are not intermediaries between Jesus and his people.

The Bible has another exciting word about angels. Eager that you and I realize just how important we are to God, the writer of the Book of Hebrews says, "surely it is not angels he helps, but Abraham's descendants" (Heb. 2:16). Jesus became a human being and underwent his sufferings not for angels, but for us. Because of Jesus you and I, whose present powers are less than those of angels, will be lifted far above them. How exciting to realize, as we turn from the fascination of speculating about the invisible world, that God's focus is on you and me and on our relationship to him. How important, then, that we keep the focus of our hearts and hopes directly on the Lord.

Angels are beings who minister to God's saints. Hebrews, in presenting Jesus as exalted above the angels, says, "Are not all angels ministering spirits sent to serve those who will inherit salvation?" (Heb. 1:14). Despite their powers, angels remain subject to the Lord and have been assigned by him to the service of his saints.

The speculation about "guardian angels" and just how angels relate to individual believers today cannot be answered from Scripture. But we can draw a portrait of ways in which angels have served God's people in the past. Angels have been agents of revelation, communicating God's will and his Word (Dan. 7:16; 10:11–12; Zech. 1:9, 13–14; Acts 7:53; Heb. 2:2). Angels have protected God's people from their enemies (2 Kings 6:15–17; Ps. 91:11–14; Dan. 6:22; Acts 5:19). Angels sustained Jesus in his temptation (Matt. 4:11; Luke 22:43). Angels accompany the dead to paradise (Luke 16:22). Angels will gather believers into God's kingdom at Christ's return (Matt. 13:39; 16:27; 24:31) and will serve as agents of his judgment on those who do not believe (2 Kings 19:35; Matt. 13:30, 49–50; 2 Thess. 1:7–9). It seems likely from this and from the fact that angels do guard children (Matt. 18:10) and churches (Rev. 2–3) that part of God's protective shield around you and me is made up of these powerful beings who are committed to do God's will and are determined to serve his saints.

ANTICHRIST

At times believers have been too quick to attach this term to contemporary enemies. Pagan emperors, Reformation popes, and modern oppressors like Hitler have all been wrongly identified as the Antichrist. What does this biblical term mean, and what does it teach us?

The word *antichrist* means "against Christ." It is found only five times in the New Testament, always in the letters of the apostle John. John uses the term in two ways: first, the term identifies a person who will appear in history; second, it characterizes people who corrupt the contemporary church. The "many antichrists" (1 John 2:18) who infect the living church can be identified by their refusal to accept that "Jesus Christ has come in the flesh" (2 John 7). In their denial of the incarnation, they reject Jesus as the Son, and they also reject the Father (1 John 4:7–15).

The Antichrist is a figure who is always found in the context of climactic judgments. The Gospels call him the *pseudochristos*, a term that means "the false Christ." This term is found in Matthew 24:24 and Mark 13:22, passages that refer to the prophetic vision in Daniel 11 and 12 of history's end. That powerful portrait of culminating judgment on an unbelieving world features a leader of mankind's last rebellion. That leader is energized by Satan to perform deceptive miracles. Paul also refers to Daniel's vision and portrays the Antichrist as one who "opposes and exalts himself over everything that is called God or is worshiped, and even sets himself up in God's temple, proclaiming himself to be God" (2 Thess. 2:4).

The Bible, then, recognizes in the church the existence of that antagonistic attitude that motivates the Antichrist. But it also indicates a specific person who bears this name. While exact details of the future remain uncertain, the Bible does indicate that an Antichrist will appear one day. Until then antichrists who claim membership in Christ's church while denying Jesus' deity remain a greater danger to people of faith.

APOLOGETICS

Apologetics is a reasoned defense or explanation of Christian faith. Christianity is not founded on human reason, but believers throughout the ages have been convinced that it is more reasonable to have faith than to deny revealed truth.

The Bible itself contains several examples of reasoning with those who do not believe. Jesus defended himself against the attacks of the Pharisees by a compelling argument (John 5:31–36). Paul in Athens adopted a familiar form of philosophical argument to present the gospel (Acts 17:16–34). And in 1 Corinthians 15, Paul carefully marshals evidence for the resurrection of Jesus and of the believer as well.

Even so, the purpose of apologetics has not been to present compelling proofs; Christianity calls for a faith commitment that can never be compelled. Reasonable argument can lead a person to doubt the reasons he or she has given for disbelief and can demonstrate that Christianity is not unreasonable. But ultimately we arrive at that moment when we realize that we must make a personal choice. Christians insist that that choice is a simple one: either we believe that God is and that he has acted in Jesus to provide human beings with forgiveness and new life, or we reject divine revelation and seek some other way to come to terms with life. Apologetics has as its goal helping persons face this choice with as few reasons for hesitation as possible.

There are, of course, reasoned arguments against basic Christian beliefs as well as for them. Arguments against Christianity have tended to question the existence of God, the Incarnation, the possibility of miracles, and the validity of Scripture. By raising the specter of evil, unbelievers have also attacked the Christian's belief in a benevolent and all-powerful deity. Quite naturally Christian apologetics has tended to focus on these same issues. It demonstrates that it is reasonable to believe in the existence of God, and it shows that the God the Bible portrays is real. ◆ EXISTENCE OF GOD, EVIL, MIRACLE, INCARNATION, REVELATION

ASCENSION

While Jesus was on earth, he told his disciples that he would return to the Father and to the Father's house (John 16:7–11, 28; 14:2). The Gospels and Acts report that after Jesus' resurrection and his appearances to the disciples, the moment came when Jesus "was taken up into heaven" (Luke 24:51; Acts 1:9–11). This historic event is reflected in the New Testament letters as well; Jesus was "taken up in glory" (1 Tim. 3:16) and is seated "at the right hand of the Majesty in heaven" (Heb. 1:3).

The great creeds of history all look back on the ascension of Jesus (as well as on his incarnation, death, and resurrection) as an actual event. Because each of these events did take place in space and time, we are assured with the saints of history that the Jesus who ascended into heaven will come again in the same literal and historic way. ◆ HISTORY, PRIESTHOOD

ASSURANCE

The word raises psychological and theological issues for the modern Christian. "Why don't I feel saved?" is a nagging question that torments some people. Often related to this question is the theological query, "How can a person know if he or she is among the elect?"

Both of these questions miss the point made by Protestant theologians from the Reformation on. Assurance isn't primarily a feeling. And one's assurance of salvation never hinges on knowledge of God's hidden will. ◗ ELECTION

During the Middle Ages the Catholic church strayed from the biblical conviction that salvation was a matter of faith in Christ alone. The church viewed salvation as a cooperative effort, and one's destiny would be determined on the basis of actions as well as belief in Jesus. Men like Martin Luther and John Calvin led the Protestant Reformation, emphasizing the biblical position that salvation is God's gift, which human beings receive by faith alone. Salvation, thus, is a matter of one's trust in Jesus. A person who has heard the good news of the gospel and who relies on Jesus for forgiveness can be completely confident that he or she is saved. Scripture says that "God so loved the world that he gave his one and only Son, that whoever believes in him shall not perish but have eternal life" (John 3:16). The passage goes on, "whoever believes in him is not condemned" (John 3:17) and "whoever believes in the Son has eternal life" (John 3:36).

Assurance, then, is implicit in Christian faith. It is not a matter of feelings or emotions. It is not a matter that hinges on one's view of election and predestination. Assurance, like salvation, flows from the conviction that Jesus is able to save us and that he does save us when we trust him. The person who has trusted in Jesus has a basis in God's Word for the quiet confidence that he or she is now one of God's own. Through faith in Jesus we are assured that at time's end we will step with Jesus into an eternity of endless joy.

Christians have gone on to add thoughts about subjective or psychological assurance. By faith believers enter a dynamic relationship to God. We are infused with God's Spirit, whose inner witness reassures us (Rom. 8:16). A new motivation toward holiness grips us (1 John 2:3; 3:2–3). As we mature in our faith, we add such traits as goodness, knowledge, self-control, perseverance, godliness, and love. These qualities "in increasing measure" keep us from being ineffective in our Christian lives and make our "calling and election sure" (2 Peter 1:5–10). How, then, are you and I to develop a sense of the assurance that can quiet our doubts and calm our fears? First, we remember that our salvation rests on what Jesus has done for us, not on what we do or do not do. Trusting him and relying on God's promise of salvation through Jesus provides the basis of our assurance. Second, we develop a sense of assurance by moving on in our faith. As God enriches and rebuilds our character, shaping us to be more and more like Jesus, that very inner transformation brings us a unique confidence. The assurance that comes through faith and with continuing commitment is far from presumption. It is, instead, an appreciation of all that Jesus has done for us and is doing in us; it is an affirmation of our conviction that God will be faithful to us to the end.

ATHEISM

Atheism is usually thought of as a denial of God's existence. Few people in our day are determined atheists, enthusiastically arguing that there is no supreme being. But practical atheism is far more common. Practical atheism simply acts as if God does not exist and holds beliefs that are inconsistent with the existence of God. Materialism and evolution are common viewpoints that implicitly deny the existence of the God that Scripture reveals.

How do we explain atheism? Psalm 14:1 uses a word that means a person who is twisted or lacking morally when it says that "the fool says in his heart, 'There is no God.'" Paul traces atheism back to the same root in Romans 1. He argues that what can be known about God is plain to mankind from what God has made because God has planted an inner witness in human nature. Rather than responding to the God they knew, human beings "exchanged the truth of God for a lie, and worshiped and served created things rather than the Creator" (Rom. 1:25).

Scripture views atheism as a moral rather than intellectual issue. The assumption that life can be lived without acknowledging God shows how deeply sin has distorted human understanding.

When we recognize the spiritual root of atheism, we realize that we can hardly argue a person into faith. ◗ REASON, TEN COMMAND-MENTS, APOLOGETICS Instead we are to witness to the reality of God and to the possibility of relationship to him, "gently instructing" those who oppose us "in the hope that God will grant them repentance leading them to a knowledge of the truth, and that they will come to their senses and escape from the trap of the devil" (2 Tim. 2:25–26).

ATONEMENT

Christians have always viewed Jesus' death as central to our faith and vital to our relationship to God. All Christians haven't held the same view of just how that death rescues us from sin and restores our relationship to the Lord. The ancient church fathers emphasized the release that Christ's death won for us from Satan and tended to think of his death as a ransom. These early Christians also saw Jesus' crucifixion as a sacrifice that in some way reconciled mankind to God. It wasn't until the eleventh century that Anselm of Canterbury focused on the notion that Jesus' death was necessary to satisfy the justice of God and to free the Lord to show mercy. Anselm, reasoning from Germanic feudal law, viewed God as an overlord whose subjects had proven disloyal and had wounded his honor immeasurably. Because human beings could not right an infinite wrong, God must become human and offer up his own life to compensate for the injury. In this way God could remain committed to justice and at the same time show mercy.

Peter Abelard, who died in A.D. 1109, focused on the moral impact of Jesus' death. He ignored the question of what Jesus' death meant to God, insisting that God's love is so great that no sacrifice for sins is needed. Instead Jesus came and died to reveal the vast extent of divine love, a revelation that awakens love in the human heart. The ground for forgiveness, Abelard taught, is that rekindled love for God is sparked when we contemplate Jesus.

Abelard's subjective view of the atonement was not accepted in his own day. While no complete theory of the atonement was developed for hundreds of years, the conviction remained that in some way the blood of Christ objectively redeems us from sin, death, and Satan's power, and it restores us to harmony with God the Father.

In the sixteenth century the great figures who led the Protestant Reformation focused anew on the Christian doctrine of salvation. Salvation is offered to all through faith in Christ, and faith alone is the means by which one must be saved. But what is the objective basis for God's offer of a free salvation? Like Christians throughout the ages, Martin Luther and John Calvin looked back to Jesus' cross, and they poured over the Scriptures to seek a fresh understanding of its meaning. The Reformers concluded that Jesus died as a vicarious sacrifice, a substitute for sinful human beings. Jesus endured the suffering that is a necessary penalty for sin, took on himself the wrath that we deserved, and bonded us forever to himself in resurrection life. Luther's *Smaller Catechism* affirms that "Christ has redeemed me a lost and condemned creature with His holy precious blood and with His innocent suffering and death" and that he has done this "in order that I may be His own and live under Him in His kingdom, and serve Him in everlasting righteousness, innocence, and blessedness."

What did the Reformers find in the Scriptures that led them to the conservative Protestant view of the atonement?

The atonement in the Old Testament. The Hebrew words translated "atonement" in our English versions are used one hundred fifty times in the Old Testament and are closely associated with forgiveness and the idea of reconciliation to God.

In the Old Testament atonement is made by sacrifice. Leviticus 4 explains how those who commit unintentional sins are to bring animals to the priests, who will offer the animals in sacrifice. "In this way he [the priest] will make atonement for the man's sin, and he will be forgiven" (Lev. 4:35). According to Leviticus 17:11, the death of a sacrificial animal is necessary for atonement: "The life of the creature is in the blood, and I have given it to you to make atonement for yourselves on the altar; it is the blood that makes atonement for one's life."

This same pattern is seen in the Old Testament's approach to intentional sins. Once a year, on the Day of Atonement, a special animal sacrifice was offered as a sin offering for "the uncleanness and rebellion of the Israelites, whatever their sins have been" (Lev. 16:21).

In this way God's Old Testament people were taught that sin results in death, but in his love God was willing to accept a substitute: the life of an innocent in place of the life of the guilty. The Old Testament animal sacrifice repeatedly prepared Israel for the ultimate revelation of the love of God in one who would be called the Lamb of God. Jesus, the ultimate innocent, would take his place on a wooden cross and there offer up his life in place of our own.

The atonement in the New Testament. The Greek words used to render the Hebrew words for atonement are translated as "atonement" in the New International Version and as "propitiation" in some other English versions (see Rom. 3:25; Heb. 2:17; 9:5; and 1 John 2:2; 4:10). What do New Testament passages teach? In Romans 3, Paul asks how God can justly leave past sins unpunished. His answer is that at last God's love and justice can be harmonized: Jesus' sacrifice of atonement shows us that God has been just to forgive those in past generations who had faith because that sacrifice provides an objective basis for the forgiveness of all sins. The writer of Hebrews shows that the animal sacrifices of the past were only "an illustration for the present time"; the repeated sacrifices of that earlier era were never able to take away sins or to "clear the conscience of the worshiper" (Heb. 9:9). But by his one sacrifice of himself, Jesus makes the believer holy and takes away all sins (Heb. 9:23–10:14). In John's first letter we are reminded that forgiveness is assured. We can come to God at any time to confess and be cleansed because Jesus, "the atoning sacrifice for our sins," comes to our defense (1 John 2:1). The ultimate demonstration of God's love is that God "sent his Son as an atoning sacrifice for our sins" (1 John 4:10).

The explicit teaching of the New Testament and the symbolism of the Old Testament both express the Reformers' conviction that Jesus died a substitutionary death. As Jesus hung on the cross, he suffered the penalty that our sins deserved, and in dying for us, he freed God to express his love for you and me in forgiveness of our sins. Isaiah's ancient words, recorded some seven hundred years before Christ, capture beautifully the meaning of the death that this great prophet foresaw:

> Surely he took up our infirmities
> and carried our sorrows,
> yet we considered him stricken by God,
> smitten by him, and afflicted.
> But he was pierced for our transgressions,
> he was crushed for our iniquities;
> the punishment that brought us peace was upon him,
> and by his wounds we are healed.
> We all, like sheep, have gone astray,
> each of us has turned to his own way;
> and the LORD has laid on him
> the iniquity of us all.
>
> (Isa. 53:4–6)

ATTRIBUTES OF GOD

Christians have a particular view of what God is like. The main qualities or characteristics we ascribe to God are called his attributes. God's attributes aren't of concern to theologians alone. Every person's concept of God is bound to influence his or her life and decisions. For instance, if you are completely convinced that God is omniscient (knows all things perfectly), then you're more likely to follow scriptural guidelines for living than if you thought that God was wise, but limited, and therefore human beings must decide moral issues as best they can. In every way what you and I think of God is going to shape the way we live our daily lives.

While some of God's qualities are similar to human qualities (God has emotions, thinks, decides, and acts), other qualities have no analogy in the human personality (God is sovereign). Yet each of the major characteristics of God does have practical implications for you and me. What are the major characteristics? The lists that we find in Christian writings through the ages differ, but most Christians would include qualities like the following:

God is personal. God thinks, chooses, loves, and hates. We, too, have the capacity of thought, will, and emotions, and so we have a basis for understanding some things about the nature of God. But while God shares personhood with us, his thoughts, his will, his love, and his hatred are not exactly like ours. Through Isaiah, God reminds his people: "My thoughts are not your thoughts, neither are my ways your ways. . . . As the heavens are higher than the earth, so are my ways higher than your ways and my thoughts than your thoughts (Isa. 55:8).

The fact that God is a person reassures us. God is no impersonal force, no abstract architect, no logical first cause so vastly different from us that we have no basis for any relationship. No, God is a person who understands our thoughts, feelings, and struggles to choose; he can relate to us on every level of our own personalities. But we must always remember that God remains the standard against which to judge our thoughts, emotions, and choices; we must resist the temptation to judge God by human thoughts and ways.

God is moral. God possesses all the moral virtues. At times some of the virtues that mark his character are listed as separate attributes by Christian theologians. However we list them, we can't think correctly about God unless we accept the Bible's description of him: loving, good, holy, righteous, forgiving, truthful, and faithful. While you and I can be merciful, truthful, and compassionate, for example, only God is perfectly good, and only God's actions are untarnished by sin. Unlike our love, God's love never fails. Unlike our forgiveness, God's forgiveness erases even the remembrance of sin. While God's holiness generates a wrath that focuses on sin and sinner, his anger is never spiteful or arbitrary, and in wrath God always remembers mercy. Only God, who is perfect, can be both wholly loving and angry at the same moment.

Each of these qualities is central to our Christian understanding of both God and morality. Each is deeply imbedded in God's revelation of his will for his people. Each is reflected in our convictions about how human beings ought to live with one another. Because God is truly moral, we can confidently trust ourselves to him. And because God is truly moral, we who are his children can "be imitators of God . . . and live a life of love, just as Christ loved us and gave himself up for us" (Eph. 5:1).

God's moral qualities are so significant in our understanding of him and of Christian experience that each is treated in a separate article in this book's vocabulary of faith.

God is sovereign. To acknowledge God as sovereign is to recognize him as supreme ruler of the universe. Ephesians 1:11 puts it powerfully: God is the one who "works out everything in conformity with the purpose of his will." To affirm God's sovereignty is to acknowledge that our universe and our individual lives have meaning and purpose. While God does not act arbitrarily to exert his control of events, we believe that through the outworking of the physical and moral laws God designed, as well as by supernatural interventions, God is working out his entire complex plan in history.

A passage that exalts God as sovereign helps us sense how wonderful it is to have a relationship to one who is truly in control of all things. Isaiah cries out to Judah, encouraging God's people not to be afraid but to catch a vision of God: "See, the Sovereign LORD comes with power, and his arm rules for him. See, his reward is with him, and his recompense accompanies him. He tends his flock like a shepherd: He gathers the lambs in his arms and carries them close to his heart; he gently leads those that have young" (Isa. 40:10–11). How wonderful to realize that the God who is the actual ruler of our universe stoops to use his power to care for his beloved own. ◗ SOVEREIGN

God is unlimited. Many of God's attributes have no corollary in human experience. We can only begin to grasp their meaning by contrast. We human beings are finite, limited to a single place and time, limited in our knowledge and our power. But God is unlimited in all these dimensions. Theologians speak of God as omniscient, omnipresent, and omnipotent.

God is omniscient; he knows everything. He knows every fact, every thought and motive in every human heart. God knows the past and the future as well as he knows the present. There are no limitations to God's full knowledge of all things.

God is omnipresent; he is present everywhere. God's presence cannot be localized as ours necessarily is. Pantheism assumes that part of God is in every material thing — rocks, trees, people. But the Christian knows a God who is above nature yet fully present at every location in the physical universe.

David, filled with wonder at the unlimited nature of God, pauses to express his thoughts: "Where can I go from your Spirit? Where can I flee from your presence? If I go up to the heavens, you are there; if I make my bed in the depths, you are there. If I rise on the wings of the dawn, if I settle on the far side of the sea, even there your hand will guide me, your right hand will hold me fast" (Ps. 139:7–10). Because God is everywhere present, he is with you and me always, whether our moments are dark or light.

God is omnipotent; he is all-powerful. God's power and ability to act are limited only by his own character. No one and nothing outside himself can place limits on the Lord; he is able to do whatever he pleases. But it is important to realize that God limits himself by his moral character; he pleases to do only what is good and right. God cannot sin, because his character is so perfectly holy that he would never choose to sin. But whatever God might choose to do, he can do. Isaiah puts into beautiful perspective the meaning of this quality:

> The LORD is the everlasting God,
>   the Creator of the ends of the earth.
> He will not grow tired or weary,
>   and his understanding no one can fathom.
> He gives strength to the weary
>   and increases the power of the weak.
> Even youths grow tired and weary,
>   and young men stumble and fall;
> But those who hope in the LORD
>   will renew their strength.
> They will soar on wings like eagles;
>   they will run and not grow weary,
>   they will walk and not be faint.
>
> (Isa. 40:28–31)

God is eternal. God is independent of time. A psalm of Moses puts it this way: "Before the mountains were born or you brought forth the earth and the world, from everlasting to everlasting you are God" (Ps. 90:2).

The eternity of God affirms that God has always existed and always will exist. While he is the source of all things, he himself has no source.

The eternity of God holds an exciting promise for us. When God offers us eternal life in Jesus, he holds out the promise of an endless existence rich with those same qualities that make his own life so rich and full.

God is free. God's freedom is seen in that he acts spontaneously, unrestricted by any consideration other than his own character and will. God's decision to save is a free choice, which does not grow out of any obligation to humanity. As a free choice, God's willingness to aid human beings who have become enemies is a demonstration of pure grace. All he has done for us is done out of his love and compassion.

Closely associated with this concept is the traditional idea of God's immutability. God does not change, and his essential character is not affected by events in this world of time and space. We can count on God to continue forever to be the kind of person that he is.

How are we so sure that God has these attributes? Basically because we are convinced that God has spoken and that he has revealed himself to us. It is by God's initiative and not through speculative imagination that our concept of God has grown and taken clearer form. The God of the Bible is the one and true God, and this God is personal, moral, sovereign, eternal, unlimited, and free.

AUTHORITY

Christians acknowledge the authority of God. We recognize that God has the right to command our total acceptance and obedience. He is Lord.

The problem is, through what means does God communicate to us? How do we know what we are to accept and obey?

Two basic answers have been suggested. The Catholic church has come to the conclusion that, ultimately, the church represents God on earth and is his authoritative voice. In making authoritative statements, the hierarchy is to consider Scripture, the historic traditions established by the church fathers (early Christian leaders), and the views of the gathered bishops and cardinals. The pope, the voice of the church (in Catholicism, Jesus' personal representative on earth), can then sum up the evidence from these sources and make authoritative pronouncements that are binding on Catholic believers.

On the other hand, in agreement with the ancient church fathers, Protestants have focused on the Scriptures themselves as the Christian's sole objective authority. Christians' opinions about the meaning of a biblical passage should be carefully considered, but human beings are prone to error. Saint Augustine, one of the greatest of the church fathers, writes, "I have learned to yield this respect and honor to the canonical books of Scripture; of these alone do I most firmly believe that the authors were completely free from error" (*Letters*, 82:3).

At critical times in our lives you and I will seek and discover God's guidance. Confirmation of his leading will come from different sources. Perhaps a passage in Scripture, perhaps a hymn, perhaps the word of a friend, perhaps circumstances will lead to the personal conviction that a particular choice is God's will, but when we look for an objective authority, a source that we can totally trust as a revelation of God's will for humankind, we always turn back to Scripture. It is in Scripture that God continues to speak to his people, and it is Scripture that can rightly command our total acceptance and obedience as the Word of God. ⬥
SCRIPTURE, INSPIRATION, ILLUMINATION

BAPTISM

It's obvious just from the names of some of our churches that Christians have held some significantly different opinions about this significant rite. To gain an understanding of the complex questions involved, we need to isolate and explore three issues: In what ways does the Bible speak of baptism? Who is to be baptized? What is the most appropriate mode (manner) of baptism?

How the Bible uses "baptize." Baptism is a distinctively New Testament practice. Neither in the Greek world nor in traditional Hebrew faith is there a true parallel to Christian baptism.

We first meet baptism in the Gospels, in their report of John the Baptist's ministry. This prophet, appearing just before Jesus began his public ministry, called on the people of Israel to turn back to God in preparation for the coming of their deliverer. Those who responded were to repent and, in acknowledgement of their sins and their personal commitment to change their way of life, to be baptized publicly by John. The ritual had no value in itself. Those who responded were warned by John to "produce fruit in keeping with repentance" (Luke 3:8). John's baptism involved both a willingness to identify publicly with the prophet's message and a public commitment to live a righteous life.

But years later the early Christian missionaries met Jewish believers who had responded to John's message without hearing about Jesus. Then "John's baptism" was set in contrast with a baptism practiced by those who had come to know Jesus and had entered into a relationship with God far deeper than that known by John's followers.

Some people have been puzzled because Jesus himself accepted baptism by John. Christ's own explanation was simply that it was the right thing to do: Every godly Jew should identify with the message of this prophet who called Israel back to righteousness (Matt. 3:15).

It is clear from Acts and the Epistles that the early church also practiced water baptism. We see it mentioned in Acts 2, 8, 9, 10, 16, 18, 19, in 1 Corinthians 1, 15, and in Hebrews 6. But this report of church practice doesn't really tell us what baptism meant to the early Christians.

To discern the meaning of water baptism, we have to note that the same word is used in the New Testament in a very different sense. John the Baptist, questioned by his critics, warned of a powerful person who would soon appear and baptize not with water "but with the Holy Spirit" (Matt. 3:11; Mark 1:8; Luke 3:16). Acts tells of a day when that promise was fulfilled (Acts 2:1–4; 10:45–47; 11:15–17). The Holy Spirit was given to the church and filled the believers. In that unique event, marked by the outward signs of visible flames and a rushing wind, a new spiritual age began. But the description of the happenings of that special day still does not define spiritual baptism.

That definition is given in 1 Corinthians 12:13: "We were all baptized by one Spirit into one body — whether Jews or Greeks, slave or free — and we were all given the one Spirit to drink." Theologically, baptism is that special work of God the Holy Spirit by which the person who believes in Jesus is joined to Jesus and his body in spiritual union.

This biblical use of baptism to express spiritual union with Jesus is reflected in another New Testament passage, in which Paul asks, "Don't you know that all of us who were baptized into Christ Jesus were baptized into his death? We were therefore buried with him through baptism into death in order that, just as Christ was raised from the dead through the glory of the Father, we too may live a new life. If we have been united with him in his death, we will certainly also be united with him in his resurrection. . . . Now if we died with Christ, we believe that we will also live with him" (Rom. 6:3–5, 8).

Other passages add their testimony. Because we experience "one baptism" (Eph. 4:5), Christians can live in unity. Because we have been united to Jesus, the power of his endless life is available to us (Col. 2:12; Gal. 3:27).

However we understand baptism and the differences within the Christian community, our view of baptism should be shaped by the deep spiritual significance of union with Jesus.

Who is to be baptized? Two views about who should be baptized have divided Christians. One view holds that all associated with the visible church — professing adult Christians and their children — should be baptized. The other view insists that baptism should be reserved for those who have made an intelligent profession of personal faith in Jesus.

The Catholic church promotes infant baptism because it views the rite as a means of salvation; baptism cleanses the infant and provides forgiveness. Protestants reject this view of baptism. While they do not believe that baptism has any power to save, many Protestants hold that infants are members of the visible church along with adult family members who are believers. Some Protestants view baptism as the symbol of a special covenant relationship that they believe God enters into with those who believe.

In Protestantism the word *covenant* is used in two primary ways. One use is strictly biblical: "the covenants" are specific promises that God made to Abraham, to David, and (in Jesus' death) to all who believe. Another use is theological: God is seen to relate to mankind through a series of covenant commitments that reflect, but are not the same as, the biblical covenants. ◆ COVENANT

Covenant theologians, who find their key for interpreting Scripture in the theological covenants, argue that just as a Jewish child was circumcised on the eighth day of his life to identify him with God's Old Testament people, so the child of believers is baptized to show his or her identity with God's New Testament people. Baptism of infants does not confer salvation on any person, but it does affirm the grace God has already given to a child born into a covenant family, who, through that birth, has become a member of the visible church.

The baptism of an infant in a Protestant church, then, is not necessary for any child's salvation and does not confer any special grace. But Protestants who teach infant baptism believe that baptism of adults who become Christians, and of children born to believers, is necessary because it is taught by Jesus, a practice to be observed out of obedience to the Lord.

Despite the fact that there is no biblical example of infant baptism and no passage that teaches infant baptism directly, Origen, one of the earliest church fathers, says in his commentary on Romans 5:9 that "the church received from the apostles the tradition to give baptism also to infants."

The view that infants should be baptized is strongly rejected by those in the Baptist tradition. They argue that Scripture is silent about infant baptism. The Old Testament commanded circumcision, but no parallel command for infant baptism is found in the New Testament. Instead, in every case in which water baptism is described in the New Testament, those baptized are adults who newly have professed faith in Christ.

The root of the Baptist position, however, is found in their historic view of the church itself. Wherever the church is found in the New Testament, they argue, what is in view is the community of actual saints. That is, only those who are true believers are members of the body of Christ. It is both confusing and wrong to speak of a "visible" church made up of true believers and of others who do not yet believe. What's more, baptism is important as a public testimony of personal conversion, and so it must be restricted to adults who can make a personal commitment to Jesus and who then follow that commitment with a public profession.

This division of opinion persists in Christianity, and it seems likely to continue. But whether baptism is a rite for infants or for adults who undertake it on conversion, it is important not to confuse the ritual with the spiritual realities that it signifies. When a person responds to the gospel message and exercises personal trust in Christ, God's Spirit unites him or her with Jesus and with other believers in the body of Christ. Faith brings this union, and the ritual of baptism symbolizes not only personal commitment to Jesus but also the link between the baptized person and others in the Christian community. We may differ in our views about who should receive water baptism, but there remains the spiritual reality that binds us into a single family: We know in truth "one faith, one Lord, one baptism, one God and Father of all, who is over all and through all and in all" (Eph. 4:5–6).

What is the most appropriate mode (manner) of baptism? The English word *baptize* comes from a Greek word that means "to dip" and was commonly used in the sense of immerse. New Testament writers use it both in its technical theological sense and to refer to the ritual washings of the Pharisees (Mark 7:4; Luke 11:38). But as a technical term, infused with fresh meaning by its adoption into the language of faith, the historic secular meanings can't be used to define the practice of baptism in the Christian church. Those people in the Baptist tradition argue that the origin of the word, the biblical incidents of baptism, and the reality of union with Jesus in his death and resurrection all suggest that the most appropriate mode of baptism is by immersion. It is clear from church history that Christians have immersed from earliest times. But they have also practiced baptism by sprinkling and pouring water on the person to be baptized.

While it is wrong to pass lightly over issues that our brothers and sisters feel are important, it is certainly true that the manner of baptism is of less concern to Christians than the issue of whether baptism is for believers only or for believers and their children.

But what is most important is the wonderful truths that this word expresses in the New Testament letters. There the focus is not on the ritual but on the reality of God's work for us and in us. You and I have been united to Jesus Christ. When we trusted Jesus, God the Holy Spirit supernaturally linked us with Jesus himself and through Jesus with all his people. Now through this supernatural union we have died with Christ, and through this union we participate in his resurrection. Because we have been baptized into Jesus, we share his life and his strength. All this comes as God's wonderful gift to us through faith. How gladly, then, do we participate in the rite of water baptism and affirm publicly the wonders of the grace that you and I enjoy.

BLOOD

Christianity is a religion of life and death. In each testament the Bible deals with life-and-death issues, and one of the most prominent terms used is *blood*.

The word *blood* is found three hundred sixty-two times in the Hebrew Old Testament. There it is used in two contexts: first, of warfare and murderous attacks that usually end in death; second, in the context of animal sacrifice. "The life of the creature is in the blood," Leviticus 17:11

affirms. And it was the life of the sacrificial animal, which sinners offered on Old Testament altars, that won atonement for sins.

The word *blood* is found ninety-seven times in the New Testament. Six times it is used in the phrase "flesh and blood" to indicate human frailty. In the Book of Revelation blood is associated with awful divine judgments. Some twenty-nine times the word refers to the Old Testament sacrificial system. But twenty-five times the New Testament speaks about the blood of Christ.

The New Testament associates Jesus' blood with two wonders. First, it is by blood that Jesus made atonement for our sins. Our salvation rests upon the significance of Jesus' sacrifice of himself, and the offering up of his life for us. Second, the New Testament teaches that Jesus' blood (the offering up of his life as a sacrifice for sins) initiated a new covenant, a new basis on which God will relate to human beings. Under the new covenant God promises both forgiveness and a "new heart": an inner transformation of our character as we become more and more like Jesus.

Many New Testament passages point up the benefits won for us through Jesus' blood. It is by his blood we are justified (Rom. 5:9), have redemption (Eph. 1:7; Heb. 9:12), and have been delivered from our old, empty way of life (1 Peter 1:18–19). Jesus' blood was the means by which we have been brought into relationship to God (Eph. 2:13) and by which peace between God and humanity has been established (Col. 1:20). It is Christ's blood that has dealt with our sin (Heb. 9:24–26), brought forgiveness (Rom. 3:25), cleansing (1 John 1:7), and release from the inner power of sin (Heb. 9:14; Rev. 1:5).

Christianity is a life-and-death faith, a religion of blood. It was the death of Jesus on Calvary and the blood he shed there that brings us the life we have in him now and in eternity. ◗ **FORGIVENESS, JUSTIFICA-TION, ATONEMENT, SACRIFICE, NEW COVENANT**

BODY OF CHRIST

In different eras different theological questions have drawn the attention of believers. For instance, in the second century, Christians' attention was focused on the trinity and on understanding the nature and person of Jesus. In the Reformation of the sixteenth century, the primary concern was salvation and the role of faith.

In our time the focus of many is drawn to the church. Believers are looking anew at the biblical images and teachings about the community of those who believe. The church has existed through all the centuries of church history, but not enough attention was paid to issues raised in Scripture.

One of the prime images in Scripture is being taken more seriously today. The Bible teaches that the church is the body of Christ. The church is a living organism, not simply a human institution. We who are Jesus' people are linked so intimately and uniquely to one another and to Jesus that together we constitute a unified and organic whole.

The image of the body emphasizes relationships. Note that Scripture does not suggest that the church is like a body: the Bible says we *are* a body. Our identity as God's people is deeply rooted in our organic relationship with each other and with Jesus.

Jesus is head of the body. In the New Testament the term *head* is never applied to human leaders of the visible church. Instead the church is everywhere viewed as an organism, and Jesus is presented as sole and living head. You and I as members of the body are so linked with Jesus that he is able to guide, direct, and strengthen us.

A number of New Testament passages help us sense the importance of recognizing Jesus as our living head. Ephesians presents Jesus as supreme, "far above all rule and authority, power and dominion, and every title that can be given, not only in the present age but also in the one to come" (Eph. 1:21). This is the person that God has given us to be "head over everything for the church, which is his body" (Eph. 1:22). Through our personal relationship to Jesus, we have a source of unimaginable power. We are invited to realize and to experience "his incomparably great power for us who believe. That power is like the working of his mighty strength, which he exerted in Christ when he raised him from the dead" (Eph. 1:19–20). In our organic relationship to Jesus, the very power of God is made available to us, and all that cripples us can be overcome through his inner strength.

Ephesians 4 focuses our attention on growth. Our relationship to Jesus is the secret of individual and congregational spiritual growth. From Jesus "the whole body . . . grows and builds itself up in love" (Eph. 4:16).

Colossians 1 lifts Jesus up, showing his supremacy over the visible and invisible creation. He is also supreme over the church; he has priority in our thinking and in our lives (Col. 1:18).

Colossians 2 warns believers that the key to our spiritual vitality and growth is found in our relationship to Jesus. We dare not lose "connection with the Head" by looking for spiritual fulfillment in ritual or religious practices (Col. 2:19). "In Christ all the fullness of the Deity lives in bodily form, and you have been given fullness in Christ, who is the head over every power and authority" (Col. 2:9–10).

These passages have implications for individuals and congregations.

We must learn to look expectantly to Jesus for his guidance, confident that whatever our head directs, he will also enable us to accomplish. Believers who view themselves as members of a living organism can never discount the supernatural. Human schemes of organization can never adequately capture this reality.

Another exciting implication of Scripture's teaching that Jesus is the living head of the church is that we are to be the living incarnation of Jesus in the world. While Christ is in heaven, Jesus' people are on earth. Through his link with believers, Jesus, even now, is vitally present on the earth. He touches others through the living people who are his body. As we live in responsive obedience to our Lord, all his good purposes for humanity will be accomplished. How important, then, that Christians recognize the headship of the living Christ and look to him for guidance, acting in total confidence in his ability to do through us what he directs us to do.

Believers are the body of Christ. A number of passages emphasize the relationships that are to exist between believers. "Each member [of the body] belongs to all the others" Romans 12:5 teaches. This New Testament chapter, together with 1 Corinthians 12 and Ephesians 4, stresses the importance of love, expressed as acceptance and mutual concern. The body is able to function as God intends when believers care for one another and commit themselves to serve each other.

The New Testament suggests that mutual love rather than organizational union or even doctrinal agreement binds the body of Christ together. Each of the three New Testament chapters that focus on the body of Christ (Rom. 12; 1 Cor. 12–13; Eph. 4) stresses the importance of love and intimate personal relationships between believers. The church cannot function as the body of Christ if our interpersonal relationships are superficial, strained, or based on sociological similarities rather than a recognition of our common participation in Jesus Christ.

Another theme linking passages that speak of the body of Christ is that of spiritual gifts. These are best understood as special enablements by the Holy Spirit by which we are equipped to serve and encourage spiritual growth in our brothers and sisters in the body of Christ.

The modern focus on the church as the body of Christ is a healthy one. As Christians sense their shared identity as members of a single organism and as they acknowledge Jesus as living head, personal spiritual growth will be stimulated, and the body of believers will become a more effective servant of God in our world. ◗ CHURCH, HEAD, SPIRITUAL GIFTS, LOVE

BONDAGE

The Bible paints a dismal picture of the human condition. We human beings have fantastic potentials. We can master the physical universe we live in, inventively reshaping metals and materials to enable us even to escape from our planet. But despite our potentials, human beings are still in bondage. We can master the material world, but we cannot master ourselves. We can reach out to the stars, but we will not reach out to God. We can design and redesign machines that alter our standard of living, but we cannot reshape the human personality to eradicate sin's flaws, which so warp and twist our relationships.

While some modern and ancient Christians have been optimistic about human spiritual potential, most Christians have taken sin more seriously. Most believers have realized that without God's special aid, individuals and society are hopelessly trapped by personal and spiritual inadequacies that often find expression in open hostility. ◆ SIN, DE-PRAVITY, FREE WILL

BORN AGAIN

The phrase is commonly recognized today, although many people misunderstand its meaning. Jesus was the first one to use it, telling a nighttime visitor that human beings must be born again (John 3:3–15). Peter picks up the same phrase, reminding believers that "you have been born again, not of perishable seed, but of imperishable, through the living and enduring word of God" (1 Peter 1:23).

The imagery reflects a basic teaching of Scripture. Human beings are portrayed in the Bible as spiritually dead, unable to please God or live a truly righteous life. Only a new spiritual life provided by God can change a person and his or her destiny. Jesus came to earth just because human beings must be born again, and only through faith in Jesus does an inner spiritual rebirth take place.

What are the signs of the new birth? John's writings portray the signs in terms of moral transformation. The person who is born of God will not "keep on sinning." The habit of moral failure so deeply ingrained in human nature will be broken, and "no one who is born of God will continue to sin, because God's seed remains in him; he cannot go on sinning, because he has been born of God" (1 John 3:9; 5:18). God's own life is introduced in the human personality through the new birth, and that dynamic vitality begins to infuse and change us. A similar expression of this new life is seen in a growing love for our fellow believers (1 John 4:7; 5:1–4). The new birth leads to both love and purity, for God's own life swells up in the twice born. ◗ LIFE, DEATH, FAITH

CALLING

The word *calling* is related to several issues in the vocabulary of Christian faith. In one context *calling* raises questions about what really happens when a person hears the gospel and responds to it with faith. In another context *calling* focuses attention on the Christian's attitude toward work, particularly toward "Christian work."

God's calling in our faith. Christians through the ages agree that salvation comes as a person hears the message about Jesus and responds to that message with a saving faith. Two things are necessary: A person must hear the gospel and must respond to that message by putting his or her trust in Jesus.

It is clear from experience as well as Scripture that not all who hear the objective message respond with faith. Yet some do. And so throughout church history some theologians have struggled with the question, "Why do some reject Jesus and others accept him?"

The biblical use of the word *call* helped to focus this argument during the Reformation. The Protestant Reformers noted that while at times the word *call* is used to indicate an objective presentation of the gospel itself (as in "many are called but few are chosen"), at other times the word *call* seems to indicate God's special work that guarantees a positive response to the message (Rom. 8:30). Theologians in the Reformed tradition then explained what happens when a person believes this way: God acted within the person to confirm the truth of the gospel message, influencing him or her (without force) to be willing to believe. Those who reject the gospel and choose not to believe, hear the external call to faith, but that external call is not accompanied by the Spirit's inner call, which is necessary to influence the free choice to believe.

This particular view of how God and human beings interact in coming to faith in Christ is not the only view we find in church history, and it is closely linked with the Reformers' belief in predestination. ◗ PREDESTINATION, FREE WILL, DEPRAVITY

What are some of the other views? We can see various ideas about what happens when we look at a hypothetical situation. Both Ken and Carl heard the gospel regularly, not only as children in their churches but also as adults through reading, radio, TV, and the testimony of friends. Ken responded to the gospel message and accepted Jesus as his Savior.

Carl simply continued to shake his head and refused to believe. What kinds of explanations have been suggested in church history to explain their opposite responses to the same objective presentations of the gospel?

Viewpoint	Ken	Carl
Pelagian	Ken willed to believe.	Carl willed to reject.
Semipelagian	Ken began to try to believe and was helped.	Carl made no effort to believe.
Arminian	Ken cooperated with the grace God gives all people.	Carl did not cooperate.
Lutheran	Ken yielded to God's grace.	Carl continually resisted God's grace.
Calvinist	Ken was given new life by God's Spirit, and so chose to believe.	Carl was not.

To some extent these various theories are irrelevant to believer and nonbeliever alike. We who are Christians simply know that we have heard God's offer of full forgiveness in Jesus and that we trust ourselves to him. We made our choice freely, not because God forced us to believe against our will. Whatever hidden influences may or may not have been at work, nothing changes the wonderful reality that now we have a new life and full salvation in Jesus Christ. As for those who are not yet Christians, speculations about what may or may not be happening inside them beg the issue. The gospel offer is objective and real. The answer to the question, "What must I do to be saved?" remains the same as ever: "Believe in the Lord Jesus Christ, and you will be saved" (Acts 16:30–31). That choice is one that must be made by everyone, and nothing can change the fact that we are responsible for the decision we alone can make.

God's calling to our occupation. The other way that Christians use the word *call* involves one's work. Martin Luther taught Christians to view every occupation as a Christian calling. Each occupation provides some opportunity for us to serve others and be God's ministers to them for good. Each occupation allows us the opportunity to excel: to do our work well and so bring glory to God, who approves of faithfulness in every situation. This view elevates every occupation — teaching, plumbing, selling — to the level of ministry, and our most ordinary tasks are transformed into Christian service.

In more recent times some believers have focused the idea of a

Christian calling much more narrowly. "Full-time Christian service" as a pastor, a missionary, or in a similar religious occupation has been seen as the object of one's "call." The question of "how were you called to the ministry" entered the vocabulary of faith.

Two things can help Christians keep work and ministry in perspective. The first is the realization that each of us has gifts and talents that enable us to contribute in different ways to others. The plumber is as necessary as the preacher (and, if your basement floods, probably more necessary!). It is wrong to think of some occupations as Christian and others as merely secular jobs. Luther was right: All work is to be undertaken as ministry, and all work is to be done with excellence, as unto the Lord. The second realization is that despite our human tendency to rank persons and occupations, God places his people as he wills. You and I are to undertake our work with as deep a sense of God's calling as are the missionaries or the pastors that we mistakenly assume to be so different from ourselves. ♦ **LAITY**

CANON

The canon is comprised of the Old and New Testament books that are acknowledged as authoritative Scripture. By Jesus' time the Jews accepted the books in our Old Testament as uniquely inspired by God. Very early in the Christian era lists of the writings that make up our New Testament appeared, and after some early hesitation over Hebrews, James, and one or two others, the twenty-seven books of our New Testament were universally accepted as God's inspired Word. ♦ **INSPI-RATION, SCRIPTURE**

CHARISMATIC

We use the word *charismatic* to describe persons who emphasize the importance of the Holy Spirit in Christian experience, worship, and witness. Charismatics also have distinctive views about the gifts of the Holy Spirit and how those gifts are to function in the church today. Charismatics are not divided from other Christians but are found in many major fellowships and traditional mainline denominations. ♦ **HOLY SPIRIT, SPIRITUAL GIFTS**

CHRIST ◆ JESUS CHRIST

CHRISTIAN

Believers were first called Christians in the pagan city of Antioch (Acts 11:26). It was intended as a joke, a bit of cynical ridicule. Christian means "little Christ," and the pagan population apparently thought it quite funny to see these disciples of a crucified Jew running around, trying to imitate him.

But what a challenge that ancient joke raises for you and me today. John raises the challenge too: "Whoever claims to live in him [Jesus] must walk as Jesus did" (1 John 2:6). We really are supposed to be little Christs, reproducing in the quality of our own relationships with others his love, compassion, and commitment to do the Father's will.

CHURCH

We use the word in a number of ways. We use it of the building where we worship, the denomination to which we belong, the whole company of believers alive in the world (the church militant), and all believers of all ages now in the presence of God (the church triumphant). But even when we use it in the most general of ways, we need to define carefully what we mean. People who speak about the church may mean very different things.

For instance in South America today many Catholic priests and missionaries speak of the mission of the church to liberate the poor and the oppressed. What do they mean by the church? In the language of liberation theology the church is the hierarchy — the priests, bishops, religious orders, cardinals, and the pope who speak for God on earth and who are charged with carrying out his will. For the church to speak or act demands that the institution and its ordained representatives become involved with the cause of the needy and exercise spiritual and, where necessary, civil power on their behalf.

This view of the church, so strange to those in the Protestant tradition, must be understood if Christians today are to understand what many Catholic priests in the third world think and mean.

How have Christians through the ages viewed the church? What has this great word meant through the various eras of church history, and what does it mean to us today?

The earliest centuries. At first the church was simply a fellowship of men and women who shared a common faith in Jesus and a commitment of love for believing brothers and sisters. The New Testament is rich in gentle instruction to believers on how to live together in fellowship. Nearly every New Testament book gives instructions: believers are to "be devoted to one another in brotherly love" (Rom. 12:10) and having been cleansed by obedience to God's truth, to "love one another deeply, from the heart" (1 Peter 1:22). The dynamic power of that loving community exploded to expand the company of believers through the known world. Committed to the apostles' teaching as it was recorded in the Scriptures, the early church knew an organic existence. Small groups met in homes. Elders in local communities guarded the purity of believers and taught them. Itinerants with special gifts and teachings traveled from place to place to enrich the faith of believers.

Christians, then, lived in community with other relatively small groups of believers. They recognized the authority of Scripture, and when heretical ideas were introduced, they relied on the teachings of Scripture and the traditions of the apostles. But the key to the early church's dynamic was found not in its structure but in the believers' commitment to each other, their fellowship with Jesus, and their responsiveness to his Word.

In that era the church was thought of and experienced as the community of faith, the fellowship of Jesus' people. It was made up of all believers, who linked themselves with Jesus' people by profession of faith in the Lord.

Hierarchical Christianity. As Christianity moved into its third century, significant changes took place. Under challenges to historic Christian doctrines, an emphasis was placed on correct interpretation of Scripture. The view developed that bishops (recognized Christian leaders of major centers of the Roman empire), the successors of the apostles, were charged with guarding the apostolic tradition. The view developed that an unbroken succession of these leaders, going back to the time of Christ himself, guaranteed the reliability of orthodox teaching. In time the church became more and more identified with the bishops and particularly with the bishop of Rome.

Parallel with this development was a transition in thinking about the priesthood. In the early church all believers were priests, called by God to minister to one another with whatever gift they had been given. With the emergence of the episcopacy (bishops), a situation developed in which only the authorized few were permitted to baptize or offer the Lord's Supper. The church became increasingly the institution in which the Word was preached and the sacraments observed, under the authority of ordained bishops and priests. One who did not identify with this visible structure was not a member of the church of Christ.

Not all Christian thinkers adopted this view of the church. Augustine, one of the greatest of the church fathers, wrote of the "mixed church" of time and the "pure church" of the future. The visible institution is a congregation that mixes the wicked with the saints. The wheat and the tares, the real and the counterfeit, are both found among those who give outward allegiance to the institutional church. But, Augustine argued, in the proper sense, God's church actually includes only the good and the holy.

The early Christian fellowship that bore the marks of mutual love and obedience to Scripture had been replaced by a structure that was marked by a hierarchical leadership that claimed unbroken succession from the apostles. This new leadership taught that only the visible institution could correctly interpret God's Word or administer the sacraments.

But throughout this era of church history, church fathers like Augustine realized that the visible church of the hierarchy could not be identified with the true church of God. Yet by the eleventh century, the church had become a powerful institution consisting of rulers and subjects.

Reformation concepts of the church. The sixteenth century's reaffirmation of salvation by faith alone resulted in a repudiation of many of the Catholic church's doctrines. Clearly one belief that had to be reexamined was the concept of the church. The hierarchical structure of Catholicism was rejected. The Reformers found Scripture to declare that all believers are priests, all believers are directly responsible to God, and all can study the Scriptures.

Martin Luther emphasized the mystical reality. The true church is composed of those who are believers, one in faith, existing on earth at all times and ages. Thus Luther writes, "I believe that there is upon earth a little holy group and congregation of pure saints, under one head, even Christ, called together by the Holy Ghost in one faith, one mind and understanding, with manifold gifts, yet agreeing in love, without sects or schisms." Luther described the visible church as a gathering of the saints, where God's pure Word is preached and the sacraments administered.

Calvin and the other Reformers viewed the church as the elect of all ages and places. But Calvin argued that the visible church is also the true church. Both are composed of believers and their children, and although there may be hypocrites among professing believers, withdrawal from the visible church is a denial of Christ. They described the marks of the true church as: the preaching of the Word, the administration of the sacraments, and the exercise of a discipline that promotes holiness. ▸
BAPTISM, CHURCH AND STATE, ISRAEL

Not all people during the Reformation were satisfied with the view adopted by the Reformers. Splinter groups like the Anabaptists called for a believers' church. Only those who made a personal, adult profession of Christ as personal Savior, and thus became members of the body of Christ, should be recognized as church members. The church should function as in New Testament times, as a living fellowship of men and women who care for one another and support each other in their desire for holiness. The assumption that the visible church, an institution, could be identified with the invisible body of Christ was strongly denounced.

The church today. Today a number of important questions are being raised and worked out in the life of many congregations. Whatever our concept of the relationship between the visible, institutional church and the mystic, true church composed of the believers of all ages, Christians are concerned with a recovery of that community we see described in the New Testament.

In our local congregations we can be again a true fellowship, loving one another, encouraging and supporting each other, ministering to each other with our spiritual gifts, and living out our obedience to Jesus and his Word.

Many very significant issues must be worked out. For instance, what are the implications of the fact that Jesus is the living head of his church? How are human leaders to exercise their influence while operating in a way that recognizes the supernatural guidance by Christ of his own body? What are the implications of the many images of the church in Scripture: images of a body, a family, a holy temple?

Our understanding of the church will shape our views of political and Christian responsibilities. Can Christ's church be identified with its visible institutional expressions? Are ministries to be undertaken by the church or by Christians? Is the church to speak out on moral and political issues? Or do we do violence to the nature of the church when Christian leaders or representative assemblies claim to speak for it? While few people would deny the believer's responsibility to be involved in good works and in shaping his or her society, many people are concerned when institutions lay claim to speak out as Jesus' contemporary voice.

We can and should struggle with such issues so that we can act in closest harmony with who we are as God's people. But we all are participants now in local congregations. Perhaps it is most important of all to commit ourselves to live together in our churches as an active faith community. Whatever our views of the theoretical issues, we must all be excited about the fresh emphasis in our day on true community. Christian assemblies are not first of all institutions. They are fellowships of men and women who through faith are joined to Jesus and to one another. To live together as the church that is the living body of Christ, we need to enrich our love for one another and to encourage each other in love for God. If in our local fellowships we focus on building these two relationships, the horizontal and the vertical, we will discover by experience what it means to be the church of Jesus Christ. ◗ BODY OF CHRIST, FELLOWSHIP

CHURCH AND STATE

In the United States the separation of church and state is established doctrine. Our society is pluralistic, and our Constitution not only guarantees freedom of religion, but it also limits the right of Congress to make any laws that might be construed as establishing any specific religion.

The implications of our separation of church and state policy are constantly being tested and refined, and sometimes changed, by the courts. Does separation of church and state mean that the schools cannot set aside a moment for silent prayer at the beginning of the school day? Does separation of church and state require schools to keep Christian groups of teens off school property, while freedom of speech requires the same schools to make the same property available if a group of young communists wants to use it for its club meeting? Does separation of church and state mean that a city cannot display a manger scene at Christmas? Does it mean that pastors should not encourage their people to vote for a particular candidate, based on his or her attitude toward such moral issues as abortion?

One reason we are uncertain of the exact meaning of our notion of separation of church and state is that this approach to church/state relationships is relatively new. Throughout history, different concepts of that relationship have emerged, have been tested, and often have been transformed by national and international events. The framers of our Constitution wrote at a time when many nations had established a particular faith or denomination as the "official" religion of the country. That religion was supported by the government and was given many legal advantages. The Constitution requires the government to avoid this common European practice. But the writers of our Constitution hardly foresaw the issues that trouble us today: Their constitutional safeguard was merely designed to guarantee that no denomination became America's official religion, so there would be freedom for all to worship as they chose.

What does history tell us about the ways believers have related to secular government? Understanding the different patterns that have emerged and what Christians have believed about the relationship between the church and the state may help us think more clearly about how we can best respond to the church/state issues we face today.

Church and state in Scripture. The law of the Old Testament was given to Israel. In Old Testament times the people of God were both a faith community and a nation. Thus the law not only regulated the religious life of God's people, but it also regulated social, civil, and other "secular" matters. As a people set apart to honor the Lord, everything in Israel's national as well as spiritual life was to bear the stamp of God's character and holiness.

In the New Testament we have a different situation. God's people are called to be his church, not a nation. This faith community is scattered, existing within every nation, a part of and yet different from every society. The New Testament commands believers to live as good citizens of their nations, subjecting themselves to human governments (Rom. 13:1-7). Christians are to pay taxes, live quiet lives committed to doing good, and show proper respect for the secular powers by submitting "for the Lord's sake to every authority instituted among men" (1 Peter 2:13-17). The emphasis in the New Testament is on the mystical but real kingdom of God, which exists in the present as well as in the future and which cannot be equated with any specific state or other human institution. ◢ CHURCH, KINGDOM OF GOD

The body of Christ and the kingdom of God are clearly mystical concepts, emphasizing on the one hand the unique organic relationship that determines interpersonal relationships in the church and on the other hand the believer's commitment to Christ as Lord. The Old Testament law that establishes Israel as an earthly nation finds no parallel teaching in the New Testament. Instead New Testament teaching focuses on how believers can live as a community of faith, affirming the rule of God by living as citizens of his kingdom in an essentially hostile world.

Church and state in conflict. In the first centuries of the Christian era, Christianity was an illicit religion. Christians rejected the traditional gods and goddesses and refused to participate in emperor worship. Thus Christians were characterized as atheists, and under several emperors, Christians were fiercely persecuted. During this era the state was clearly the enemy of the church. Yet believers attempted to follow the dictates of Scripture and live as good citizens, coming into conflict only in those areas where the government demanded actions that Christians saw as violations of God's higher law.

Church and state in union. By A.D. 320, the Emperor Constantine had professed Christianity and he began to take a hand in church affairs. The emperor actually gave legal force to the decrees of church councils. In A.D. 381 another emperor announced, "What I desire, that is canon." While the state took the side of orthodoxy in the doctrinal conflicts of the era, by the time of Justin I (A.D. 518–527), a clear political demand for harmony in government, laws, and church had emerged. Justin strengthened the power of the institutional church and the clergy, but in exchange, the church surrendered independence. At this time, too, it was affirmed that the bishop of Rome "is the first of all priests." While a few, like Augustine, caught glimpses of the New Testament vision of the church as a community of faith, that biblical vision was replaced by the notion of a visible, hierarchical structure supported by the secular power. As the secular power of the visible church increased, the spiritual power of the mystical decreased. Church and state were wedded. History shows struggles for dominance between secular and church powers, but it does not record an attempt by the church to recover its true biblical identity.

Church and state in the Reformation. The Reformers saw the church as the company of the saved of all ages. But they also argued that the visible company of those who professed Christ, even though that company might contain hypocrites, must also be considered the church. ♦ CHURCH

While the marks of the true church are primarily spiritual (the preaching of the Word, the proper discipline of members, and the administration of the sacraments), the visible church must also have a relationship with the secular power. The Reformers made a distinction between government of the inner person and "that which relates to civil justice, and the regulation of external conduct." But the Reformers also believed that regulation of conduct was a church concern and that civil government has a responsibility to uphold true religion. Zwingli, the Swiss Reformer, argued that a government that refuses to cooperate with the church should be overthrown. Calvin called on his followers to obey the magistrates, "whatever their character," as long as they do not call on believers to be disobedient to God.

Both these Reformers, however, were captivated by the notion of a theocracy: a nation of believers led by a church and government that were together committed to produce a people of God. In this ideal state the church would be supreme in matters of doctrine, and the civil authority would undertake the discipline of those who stray from the path of godliness. Both Zwingli and Calvin attempted to shape theocratic states, while Luther accepted the support of Lutheran princes and the resultant practice that the ruler's faith should be the faith of his or her subjects.

During this era it was the Anabaptists and other splinter groups that rejected the notion of any kind of union between church and state. These dissenters believed strongly that the church is solely a community of faith and that to identify a visible institution as "the church" of God is terrible error. Christians should expect to live in a hostile world and should have nothing to do with this world's institutions. Only a strict separation between church and state could preserve the unique identity of God's people and could protect them from corruption by the world.

In general the view of the Reformers has dominated the European church scene, marked as it still is by the existence of state churches. On the other hand, in the thinking of Americans has been imbedded the vision of a church that exists in our world but cannot be identified with any political movement without suffering loss of its distinctive identity.

Church and state today. This brief sketch leaves out many important interactions between church and state. It eliminates the struggle between the Roman Catholic church and later rulers for supremacy in sacred and secular realms. It leaves out the early history of our country and the struggle to establish religious liberty in colonies that were established specifically to enflesh the theocratic theories of their founders. But it does help us to focus on several critical issues.

First, how are we to view the church? Is our vision to incorporate elements that characterized Israel as a nation? Or are we to limit ourselves to New Testament teachings and focus our understanding on the church as an organism? ▸ **ISRAEL**

Second, how are we to see the relationship of the church to human governments and political systems? Those who have tended to stress the importance of the visible church generally argue that state and church are to cooperate in establishing a godly society. Those who have tended to stress the invisible church and invisible kingdom of God have generally believed that there is no basis for harmony between the church and the state.

Third, is it really the responsibility of the state to affirm biblical values and to implement them as civil laws? This becomes particularly significant when states take legal stands on moral issues (like abortion and homosexuality) and/or when a state's laws call on citizens to act against their religious convictions. How are Christians to respond in such situations? If the visible church as an institution can speak for God or for his people, should the church take a stand?

Each of these issues is essentially theological, rooted in a vision of the nature of Christ's church. Persons in different religious traditions are apt to answer these questions in very different ways. But at the same time, there may be a surprising unity among Christians who have to deal with the practical issues.

We Christians are citizens not only of God's kingdom but also of our nation. As such we are to live as good citizens, obedient to the laws of the nation and seeking the good of its leaders. In an open and democratic society, good citizenship implies involvement by the individual in the political process. Each person in the United States has an opportunity to influence the making of laws by his or her vote and also by more direct kinds of involvement. It is thus important that the individual Christian act as a responsible citizen to seek the passage of laws that express his or her moral convictions and his or her vision of a just society. In practice, Christian citizens are to act on their convictions and seek to affect the course of the nation for good.

This "Christian individual" approach does bypass important questions about whether the church as an institution has a role in seeking to shape the state. It does not, however, make the mistake of identifying pastors who express their moral convictions and beliefs as "the church." It does not view the prophetic role of Christian leaders as an attempt by the church to control the state. Believers do not violate church/state separation when as individuals — whatever their institutional role — they call other believers to participate in or attempt to influence the process by which our nation's laws are shaped.

Christians may never agree on how the church and the state should relate to one another. In the United States we are likely to remain suspicious of those who claim to speak for all Christians or claim to present the church's moral position. But certainly we cannot ask Christians whose moral convictions are subject to Scripture's teachings to refuse to speak about or to act on those moral convictions. And certainly, in a pluralistic society in which all have been guaranteed equal access to the political process through which laws are shaped, we cannot ask Christians to be silent. Whatever the appropriate relationship between the church and state may be, it is always appropriate for individual Christians to become actively involved in affirming what they believe to be the divine standards for humankind. Any laws that result would no more be "imposed" by Christians on those with different beliefs than laws with which Christians may disagree have been "imposed" on believers. In a democratic process where all beliefs are argued in the open, resultant laws reflect the will of the majority, not the convictions of a religious minority.

CLERGY ♦ PRIESTHOOD

CONFESSION

When Christians think about confession, we think about confessing our sins. In the New Testament confess can mean "to publicly acknowledge" ("confess Christ"). But in the vocabulary of faith, confession is linked intimately with human fault and failure. What have Christians thought about confession, and what does the Bible teach?

The Catholic doctrine of confession is rooted in its sacrament of repentance, first given clear expression by Pope Gregory the Great (c. A.D. 604). Gregory taught that when a person sins, he or she offends God and must make satisfaction. This requires a change of mind (or at least an unease about sinful acts), a verbal confession, and punishment (works of penance). The process issues in forgiveness and a return to good works. At various times in church history Catholics have emphasized different aspects of this process. In practice, Catholics go to a priest and confess the sins they have committed since their last confession. The priest gives them some task to perform as penance ("Say twelve Hail Mary's") and announces absolution. The sacrament becomes the means by which believers receive forgiveness and salvation.

In one of the earliest Christian documents (an instructional monograph called the "Didache"), public confession of sins in the congregation is encouraged in association with public prayer. Confession is also taught by the early church father Origen, who links it with repentance. Origen views confession as an inward act, an exchange between the individual and God. But Origen does encourage individuals to confess their sins to others (clergy or laypersons) who have the qualities of Jesus our High Priest, who sympathizes with us in our weaknesses (Heb. 2:17–18). This early sensitivity to sin and to the awareness that it is appropriate to confess sin was later transformed into the Catholic doctrine. The critical difference in the early church and Catholic view is that the Roman Catholic sacrament came to be viewed as a means of salvation through which human beings received forgiveness. The sacrament itself, with slight contrition or faith on the part of the sinner, was viewed as efficacious. In the writings of the early Christians, confession is made to God by believers who have trusted in Christ and thus have already received forgiveness for their sins.

At the time of the Protestant Reformation, the recovery of the biblical doctrine of salvation by faith alone led to a rethinking of repentance and confession. Luther came to the conviction that we are to confess our sins only to God, and that any additional confession required by a church is a mere human ordinance. It is not the sacrament of repentance, undergone because of discontent or fear of punishment, that brings salvation. It is the gospel of Jesus, the Word of God announcing that all who believe already stand forgiven on the basis of Jesus' sacrifice for their sins. Whatever the role of confession in Christian experience, it cannot be a means of salvation.

The Reformation drove Christians back to Scripture to rethink the role of confession and its meaning. That meaning is first established by the Greek term translated by our English word *confess*. The original meaning is drawn from the contemporary legal system: to confess meant "to agree with a charge brought against you." Confession was acknowledging guilt before a court. Confession of sins, then, means to admit to God that a particular action or thought is indeed sin. The notion that confession means feeling sorry or promising never to commit a particular sin again is foreign to the meaning of the original term.

The New Testament passage that deals with Christian confession of sins is 1 John 1:5–2:2. There John points out that fellowship with the Lord depends not on sinlessness but on "walking in the light." This phrase suggests complete honesty with ourselves and with God. Rather than deceiving ourselves and trying to deceive God when we fail, we are to acknowledge our sin to God. When we bring our failure to the Lord, he "is faithful and just and will forgive us our sins, and purify us from all unrighteousness" (1 John 1:9). Jesus has dealt decisively with our sins. He has paid for them and is our advocate, standing with us against any accusations. When we come to God and acknowledge our failures openly, we experience the forgiveness that is already ours in Jesus. We also experience God's own cleansing work within our personality.

What, then, about public confession? Both the Old Testament (Ps. 51 and 2 Sam. 11) and the New Testament (James 5:16) seem to encourage it. In the Old Testament public confession is appropriate in the case of public sins. When a community is aware of a person's sins and is affected by them, public confession is necessary. In the New Testament public confession may be implicit in the calling of Christians to live open, honest lives with one another (Eph. 4:25).

The tone of confession as we read of it in Scripture is surprisingly different from what we might expect. In the centuries immediately following the New Testament era, teaching on confession seems to flow from a deep sense of personal sin. In the developed Catholic era confession is a mechanism by which the institutional church is maintained; power is vested in the sacrament itself at the expense of the personal faith of the believer. But in Scripture confession is an outgrowth of intimacy and confidence. Believers know Jesus forgives their sins and assures them of heaven. ◗ ASSURANCE

Within this relationship the believer is free to "approach the throne of grace with confidence," whether in need of mercy or of grace (Heb. 4:16). The motivation for confession is a realization that one has failed and that only by taking a stand with God and acknowledging guilt can the intimacy of fellowship with the Lord be maintained. We confess our sin, not out of fear but out of love. In confession we experience a forgiveness that is already ours in Christ, and we open up our lives to God's transforming power.

CONFESSIONS ◆ CREEDS

CONFIRMATION

In the Catholic church confirmation is considered one of seven sacraments by which God's grace is communicated to members. Confirmation is administered by a bishop and is viewed as giving the Holy Spirit to the individual to strengthen him or her for godly living.

During the Reformation this sacramental concept was challenged. In many Protestant churches today confirmation classes for adolescents are used to give special instruction in Christian beliefs before accepting a young person as a church member. This Protestant practice reflects the situation in the early church, in which new believers were given instruction in the faith they had professed.

CONSCIENCE

Both psychology and theology take an interest in conscience. In a sense both are interested in morality and in moral action. Psychologists have been fascinated by conscience, not so much because it produces moral actions but because so many things can go wrong with it. Conscience can be distorted, produce neurotic guilt, and fail to counter impulses. Conscience can even actively condemn delinquents into actions that are wrong just so they can be punished! But in the vocabulary of faith, conscience points up both the glory and the tragedy of being human.

The glory of human conscience. Conscience is a Greek concept. In that culture the notion of a conscience was distasteful, for it meant looking back and evaluating remembered events. Greek literature refers to the "bad conscience," which plagues its owner about past failures.

But in Scripture, conscience, which points to human moral faculty, is a witness to the image of God. Human beings alone of all creation share with the Lord a moral sense, intuitively recognizing the moral nature of many choices. Paul makes it clear that even the pagans who have no contact with divine revelation have an inner witness to morality planted within their very nature (Rom. 2:14–15).

The existence of conscience, then, gives constant testimony to the truth that human beings are more than animals: The mark of the eternal is stamped indelibly on the human personality.

The tragedy of human conscience. The tragedy of conscience is found in its inability to cause human beings to be truly good.

On the one hand, the content of conscience (one's moral beliefs) may be faulty. God's revelation has given human beings instruction that is designed to inform the conscience. Through God's Word we have authoritative information about what is truly good and truly bad. But not all people know or accept the divine revelation of moral truth. Paul teaches in Romans 2 that even those without revelation recognize moral issues. Every culture has notions of right and wrong associated with sex, property rights, and other rights of the individual. The specific beliefs about what is right (one wife or four, as in Muslim countries) may differ. But all people recognize the same issues as having moral dimensions. Yet, even when information is available from revelation as to the right content for the conscience, human beings may refuse to accept that information. The Bible describes the understanding of humanity as "darkened" because "of the ignorance that is in them due to the hardening of their hearts" (Eph. 4:18). The human conscience is not corrupted just by a lack of information about right and wrong but by an unwillingness to understand God's ways.

The tragedy is compounded by the fact that moral knowledge carries no guarantee that one will act morally. Paul in Romans recognizes the Jew's knowledge of God's will. They "approve what is superior because they are instructed by the law" (Rom. 2:18). The problem here is a misuse of knowledge. Some treat moral knowledge as if it were the basis on which to judge others. But they, like everyone else, actually fall short of doing what they know to be right. Paul's conclusion is that all have sinned and fallen short of the revealed morality of God. As a result all that the knowledge of good can do is to inform the person of his or her failures. "Whatever the law says, it says to those who are under the law, so that every mouth may be silenced and the whole world held accountable to God" (Rom. 3:19). An informed conscience can only condemn and never can cause a person to become righteous, for no one does perfectly what conscience tells him or her is right.

The New Testament has other descriptive terms that focus our attention on the inadequacy of conscience. The Bible speaks of a defiled conscience. When we violate our sense of right and wrong by regularly choosing to do wrong, our conscience becomes scarred — so defiled that we lose all sense of moral direction (1 Cor. 8:7; Titus 1:15). Even the conscience of a believer may be "weak" (Rom. 14:1–10). In context the weak conscience is troubled because it is not yet aware of biblical principles that could guide to appropriate choices. The weak conscience is vulnerable, sometimes leading a person to act against his or her convictions and often leading a person to judge others in matters in which believers are to exercise individual freedom.

The Christian's conscience. The New Testament speaks positively about both a cleansed and a good conscience. The writer of Hebrews looks back at the animal sacrifices of the Old Testament and notes that they were "not able to clear the conscience of the worshiper" (Heb. 9:9). The repeated sacrifices of the Old Testament system simply reminded the worshiper that he or she was guilty before God. Past failures were stored up in the person's memory, shouting guilt and draining confidence in a transformed future. ▶ GUILT

The writer goes on to point out that the blood of Christ accomplished what the Old Testament sacrifices could not. Jesus' blood is able to "cleanse our conscience from acts that lead to death, so that we may serve the living God" (Heb. 9:14). This cleansing is both objective and subjective. Objectively, Jesus' death brings a full forgiveness of sins, so that God himself "remembers our lawless acts no more" (Heb. 10:17). Subjectively, cleansing makes forgiveness available to us so that the burden of our past failures is removed. When we remember that we are forgiven, we are released from the bondage of that "bad conscience" that so plagued the Greeks, and we are able to look ahead eagerly, confident that we truly can serve God. The passage goes on to assure us: As we live now to please God, we will receive the promise (Heb. 10:35–36). We will be freed from our past by the cleansing of our conscience; we will learn to look forward with optimism to a full, meaningful life.

Paul writes about the clear conscience, which a Christian maintains by living in harmony with the truth of God's Word (Acts 24:16; 2 Cor. 1:12; 1 Tim. 1:5–19; 2 Tim. 1:3; 1 Peter 3:16–21). As we act on what we believe to be right, we maintain a clear conscience and have confidence in our relationships with others and with God (but see 1 Cor. 4:4–5).

One important theme in Scripture reminds us that we are responsible only to our own conscience. In some areas the Bible speaks plainly about what is right and wrong. In these areas our choices are not so much a matter of conscience (e.g., moral sensibilities) as they are matters for obedience. But in some areas, like the eating of meat and keeping of holy days (Rom. 14), Scripture provides no definitive right/wrong guidance. How are decisions to be made in such areas? Paul treats such things as issues to be decided by the individual on the basis of his or her own best judgment of what will please God (Rom. 14:5–6). One must act on personal convictions in such areas, for going against conscience involves sin, for "everything that does not come from faith is sin" (Rom. 14:23). But at the same time Paul makes it very clear that one person's conscience is not a basis on which he or she can judge others. Any condemning or contempt for another believer based on personal conscience is strictly forbidden, for believers are called to give account in such areas only to God (Rom. 14:3–4, 8–10).

What, then, are we to think about conscience? Conscience provides testimony to our moral nature, but conscience is not a safe guide to behavior. Its judgments may be faulty, and it will not motivate a person to do what is right.

Conscience is important, however, in unbeliever and believer alike. In one who does not yet know Jesus, the nagging of a guilty conscience may turn attention to the possibility of forgiveness. That forgiveness can be found only in Jesus, who wipes away our past and cleanses our conscience. While believers are to recognize the inadequacy of conscience, they are to keep a clear conscience by doing what they believe is right. As a person grows in Christian faith, the conscience will gradually be strengthened and the understanding of right and wrong will be reshaped by a growing understanding of God and his Word. While Christians are to be responsive to their consciences in making personal decisions, we are not to impose our own sense of right and wrong on the Christian community. Jesus is Lord, and he exercises his lordship over the church through his Word. On issues about which the Scriptures are silent, Christians are to give one another the freedom to be responsible to Jesus himself.

CONVERSION

It does happen. A person experiences an inner change, sometimes radical, and his or her life is reoriented. A person moves from unbelief to belief, from a sense of guilt and alienation from God to an awareness of forgiveness and joy.

Sometimes conversion is revolutionary. Augustine, struggling in the fourth century with his own doubt and sin, wept under a fig tree until he picked up the Scriptures and read, "Put on the Lord Jesus Christ and make no provision for the flesh." Augustine later writes: "No further would I read, nor did I need, for instantly, as the sentence ended — by a light, as it were, of security infused into my heart, — all the gloom of doubt vanished away" (*Confessions* VIII.12.29). Great Christian leaders like the apostle Paul, Martin Luther, and John Wesley experienced the same kind of sudden conversion. For other believers, conversion has been gradual, whispered, coming unnoticed in childhood or coming so gradually that the time of passage was never recognized in the adult. And yet Christians have been deeply aware that conversion is necessary.

Historically conversion was looked at primarily from a theological perspective. What actually happens when a person comes to faith and enters a relationship with God? More recently conversion has been examined from a psychological perspective. What experiences seem to be associated most often with religious conversion, and what changes can we observe in a person who experiences it?

Theological views of conversion. In traditions in which conversion is emphasized, we find a serious view of humanity's sinful condition. A number of biblical images provide background. The natural state of fallen humanity is "dead in transgressions and sins" (Eph. 2:1), willingly following the ways of this world and the cravings of a sin-warped nature. This spiritual death can only be overcome by the mercy of God, who acts in love to make us "alive in Christ" (Eph. 2:5). Other verses emphasize human powerlessness (Rom. 5:6), complicated by the fact that in our natural state, we human beings are the active enemies of God (Rom. 5:10). So Scripture affirms that "the mind of sinful man is death . . . because the sinful mind is hostile to God. It does not submit to God's law, nor can it do so" (Rom. 8:6–7). Whenever Christians have taken this portrait of humanity seriously, they realize that Scripture describes a radical change in both state and attitude. We must pass from death to life. We must change from God's enemies into his friends. We must reject the cravings of sin within and submit to God's law. In short, the notion of an inner transformation of the individual believer is basic to Christian faith.

The early church fathers believed in conversion and wrote of faith's new birth. But little attention was given to the specific role of the individual and the Holy Spirit in the process by which a person came to new life in Christ. In the Catholic era the concept of salvation by sacrament (the belief that saving grace was transmitted by rites conducted by priests and bishops of the church) dominated. Personal conversion did not seem necessary. Original sin was assumed to be purged by baptism, and other sins were forgiven through the sacrament of repentance. With the Reformation came a recovery of the Bible's teaching that salvation comes to human beings through faith in Christ and through faith alone. This teaching drew fresh attention to conversion. Clearly some people responded with faith to the word of the gospel. These were assured of salvation and given new life by God. Just as clearly some rejected the gospel offer. The mystery of why some believed while others did not was a major concern of the Reformers. ◆ CALLING

In general the Reformers believed that human beings were so ruined by the Fall that no one would or could respond to the gospel unless God intervened. Augustine also held this view, teaching in the fourth century that human will was bound by sin and lacked the power of self-deliverance. In Augustine's day this view was opposed by Pelagius, who insisted that human beings can do all that God commands. Pelagius argued that persons are free to choose good or evil and are born without any bias toward either good or evil. To Pelagius the human will determined salvation, for individual initiative and choice are sufficient for any person's conversion. Against this concept Augustine argued that the human will is in bondage to sin, which has taken deep root within the human personality. Adam's sinful nature was transmitted to his offspring. Human moral bondage can be broken only by an act of God's grace; the Holy Spirit generates a renewal within, freeing the will to choose faith.

The Reformers held an essentially Augustinian position. They, too, believed that fallen human beings have no ability to do anything that is spiritually good. Instead freedom of the will is only freedom to willingly choose to do evil. When the the gospel comes, that external message must be accompanied in some way by an internal work of the Holy Spirit. "When the Father is heard within, he takes away the heart of stone and gives a heart of flesh," John Calvin writes. God's inner work leads to faith and repentance. A person believes in Jesus, recognizes his or her sin, and cries out to God for deliverance.

In some sense, then, the Word of God (which brings the message of Christ), the Holy Spirit (who works within the person), and the will of the person interact. The person believes and with faith comes an inner spiritual transformation: a new life that releases the new Christian to choose to respond to God and to actively seek to do what is truly good. Conversion is not simply a change of beliefs. It is an inner transformation that refocuses a person's life on Jesus Christ. While the specific role of the Word, the Spirit, and the human will in conversion may be debated, millions of people have experienced the reality of the transformation that conversion promises to anyone who believes. ◆ FAITH, REPENTANCE, FREE WILL

Psychological views of conversion. Psychologists have been interested in conversion, but they tend to view conversion broadly. To some people conversion is simply a reordering of priorities and attitudes; conversion, therefore, can be religious, political, ethical, or aesthetic in nature.

Christian conversion is unique in two ways. First, the content of the conversion is Christ: Christian conversion is focused as a personal commitment to Jesus. Second, the psychological fruits of Christian conversion are typically peace, love, joy, longsuffering, goodness, gentleness, and other similar qualities (Gal. 5:22–23). Personality and character changes are a common outgrowth of Christian conversion, just as a growing sense of need, or guilt, or a strong desire for a better self are often experienced before conversion. The harmony of Christian experience with Scripture in conversion is striking. The Bible portrays coming to Jesus as a new birth, an entrance into a new kind and quality of life. "If anyone is in Christ, he is a new creation," Paul writes, "the old has gone, the new has come" (2 Cor. 5:17). The experience of countless millions testifies to this reality. With conversion to Christ comes a new personality, gradually in some people, suddenly in others. Life is redirected, values change, and the inner quality of the person's experience is transformed as anxiety gives way to peace and hostility gives way to love. Christian conversion truly unlocks the potential of human beings to develop in the image of God and to grow in the likeness of Jesus Christ.

CONVICTION

Conviction is closely associated with conversion. Conviction is generally understood as God's work in a person's life, preparing him or her to hear the gospel message.

In the New Testament era the Greek word translated "convict" meant "to confront or correct." In Greek culture it came to mean "to accuse" and then "to convict before a court." The Bible teaches that God's Spirit "will convict the world of guilt in regard to sin and righteousness and judgment" (John 16:8). In this powerful ministry, God's Spirit confronts human beings to help them recognize their personal sin and need for salvation. Yet conviction is simply preparatory. Each person remains responsible for the choice he or she ultimately makes. ◆ FAITH

COVENANT

The word *covenant* is important in the vocabulary of Christian faith. Christianity affirms that not only is God personal, he is also the all-powerful ruler of our universe. This God has chosen to reveal himself to human beings. In doing so, God has shown us that he invites us to have a personal relationship with him. In Scripture and in various Christian theological systems, covenants are basic, for they establish the basis on which personal relationships between God and humanity are possible. To understand the meaning of this important biblical and theological word, we need to look at relevant Hebrew and Greek words, at the theological covenants suggested by the Reformers, at three specific Old Testament covenants, and at the new covenant explained in both testaments.

The Hebrew and Greek words translated "covenant." In Old Testament times ancient cultures adopted the concept of a covenant (*berit*) to express a range of interpersonal and social relationships. A covenant between nations was a treaty (Gen. 14:13; 31:44–55). Between persons, a covenant might express a business contract or a pledge of friendship (1 Sam. 18:3; 23:18). A covenant between a ruler and the subjects served as the constitution of states, spelling out the responsibilities of both the ruler and the ruled (2 Sam. 3:21; 5:3). This fundamental relational concept was adopted by God to express truths about his relationship with human beings.

While the concept of covenant was familiar to the Old Testament people, the covenants between God and humanity have unique elements. You will remember that the word *covenant* has different shades of meaning: "contract," "constitution," and "pledge of friendship." We shouldn't be surprised if there are distinctive aspects to the word *covenant* when it is applied to relationships between God and humanity. The distinctives are captured in this definition of a biblical (divine/human) covenant: A biblical covenant is a clear statement by God of his purposes and intentions, expressed in terms that bind God by solemn oath to perform what he has promised.

The Bible identifies four major covenants. In each of them the Lord states what he intends to and most certainly will do. It is through these great covenant promises that we learn who God is and what his plans and purposes for us are. God's commitment to do as he has promised provides a firm basis for our faith.

Covenant has the same meaning in the New Testament. There the Greek word *diatheke* is used. The Greeks used this word in the sense of a will, by which a person chose how to dispose of property. That decision, put into effect when a person died, could not be changed by anyone else. Jesus' death put into force what both testaments call a "new covenant." In Hebrews another Greek word is used: God's Old Testament covenant is called an *orkos* (Heb. 6:17). This word meant "a legally binding guarantee." Hebrews says, "because God wanted to make the unchanging nature of his purpose very clear to the heirs of what was promised, he confirmed it with an oath."

The emphasis in both testaments, then, is on the fact that God has expressed his purposes and announced his plans in the form of covenant promises. These covenant promises provide a firm basis for our faith and enable us to define our relationship with the Lord.

The theological covenants. The Reformers of the sixteenth century were well aware of the significance of the covenants. They expressed their understanding of what the Bible teaches about relationships between God and human beings by summing up that teaching in two basic covenants: a covenant of works and a covenant of grace. These theological covenants are not the same as the biblical covenants. But the Reformers believed that their statement of the theological covenants effectively and accurately summed up what the Bible teaches about salvation. What are the theological covenants?

The covenant of works, the Reformers taught, was a conditional promise made by God to Adam, who was a free moral agent. In effect this covenant was a contract that included conditions. God promised eternal life and endless fellowship with him on the condition that Adam would be obedient and not eat the fruit of a particular tree that was planted in the Garden of Eden (Gen. 2–3). If Adam violated the condition, the consequences would be his death, with all that "death" in Scripture implies. ◆ DEATH

The Reformers taught that as far as the unsaved are concerned, this covenant of works is still in force, with all its binding conditions. Disobedience and unrighteousness still bring God's condemnation. But the situation has changed for the saved. The Reformers realized that Jesus came to earth and lived a perfect life, fulfilling by his obedience every condition of the covenant of works. Then Jesus died for the sins of humankind, not only taking our sins on himself but also offering his own righteousness to us. Believers, who through faith are united to Christ, are released from the covenant of works. That covenant of works is abrogated by the gospel.

To explain what Jesus has done, the Reformers thought in terms of a covenant of grace. This covenant relates specifically to God's plan of redemption. The Reformers saw this covenant as a contract concluded between God the Father (representing the Godhead) and God the Son (representing all the redeemed). Jesus covenanted to fulfill all the obligations of the covenant of works on behalf of his people. Jesus took on all our responsibilities, satisfied all God's conditions (including the condition that sin must be punished by death), and thus won eternal life for his own.

Nearly all aspects of Reformed theology grow out of the way that the Reformers organized their teaching about salvation under these two theological covenants. For instance, infant baptism is practiced as the visible sign and seal of the covenant of grace, just as circumcision functioned in Old Testament times as a sign that the child was a member of Israel's covenant community. ⟩ ISRAEL, BAPTISM

The conviction that a covenant exists between God and humanity is basic in every Christian theological system. But differences about the nature of that covenant (or those covenants) has led to many differences in specifics of Christian beliefs and convictions.

The Old Testament covenants. When we hear Christians speak about covenants, it is important to know whether they are speaking of the theological covenants, described above, or of biblical covenants.

The theological covenants sum up much biblical truth in a significant, systematic way. But the theological covenants are not the same as the biblical covenants, although they are modeled on them. What are the biblical covenants, and what do we need to know to understand each of them?

The Abrahamic covenant is the first of the biblical covenants. God appeared to pagan Abraham, who worshiped the moon god in his native Ur. God told Abraham to leave his homeland and travel to "the land I will show you." At that first contact, God made promises to Abraham that were later confirmed, following human custom to make a binding oath (Gen. 12:2–3; 15:1–21). Still later God instructed Abraham to circumcise all male offspring as a sign that they belonged to the family line to which the covenant promises were given (Gen. 17:1–22).

The promises given to Abraham will be fulfilled at history's end. They tell what God intends to do for the Jewish people then. They also show blessings God offers to Abraham and Jewish generations between Abraham and history's end. What are the promises given in the Abrahamic covenant? "I will make you into a great nation and I will bless you; I will make your name great, and you will be a blessing. I will bless those who bless you, and whoever curses you I will curse; and all peoples on earth will be blessed through you" (Gen. 12:2–3). One other clause is added to the covenant and is also confirmed by covenant oath: "To your offspring I will give this land" (Gen. 12:7).

The firm conviction that God spoke to Abraham and made promises to him about his offspring has given the Jewish people a sense of special identity that has preserved God's Old Testament people as a faith and a race to this day. Also, this covenant is the key to our understanding of the Old Testament, that story of how God has been working out his promises to Israel in history.

Stories telling of God's covenant with Abraham are also our key to understanding personal relationship with God. Abraham heard God announce his purposes and state his promises. The Bible tells us that Abraham responded with faith. "Abram believed the LORD, and he credited it to him as righteousness" (Gen. 15:6). Thus God showed himself willing to accept faith in his promises instead of a righteousness that Abraham did not possess. In Romans, Paul teaches that "the words, 'it was credited to him' were written not for him [Abraham] alone, but also for us, to whom God will credit righteousness for us who believe in him who raised Jesus our Lord from the dead" (Rom. 4:23–24). Faith in God's promise is the key to salvation.

The Mosaic or Law covenant is distinctive in several ways. After four hundred years in Egypt, Abraham's descendants were led out to freedom by Moses. God intended to lead them to the land that he promised to Abraham centuries before. On the way God gave this people a law patterned after the suzerainty treaties of the ancient Middle East. Such covenants were developed between rulers (called suzerains or sovereigns) and subjects. They spelled out the obligations of each party and defined what would happen if subjects kept or violated covenant conditions. The Law covenant, Israel's national constitution, was between God and Israel. It regulated the personal, social, and civil life of Israel as well as defined religious duties. But this covenant was both different from and similar to God's covenant with Abraham.

Like the other biblical covenants, the Mosaic covenant includes an announcement by God of what he intends to do. This statement of God's intentions in the law is unconditional. God will do what he states he will do in the law.

Unlike other biblical covenants, the Law covenant focuses on the present experience of each Israeli generation. The other covenants announce what God will do at history's end. This covenant explains what God will do in history as succeeding generations are either obedient to or disobedient to his law.

Unlike other biblical covenants, the Law covenant was ratified (renewed or confirmed) by the people. Each generation must choose to commit itself to live by the Sinai Law (Exod. 24; Deut. 29; Josh. 24). Today in Jewish society, a child who is twelve years old makes a similar choice and becomes "bar mitzvah," a son of the commandment.

Law, then, defined how Israel was to live as a nation under God. It provided a full set of laws and regulations to govern every aspect of national and personal life. It was a covenant in the sense of a national constitution, and God, the ruler of Israel, specified not only how his subjects were to live but also committed himself to bless the obedient and punish the disobedient. Unlike every other biblical covenant, the Old Testament says that this Law covenant was temporary, to be replaced by a new covenant (Jer. 31:31–32). ◆ **LAW**

The Mosaic covenant was a temporary covenant, designed to function during Israel's centuries as a nation until the Savior would come to introduce a new and better basis for a person's daily relationship with the Lord.

The third biblical covenant is the Davidic covenant. David was Israel's ideal or model king. Under David the tiny country expanded tenfold to become a powerful state. David's faithfulness to God and his love for the Lord were the key to his effectiveness as a monarch.

The Bible tells us that the prophet Nathan was sent by God to David with a special promise: "Your house and your kingdom will endure forever before me; your throne will be established forever" (2 Sam. 7:16). This commitment is celebrated in the Psalms as a covenant promise (Ps. 89:2–4; 105:8–10). On the basis of this covenant promise, the Jewish people believed firmly that their Messiah (God's anointed deliverer) would be a ruler from David's line and would establish a kingdom ruled perfectly by God. ◆ **KINGDOM**

The genealogies of Jesus contained in Matthew and Luke are there in part to establish Jesus' descent from King David and thus establish Jesus' hereditary right to the throne of the Old Testament's promised kingdom.

Like the Abrahamic covenant this covenant is God's promise about his plans and his purposes to human beings. Like the Abrahamic covenant also, the Davidic covenant will find its complete fulfillment only when Jesus returns to actually take the throne of the kingdom he alone is qualified to rule.

The new covenant. The new covenant is the most significant of the biblical covenants for believers today. The new covenant was promised by the Old Testament prophet Jeremiah at a critical time in Israel's history. Mosaic law was given about 1450 B.C., but the people of Israel were constantly unfaithful to their obligations under that covenant. Their disobedience led to national judgments. The culminating judgments were military defeats and exile from the promised land. Part of the nation was deported by the Assyrians in 722 B.C., while the remaining Jews continued the plunge into idolatry, immorality, and injustice. Finally, in the days of Jeremiah, the remaining Jews were crushed by Babylon. The great Jerusalem temple was destroyed, and in 586 B.C. the last of God's people were carried into captivity.

For the first time in nearly a thousand years, the Jewish people no longer lived in the promised land so intimately associated with God's covenant promises to Abraham and David. How did this happen? the exiles must have wondered. Had their disobedience caused God to change his plan and withdraw his promises?

God used the prophet Jeremiah to answer this pressing question. First, God's people had broken his covenant and must be punished. But God's promises and his purposes still stand: "Only if the heavens above can be measured and the foundations of the earth below be searched out will I reject all the descendants of Israel because of all they have done" (Jer. 31:37).

But God has another, surprising word for Israel. He promises through the prophet that "the time is coming when I will make a new covenant with the house of Israel" (Jer. 31:31). The law, under which blessing in this life depended on human performance, has not produced a righteous people. God will replace the Mosaic covenant with a more effective approach.

Like other covenants the new covenant states plainly what God intends to do. Jeremiah emphasizes God's work in the life of people: "I will put my law in their minds and write it on their hearts. I will be their God, and they will be my people. No longer will a man teach his neighbor, or a man his brother, saying 'Know the LORD,' because they will all know me, from the least of them to the greatest. . . . For I will forgive their wickedness and I will remember their sins no more" (Jer. 31:33–34).

It is not until the New Testament that we read of this new covenant actually being made. There we hear Jesus, on the night before his crucifixion, explain to his followers as he held up the communion cup, "This is the blood of the [new] covenant, which is poured out for many for the forgiveness of sins" (Matt. 26:28; Mark 14:24; Luke 22:20; 1 Cor. 11:25).

Like the Abrahamic covenant, this new covenant was initiated by a sacrifice (Gen. 15). But this time the sacrificial blood, which sealed the divine promise, was that of God's own Son. On the basis of that sacrifice, the promised forgiveness was won for humanity, to be appropriated by faith, just as Abraham had believed God and was credited with righteousness.

The new covenant, then, replaces the Mosaic Law. That law, carved in stone tablets, expressed objectively the righteousness that God's holiness requires. But the law's statement of external standards was unable to produce righteousness in human beings. The new covenant takes a radically different approach. It takes the righteousness that was expressed in law, and it supernaturally infuses that righteousness into the very character of the believer. The Book of Hebrews sums up the new covenant's key provisions: "I will put my laws in their hearts and I will write them on their minds. ... Their sins and lawless acts I will remember no more" (Heb. 10:16–17). Rather than the law's word — "do this, and live" — the new covenant majestically states God's intention: "I will write righteousness on their hearts!" God has promised that he will work within the lives of his new covenant people to transform us from within.

It is important to remember that the appropriate response to all God's covenant promises is faith. God has announced what he will do. We human beings can only take him at his Word. It is not surprising, then, that in both Romans 4 and Galatians 3, the New Testament argues that since the essence of covenant is promise, all that human beings can possibly do is to believe.

God promised Abraham that he and his descendants would be blessed. That promise stands, and full blessing will come at history's end. But as an individual, Abraham began to experience the blessings promised because he believed. The Mosaic Law expressed the divine commitment to blessing and punishment following obedience or disobedience. Those who heard and believed God's promises to Abraham followed the law willingly, and when they failed, they offered the required sacrifices for sin. Faith moved them to obedience and brought them the promised blessings.

The new covenant states God's plan and purpose for the restoration of humankind. Through Jesus, God provides forgiveness and an inner dynamic that will actually make human beings righteous. While the ultimate fulfillment of that promise awaits Jesus' return and our resurrection, faith wins the believer a present experience of new covenant blessings. When you and I believe God's promise in Jesus, the benefits won by his death and resurrection become our own.

The covenants in summary. Biblically covenants are statements of God's purposes, which are expressed as promises, often associated with binding oaths. The Abrahamic, Davidic, and new covenants look forward to history's end for their fulfillment. But faith brings a person into covenant relationship with the Lord. God graciously makes available now to those who believe in him many of the benefits intended for a redeemed mankind when Jesus returns.

The Mosaic covenant was temporary, designed to serve as Israel's constitution as a nation until Christ should come. It was different from the others in that, according to the New Testament, it is not based on promise. Instead of stating what God intends to do in the form of a promise, it stated what God would do in response to specified human behaviors. While people who had a faith relationship with God (like David) did seek to be obedient, the Old Testament system had to include sacrifices that could be made when they failed. Faith led a person to obey, and faith led that same person to bring the required sacrifices when he or she failed. Thus faith was critical in the age of law even as it has been in every age.

Faith alone, then, is the response that human beings can make when God speaks in promise. Faith alone can bring us into personal relationship with God. Faith alone enables us to experience in our present life those benefits and blessings that God has promised to bring to humankind.

While the theological covenants developed by the Reformers are not the same as the covenants spoken of in the Bible, they do express vital truths about personal relationship with God. They capture the basic Bible teaching that relationship with God must depend on faith and faith alone. The salvation that we can know as individuals flows from a faith appropriation of that commitment God has chosen to make to humankind in Jesus Christ.

CREATION

Across the milleniums believers have sensed God through his creation. With the psalmist we have felt the wonder and awe often expressed as praise: "O LORD my God, you are very great; . . . He set the earth on its foundations; it can never be moved. You covered it with the deep as with a garment; the waters stood above the mountains. But at your rebuke the waters fled, at the sound of your thunder they took flight" (Ps. 104:1, 5–7). When troubles came, the prophets of Israel often called on their people to remember that their God was the Creator, that all that exists demonstrates his power. How confident the believer can be, for we rely on one who holds all power in his hands.

> Lift your eyes and look to the heavens:
> 　Who created all these?
> He who brings out the starry host one by one,
> 　and calls them each by name.
> Do you not know?

> Have you not heard?
> The LORD is the everlasting God,
>   the Creator of the ends of the earth.
> He will not grow tired or weary,
>   and his understanding no one can fathom.
>
> (Isa.40:26, 28)

The conviction that our God is Creator of the material universe and remains its governor is basic to Christian faith. Looking back to the beginning and looking at the world around us, we gain a fresh appreciation for the awesome power of the one we know and worship in Jesus Christ.

Creation and the Old Testament. People of every age have developed theories to explain the origin of the world and of life. In the ancient Near East, the world in which the Old Testament originated, the commonly accepted theory bore a close resemblance to the modern theory of evolution. Near Eastern myths and creation tales began with preexisting matter. This matter surged and writhed with energy (chaos), finally generating the gods, whose activity led to the emergence of human beings and the orderly universe we now know. ♦ EVOLUTION

Old Testament teaching is a dramatic contrast. In simple words the Old Testament states, "In the beginning God created" (Gen. 1:1). Before time began, before the stars flared, before the planets swung in their courses, there was God. All the energy that infuses existence was his energy, not an energy inherent in matter. Even after God first spoke and matter flashed into existence, it lay inert and unmoving, formless and empty and dark until God's Spirit molded it and set what we know as natural laws in motion (Gen. 1:1–2).

Christians have disagreed over certain details. How long did the Creation take? Was the universe ordered in seven literal days or over long ages? But these differences of opinion about the when and how of creation do not shake Christians' common conviction that God did create. Christians are convinced that everything owes its existence to God and to God alone. In the words of the psalmist, "By the word of the LORD were the heavens made, their starry host by the breath of his mouth. . . . Let all the earth fear the LORD; let all the people of the world revere him. For he spoke, and it came to be; he commanded, and it stood firm" (Ps. 33:6, 8–9).

Creation and the New Testament. While Christians have presented arguments showing that belief in a Creator is reasonable, the New Testament teaches that belief in the Creation is a matter for faith. ♦ EXISTENCE OF GOD It is "by faith we understand that the universe was formed at God's command, so that what is seen was not made out of what is visible" (Heb. 11:3).

Faith is essential because human beings, despite plain evidence in the creation of the Creator (Rom. 1:18–20), "did not think it worthwhile" to retain the knowledge of God (Rom. 1:28). In this critical passage Paul argues that humanity has been so warped by sin that societies and cultures willfully seek reasons to ignore the Creation's testimony to God and thus "exchange the truth of God for a lie" (Rom. 1:25).

Faith, however, recognizes and affirms God as the invisible cause of the visible universe. And the New Testament goes on to teach us more about God's creative work than was revealed in the Old Testament.

The Gospel of John, like Genesis, looks back beyond the beginning, teaching us that God the Son, the eternal Word, was (along with God the Father) the source of creation. "Through him all things were made," John writes, and "without him nothing was made that has been made" (John 1:3). Colossians picks up the same theme, saying of Jesus that "by him all things were created: things in heaven and on earth, visible and invisible, whether thrones or powers or rulers or authorities; all things were created by him and for him" (Col. 1:16).

When we look at the total testimony of Scripture, we realize that each person of the Godhead was involved in the Creation (the Father, 1 Cor. 8:6; the Son, John 1:3 and Col. 1:16–17; the Spirit, Gen. 1:2 along with Job 26:13 and Ps. 104:30).

Theologians have summed up the Scripture's teaching by affirming that God created the material universe *ex nihilo*, from nothing. This Latin phrase emphasizes the difference between biblical and alternate views of the universe. God created the universe from nothing, without the use of previously existing materials. Every thing, material and immaterial, has its ultimate origin in God.

Christian attitudes toward the Creation. We have in the Old Testament, and especially in the Psalms, a model for an appropriate attitude toward God's creation. There we see again and again expressions of wonder, awe, and celebration.

The elemental power of the storm reminds the believer of the far greater powers of God. The vastness and beauty of the wilderness, the majesty of towering mountains, and the surging seas turn the eyes of faith to the Lord.

> How many are your works, O LORD!
> In wisdom you made them all;
> the earth is full of your creatures.

> There is the sea, vast and spacious,
> teeming with creatures beyond number —
> living things both large and small.
>
> (Ps. 104:24–25)

The sense of wonder generated by the Creation helped to form in the Old Testament believer a healthy attitude toward life in this world. That attitude can be characterized as one of joy and celebration. As the psalmist says, "Great are the works of the LORD; they are pondered by all who delight in them" (Ps. 111:2).

While at times Christians have adopted a gloomy attitude or a moody asceticism toward life in this world, recognition of God's good hand in shaping our world as a home for mankind has more often opened the way to a positive and joyful view of our present life. Our days must have significance since God has so carefully designed the stage on which we each play our part. Pleasure must be God's good will, since our bodies have been shaped to enjoy the tastes and to thrill to the beauty God has planned. No wonder, then, the New Testament affirms God as the one "who richly provides us with everything for our enjoyment" (1 Tim. 6:17).

The beauty and harmony of the creation have been distorted by sin. The New Testament pictures creation as frustrated, awaiting liberation from its bondage to decay (Rom. 8:19–21). The message that creation gives is mixed, evidence of both God's goodness and of the existence of evil. ◆ EVIL Yet the basic message of creation remains clear. God exists, and he is the source of all that is. God exists, and because he is loving and good, filled with a love of beauty and the joy of life, the world that he shaped is also good, a fitting setting for rejoicing in his works and celebrating the life we have here and now.

God's new creation. The Bible looks back to the beginning and presents God as the creative force bringing existence and vitality to all that exists. God spoke, and the material universe burst into existence. God spoke, and living creatures populated the earth and skies and seas. God stooped, and in a special creative act, he shaped mankind. God, thus, is the source of all that is fresh and new and good.

It is not surprising then, in view of the impact of sin on this creation, to discover that the Bible promises a new creation. By another exercise of divine power, all that is warped and twisted will be set aside, and God will speak again, bringing a fresh newness to the universe. The fact that God is and remains the Creator is one source of the Christian's optimism and hope that remains vital despite the corruption and pain so visible in nature and society.

The Old Testament speaks of a day when God will speak again and create a new heaven and a new earth. In that new creation every cause of sorrow and sadness will be removed. "Behold, I will create new heavens and a new earth. The former things will not be remembered, nor will they come to mind. But be glad and rejoice forever in what I will create, for I will create Jerusalem to be a delight and its people a joy" (Isa. 65:17–18).

The New Testament adds its testimony to the Old Testament vision. Peter reminds his readers that the Lord will keep his promises in his own time. Then "the heavens will disappear with a roar; the elements will be destroyed by fire, and the earth and everything in it will be laid bare" (2 Peter 3:10). While the old creation will be destroyed, we "in keeping with his promises" are "looking forward to a new heaven and a new earth, the home of righteousness" (2 Peter 3:13). In that day, toward which all history moves, we will hear God announce, "I am making everything new" (Rev. 21:5).

The Christian doctrine of creation, then, is not limited to beliefs about the origin of the universe and of life. We believe in a Creator God whose limitless power has been and will be exercised to give vitality and shape to existence now and in eternity.

Strikingly the Bible and our experience teach us that God's work of re-creation has already begun. We see that work not in the world around us but within the hearts of believers. The Scriptures teach that when a person puts his or her trust in Jesus, that person is given new life by God. ◗ BORN AGAIN, LIFE One image used in speaking of this new life is the image of creation. "If anyone is in Christ," the Bible says, "he is a new creation; the old has gone, the new has come!" (2 Cor. 5:17). The new self we are given by God has been "created to be like God in true righteousness and holiness" (Eph. 4:24). Because God has acted to create a fresh newness within us, we can now be "transformed into his [Jesus'] likeness with ever-increasing glory, which comes from the Lord, who is the Spirit" (2 Cor. 3:18).

God's power, exercised in the creation of our universe, is exercised today as he creates new life in those who come to Jesus. And God's power will be exercised in the future, shaping a new universe, the home of righteousness, to be our home through all eternity.

CREEDS

A creed makes a concise statement, summing up what Christians believe. The form was probably used first for teaching and as the basis for a baptismal candidate's declaration of his or her own faith. During the early centuries of the Christian era, several important creeds developed to clarify several critical church doctrines.

The earliest of the creeds was the Apostles' Creed. Its earliest form, which goes back to about A.D. 140, was shorter than the form we know today. That early form reads:

> I believe in God the Father Almighty, and in Jesus Christ His Only Son our Lord, who was born of the Holy Ghost and Virgin Mary; crucified under Pontius Pilate, and buried; the third day He rose from the dead; He ascended into heaven and sitteth at the right hand of the Father; from thence He shall come to judge the quick and the dead. And in the Holy Ghost; the holy church; the forgiveness of sins; the resurrection of the body; the life everlasting.

The expanded form that we use in our churches today did not take its present form until the sixth or seventh century.

During the fourth and fifth centuries, controversies over critical issues, such as the nature of Jesus and his relationship to other persons in the Godhead, were settled in counsels that summed up their findings in creeds. The two major creeds of this era are the Nicene Creed (which defined Jesus as being of one substance with the Father) and the Athanasian Creed (which clarifies and affirms the doctrine of the Trinity).

While the earlier centuries saw theological formulations expressed in creeds, the Reformation led to the development of Confessions. Creeds were brief, summary statements of the basic truths that orthodox Christians hold in common. In contrast to this simplicity the Confessions of the sixteenth and seventeenth centuries were detailed documents. In contrast, too, the Confessions focus on issues that divide denominations. Rather than being documents unifying all Christians, Confessions are documents designed to unify Presbyterians or Lutherans.

While Christians will always disagree about certain issues, the creeds of the church remind us that Christianity remains one faith. On the basic truths expressed in history's great creeds, we are and will remain one.

CROSS

With Christians throughout the ages, we sing of the cross:

> In the cross of Christ I glory,
> Tow'ring o'er the wrecks of time,
> All the light of sacred story
> Gathers round its head sublime.

and

> When I survey the wondrous cross,
> On which the Prince of glory died,
> My richest gain I count but loss,
> And pour contempt on all my pride.
>
> Forbid it, Lord, that I should boast,
> Save in the death of Christ my God;
> All the vain things that charm me most,
> I sacrifice them to His blood.

No one can grasp the meaning of Christianity without discovering the significance of the cross and the meaning of Jesus' death.

Public execution of criminals. In the time of Jesus, Palestine was part of the Roman Empire, which used crucifixion to execute the dregs of society: the slaves, robbers, assassins, and rebels among the foreign populations controlled by Rome.

Crucifixion was a painful as well as shameful method of execution. The criminal was first beaten with a metal-studded leather whip to weaken him. He was then nailed to a wooden crossbar that was lifted to the top of a post, high enough to keep his feet off the ground. Death came slowly and painfully as the position forced oxygen starvation.

The Jews found crucifixion especially repellent; the Old Testament taught, "If a man guilty of a capital offense is put to death and his body is hung on a tree, you must not leave his body on the tree overnight. Be sure to bury him that same day, because anyone who is hung on a tree is under God's curse" (Deut. 21:22-23). Crucifixion desecrated the land and was the most shameful death a Jew could die. Romans, too, were repelled, and only in the most extreme circumstances would a Roman citizen be so executed.

The cross of which Christians sing and in which songwriters "glory" and consider "wondrous" was fearful and repellent in the first-century world. It is the death's significance that has transformed shame into wonder and disgust into praise.

The significance of Christ's cross. The cross in Scripture is linked with other vital terms like *blood, sacrifice,* and *atonement.* A few verses from each testament reveal clearly that Jesus' crucifixion was the means by which you and I are saved from the sin that holds all mankind in its grip.

> He himself bore our sins in his body on the tree, so that we might die
> to sins and live for righteousness; by his wounds you have been
> healed. (1 Peter 2:24)

He was pierced for our transgressions, he was crushed for our iniquities; the punishment that brought us peace was upon him, and by his wounds we are healed. (Isa. 53:5)

God was pleased to have all his fullness dwell in him, and through him to reconcile to himself all things, whether things on earth or things in heaven, by making peace through his blood, shed on the cross. (Col. 1:19-20)

The wonder of the cross is Christ's willingness to accept the pain and the shame and the weight of our sins. The glory of the cross is in the love it demonstrates and the salvation that it won for all who will believe. ♦ SALVATION, SIN, ATONEMENT, BLOOD

The cross stands as history's single most significant image of love and deliverance. But there are other scriptural images associated with the cross. Among the most significant images are those of commitment and obedience.

The Bible makes it clear that the cross was God's will for Jesus. Christ was handed over to his enemies "by God's set purpose and foreknowledge" (Acts 2:23). And Christ remained ever responsive to the Father's will. During his days on earth, Jesus spoke of his relationship to the Father and said, "I always do what pleases him" (John 8:29). Looking back at the cross, the New Testament sees Jesus' voluntary self-sacrifice as the ultimate act of obedience: "He humbled himself and became obedient to death — even death on a cross" (Phil. 2:8). And Romans adds, "Just as through the disobedience of the one man [Adam] the many were made sinners, so also through the obedience of the one man [Jesus] the many will be made righteous" (Rom. 5:19).

When the Bible speaks of the Christian's cross, it is the image of full commitment that is primarily intended. As Jesus was obedient to the Father and willing to pick up his cross, so you and I are to be obedient, willingly picking up our own crosses and following his example (Matt. 16:24). The Christian's cross is whatever challenges us to deny ourselves and commit ourselves to complete loyalty to God (Mark 8:34-36).

The cross is also a symbol of shame, reminding us that we, too, may be ridiculed by society for following Jesus (Heb. 12:2; 13:12, 13). It is a symbol of death, even as believers are called on to deny old desires and evil impulses to live the new life, which is ours through union with Jesus (Rom. 6:6; Gal. 2:19-20). ♦ UNION WITH JESUS

The cross, then, is rich in meaning for the Christian. It has been transformed by Jesus from an image of shame to history's ultimate expression of love. It has been transformed by Jesus from a means of execution, agonizingly stripping away the victim's life, to the very source of life for a lost humanity. And the cross has been transformed by Jesus into a symbol of the obedience that you and I, because of Jesus' gift of eternal life, can now gratefully render to our God.

DAY OF THE LORD

The Old Testament prophets looked forward to something they called the Day of the Lord, or "that day." Isaiah's powerful voice says, "The LORD Almighty has a day in store for all the proud and lofty, for all that is exalted (and they will be humbled)." When that day comes, "the arrogance of man will be brought low and the pride of men humbled; the LORD alone will be exalted in that day, and the idols will totally disappear" (Isa. 2:12, 17).

The twin themes seen here sum up scriptural teachings about the Day of the Lord. It is the time when God finally acts to judge a sinning humanity, and it is a time when God will be exalted and his righteous kingdom established.

The Day of the Lord, then, focuses our attention on the climax of history and encompasses all that God will do at that time. In many Old Testament passages the emphasis is on the judgments associated with the Day of the Lord, but in other passages the emphasis shifts to the blessings that the Lord will introduce when Jesus' kingdom is established. ▸ **PROPHECY, JUDGMENT**

DEATH

The very word is grim. To some it means "the end." To everyone it means "separation," "loss." For most of humanity death is the great unknown, a realm of shadowy uncertainty to which each of us must sooner or later go.

Some cultures, like the ancient Egyptians, were so fascinated with death that their religion and culture was focused on it. The great pyramids that lie on hot desert sands are nothing but the tombs of kings who hoped that somehow their mummified bodies would, like the piled rocks above them, last through eternity.

Christians, too, have a perspective of death. We agree that death is grim: It is, after all, an enemy. But Christians look at death as a doorway, not to uncertainty but to a richer experience of the eternal life won for us by Jesus. We sorrow when a loved one dies, but we do not grieve as some do. We know that a great reunion lies ahead. When Jesus comes, the dead will rise, and we will be with our loved ones forever.

The Bible has deepened our understanding of death. Death is not merely what happens when bodies die. Scripture uses the word *death* both to describe the lost state of humanity and to sum up the impact of sin on mankind. Death's grim reality is not simply that every person faces physical dissolution. The reality is that all human beings are born and live in a state of spiritual death. When we understand the full meaning of death as that term is used in Scripture, we realize how great God's gift of life in Jesus truly is.

Physical death. Physical death is the end of biological life. In the Old Testament life on earth is viewed as a good in itself. A person might have troubles and experience tragedy, but to live is good. Life is a gift of God. In contrast death is an enemy, robbing a person of the opportunity to use the capacities God has given him or her. While the Old Testament gives evidence of a belief in resurrection, the end of life was viewed as a tragedy:

> My soul is full of trouble
>   and my life draws near the grave.
> I am counted among those who go down to the pit;
>   I am like a man without strength.
> I am set apart with the dead,
>   like the slain who lie in the grave,
> whom you remember no more,
>   who are cut off from your care. . . .
> Do you show your wonders to the dead?
>   Do those who are dead rise up and praise you?
> Is your love declared in the grave,
>   your faithfulness in Destruction?
> Are your wonders known in the place of darkness,
>   or your righteous deeds in the land of oblivion?
>
> (Ps. 88:3–5, 9–12)

Whatever else death meant to the Old Testament saint, it meant that the person was cut off from life, unable even to participate in the community's worship of God.

In the New Testament era the Greeks saw death simply as the end. When biological death came, existence stopped. The Greeks struggled for ways to deal with this grim reality. Some argued that death is natural and thus right. Others tried to find comfort in the idea that a person lives on in his or her children. Some insisted that death should be welcomed as an end to our struggles and our pain in this uncaring universe. While Plato argued that the personality might continue after the body's death, there was no common belief in immortality, and the idea of resurrection seemed utterly foolish. In the Greek language death was *nekros,* "dead matter." Whatever gives vitality to the body leaves with death; the corpse is no longer a person.

The Old Testament views death as an enemy. But death is an enemy because it is not natural. The Old Testament teaches that death was introduced because of human sin; it was not intrinsic to creation as God originally designed it. How God would ultimately deal with death had not been fully revealed. But human beings were not destined to become nothing. Despite the wrongness of death and despite its terrors, the believer has a hope for the future: "He asked you for life, and you gave it to him — length of days, for ever and ever. . . . Surely you have granted him eternal blessings and made him glad with the joy of your presence. For the king trusts in the LORD, through the unfailing love of the Most High he will not be shaken" (Ps. 21:4, 6–7).

And what about the New Testament? Of the one hundred thirty times that *nekros* is found there, one half of them are linked with the assurance that God can raise the dead. God raised the body of Jesus and he will raise our dead bodies as well (Acts 13:30; 1 Cor. 15:12–55). ♦

RESURRECTION, LIFE

The New Testament makes very clear the Old Testament's teaching that death really is not "natural." Romans 5:12 goes back to the story of the Fall and explains that "just as sin entered the world through one man, and death through sin, in this way death came to all men." Death is something unnatural, brought on humanity by a shattering event that corrupted the whole material universe (Rom. 8:19–22). Physical death and all its pangs are a result of sin. Only God, who dealt with sin in Jesus' death for us, can reverse the process of corruption and raise the dead.

In one major sense, then, death is the biological end of life. This death is somehow "wrong," as most of us intuitively sense. Each human being is too significant to simply be snuffed out. The Christian understands the wrongness of death and traces death back to sin. Death passed into the race through Adam's failure, and only the work of Jesus can bring a return of that original vitality. Only through Jesus can believers receive the promise of a biological resurrection and an endless life.

Spiritual death. The Genesis account of the Fall immediately alerts us to the fact that death is more than the termination of biological life. God warns Adam about eating fruit from the forbidden tree: "When you eat of it you will surely die" (Gen. 2:17). Adam does eat. Centuries later did Adam actually die.

Yet something analogous to death is seen in the Genesis account. Immediately after taking the fruit, Adam and Eve are gripped by shame. They run from God when they hear him in the garden. When God confronts them, they accuse each other. Somehow the harmony of life has been shattered, and the first pair are alienated from God and from each other. The text goes on to tell of Adam and Eve's struggle to live on an unfriendly earth, of the jealousy and anger that lead Cain to murder his brother, and of the corrupt society established by their descendants.

In the New Testament the death imagery is picked up and amplified. Death is a theological term, portraying a humanity unresponsive to God, filled with corrupt cravings, desires, and thoughts. Human society is warped and twisted, reflecting the outlook of Satan rather than God. The New Testament describes humankind as "dead in your transgressions and sins, in which you used to live when you followed the ways of this world and of the ruler of the kingdom of the air, the spirit who is now at work in those who are disobedient. All of us also lived among them at one time, gratifying the cravings of our sinful nature and following its desires and thoughts" (Eph. 2:1–3). Death has become symbolic, the only term capable of adequately describing humanity's inner moral corruption and unresponsiveness to God.

What are the implications of this spiritual death? The New Testament shows us that the spiritual death caused by sin involves a state of actual antagonism toward God (Rom. 1:18–20). Rather than responding to God as he reveals himself, human beings reject him and are carried inevitably into a religious and moral cesspool (Rom. 1:21–32). In this state human beings lie condemned, rightly objects of the divine wrath (Eph. 2:3).

This biblical vision of the human condition has led Christians to a realistic appraisal of human potential. Our race may master the physical universe, but it will never master itself. The utopias of which people dream will continue to crumble under the weight of humanity's inner corruption. Neither crime nor war will be put aside by mere human effort. But Christian realism is not hopelessness. When we understand how firm the grip of death is, we look away from ourselves to God. The God who gave life to the original creation is able to infuse new life into the spiritually dead.

But what about the new life that Christians are given in Jesus? It does not cancel out every impact of death. Death retains a foothold in our personality, to be erradicated only with the biological transformation that is to be ours at the resurrection. But with our new life in Jesus, God gives us his Holy Spirit. The Spirit is able to "give life to your mortal bodies" (Rom. 8:11). Even now, as we depend on God for enablement, the impact of death within can be blunted, and we can actually respond to him and live holy lives. ◆ SANCTIFICATION

A number of New Testament passages are critical to an understanding of spiritual death. Romans 5:12–21 focuses on two events that dominate history. Adam sinned and so introduced death into the race, but Christ came, defeating death and restoring life. Romans 6:1–10 teaches that believers are so completely identified with Jesus that the death he died is considered ours, and the resurrection that Jesus experienced is the source of our new life. Romans 7:7–25 shows that the death principle is still active in believers. Our lives are ineffective and unproductive without the daily aid of God's Spirit. Romans 8:1–11 shows how the Holy Spirit acts to break the grip of sin in the Christian's personality. Even our mortal bodies, still corrupted by the principle of death, can be quickened. We can live a righteous and fulfilling life. With our biological resurrection, every taint of sin will be gone, and death, in all its senses, will be "swallowed up in victory" (1 Cor. 15:12–57).

Death, then, is a central biblical image that helps to shape the Christian's understanding of life and its meaning. Death is the biological end of life on earth. But death also speaks of our spiritual state. Mankind has been corrupted morally and spiritually by sin, and this corruption is the source of personal and social sins. Death also describes human relationship with God. We are dead to God, not only unresponsive but actively hostile. Without God's intervention, death will retain its grip on us, and physical death will catapult us into an eternity of alienation from the Lord. We can only imagine the horrors of that fate, but the Bible calls it the "second death" (Rev. 20:14).

The death of Christ. In view of the varied ways the Bible uses the word *death*, it would be wrong for us to see Jesus' death on Calvary as a mere biological event. The Christian understands Jesus' death as our Lord's full experience of everything that death implies, even of that awful separation from God. On the cross Jesus took on himself the full weight of our sin and died our death. Emerging victorious from the grave, he gives us a new life that flows from his own resurrection.

Christ's death breaks the power of death over human beings. We are reconciled to God "through the death of his Son" (Rom. 5:10). Even our present bondage is relieved. "By sending his own Son in the likeness of sinful man to be a sin offering," God "condemned sin in sinful man, in order that the righteous requirements of the law might be fully met in us" (Rom. 8:3–4). God has acted in Christ, and "by Christ's physical body through death" is able to "present you holy in his sight" (Col. 1:22). Perhaps the meaning of Jesus' matchless life and sacrificial death are best summed up in Hebrews 2:14–15: "Since the children have flesh and blood, he too shared in their humanity so that by his death he might destroy him who holds the power of death — that is, the devil — and free those who all their lives were held in slavery by their fear of death." Jesus experienced death in all its meanings for us. His resurrection to new life shattered the power of death. Biologically and spiritually you and I can look ahead to endless life because of Jesus' death for us.

What happens to us when we die? Christians through the ages have retained the firm confidence that resurrection lies ahead. Death of the body is not the end. But believers have differed about what happens to a person when he or she dies.

The reason for this uncertainty is that there is, and must be, an intermediate state between death and resurrection. Scripture speaks of Jesus' return, and it promises a joyous resurrection for Jesus' own (1 Thess. 4:13–18). If resurrection comes *then*, what happens to us when we die *now?*

The traditional Roman Catholic answer is found in the concept of purgatory. This notion assumes that those who die in the church but who are not pure enough to enter heaven pass through purgatory, where minor sins and impurities are cleansed by literal fires. This doctrine has no solid biblical support and, in effect, denies the Bible's teaching that Jesus provides a salvation that "purifies us from every sin" (1 John 1:7; Heb. 9:28). Protestants share the early church's conviction that full salvation is offered to human beings on the sole condition of faith in Jesus Christ. ◆ FAITH

While a few Christians have suggested the notion that souls "sleep" between the time of physical death and the resurrection, most believers have been convinced by Scripture that our personality remains intact and conscious. This certainly was the case in the story Jesus told of rich Abraham and the beggar named Lazarus (Luke 16:19–31). Each person was alert, conversed, and experienced either comforts or torment. The expectation of the apostle Paul is stated very clearly in Philippians 1:23. He desires "to depart and be with Christ, which is far better" than to remain here on earth in this body. Perhaps most Christians understand 2 Corinthians 5:1–10 to suggest that God has planned a temporary body for us (just as our present body is temporary), so that our personality will not be "unclothed but clothed with our heavenly dwelling" until the time for resurrection comes.

When we add this to the promise that when Jesus returns he will "bring with" him those who die, so that we who are still living will not precede them in resurrection (1 Tim. 4:14), we have solid grounds for the conviction that physical death launches the believer into the presence of the Lord. We do not know exactly what we will experience during the time between our death and our resurrection. But it is enough to know that we will be ourselves, conscious, cleansed, and enjoying the presence of our Lord.

The Christian's attitude toward death. Christians need to maintain a healthy attitude toward death and dying. That attitude should recognize that while death is an enemy, it is also the doorway to a fuller experience of the endless life won for us by Jesus.

Death is separation, and because it separates us from all that we hold dear in this life, death is painful. The death of loved ones rightly brings us sorrow and pain.

At the same time physical death is one of God's gifts. The deterioration that grips our race because of sin means that our powers and vitality will inevitably be drained. For many death comes as a welcome release. Isaiah puts it graphically: "The righteous perish, and no one ponders it in his heart; devout men are taken away, and no one understands that the righteous are taken away to be spared from evil. Those who walk uprightly enter into peace; they find rest as they lie in death" (Isa. 57:1–2).

Rather than shy away from the prospect of death, the Christian can look realistically at the fact that life on earth is fleeting. In one Psalm, David asks God,

> Show me, O LORD, my life's end
>   and the number of my days;
>   let me know how fleeting is my life.
> You have made my days a mere handbreadth;
>   the span of my years is as nothing before you.
>   Each man's life is but a breath.
> Man is a mere phantom as he goes to and fro:
>   He bustles about, but only in vain;
>   he heaps up wealth, not knowing who will get it.
> But now, LORD, what do I look for?
>   My hope is in you.
>
> (Ps. 39:4–7)

With life so brief, how foolish it would be to seek meaning in the here and now rather than in a relationship with the living God.

When we have a personal relationship with God through Jesus Christ, we can look without terror at death. Fears are natural and may still come, but we realize that death brings us face to face with our Savior. Death ushers us into a state that truly is "far better" than the life we know on earth. Death's sting has been removed (1 Cor. 15:55), and death has no power to separate us from the love of God in Christ Jesus our Lord (Rom. 8:38–39).

DECREES ♦ PREDESTINATION

DEMONS

Christians through the ages have taken biblical stories about evil spirits and demons seriously. At times, like the Middle Ages, the biblical images have been corrupted by crude, popular notions. But the conviction has remained that hostile evil beings populate the spirit world and that these beings can influence humans.

In general demons have been identified with the angels who followed Satan in his rebellion against God. ♦ SATAN, ANGELS No specific passages deal with their origin, but Mark 5:1–17 and Luke 8:26–39 use the terms *evil spirits, demons, devils,* and *unclean spirits* interchangeably.

Volume II of *A Contemporary Wesleyan Theology* sums up the New Testament's teaching about demons this way:

> As spiritual beings, demons are unclean, they are vicious, intelligent, and able to attack human persons with moral and spiritual pollution as well as with physical harm and abuse. Throughout the Gospels (Matt. 8:16; 17:18; Mark 9:25; Luke 10:17, 20), demons are shown to be spiritual beings. In some cases — e.g., the Gadarene demoniac (Mark 5:2–16; Luke 8:27–38) and Mary Magdalene, out of whom Jesus cast seven demons (Mark 16:9; Luke 8:2) — numerous demons may possess one person. The apostles Paul and John likewise lend support to the spiritual nature of demons in such passages as Ephesians 2:2; 6:12; and Revelation 16:14, among others.

> Furthermore, demons in their possession of human beings are unclean (Mark 3:11–12; Luke 4:36); they are violent and malicious (Matt. 8:28); they are agents or emissaries of Satan (Matt. 12:26–27; 25:41); they afflict the human body with various physical maladies (Matt. 4:24; 12:22; 17:15–18); they obstruct the truth and lead people into personal corruption (1 Tim. 4:1–3; 2 Peter 2:10–12); and they strive to prevent believers from living clean, spiritual lives (Eph. 6:12; 1 Tim. 4:1).

The Bible makes very clear what attitude the Christian should have toward these beings. God forbids Israel to resort to any means — spiritism, mediums, witchcraft — that might promise secret powers or information. "Anyone who does these things is detestable to the LORD" the Old Testament says (Deut. 18:12).

This blunt warning is given out of love. God has his people's best interests at heart, and whatever the demonic may seem to promise, these spirit beings are basically hostile to human beings. How foolish, then, for anyone to turn from God to other sources for supernatural aid or guidance. And how great an insult to the Lord.

The New Testament also encourages withdrawal from anything involving the demonic. Paul looks at the people in his culture who honor pagan idols with feasts, and says, "The sacrifices of pagans are offered to demons, not to God, and I do not want you to be participants with demons. You cannot drink the cup of the Lord and the cup of demons too; you cannot have a part in both the Lord's table and the table of demons" (1 Cor. 10:20–21).

If Christians are not to associate themselves with the demonic voluntarily, what about involuntary demon oppression or demon possession? A survey of Gospel references shows that demons both oppress and possess human beings (Matt. 8:16, 28; 9:32; 12:22–27; Mark 1:32; 5:1–5; 8:27–29, 36). This kind of demonic activity is related both to various kinds of sickness and to madness. Are believers today subject to the malignant powers of Satan and his fallen angels?

Christians differ, often strongly, on this issue. Some point to the fact that Jesus is Lord, and he drove out demons wherever he found them oppressing human beings (Matt. 9:33; 17:18; Mark 7:26, 29–30; Luke 11:14). Surely Jesus, who is Lord of the invisible as well as visible realms, protects his own from these evil beings. But others note that Job was not immune to Satan's efforts, and Saul was tormented by an evil spirit. God may permit demons a foothold even in a believer's life. And what about the woman of faith (the implication of Jesus' phrase "a daughter of Abraham") who had been crippled by a spirit for eighteen years until Jesus set her body free (Luke 13:10–16)? Even Paul experienced a "thorn in the flesh, a messenger from Satan" (2 Cor. 12:7).

Whatever the actual situation of believers, biblical teaching about exorcism parallels teaching about possession. Jesus, Lord of all, exercised ultimate power in every confrontation with the demonic. Later the disciples cast out demons, commanding them in Jesus' name and authority. The name of Jesus was not used in a magical formula, for when some treated it that way, we are told that the "evil spirit answered them, 'Jesus I know and Paul I know about, but who are you?' Then the man who had the evil spirit jumped on them and overpowered them all" (Acts 19:15–16). The principle we derive is simple but basic. The method for exorcizing demons is found in Paul's words in Acts 16:18: "In the name of Jesus Christ I command you to come out of her!" But these words have impact only when uttered by a person who has a personal relationship to Jesus, a person in whom Jesus dwells.

What, then, is the Christian's attitude toward the demonic? The epistles say very little about demons, and so we may suspect that their influence in the Christian life is less than some fear. But we do recognize the existence of these beings and understand their basic hostility toward human beings and the Lord. We follow the Bible's injunctions and withdraw from any contact or association with things demonic. Should we ever be touched by what we suspect is demonic, we can call on Jesus and command the demons in Jesus' name, trusting in his power and in his cleansing. We walk confidently in this world, reminded that "the one who is in you is greater than the one who is in the world" (1 John 4:4).

DEPRAVITY

Christians have been known for a pessimistic (or more accurately, realistic) view of human moral potential. Without denying others a moral vision, conscience, or even admirable choices, we consider human beings to be trapped in sin and "totally depraved."

That phrase is so easy to misunderstand. Jesus implied it when he made what seemed to be a contradictory statement. Urging his listeners to come to God, he said, "If you, then, though you are evil, know how to give good gifts to your children, how much more will your Father in heaven give good gifts to those who ask him?" (Matt. 7:11). And so the contradiction: The evil know how to give good gifts.

Whatever the Christian's belief in the depravity of mankind may be, it does not deny that human beings are capable of and often do good in their interpersonal relationships. If every person were as evil as he or she were capable of being, society itself would be destroyed.

And yet Christians still speak of depravity. In John Wesley's evangelistic preaching, he would say to his listeners, "Know that thou art corrupt in every power, in every faculty of thy soul; that thou art totally corrupted in every one of these, all foundations being out of course. . . . Such is the inbred corruption of thy heart, of thy very inmost nature."

A. A. Hodge, a Calvinist, agrees. Depravity means that humanity has turned from allegiance to God and by nature is totally alienated in the "governing dispositions" from God. In this state of rebellion, no human act can be pleasing to God. By nature human beings tend toward moral corruption. Only the gracious ministry of God's Spirit prevents a more rapid deterioration of the individual and society.

Total depravity, then, does not mean that persons are as bad as they can be, or that persons without a relationship to God cannot perform admirable actions. But it does mean that all human beings are born alienated from God; the human tendency to sin is so great that we, in fact, do choose to sin, and we do not have any basis within ourselves for a moral recovery. When we are judged by God's standards of perfection, the divine verdict stands: "There is no one righteous, not even one; there is no one who understands, no one who seeks God. All have turned away, they have together become worthless; there is no one who does good, not even one" (Rom. 3:10–12).

The Christian conviction that all have sinned underlies our certainty that every human being needs salvation. We cannot reform ourselves, but God can effect a new creation. Through Jesus, God not only forgives our sins, but he also works within us to provide a new life. From this new life flow actions that are truly godly and good. How wonderful that God, seeing clearly the sin that warps and twists mankind, still loved us enough to send his Son. Even in depravity, we remain the objects of God's matchless love. ◗ SIN, SALVATION

DISCIPLESHIP

Perhaps the simplest definition of discipleship is this: A disciple is a follower. Few of history's theological movements have focused on discipleship. But Christians through the centuries have realized that believers are called to follow Jesus. Christianity is a call to a new way of life, not merely an invitation to agree with church dogma.

Probably the best way to understand discipleship is to look into the New Testament and see how the word is used there. The Greek word translated "disciple" is *mathetes*, from a verb meaning "to learn." A disciple would attach himself to another to gain some practical or theoretical knowledge, either by instruction or experience. In Jesus' time rabbis (teachers) had disciples who studied with them. The teacher/disciple relationship was well-defined in New Testament times. The disciple left home and moved in with the teacher. The disciple served the teacher, treating the teacher as an absolute authority. By living with the teacher, the disciple expected not only to learn all that the rabbi knew but also to become like him (Luke 6:40). In return, the rabbi provided food and lodging and saw that his own understanding of the Scripture was passed on. Mark's comment that Jesus "chose twelve men that they might be with him" accurately reflects the practice of discipling in that day. This was the way future leaders of any movement were trained.

But the word *disciple* is used in several ways in the Gospels. It most often designates the twelve people whom Jesus chose to be with him. These twelve made the disciple's full commitment: They gave up everything to follow Jesus and obey him (Luke 14:26; Matt. 10:24; Mark 3:31–35; Luke 9:59–62; John 11:16). In some uses, *disciple* simply indicates a person who identifies with a particular movement. In this sense the Pharisees had disciples (Matt. 22:16; Mark 2:18), as did John the Baptist (Matt. 11:2; Mark 2:18). At other times the Gospels use *disciples* to describe those who identified with Jesus and his teaching. In this context the word almost means "believers" (as in John 8:31; 13:35; 15:8). But not all such followers had made a firm commitment to Jesus. When some people found Jesus' teaching about the "bread of life" hard to understand, they "turned back, and no longer followed him" (John 6:66).

After the resurrection, Jesus gave the twelve disciples what has come to be known as the Great Commission. "Go," Jesus said, "and make disciples of all nations." This was no charge to gain adherents for a movement. Jesus' commission was to teach those who believe "to obey everything I have commanded you" (Matt. 28:20). Christian discipleship is a call to full commitment and obedience; it is a call through which believers can become more and more like their teacher and Lord.

The goal of discipleship is to become like the teacher. Jesus defined that goal this way: "A student [literally, a "disciple" or "learner"] is not above his teacher, but everyone who is fully trained will be like his teacher" (Luke 6:40). Likeness rather than mere knowledge was the goal of Jewish discipleship, and it is the goal of Christian discipleship as well.

One striking feature of the New Testament is that we find the word *disciple* only in the Gospels and in Acts. Even John, who uses the word so often in his gospel, does not use it in his letters or in Revelation. Why? Perhaps the reason is because other images have replaced the image of the disciple with a single teacher. After all, Jesus has returned to heaven. In place of that one teacher with disciples, the Epistles portray a fellowship, a body of believers. It is in the fellowship of other believers, committed as we are to follow Jesus in obedience, that you and I grow toward Christlikeness and experience transformation into Jesus' image (Eph. 4:11–16; 2 Cor. 3:18; Heb. 10:24–25). ◗ **TRANSFORMATION, BODY OF CHRIST, OBEDIENCE**

DISCIPLINE

We are familiar with discipline. We discipline our children, and we discipline ourselves to get our work done. When we speak about discipline, we can mean punishment, training, or simply strict control.

The Bible describes God as a good Father who brings us experiences through which we are disciplined and trained in righteousness. Such experiences generally seem unpleasant and painful at the time. But we're told that "God disciplines us for our good, that we may share in his holiness" (Heb. 12:10).

It is this model of discipline that both helps and troubles us when we come to the issue of church discipline. We realize that the church, the body of Christ, is to be holy. How do we act as God's special people, loving and accepting one another, while still being faithful to the challenge of mutual and corporate discipline?

In the early church one era of persecution caused many people to abandon their profession of Christianity. When the persecution ended, many people wanted to return. The dispute over whether or not to accept them literally divided the church.

In the time of the Reformation, Luther believed that public discipline was one mark of the true church. He writes, "The people of God, or holy Christians, are known by the keys, which they publicly use. Christ decrees, in Matthew xviii that if a Christian sins, he shall be rebuked, and if he does not amend his ways, he shall be bound and cast out; but if he amends, he shall be set free. This is the power of the keys. . . . Now wherever you see the sins of some persons forgiven or rebuked, publicly or privately, know that God's people is there" (*On the Councils and the Churches*).

Calvin gives a similar emphasis. Both men believed that the invisible church, a spiritual reality, took visible form. The visible church could and should be identified as the true, invisible church and should be recognized by certain marks: the preaching of the Word, the administration of the sacraments, and the exercise of church discipline.

While the church is called to be a holy fellowship, it remains imperfect. Believers should pray daily for the forgiveness of their own sins. Calvin taught that "Each should begin with himself. If then I wish to be a good judge of my neighbors to judge their faults, I must know my own and condemn them first." Yet Calvin established a church court to censure sinners and help them amend their ways. While sensitive to people and their weaknesses, early Calvinism encouraged a rather strict discipline in the conviction that this was "holy and healthful" for the church.

What does the New Testament say about church discipline? First, discipline is clearly a matter of training rather than of punishing. The Scriptures themselves are given to us for "teaching, rebuking, and training [discipline], which leads to righteousness" (2 Tim. 3:16). Discipline is guidance toward holiness. In this context, church discipline involves correcting a person when he or she strays from righteousness into sin.

The clearest scriptural picture of church discipline is found in 1 Corinthians. The church in Corinth was passively accepting a situation of open sexual immorality. Paul writes, "I have already passed judgment on the one who did this, just as if I were present." Paul commands that "when you are assembled in the name of our Lord Jesus . . . hand this man over to Satan" (1 Cor. 5:3–5). The congregation is called to expel this person and "not to associate with anyone who calls himself a brother" but consistently practices sin. Paul says, "with such a man do not even eat" (1 Cor. 5:11).

It is important to understand the rationale for this action. Scriptures teach that God is the moral judge of the universe. His authoritative Word has identified certain acts as sin. What Paul has done, and what Paul calls on the church to do, is to agree with God's assessment of the action of this person "who calls himself a brother." The Christian community must both expel this person who openly practices sin and have no relationship with him or her.

The goal of this action is not punishment but restoration. The Bible teaches that sin breaks the believer's fellowship with God. The church is to act out this reality by withdrawing its fellowship from such a person. The intention is to so clearly confront the person with his or her sin and with its consequences that the person will confess and abandon the sin. We look again to 2 Corinthians for the outcome of this particular case. The "punishment inflicted by the majority" had its desired results. The guilty man repented, and Paul calls on the church to welcome him back and to "reaffirm your love for him" (2 Cor. 2:6–11).

Church discipline, then, calls the congregation to take a stand with God on what is holy and what is unholy. At the same time church discipline becomes a powerful aid to motivate the true believer to repent.

It is important for us to realize that in Scripture there is really only one basis for church discipline. Discipline isn't exercised when Christians disagree about personal convictions or even about doctrines; church discipline is reserved for those things that Scripture clearly and unequivocally identifies as sin.

Matthew 18:15–17 is generally understood to outline a process by which a local congregation can exercise its responsibility to discipline its members. Anyone aware of another's sin is instructed to go to him or her. If the person does not listen, several people go together. If the person still does not respond, the whole community is to be involved and the person is to be ostracized. This shared responsibility is reflected in Paul's words, "when you are assembled in the name of the Lord Jesus" (1 Cor. 5:4).

How does this vision of discipline fit with the biblical image of the church as a forgiving, forbearing fellowship composed of imperfect people who are still growing? Very well, if we remember that discipline is exercised only when a person refuses to acknowledge or to try to deal with personal sins. A person who is in the grip of some temptation may slip and fall again and again. As Jesus told Peter, a person might sin seventy times seven, and yet be freely forgiven. But when we fail to judge ourselves or face the fact that our sinful act is sin, then we must be confronted. The person who is struggling with sin is given unqualified support. It is only the person who will not admit to sin who must be helped toward holiness by the church's discipline.

DOCTRINE

Doctrine is a slippery term. The word translated "doctrine" in the New Testament is a word that simply means "the teaching." In 2 Timothy, Paul speaks of good news revealed to us through the appearing of Jesus. Paul has been appointed a herald, an apostle, and a teacher of "this gospel." What Paul has taught is "the pattern of sound teaching"—the basic truth about Jesus. This truth, publicly taught by the apostle, is to be entrusted to "reliable men who will be able to teach others."

Part of our problem is that we sometimes fail to make a distinction between this basic Christian teaching, which expresses the common faith of the church, and our explanations of the truth, which we are all too likely to call our doctrines.

Perhaps the best way to sense the distinction is to look at an early affirmation of the faith of the Christian community. One such statement or "rule of faith" was written by Irenaeus about A.D. 190. Here is his formulation of that true teaching with which all Christians agree:

> The church, though dispersed throughout the whole world, even to the ends of the earth, has received from the apostles and their disciples this faith: [She believes] in one God, the Father Almighty, Maker of heaven, and earth, and the sea, and all things that are in them, and in one Christ Jesus, the Son of God, who became incarnate for our salvation, and in the Holy Spirit, who proclaimed through the prophets the dispensations of God, and the advent, and the birth from a virgin, and the passion, and the resurrection from the dead, and the ascension into heaven in the flesh of the beloved Christ Jesus, our Lord, and His [future] manifestation from heaven in the glory of the Father "to gather all things in one," and to raise up anew all flesh of the whole human race, in order that to Christ Jesus, our Lord, and God, and Savior, and King, according to the will of the invisible Father, "every knee should bow, of things in heaven, and things in

earth, and things under the earth, and that every tongue should confess" to Him, and that He should execute just judgment towards all; that he may send "spiritual wickedness," and the angels who transgressed and became apostates, together with the ungodly, and unrighteous, and wicked and profane among men, into everlasting fire; but may, in the exercise of His grace, confer immortality on the righteous, and holy, and those who have kept His commandments, and have persevered in His love, some from the beginning [of their Christian course], and others from the date of their repentance, and may surround them with everlasting glory.

In this expression of his rule of faith, Irenaeus attempts to state as clearly as possible what the whole church of his day agreed to. This is foundational truth: truths taught by Christ's apostles and received by all Christians everywhere. Even though there was no unified church organization at this time, a person could travel throughout the known world and find that any Christian group held these very truths as the basis of their faith and the framework of their thinking.

And Christians have gone on to think about their faith. They have attempted to explain, amplify, develop, and define their beliefs. In the process of thinking about the common faith of Christians, and in their study of the Scriptures, different people have developed different categories and systems. Again and again church history has shown that human beings think in systematic ways. History shows the development of theological systems. Among the great Christian systematic thinkers, we would list Augustine, Thomas Aquinas, Luther, Calvin, Arminius, and a number of lesser-known figures like Menno Simons. Though not a systematic thinker, John Wesley's writings, preaching, and thought have also shaped Christian thought. Usually what people mean by the word *doctrine* is that particular way of formulating thought about basic Christian truth that is expressed in one of these systems.

Systematic thinking about faith meets a basic human need. And it surely is not wrong to seek deeper understanding of revealed truth or to express our understanding in systematic ways. The problem comes when we begin to think of our particular formulation, our particular doctrines, as "the" truth. Then, sure that our way of thinking about Christian faith is correct and that others are wrong, we find ourselves forming exclusive groups, cutting ourselves off from other Christians who may not hold our doctrines.

In fact, however, our doctrines are all too often inadequate human ways of thinking about God's truth, and they are certainly not the truth itself. Because even the best human mind is finite and fallible, we have to conclude with the apostle Paul that "the man who thinks he knows something does not yet know as he ought to know" (1 Cor. 8:2).

What then about those truths that Paul taught and that he urged Timothy to commit to faithful men who could teach others? First of all, we have the teaching of the apostles, preserved for us as our New Testament. Second, we also have, preserved in church history, a number of rules of faith and creeds that state and restate the core truths believers throughout the ages have affirmed. The wonderful truth is that, Calvinist or Arminian, Baptist or Methodist, Pentecostal or Adventist, Christians everywhere find in these simple statements an accurate expression of their own faith. The details and the explanations may vary, but the faith of Christians remains one.

Our doctrines are important, and our systems of thought may very well enrich our understanding of Scripture and our pursuit of holiness. But we need to remember that underneath the differences that sometimes divide and confuse us lies a common foundation. There is a faith, delivered once for all and acknowledged by the church of all places and all times.

DOMINION

The concept of dominion has never been a major doctrine of the church. But it has always been there, usually overlooked by a humanity eager to tear every resource from our earth. God shaped Adam and Eve in his own image and said, "Let them rule over the fish of the sea and the birds of the air, over the livestock, over all the earth, and over all the creatures that move along the ground" (Gen. 1:26).

How do we understand that directive, along with God's commission to "fill the earth and subdue it" (Gen. 1:28)? God placed Adam in the Garden of Eden and told him "to work it and take care of it" (Gen. 2:15). God provided the basic resources. Now Adam and his descendants would care for the creation and draw from it not only their living but also the satisfaction of working and of enjoying beauty.

Sin shattered the idyllic picture of a perfect original creation. The work that human beings must do to sustain themselves was multiplied, and the creation itself would resist their efforts. But humans and God's creation were never enemies. Human beings always were to live in harmony with and to care for the world entrusted to them.

Perhaps it is time now for Christians to develop and affirm a theology of dominion and to help us understand and respect the role that God has given us as rulers of the world that his wisdom shaped.

DOUBT

Most of us have pangs of doubt at one time or another. When we do, it is comforting to remember a number of biblical incidents.

David's son Absalom led a rebellion against the aging king. Fleeing from Jerusalem, David was cursed and ridiculed by Shimei. When one of David's few remaining followers wanted to go and "cut off his [Shimei's] head," David held his follower back. Perhaps the Lord had told Shimei to curse the king. Under the pressure of David's tragedy and with the memory of his past failures, even this king who loved God dearly felt the pangs of doubt.

When the father of a demon-possessed boy brought his son to Jesus' disciples, they were unable to help. Jesus commanded the child be brought to him. When the father, torn between hope and despair, expressed doubt, Jesus confronted him: "Everything is possible to him who believes." Tearfully the father cried out, "I do believe; help me overcome my unbelief" (Mark 9:24). Then Jesus spoke, and the evil spirit was thrown from the boy's body.

Jesus' disciple Thomas had lived with the Lord for three years. Thomas, like the others, had heard all Jesus' words and had seen all Jesus' miracles. Even Thomas was gripped with doubt when his fellow disciples told him Jesus had risen from the dead. Thomas' response to the news of the resurrection was, "Unless I see the nail marks in his hands and put my finger where the nails were, and put my hand in his side, I will not believe it" (John 20:25).

These incidents are comforting because they show us that true believers can have times of doubt. Such times can be stimulated by tragedy, as in David's case. They can come when we're under special tension, as in the case of the father who came to Jesus. They can even come when, like Thomas, we really do know the power of Jesus. Perhaps even more comforting is looking at the outcome of these incidents. David, on the very evening of his despair, found peace in remembering God's faithfulness (Ps. 3:4). Within a few weeks the rebellion was put down, and David was restored to his throne. The father cried out to Jesus even in his doubt. Jesus acted, and the boy was delivered. And Thomas? Jesus appeared to Thomas, and that disciple needed no more proof. He fell on his knees, acknowledging Jesus as Lord.

You and I can have dark days of doubt, but God isn't going to be angry with us any more than he was angry with David and the others. The writer of Hebrews invites us to see Jesus in the special role of high priest. Remember, he says, "We do not have a high priest who is unable to sympathize with our weakness" (Heb. 4:15). Christ recognizes our doubts, sympathizes with our weakness, and always remains faithful.

How wonderful to remember that the foundation of our relationship to God is not subjective, resting on how we feel at the moment, but it rests on the objective foundation of God's faithfulness to those who are Jesus' own. ◗ FAITH, UNBELIEF

EARTH

Christians have the notion that somehow earth is the center of the universe. Others speculate about alien races and galactic empires. The Christian shrugs and says no, our planet is the focus of God's attention. Others laugh. One tiny speck of dust circling a minor sun on the spiraling arm of one of millions of galaxies of stars? Why should our speck be so important in an endless universe?

At times believers have been a little illogical about it. The ancient Catholic church denounced Copernicus when he showed that the earth revolves around the sun. (The good fathers failed to note that the theological or philosophical center of something need not be at the geographic or physical center.) Modern Christians have been drawn into furious but futile arguments about how long God took to shape the earth and just how he did it. The seven days of Genesis have been variously understood to indicate (1) a literal seven days' reconstruction of a creation ruined at Satan's fall, (2) a series of geological eras with "day" used in a figurative sense, and (3) indefinite ages punctuated by literal creative days. In addition Christians have proposed (4) creation *in situ* (Latin for "in its original place"), which means that a few thousand years ago creation occurred with coal, fossils, etc., created *in place* to give the appearance of age, (5) a series of seven revelatory days (days in which God revealed his creative work to Moses), and even (6) the notion that the days of Genesis are simply a handy approach the writer took to organize his material.

We can get so caught up in such speculation that we miss both the main point of the biblical story and the significance of planet earth. The Bible tells us that God created the far-flung material universe, but his efforts focused on our planet. It was this planet that God molded into an environment for living things. It was here that life sprang into existence when God spoke. It was here he came to scoop up the dust into which he breathed the breath of life. It was to planet earth God came to walk with Adam and Eve in the Garden. It was this earth that shared ruin as a consequence of Adam's sin, and it was on this earth that the drama of redemption has been acted out. It was on this tiny planet, in a Middle Eastern backwater of world culture, that God chose to take on human form, and here on this planet Christ died on the cross. Earth is the center of the universe simply because the grand drama of sin and salvation has been acted out on its stage. Compared to what has taken place on earth, the ravening furnaces of a billion stars pale to insignificance.

For some mysterious reason God has determined that earth will always be the center. One day the first creation, warped as it is by sin, will be dissolved, its very elements destroyed by atomic fires. And then God will speak again, calling into existence a fresh universe, and in that fresh universe there will be a new earth (Rev. 21:1). That earth also will be the center of the new universe, just as our earth is the center of the old. Revelation looks ahead and tells us what will be on this renewed world of ours: "Now the dwelling of God is with men, and he will live with them. They will be his people, and God himself will be with them and be their God. He will wipe every tear from their eyes. There will be no more death or mourning or crying or pain, for the old order of things has passed away" (Rev. 21:3–4). Earth will be the center of all, for God will dwell there with his creation.

ECUMENICAL ◆ UNITY

ELECTION ◆ PREDESTINATION

ETERNAL LIFE ◆ LIFE, ETERNITY

ETERNITY

The Bible nowhere explains eternity. It simply affirms that God existed before the Creation, before time began. And it affirms that God will exist endlessly after this universe has been folded up, like a wornout tent, and put away. The psalmist finds a great sense of security in knowing that God inhabits eternity, unmoved by the changes taking place in time: "LORD, you have been our dwelling place throughout all generations. Before the mountains were born or you brought forth the earth and the world, from everlasting to everlasting you are God" (Ps. 90:1–2; see also Isa. 57:15).

A number of concepts are linked with the concept of time and eternity. Scripture does not look at either in a philosophical way. But what the Bible does say about God, time, and eternity has great practical importance to the Christian.

Paul carefully explains God's intention to transform Christians to be like Jesus. The process may be painful and slow, and it may be easy to lose heart, but Paul reminds us not to be discouraged. He says, "We fix our eyes not on what is seen, but on what is unseen. For what is seen is temporary, but what is unseen is eternal" (2 Cor. 4:18).

Anything that exists in this world of space and time is caught up in processes of change. This means that anything we can touch or see or experience is necessarily temporary. But God and those unseen spiritual realities that participate in his nature are not subject to change. They are eternal.

So God stands outside of time and thus is unchangeable. This conviction is important to our faith. You and I are constantly changing. Our bodies, our experiences, and our feelings are affected by the passage of time. But God is immutable: he never changes. He is outside of time and unaffected by its flow. Since God never changes, we can be sure that he who has loved us in Jesus will never change his mind or withdraw his promises.

The writer of Hebrews builds on this fact when he reminds us that God has said, "Never will I leave you; never will I forsake you." The writer then tells us how we can be so sure: "Jesus Christ is the same yesterday and today and forever" (Heb. 13:6, 8).

The eternity of God, his immutability as one standing outside of time and unaffected by it, means that you and I can have complete confidence in his endless love. God never will leave or forsake us.

This particular view of eternity helps us understand the implications of God's gift of eternal life. God has given those who believe in him a new kind of life, a life that is untouched by time or the course of events. This is, in fact, the basis of Paul's argument in 2 Corinthians 4. Later Paul contrasts what is seen in a person's life with "what is in the heart" (2 Cor. 5:12). "If anyone is in Christ," the passage says, "he is a new creation; the old has gone, the new has come" (2 Cor. 5:17). God has changed you and me by giving us a new life that is unaffected by events in this world and that must grow stronger and stronger, enabling us to reflect Jesus.

Peter picks up the same theme and expresses it this way: "You have been born again, not of perishable seed, but of imperishable, through the living and enduring word of God" (1 Peter 1:23). God has taken something of his own enduring life, something imperishable, and has given it to you and me through the new birth. Somehow we have eternity in our hearts, and we know that we will never perish but live endlessly with our God.

Eternal life, then, isn't something that starts when a person dies or that begins after God's final judgment on humanity. Eternal life begins at the new birth, as God plants something of Jesus in our personalities;

something that cannot be destroyed or changed by our experiences in time. To have eternal life means that our present relationship to God cannot be affected by the circumstances of our lives. Because we have this kind of permanent relationship to the Lord, we have confidence and hope, no matter what our days in time may bring.

To survey what the Bible says about eternal life, see Matthew 19:16, 29; 25:46; Mark 10:17, 30; Luke 10:25; 18:18, 30; John 3:15, 16, 36; 4:14, 36; 5:24, 39; 6:27, 40, 47, 54, 68; 10:28; 12:25, 50; 17:2, 3; Acts 13:46, 48; Romans 2:7; 5:21; 6:22, 23; Galatians 6:8; 1 Timothy 1:16; 6:12, 19; Timothy 1:2; 3:7; 1 John 1:2; 2:25; 3:15; 5:11, 13, 20; and Jude 21.

ETHICS

The study of ethics discusses what we consider right or wrong. It includes big questions, such as what is the nature of "the Good." And it asks how human beings should live their lives. Ethics examines human motives and probes personal and social responsibilities. Because issues like these are so basic to the human experience, ethics is considered to be a major branch of philosophy. Because Christians are concerned about doing right, ethics is a Christian concern also. Ethics has been a concern of great Christian thinkers and as a practical study, is important to every believer. How can we tell what is the best thing to do? How do we make daily decisions that reflect our faith's concern with pleasing God and with caring deeply for human beings?

To help us think about ethics, we need to look at the distinctive basis that Christianity provides for our own ethical thinking and actions. And we need to raise some practical questions about how a Christian goes about making decisions.

The basis of ethical thought. Ethical systems are constructed on only two foundations. The first basis includes both speculation about reality and notions derived from observing societies. Plato's philosophical speculations led him to ideas about the nature of things. These ideas served as the foundation for his ethical teaching about individuals and the state. Thomas Hobbes argued that ethics should rest on a description of what people actually do, not on notions about what they ought to do. Thus scientific observation was to be the basis for ethics. Jeremy Bentham thought that such observation proved that persons seek only one thing: pleasure. So ethics ought to spell out how human beings might achieve the greatest pleasure for the greatest number. We can multiply examples. But it's clear, despite the differences in various systems, each rests on the conviction that human beings must devise their own ethical systems. They may do this in the manner of a philosopher, developing a system to explain reality and then applying the system to ethics. Or they may do it in a more modern, scientific way, observing how people behave and reasoning from that to an ethical explanation of the behavior. But each approach relies wholly on human powers and assumes that ethical concerns have no necessary link to God.

The Christian, on the other hand, is convinced that standards of right and wrong come from outside the natural realm. Right and wrong are rooted in the very character of God. We know right from wrong because God has acted to reveal himself and his standards to us. Throughout the ages many Christians have been convinced that God has not only revealed morality in Scripture, but he has also planted in human beings a sense of right and wrong (Rom. 2:14–15). For Christians, then, ethical puzzles have not focused on "how do we know right from wrong." A moral Creator has revealed his own standards of right and wrong to us. Christian ethics are based squarely on the revelation of God's will given to us in the Bible.

The biblical perspective of ethics. Before we can deal with the specific content of biblical ethical teaching, we must understand the Bible's teaching about humanity. All human beings are born with a moral flaw. While every culture demonstrates the fact that humanity does have an innate awareness that certain issues are moral (that is, that there is such a thing as right and wrong), every culture also demonstrates the fact that "all have sinned and fallen short of the glory of God" (Rom. 3:23). Having a sense of right and wrong, and even having correct beliefs about what is right and wrong, does not produce moral actions. There is, in fact, in every human society and in the experience of every person a "morality gap." No one ever lives up even to his or her own standards, much less to God's standards.

This morality gap points to several basic Christian beliefs. We believe that the Creator, who made us in his own image, is a moral being. Human moral sensitivity is evidence of the divine source of human nature. We believe that human beings are corrupted by sin. The fact that utopia remains beyond our grasp and that every one of us is aware of falling short of our own standards is evidence of the reality of sin and its grip on human nature. The ethical experience of the individual and society provides compelling evidence that the biblical portrait of a lost humanity is truly accurate.

Another perspective on ethics is expressed in Romans 1. There Paul argues that racial history demonstrates that human beings have turned away from God, willfully rejecting what they know of him intuitively and through the testimony of nature. There, too, Paul argues that a mind that shuts God out becomes depraved: "Since they did not think it worthwhile to retain the knowledge of God, he gave them over to a depraved mind, to do what ought not to be done. They have become filled with every kind of wickedness, evil, greed, and depravity. They are full of envy, murders, strife, deceit, and malice. They are gossips, slanderers, God-haters, insolent, arrogant, and boastful; they invent ways of doing evil; they disobey their parents; they are senseless, faithless, heartless, ruthless. Although they know God's righteous decree that those who do such things deserve death, they not only continue to do these very things but also approve of those who practice them" (Rom. 1:28-32).

Without God human beings have no moral anchor, and they and their civilizations will be drawn increasingly into evil. Thus the Christian is convinced that we can have no sure moral standards without divine revelation, and that we can have no true moral experience or growth apart from a personal relationship to the Lord.

All Christian ethical thinking must operate within the framework provided by these revealed truths. God has shown us standards of right and wrong. Human beings, while possessing a moral sense, are twisted by sin. As a result no one chooses to do all that he or she believes to be good. The best that a person can do falls short of what is truly good. This does not, of course, imply that all persons always choose to do what is truly evil. ◆ DEPRAVITY But it does mean that to move toward the ethical ideal of right action from right motives, a personal relationship with God is necessary to free us from our bondage to sin within.

Ethical issues: knowing right and wrong. Most societies have established standards of right and wrong in the same areas. That is, societies have set standards related to sexual behavior, property rights, contracts and agreements, and the like. The content of right and wrong will vary among societies, but the areas that are viewed as ethical in nature are pretty much the same. Thus a Muslim may have four wives, and a Christian will have only one. But in no culture can a man have any woman he wants, whenever he wishes. Every culture establishes some sexual standards, whether or not members of that society live by their standards.

Christians are convinced that God has given us an authoritative revelation of what constitutes ethical and moral behavior. We are not left to guess at the content of ethics or to wonder if one set of ethical notions is really as good as another. Scripture limits sexual relations to marriage, and intercourse before marriage or with a partner other than one's spouse is wrong.

There are parallels from Scripture in most ethical and moral areas. Persons are to be faithful to the contracts they make. A person is not to lie to favor the rich or to favor the poor. A person is not to fraudulently take another's possessions; stealing is wrong. Both the individual and society are to have compassion on the poor and powerless. A person is responsible for what he or she has borrowed and is to return it in good condition. A person must be truthful in relationships with others; lying is forbidden. No one can read the Bible without becoming aware of the many expressions that define the content of right and wrong. The Bible states general principles ("love your neighbor as yourself"), but the Bible also provides many specific illustrations to define for us what actions really express love.

While Christians debate which Old Testament laws, for instance, apply to believers today, they agree that a study of Scripture provides a clear picture of moral and ethical norms. We believe that a person can know right from wrong if he or she will simply look into the Bible and come to understand those standards that God has communicated in his Word.

Ethical issues: motivation for right action. An ethical action has at least two elements. One is behavioral (the person does what is right); the other is motivational (the person does what is right from the right motive).

A significant question for Christians as well as other ethical thinkers is, What is right motivation? And what is wrong motivation?

Superficially some Christians have argued that right motivation is implicit in the concept of obedience. God, the moral governor of the race, has given his people instructions on how to live. The believer is obligated to obey. When you or I choose to do what is right as an act of obedience to God, then our action is truly moral. ◗ OBEDIENCE

Obedience surely is a basic concept, intimately linked with Christian ethics. But the question of motives probes more deeply. *Why* do we choose to obey God? Is it out of fear of punishment? Is it because we want to establish our righteousness so God will accept us and grant us heaven? Each of these motives for obedience is flawed. And because God considers our hearts (our inner orientation, our thoughts and motivations), an obedience that consists in outward conformity but flows from faulty motives simply is not acceptable to God.

The key to Christian motivation in ethical behavior seems more appropriately located in faith and love. Faith acknowledges God as moral governor, but it also recognizes God as one who justifies the ungodly. ◗ JUSTIFICATION Faith appropriates God's promise and shifts the basis of relationship to God from a foundation laid in human actions to the foundation laid in Jesus and in God's eternal promise. The person with faith does not obey God in an attempt to establish personal righteousness, because faith recognizes a righteousness that comes as a gift from God.

◆ RIGHTEOUSNESS, FAITH

In both Old and New Testaments, love is explicitly linked with obedience. Love motivated God to choose Israel and to reveal his moral standards so that obedience to God's laws might bring his people blessing (Deut. 4:37–40). And our love for God is a prerequisite to taking God's commandments to heart (Deut. 6:4–6). "Love the LORD your God and keep his requirements, his decrees, his laws, and his commands" is foundational to Old Testament ethics (Deut. 11:1). Love without obedience is unthinkable, and obedience without love is impossible.

In the New Testament this linkage is made even more explicit. Jesus told his disciples, "If you love me, you will obey what I command" (John 14:15). In the same passage he adds, "Whoever has my commands and obeys them, he is the one who loves me," and, "If anyone loves me, he will obey my teaching" (John 14:21, 23). In a powerful statement, the apostle Paul dismisses any actions not rooted in love as ethically and spiritually meaningless: "If I speak with the tongues of men and of angels, but have not love, I am only a resounding gong or a clanging cymbal. If I have the gift of prophecy and can fathom all mysteries and all knowledge, and if I have faith that can move mountains, but have not love, I am nothing. If I give all I possess to the poor and surrender my body to the flames, but have not love, I gain nothing (1 Cor. 13:1–3).

Love also speaks to the obedience that is motivated by fear. In 1 John the apostle says, "There is no fear in love. But perfect love drives out fear, because fear has to do with punishment" (1 John 4:18). Knowing that our relationship to God is based on God's loving promise rather than on our performance, we have no more reason to fear. We are freed to act spontaneously out of love for the God who has loved us so freely and so completely.

In Christian thought, then, love for God is viewed as the wellspring of ethical and moral behavior. Our perception of what is right and wrong is shaped by God's revelation of his standards. Our choices to act in obedience to that revelation are motivated by love. Truly ethical acts involve obedience that is motivated by love for God.

Ethical issues: moral dilemmas. Sooner or later every Christian faces decisions in which what is right and wrong is unclear. The choice may be between two things, each of which seems good. The choice may be between two things, each of which seems bad. The choice may be between a good and a bad, but the good may appear to bring pain to a neighbor we are commanded to love. It is easy to know what we should do when the right and wrong issues are clear (although it may not be easy to actually make the right choice). What is not so easy is to make those ambiguous ethical choices (those that we sense involve right/wrong but are unsure about the right thing to do). Often, we are not only uncertain, we are not even sure how to go about making our decision.

For instance let us suppose a young Christian woman has been asked to join the office bowling team. There's nothing intrinsically right or wrong about bowling. But she has heard that the league is a rowdy and rather unsavory one. So she wonders, Would it be right to join the team and take part in that particular league?

How is she going to tell if joining that team would be right or wrong? Some people would say, "Just look up a verse in the Bible and do what it says." Others would have her appeal to a hierarchy of values; still others would say, "Oh, just do the loving thing." But there are problems with each of these ways of resolving ethical dilemmas.

Let us suppose that as she has been thinking about joining the team, she remembers 1 Thessalonians 5:22, "Avoid every kind of evil." So she decides she better not join the team. But then a friend points out that when Paul said not to associate with the immoral, he did it "not at all meaning the people of this world who are immoral" (1 Cor. 5:10). This friend goes on to remind her that Jesus was considered a friend of sinners. Building relationships with the office bowling team is simply a response to Jesus' command, "Go ye into all the world." So she decides she will join the team. But then a third friend objects, reminding her that Paul also told the Corinthians not to be "unequally yoked together with unbelievers." This friend says she should join a bowling team made up of Christians.

Here we see the problem with the "just-find-a-verse-and-obey-the-Lord" approach. The problem is, which verse? A number of Bible precepts and principles are likely to relate to any given situation. How can a person tell which verse he or she is to obey?

At this point some Christian ethicists suggest an interesting answer. You organize the principles and precepts of Scripture into hierarchies. Then you find the highest principle that applies and follow it.

Suppose that in this case, people agree that several principles apply: witness by building relationships, witness by the purity of your life, and witness by avoiding every appearance of evil. Let's suppose that in this particular system, "witness by building relationships" is considered the highest item in the sequence. Now the decision is easy. It is true that some might misunderstand our friend's membership on this particular team. But it is more important to build relationships that could lead to a personal sharing of Jesus. So, following this approach, the dilemma is resolved, and she joins the team.

But there is a problem. Let us also suppose that our young friend is a new Christian, easily tempted back into a way of life she abandoned when she was converted. Let us suppose that under the influence of the team and the league, she slips back into her old way of life. Was her decision really right?

The problem with the hierarchical approach is that it offers us no way to deal with the individual differences that make ethical choices unique. The appeal to higher principles makes no adjustment for the spiritual and personal strength of the person or for the attitudes of the other team members, for instance. As a way of going about making ethical decisions, appeal to a hierarchy of principles is mechanical, impersonal, uncertain, and dangerous.

Unhappy with complexities like these, some people have thrown up their hands and said, "Oh, just do the loving thing." In this they claim biblical justification. Paul says in Romans 13:10, "Love does no harm to its neighbor. Therefore love is the fulfillment of the law." So those of this persuasion argue, "Just look ahead, figure out the results your actions will have, and do what will be loving toward others."

But now we have two problems. First, you and I really can't look ahead and know the results of our actions. We are finite and limited, and life is very complicated. If we have to rely on our ability to know how our actions will really affect others, in long-term rather than superficial ways, we're really in trouble. Second, this solution misses something important in Romans 13. That verse says love fulfills the law. That is, love and law are intimately linked. God gave us his law for the purpose of telling us what the loving thing to do really is.

Love is an adequate motive for moral action. Love can make us want to do what is good and right. But love alone can't tell us what the "good" and "right" are!

So the Christian returns to the basics. God has given us a revelation of moral and ethical behavior. Somehow our decision making has to take that revelation into account.

How, then, can we go about making decisions? The Christian has two great ethical advantages. First, we believe in objective, revealed moral standards. Second, we have a personal relationship to God — a living God. Jesus is Lord, and he is alive. You and I, linked with Jesus by the Holy Spirit, have access to his wisdom. The Book of Proverbs puts it this way: "Trust in the LORD with all your heart and lean not on your own understanding; in all your ways acknowledge him, and he will make your paths straight" (Prov. 3:5–6).

In the New Testament the same truth is emphasized. Because the Christian is related to the Spirit of God, we are able to make judgments about all things. This is because "we have the mind of Christ" (1 Cor. 2:15–16).

Christian ethics has a supernatural dimension. We believe in a God who is, and who lives to guide us daily. We are not mystics. We study the Bible to learn more about how God thinks and what he expects of us. We talk with Christian friends to gain insights from their wisdom. But ultimately each one of us is responsible to God to make each personal decision. And each of us, as we look to the Lord and desire to do his will, can expect God to guide us. We study, think, and pray over our decisions. And then, in faith, we do what seems best, always open to hear God's voice and ready to change direction if we are convinced it is God's will. ◆ GUIDANCE

Summary. The subject of ethics is broad and complex. It asks questions about right and wrong, about the nature of the good, and about what is the best way to live one's life. In its most practical expression, ethics deals with how we make daily decisions in areas where we feel that right and wrong are involved.

The Christian has a number of advantages in the area of ethics. First, we believe that right and wrong can be known objectively, for God has revealed his own moral standards to us. Second, we recognize the ruin that sin has worked in our race. We understand that knowing what is good does not imply anyone will choose what is good. In fact we believe that the secret of living truly good lives is found in our personal relationship to God. Love for God will motivate us to obedience, and God himself will work within to enable us to do what is right.

We also have another advantage. When we come to complex situations in which the right and wrong are unclear, we can look to our living God, to whom all things are clear. As we look to God in prayer, study to understand his ways, and discuss our choices with other Christians, we will experience his leading.

We may not always be sure about every decision we make, for we are called to walk by faith and not by sight. But as we remain open to God, we know that he truly will make our "paths straight."

EVANGELISM

Evangelism means "sharing the good news." Christians have always believed that our faith is good news and have been enthusiastic about communicating that news to others. It is not that we are simply advocates of a system of belief. We are convinced that in Jesus, God has acted to meet the deepest needs of human beings and to rescue us from a truly lost condition. ◆ LOST, SALVATION

Still many Christians are a little uncertain about evangelism. What exactly is it? Is it passing out tracts? Inviting people to church? Explaining to people how they can be saved? ◆ SAVED

To understand the nature of evangelism, we must examine the meaning of the Bible's key words associated with evangelism, the content of the evangelistic message, the goal of evangelism, and the methods used to spread the gospel in the early, explosive days of Christianity.

Biblical words associated with evangelism. The New Testament uses three Greek words closely associated with the evangelism of the early church. The first of these is *euangelizesthai*, meaning "to tell the good news." In the New Testament the good news invariably focuses on Jesus. It may be good news that God's kingdom is near, but Jesus is the king (Acts 17:7). It may be good news about peace, but that peace comes "through Jesus Christ, who is Lord of all" (Acts 10:36). The good news that Christians have for the world always focuses on Jesus and what his life, death, and resurrection mean to humanity.

The second word is from the root *kerussein*, which means "to herald or to announce." Its noun form is "the message," a synonym for the good news itself (as in Rom. 16:25). The power of the message is found in the reality of the resurrection of the Jesus it proclaims (1 Cor. 15:14). The verb form is used as often as *euangelizesthai* and in the same way. Twelve times the two words are linked in a form that means "to preach the good news," and nine times they are linked to speak of people preaching Jesus. It is important to note that when the Christian community heralds its message to the world, the focus of that message is always Jesus.

The third word is from the root *martureo*, meaning "to witness or give testimony." This word group had legal connotations, indicating those who on the basis of a personal involvement in events could give witness and evidence of them. The word is often used in contexts that focus on the historic events on which our faith is founded: the life, words, actions, death, and resurrection of Jesus. But the early believers also gave witness to the fact that they had trusted Jesus and had found the gospel claims verified in their own experience.

Evangelism, then, involves us in sharing the good news about Jesus, announcing him to others, and giving personal witness to his impact in our own lives.

The content of the evangelistic message. It is clear that the content of the Christian's good news is nothing less than Jesus himself. The

Christian message does not just present a better philosophy, a higher moral vision, or a more pleasant prospect for life after death. The Christian message presents Jesus Christ, God's Son, as one in whom a person can trust, as one whom a person can serve. In Jesus we meet God in the flesh. In Jesus we meet sacrificial love. In Jesus we meet forgiving grace. In Jesus we meet resurrection power. In Jesus we meet a living Lord. The only message the Christian has is Jesus.

The more clearly we help others to understand who Jesus is, what his attitude toward us is, what he has done for us, and how we are called now to live in and for him, the more clearly we present a gospel message that truly is good news for humanity.

Some have tried to summarize the gospel and identify it as certain facts about Jesus and his work on the cross. Certainly Jesus' cross and resurrection are central to the gospel. While I may be told that "Christ died for my sins," without a better understanding of who Jesus is, I may fail to grasp or to accept that central gospel fact. In a significant way everything that helps another person understand and know Jesus is the gospel, for the gospel is Jesus. To limit evangelism to presenting a limited number of facts about him, no matter how important those facts may be, will distort our understanding of how Christians can share their Lord and the good news about him with others.

In a more limited context some have argued that evangelistic preaching has a specific content. This argument is based on a study of the evangelistic sermons that Luke reports in Acts. There, speaking to an audience that was familiar with Jesus' life, teaching, and recent death, Peter concentrated on several recurring themes. Jesus was accredited by God as his messenger through the miracles and wonders that they themselves had witnessed. Jesus' death was permitted by God and foretold in the Scriptures. Jesus was raised from the dead and thus shown to be God's promised Christ (Messiah), as was also foretold by the Scriptures. Jesus is thus Lord and Christ, and hearers must repent (in context, abandon their earlier opinion about Jesus) and be baptized as an open sign of allegiance to Jesus. Those who turn to him will have their sins forgiven, and they will receive the Holy Spirit (Acts 2–3).

While others have noted that Paul used a different approach in speaking to a different audience in Athens (Acts 17:16–34), what we find is that wherever the good news is shared with those who are not yet Christians, the message is always about Jesus. Jesus is the one we talk about — not our doctrines, not our churches and their programs, but Jesus. It isn't wrong to talk about doctrines. And its not wrong to talk about the things we like about our church or to invite friends to come. But this isn't evangelism. Evangelism is always sharing or showing others more about Jesus, our Lord.

The goal of evangelism. The goal of evangelism is conversion. Christians do not operate out of a relativistic framework, which assumes that one religion is as good as another and that any faith is simply a different path leading to the same God. The Christian is bound by Jesus' own teaching: "I am the way and the truth and the life. No one comes to the Father except through me" (John 14:6). Because of this, and because we believe that personal relationship to God is the central issue of life, our goal in evangelism is to lead people to a personal, faith relationship to Jesus Christ and all that relationship implies. ♦ CONVERSION

Methods used in evangelism. Evangelism is communicating the good news about Jesus; Jesus is the content of evangelism, and conversion is evangelism's goal. What does the New Testament suggest to help us understand how to share about Jesus?

In the first place we read about some people in the church who are especially gifted as evangelists. For instance, Philip (Acts 8) had an effective ministry in preaching about Jesus outside of Israel; Philip was also gifted in what has been called personal evangelism — talking to people about Jesus. A modern parallel might be Billy Graham, whose public meetings around the world and on television have been used to introduce millions to Jesus. But evangelism is not the sole responsibility of evangelists.

Acts 8 also notes that when a persecution of Christians broke out in Jerusalem, most of the believers were scattered throughout Judea and Samaria. The chapter says, "Those who had been scattered preached the word wherever they went" (Acts 8:4). The original text here suggests not public meetings but gossiping on street corners. Average Christians found that wherever they went, they simply talked about Jesus. The secret of the church's explosive early growth is not found in its clergy or missionaries or evangelists alone. The secret is found in the practice of God's informal missionaries, the average believers, simply talking about Jesus to those with whom they come in contact.

But the secret of effective evangelism lies in more than talk. A number of New Testament passages point to the witness of transformed lives and loving community.

Paul writes, of himself and of Christians in general, "We have renounced secret and shameful ways, we do not use deception, nor do we distort the word of God. On the contrary, by setting forth the truth plainly [by word and by life] we commend ourselves to every man's conscience in the sight of God" (2 Cor. 4:2).

Peter echoes the same theme. Non-Christians may be puzzled about the holiness of the Christian's life, but when troubles come and non-

Christians see how the Christian approaches the future with hope, non-Christians will "ask you to give a reason for the hope that you have." At such times the Christian is to respond "with gentleness and respect, keeping a clear conscience, so that those who speak maliciously against your good behavior in Christ may be ashamed of their slander" (1 Pet. 3:15–16). The transformation of behavior, which is always associated with a true belief in Jesus, is one of the most powerful of all testimonies. This transformation will provide many opportunities to speak openly about our Lord.

The same silent witness is to be provided by the Christian community. The New Testament stresses the love and acceptance found in the fellowship of believers. As Jesus promised, "All men will know that you are my disciples if you love one another" (John 13:34). ▸ FELLOWSHIP, LOVE

Within this context of public evangelism by gifted people and the daily evangelism by typical believers, the good news about Jesus permeated the world of the New Testament. It wasn't easy. And it wasn't something that happened overnight. Preaching, teaching, and writing all were involved. Probably most evangelism during the New Testament era took place in homes. Christians met in homes and invited neighbors. The children were taught in the home. Friends and neighbors visited in homes. Personal evangelism took place; people engaged in conversations equivalent to our back-fence chats or phone conversations. In Christians' daily contact, they naturally talked about Jesus, who was so much a focus of their lives.

Summary. Christians are convinced they have good news to share with others. This good news is about Jesus, who is the sole avenue humanity has to personal relationship with God. The good news has always been announced by some people in the church who are especially gifted for this task. But the most effective evangelism has always been done by average Christians who know and love Jesus and whose lives as well as their talk reflect that relationship.

EVIL

Evil has spawned one of the classical arguments against the existence of God. It is a simple argument. If your God is both good and all-powerful, he wouldn't permit evil. But evil does exist in the universe. Therefore the good and all-powerful God that Christians believe in cannot exist.

It is an interesting argument, but it has problems. The first is that it makes God a two-dimensional caricature. Christians also believe in a God of infinite wisdom. Simply because something may appear to be a contradiction to limited, finite human beings doesn't mean that it is a contradiction to God. In talking about God, we can never limit ourselves to a two-dimensional caricature.

The other problem is linked to the word *evil*. In this argument it is used in a slippery way. Often when we speak of evil, we are really talking about evils: about sickness and sorrow, about pain and tragedy, and about distress and death. At other times when we speak of evil, we mean things like jealousy and injustice, hatred and anger, and murder and theft. On the one hand, evil includes all those ills and troubles to which human beings are subject. On the other hand, evil involves all those wicked acts of which human beings are capable. It is important when we discuss evil to be clear what we are talking about.

Of course evil in both senses does exist. To some extent every philosophy and every religion must face that fact and deal with it. Every system of thought must provide some answer to the question, "Why evil?" Every system must provide some answer to the person who cries out, "How do I deal with the evil and the evils that plague me?"

The answer to these questions is never simple. But we are convinced that our faith provides the best answers possible. Our answers square with what we know about evil. And our answers satisfy the hearts of those caught in the web that evil of both types spins to trap each person who comes into our less-than-perfect world.

To catch a glimpse of the Christian perspective on evil, we need to look at several issues: What is the nature of evil? What is the origin of evil? What is the impact of evil on humanity? How does the Bible use words related to evil? And what is God's solution to the problem of evil?

The nature of evil. Many people have struggled to define evil. To some, evil seems best understood as the absence or the lack of good. Bad fishing is simply the lack of good fishing (of catching fish). Similarly, bad behavior would simply be the lack of good behavior. In this framework evil actions grow out of human limitations and finitude, from the fact that we are becoming and have not yet arrived at the divine perfection.

But evil cannot be so easily explained. If the argument were valid, we would call a fetus and a three-year-old child evil because they have not yet reached their adult potential. Instead we can speak of a good (healthy) fetus and even of a (morally) good three-year-old child, meaning that each functions appropriately at the level currently attained. Looking at the innocent Adam, who like us was finite and imperfect, God did not call his creation evil, but God called it "very good" (Gen.

1:27–28). Whatever evil may be, we cannot explain it merely as a lack or absence of good.

One long tradition views evil as a principle inherent in matter, while the immaterial or the spiritual is good. In church history this view was expressed in the Gnostic corruption of Christianity. In such dualistic systems, God is not viewed as the direct Creator of the material universe. Instead he is distanced from his creation; the "good" spiritual principle is thought to be repelled by the "evil" material world. In such systems human beings are viewed as good spirits trapped in evil physical bodies. One either denies bodily needs and desires to gain mastery over evil physical nature (asceticism), or else one permits any physical excess, because the "real" immaterial person within isn't affected by what the body does (libertarianism). But this view, too, is inadequate. It is clear that the immaterial part of humanity, if we can use this language, is moral arbiter of the material. That is, when tempted by some passion rooted in the physical nature, one does not have to give in. The "inner me" rules the body and decides whether or not to respond to its urgings. Thus we can choose to do good with our bodies, or we can choose to do evil with them. To say that evil resides in the material and good resides in the immaterial fails to reckon with the fact that we exercise an immaterial moral judgment and that our immaterial will makes choices about what the body does. Somehow the notion that evil is intrinsic in the material of the universe while good is intrinsic to a spiritual dimension simply cannot be upheld.

Others have presented a variation of the first argument, that evil should be viewed as the absence or lack of good. They have said that evil is moral ignorance or the absence of adequate experience. Plato, the classic proponent of this view, argued that if only human beings knew the good, they would choose it. But this concept also fails to fit the facts. Many people who know that smoking cigarettes shortens life continue to smoke, and all the oversized warnings the Surgeon General places on cigarette packages will not deter them. Somehow knowing what is good or what is best never succeeds in bringing Utopia. Despite our knowledge human beings still choose to do things they know are wrong and harmful.

Another popular notion is that evil in human beings is the residue of the evolutionary process. Evil is the relic of the animal, not yet outgrown by a human race moving toward biological perfection. This is an attractive option because it excuses humanity from moral responsibility. It is not really our fault; evil is just a remnant of the savage. But this view is hardly sustainable or relevant. What the animals do, they do by instinct. What human beings do, they do with a knowledge of moral implications. We can hardly argue that human beings received their moral sense from animals who have no such sense. We cannot argue that our choices to do what we recognize as evil are made under the influence of uncontrollable instinct. Instead all human law and custom is based on the idea that the individual is responsible for what he or she does, unless insanity removes the burden of responsibility. Human evil is not done by instinct at all; it is done responsibly, with and in spite of all our uniquely human capacities.

Other people have offered views about the nature of evil. Rousseau felt that evil was a creation of culture: that left alone, living in a primitive state, humans would not be warped by evil. But no culture, however primitive, has ever been void of evil. Marx argued that evil was an economic creation: Capitalism created inequities, leading to social injustice and all kinds of social and personal evils. If only human beings would turn to communism, where no issue of personal property could be raised, evil would be put aside and the golden age would emerge. Soviet Russia gives dark testimony to the validity of that view.

These and other attempts to explain the nature of evil all prove inadequate. While each approach recognizes the existence of evil, none is willing to go beyond the limits of the material universe in an effort to understand it. But the fact is, only when we take the God of the Bible and his revelation seriously can we begin to understand evil and see how we must deal with it.

The origin of evil. The Bible does not provide any philosophical or theoretical treatise on evil. Instead it speaks of God, who is perfectly good and who created a good and beautiful universe. Evil is an intruder in this universe, a distortion introduced by creatures and not by God.

On a cosmic scale, evil was introduced in the universe by Satan. Many people take Isaiah 14 as a description of Satan's self-transformation from a powerful angel (Lucifer) into God's implacable enemy:

> How you have fallen from heaven,
> O morning star, son of the dawn!
> You have been cast down to the earth,
> you who once laid low the nations!
> You said in your heart,
> "I will ascend to heaven;
> I will raise my throne
> above the stars of God
> I will sit enthroned on the mount of
> assembly,
> on the utmost heights of the sacred mountains.
> I will ascend above the tops of the clouds;
> I will make myself like the Most High."
>
> (Isa. 14:11–14)

If this description is of Satan's fall, then we see evil spring into being in the heart of a living creature. Evil, like creation itself and like good, has a personal origin. Evil has nothing to do with any inherent qualities residing in matter.

What's more, evil is defined in this passage of "I wills." Evil is the creature demanding the place of the Creator. Evil is the will of the creature substituting for the will of the Creator. Evil is the shattering of the divine order, as contrary wills emerge to warp and distort the original harmony. In this view evil is an active rather than a passive force; it is rebellion against God's will and desires.

The pattern, set on a cosmic scale in Satan's rebellion, is duplicated in the events reported in Genesis 1–3. God has shaped the material creation into perfect form. He has hung earth in space and has molded the planet into friendly form. He populated it with animal life, and as a culminating act, he formed Adam and later Eve to share his image. God places the happy pair in a beautiful garden; he gives them responsibility for the earth and the opportunity to live in obedient relationship with God and so preserve their innocence and the harmony of this fresh creation. But Satan slips into the garden, and Adam and Eve make a tragic choice. Like Satan before them, they choose to rebel against the will of God. Their act, like Satan's, shatters the harmony of the universe and introduces discord and pain. Their act, like Satan's first sin, warps the nature of the sinner and leads to continuing rebellion against God's will and purposes.

In the cosmic and the experiential realm, evil is intimately linked with sin. By nature, evil acts are sin, and evil itself is the rebellious insistence on exercising the will of the creature against that of the Creator. Evils, those tragedies and pains that plague humankind, result directly or indirectly from evil acts and especially from that first sin, which introduced discord into the original creation. Adam's fall affected all the world, even as the misjudgment of a sea captain brings his ship to a watery grave.

This sketch of the Christian view of the nature and origin of evil makes several important points. First, Christians see both evil and evils as rooted in sin. The evil that we do is done because we refuse to subject our will to the good will of God. The evils that befall us can be traced directly to some person's evil acts or indirectly to the warping of nature, which was the result of Adam's sin. To understand evil, a person must study and come to understand sin. ◗ SIN

Second, Christians believe in a personal universe. That is, reality cannot be explained in terms of impersonal or "natural" processes. When we seek to understand the nature and origin of the universe, we are forced back to God. When we seek to understand the nature and origin of good and evil, we are also forced back to examine the relationship of God's creatures with the Lord. Third, in seeking to come to grips with evil and with evils, Christians are willing to accept personal responsibility. We do not blame some savage remnant or excuse ourselves as good but helpless creatures trapped in a material tomb. We understand the sinful nature of the evil urges that we feel, and we know that we must be responsible for our choices. Most of all we rely on God to break the bonds that evil has forged.

The impact of evil. Evil shrouds every corner of our universe. Everything that we know or experience has been distorted by evil; sin has torn our world from its moorings and has twisted it out of shape. The beauty and harmony of the original creation is gone, and we can hardly imagine Eden. The purity of a humanity fresh from the Creator's hand is lost, and we can hardly imagine innocence. Bluntly put, nothing in our experience or in our nature is free of the taint of evil; everything in human life is flawed and marred.

Evil appears in the passions that tug at us, tempting us away from good. Evil appears in the hidden motives that lie behind our actions. Evil appears in the choices that hurt others or that selfishly set our own desires above the desires of God. Evil appears in the hurts we suffer at the hands of others and in the injustices that social systems perpetuate. Evil lies within us and around us, wearing the common face of sin. When evil is seen as sin and as rooted in sin and when the impact of sin is fully understood, then we will understand evil and begin to realize how desperately we need Christ to rescue us. ◆ SIN, SOCIAL JUSTICE

Bible's words for evil. In the Old Testament one family of Hebrew words expresses the notion of evil. The same root indicates both wickedness and misery or distress. Wicked acts violate God's intentions for humankind. The physical and emotional pains that we experience are evils, viewed in the Old Testament as a consequence of doing evil. Everywhere in the Old Testament doing evil is defined in a simple way. Certain acts are wrong because they are evil "in the eyes of the Lord" (Num. 32:13; Deut. 4:25; Judg. 2:11; 2 Sam. 3:39; 1 Kings 15:26). God and his will are the standard of good; evil is any variation from that standard or any violation of that will. Moral evil, then, is whatever God views as wrong.

In its second major use, this Hebrew word group identifies the consequences of wicked choices. The Old Testament teaches that evil (moral) choices ultimately bring evil (painful) results. Total physical and psychological disaster result from abandoning God's way.

The interplay of these two meanings of the word *evil* explains puzzling statements in the Old Testament about God's involvement with evil. For instance some versions of the Old Testament read, "I form the light and create darkness; I bring prosperity and create evil: I the LORD do all these things" (Isa. 45:7 KJV) and, "When evil comes to a city, has the LORD not caused it?" (Amos 3:6 KJV). Statements like these refer to the believer's conviction that God is moral judge of his universe. He is not only the standard of good but also the one who will punish evil. God takes responsibility for ordering a universe in which evil acts invariably result in evil consequences of some sort. God does not act wickedly. But God does bring upon a sinning humanity the evils that are the result of sin.

Two Greek word groups are used in the New Testament to express the idea of evil. While they can be used as synonyms, the two have different shades of meaning. *Kakos* looks at a thing's nature and evaluates it as damaged. According to Romans 7:7–25, human beings are evil in that they are damaged, damaged to the extent that they are flawed and unable to do even the good they wish to do. From this flawed nature flow the evil acts of wickedness and malice that harm others. *Poneros* is a stronger, more active word, which portrays hostility. Not only are human beings flawed, but they are also in active rebellion against God. Wickedness is rooted in our evil will as well as in our flawed nature.

So again we are forced to face the personal nature of evil. Evil is not some impersonal thing, some irresistible force, some characteristic of matter, or some natural consequence of incomplete evolution. Evil is rooted in the creature's rebellion against the Creator. Evil is rebellion against the standards of God, a shattering of the harmony of original creation. And evil in this active, personal sense is the cause of all the pain and evils to which mankind is subject.

God's solution to the problem of evil. Proposed solutions to the problem of evil are directly related to one's theory of its nature. The evolutionist suggests that we must wait until moral development catches up with us. The communist calls for economic reform. But the Christian, who understands evil as rooted in the·creature's relationship with the Creator, calls for a radical conversion from hostility toward God to a love for him.

Actually evil must be dealt with on both the cosmic and the experiential levels. On the cosmic level God will one day exercise his power and judge all sin. Then every contrary will shall be forced to submit to God's will, and every rebellious creature will be bound forever, isolated in what the Bible calls the "lake of fire." ◆ HELL God will create a new universe to be the home of righteousness and joy, and every kind of evil will be a stranger to God's new heaven and new earth (Isa. 65:17–25).

On the experiential level God has acted to make reconciliation possible. In Jesus, God has punished sin and has laid the basis for restored relationship. Our hostile, evil will can be changed by conversion. When we put our faith in Jesus, God begins a process of transformation, to be completed at the resurrection. We come to love God, and we want to please him. As we continue to surrender to him, God works within us to enable us to do good. With rebelliousness replaced by love for God (2 Cor. 5:11–12) and with our human inadequacy overcome by the power of the indwelling Spirit of God (Rom. 8:1–11), we can actually begin to do good.

Even though the believer is made new and the power of the evil that distorts human personality is withdrawn, Christians still live in an evil world. Life still holds its tragedies. Every relationship has its pain. Sickness and death are still with us. But relationship with God even provides an answer to the hurts that flow from evil. Christians are not immune to evils. Instead we are told that God will sovereignly use even the evils to work his good (Rom. 8:28–29). God will so weave the experiences that come to us in our life that his good purpose for us and in us will be achieved. To transform evils into good stands forever as one of the great triumphs of our God.

In summary, then, Christians acknowledge the reality of evil and are fully aware of the evils to which humankind is subject. But we understand evil as sin, the rebellious interposition of the creature's will that is contrary to the will of the Creator. From that rebelliousness, all evil (wickedness) stems, and from wicked acts, directly or indirectly, come all the evils that mankind knows.

But God is God, and evil is destined to be put down. The cosmos will be purified of evil by a cataclysmic final judgment, and evil beings will be isolated in the lake of fire. Until then humanity can find release from the evil within through a faith relationship with God. In Jesus we have the offer of forgiveness and re-creation, the promise of a changed heart and of a divine enablement that releases us to do good. Until then even the evils that trouble mankind are transformed for us, for God has promised that "in all things God works for the good of those who love him, who have been called according to his purpose" (Rom. 8:28).

Is the existence of evil, then, a compelling argument against the existence of God? Hardly. The opposite is true. Only when we meet the God of the Bible and sense the personal origin of all things, can we fully understand the nature of evil and its workings. Only in God do we find not only an end to the philosophers' quest but also relief for the hurting heart. In God we find the message of love and salvation that can free us from the evil we sense within ourselves. In God we find the calm assurance that the evils we experience in life will be transformed by our Lord into gifts that bring us good.

EVOLUTION

We think of evolution as modern or even as scientific. Actually it is neither.

Many centuries before Christ, the Greek philosophers speculated that humanity may have evolved from porpoises. These ancient Near Eastern ideas were philosophically equivalent to that of the modern scientific evolutionist.

What I mean by philosophically equivalent is that each makes the same basic assumptions even though the theories developed from the assumptions may differ. For instance modern evolutionists and the ancient worshipers of gods and goddesses viewed matter as existing first, before life. Matter was uncreated and eternal. Out of this matter, the ancients thought, the gods were somehow generated, just as the modern evolutionist thinks that life was somehow generated from inert, lifeless matter. In both systems the individual human being has little worth, for each will die, even though mankind (the race) may continue. In both schemes good and evil are subjective, for no absolute moral standards exist. Thus the world is neither good nor evil, but it is a great impersonal entity to which human beings must adjust before their momentary life snuffs out. In neither set of presuppositions is there purpose or goal beyond whatever good can be found in the experience of life itself.

Philosophically evolution is not new at all. The scientific jargon correctly used to talk of evolution may be different from the way people talked about their beliefs three thousand years ago, but the core content of the belief systems is remarkably alike.

The similarities between modern and ancient beliefs and the contrast of the biblical account of origins is shown on the chart on page 122.

However apologists may view evolutionary theory as something new and scientific, its foundations are as ancient as the most superstitious attempts to explain the existence of the universe and mankind's place in it. The mechanisms that ancients and moderns use to explain how the present world was formed may differ, but the foundational beliefs and presuppositions are the same.

BELIEFS ABOUT ORIGINS

Ancient Beliefs	Evolutionary Beliefs	Biblical Teaching
1. Matter is first, uncreated.	1. Matter is first, uncreated.	1. Matter is created by God.
2. The gods sprang from dead matter.	2. Humans invented the gods and religion.	2. God is first, uncreated.
3. Creation is shaping matter that already exists.	3. Creation is a religious word for the natural processes by which matter took its present form.	3. God spoke, and matter came into existence and was given form.
4. Life was generated in some unexplained manner.	4. Life was generated in some unexplained manner.	4. Life came into being at God's will and command.
5. Humans have little worth and value.	5. Humans are animals of no more worth or value than other animals.	5. Humans were created in God's image, and each person has infinite worth and value.
6. Humans die and death is the end.	6. Humans die and death is the end.	6. Human existence is endless, and each person will know eternal life or judgment.
7. Moral values have little impact on human experience.	7. Moral values are relative, subjective, changing.	7. Moral value is absolute, built into humans and into the universe.

Evolution and evolution. One of the things that is so confusing about the theory of evolution is that the same word is used to speak of distinctly different things.

Evolution (with a capital "E") is a theory about origins, and in particular the notion that life was somehow spontaneously generated from inert, non-living matter. The theory, then, goes on to suppose that every living being, from the most minute to the most complex, developed from that first living cell or cluster of cells by natural process. That word *natural* is also slippery. By natural, you and I usually mean something that is ordinary, common. But in this case the natural process is not ordinary or common at all. In fact no one can even say for sure what process might have caused changes from simple cells to complex life forms. In this case the word *natural* means something that can be fully explained by nature, something that is an effect of causes located within the material universe and thus needs no external, supernatural cause.

Book upon book has been written pointing out the problems with Evolution. The critical change forms (missing links) have not been found. The laws of thermodynamics suggest it is impossible for the simpler forms to generate the more complex. The complexity and interrelationships of body structures (such as the human eye) make it statistically nonsense to suppose that every interrelated element would generate spontaneously at the same time and would be so imbedded in genes that the whole would be passed on to succeeding generations.

Scientists who are Evolutionists are not unaware of the problems. But the textbooks that schoolchildren read and the popularizers of scientific theory like Carl Sagan boldly speak of Evolution as if the theory were proven fact and any other view of origins were proof of ignorance.

Used in another sense, however, evolution (with a lowercase "e") *is* established. Changes do take place in species of living things, and we understand some of the mechanisms by which those changes are generated. Charles Darwin pointed many of them out, and since then they have become better understood.

The problem is that some people take evidence for evolution to be evidence for Evolution. And this does not necessarily follow. For instance we can breed dogs so that some are tiny and hairless and others are giant and hairy. These very different dogs may have come from the same parents generations ago, but they have "evolved" their own unique characteristics. But it would be quite different to say that we have noticed or guided evolutionary changes by which a dog emerged from an alligator, from a dolphin, or even from a cat. What we have learned about the process of change within plants or animals really cannot validly be extended to explain changes between kinds.

. At best it is sloppy thinking to assume that evolution proves Evolution. At worst it is raw deceit.

What we need to do, then, is to be sure that when we're talking or thinking about evolution, we identify whether Evolution or evolution is involved. If we talk about Evolution, then we are talking about a theory of origins that does not rest on a scientific base but instead is simply a modern variation of an ancient faith. Today human beings still try to explain the material universe apart from God. ◆ **EXISTENCE OF GOD, SCIENCE** If we are talking about evolution, then whatever we discover has value for our understanding of the laws by which God governs the world, but it has nothing to do with one's theory of origins.

I should perhaps note that some Christian scientists have suggested Theistic Evolution. That is, they accept the ideas that the earth is extremely old and that processes that we can observe today account for most of the way that the world is. They also agree that very great changes can take place naturally within species. But they argue either that God superintended the changes or that at each point of radical change God intervened with a creative act. Enough books have been written debating the pros and cons of this Christian variation of the theory of Evolution. What's important to note is that, whether or not we agree with the Evolutionary framework, Christians still go back to the basic issue. It is not important how God created, but that God is the Creator. It is not important how changes took place in living things, but that God is the source of life. It is not important when mankind originated on planet earth, but that human beings are the special creation of God, shaped in his image, bearing now and always the stamp of eternity.

It is strange that believers seems always to find themselves out of step with the world. In Old Testament times the believer's faith in a God who spoke the material universe into existence ran counter to the common notion that matter was the uncreated ground of reality. Today, too, we look back and affirm our faith in a God who is himself the personal ground of reality, the source of the material. Against the wise of this world, who insist that dead matter generated life, we believe in an unseen God who is the source of all that is. And we are comfortable in this faith. In fact we are "sure of what we hope for and certain of what we do not see," understanding "that the universe was formed at God's command, so that what is seen was not made out of what was visible" (Heb. 11:1, 3). By faith, we know. The godless universe of human speculation is not the universe in which we live. The universe and you and I come from the hand of the living God.

EXISTENCE OF GOD

The Bible doesn't argue the existence of God. Scripture simply states, "God is." Beyond the beginning, the cause of all, there looms the image of a God who later broke through all the barriers between time and eternity to reveal himself to the human beings he had created.

Scripture assumes that creation itself gives compelling evidence that

God is. This theme is found in passages like Psalm 19 and Romans 1. The psalmist says, "The heavens declare the glory of God; the skies proclaim the work of his hands. Day after day they pour forth speech; night after night they display knowledge. There is no speech or language where their voice is not heard. Their voice goes out into all the earth, their words to the ends of the world" (Ps. 19:1–4).

And Paul argues that "what may be known about God is plain to them, because God has made it plain to them. For since the creation of the world, God's invisible qualities — his eternal power and divine nature — have been clearly seen, being understood from what has been made, so that men are without excuse" (Rom. 1:19–20).

The classic arguments. Three different kinds of arguments have been advanced to "prove" the existence of God. One rests on a kind of logic, and the other two rely on arguments drawn from experience.

The ontological argument, presented first in the eleventh century by Anselm, goes like this: "We can conceive of a perfect being, one who is so great and perfect that there could be none greater. Such a being must have existence as one characteristic. Therefore such a being must exist." The argument is abstract and hard to grasp. Unlike the other arguments for God's existence, this one has only tenuous roots in Scripture. Anselm thought that his argument was implied by Scripture's comment that "the fool has said in his heart, 'there is no God'" (Ps. 14:1). How clear it seemed to Anselm: Only a fool could conceive of God and then deny him. Only a fool would fail to realize that the being he denied must in fact exist, for the very concept of such a being demonstrates his existence.

Cosmological and teleological arguments appeal to the order observable in the universe. The cosmological arguments observe the orderliness of events and note that cause and effect rule. Moderns note the first law of thermodynamics and observe that energy is lost in each transaction so that the universe is, in essence, running down. Somehow, then, there must have been a first cause of the cause/effect chain we see in our universe; somehow there must have been a first burst of energy to explain the existence of that receding flow of energy we now observe. Whatever one wants to call that first cause, the believer is convinced that the self-existent Creator our universe calls for is in fact the God who has revealed himself to us in Scripture.

The teleological arguments note orderliness and its testimony to a shaping mind who made things as they are to fulfill their purpose in his scheme of things. This argument is often put in simple forms. "You can no more explain the design of the stars and the structure of living beings by chance than you could expect a tornado to hit a junkyard and put together a new car." Or "If you walk through a field and find a clod of dirt, you suspect nothing special. But if you find a ticking watch, you know it didn't just happen. There must have been a watchmaker." So, this argument insists, the complex design and order exhibited in the world demand a maker who shaped things for the purpose they fulfill in his creation.

The third kind of argument rests on observance of human beliefs and behavior. The human race exhibits a sense of morality, an awareness of right and wrong. This moral sense implies the existence of a moral source, and thus human nature itself testifies to the necessity of a personal and moral Creator.

The value of the arguments. Christians have disagreed over the value of these arguments for the existence of God. Some insist that they effectively prove God must exist. The problem is that proof does not compel belief. It is still the "fool" (our translation of a Hebrew word indicating a person who is morally and spiritually — not necessarily mentally — deficient) who refuses to accept the evidence inherent in creation. As Hebrews asserts, "By faith we understand that the universe was formed at God's command, so that what is seen was not made out of what was visible" (Heb. 11:3). A faith response to God so changes our perspective that we can at last see clearly what was obvious all along. ◗ EVOLUTION, CREATION, FAITH

At the same time the arguments for God's existence do have value in pre-evangelism. They can help us show that Christian faith is reasonable and defensible; we can show that the world we live in is best understood by considering the existence of God. The modern is likely to dismiss the idea of God as old and discredited by "science." Taking the arguments for God's existence seriously and presenting them to young people or old may open minds that have been closed to the gospel message.

The believer also finds value in these arguments. The arguments confirm the confidence that we already have in God. Reasonable arguments for God's existence will never replace Scripture's revelation as a basis for our faith. But such arguments remind us that our faith is more reasonable than all the scornful world's confidence in disbelief.

EXODUS

Exodus means "going out." After centuries in Egypt the Jewish people were suddenly torn away from their slave masters and set on a journey toward freedom. On the way they were given a law and a lifestyle, were taught obedience, and were led victorious into the land promised to their forefather Abraham. Through the events of some fifty years, the people of Israel came to know their God in a unique way as he revealed himself to them in mighty acts, moral code, and purifying judgments.

The significance of the Exodus is seen in the way the Old Testament poets and prophets repeatedly return to its events. The God of Israel, known during the generations in Egypt only through the tales told by parents to their children, had appeared in space and time. In ten stunning and miraculous plagues, God judged Egypt and its gods and revealed his power to his people. ◆ **MIRACLE** God, known before as Creator, was unveiled as Redeemer, who uses his power to rescue his people. God, known before as the giver of a covenant promise to Abraham, was unveiled as moral judge, who not only chiseled his standards in stone but also punished when his people were disobedient. The distant God of the Exodus suddenly became the God who is present with his people. Forever, God would be defined by his words and actions as he delivered his people, taking them as his own special possession, calling them to love and to serve him in holiness.

It was in the Exodus that God became known to all people and for all time as one who, though beyond history, is free to act in it; it was in the Exodus that God became known as one who surely will act in history on behalf of those who through faith are his own.

We need to sense the theological significance of the Exodus. It is crucial to our understanding of who God is. It is crucial to our understanding of morality. It is crucial to the flow of history; here the vast family of Abraham was launched on its path toward becoming a nation as well as a people and a religion. But it is also important to sense the personal significance of knowing God as the God of the Exodus. That significance is captured beautifully in Psalm 77. The writer, close to despair and fearful that even the Lord had rejected him, remembered the Exodus and God's power unleashed on behalf of his people:

> When I was in distress, I sought the LORD;
>> at night I stretched out untiring hands
>> and my soul refused to be comforted.
> I remembered you, O God, and I groaned;
>> I mused, and my spirit grew faint.
> You kept my eyes from closing;
>> I was too troubled to speak.
> Then I thought, "To this I will appeal:
>> the years of the right hand of the Most High."
> I will remember the deeds of the LORD;
>> yes, I will remember your miracles of long ago.

I will meditate on all your works
    and consider all your mighty deeds.
Your ways, O God, are holy.
    What god is so great as our God?
You are the God who performs miracles;
    you display your power among the peoples.
With your mighty arm you redeemed
    your people,
the descendants of Jacob and Joseph.

(Ps. 77:2–4, 10–15)

Whatever our circumstances, we can appeal to God. Remembering his deeds, and meditating on all his works, we can rest, confident that "the God who performs miracles" has all things under control.

FAITH/BELIEF

Christians are convinced that faith is the key to personal relationship with God. But not every believer grasps what faith, in a biblical, saving sense, really is. Sometimes believers even wonder if their faith is "strong" enough, or if they have "enough" faith. Outsiders often misunderstand too. "Just believe?" they ask. "If that were all there is to it, a person could believe and commit any crimes he wanted to and still go to heaven!"

An understanding of the nature of Christian faith quiets the doubts and uncertainties of the believer and answers the objections of the unbeliever as well. Thus we need to trace carefully what the Bible teaches and what Christians have believed about faith.

It is the business of theologians to probe deeply into the kinds of issues that philosophers speculate about. If we were to look at faith/belief in a speculative way, a number of questions must be asked. For instance what is the relationship of faith, understanding, and the will? How much must a person know to be able to believe? Can we make the Catholic distinction between explicit faith (in what is apprehended by the mind) and implicit faith (exercised in the truth of propositions of which a person knows nothing)? What is the difference between intellectual assent and faith?

While people from different Christian traditions may answer those questions a bit differently, Christian theologians are convinced that "interpersonal trust is the dynamic that unites the believer to Christ" (*A Contemporary Wesleyan Theology*, Vol. I, Francis Asbury Press, p. 351). Martin Luther, in his *Brief Explanation of the Ten Commandments, the Creed, and the Lord's Prayer*, makes this basic distinction:

We should note that there are two ways of believing. One way is to believe *about* God, as I do when I believe that what is said of God is true; just as I do when I believe what is said about the Turk, the devil or hell. This faith is knowledge or observation rather than faith. The other way is to believe *in* God, as I do when I not only believe that what is said about Him is true, but put my trust in Him, surrender myself to Him and make bold to deal with Him, believing without doubt that He will be to me and do to me just what is said of Him. (*Works*, Vol. II, p. 368)

It is this, believing *in* rather than simply believing *about*, that Christians mean when we talk about faith and belief. When we understand what believing *in* God implies, our doubts are relieved and the objections of non-Christians about an "easy" salvation are answered.

Faith viewed in the Old Testament. The Hebrew word usually translated "belief" and "faith" in the Old Testament conveys the idea of certainty and firmness. It means "to be certain," "to believe in," or "to be assured." Faith is a firm conviction based on the reliability of what is believed.

When the Old Testament speaks of faith, it focuses on who God is, not on our own subjective act of believing. Faith is valid not because human believing is strong or deep or real enough. Faith is valid because it is placed in God who by his nature is the sole, sure, and certain reality in our universe. God, the faithful and unchanging person, is one to whom we can safely commit ourselves. Thus the Old Testament invites us to look away from ourselves and from subjective analysis to realize that we are safe, not because we believe but because God is utterly faithful and trustworthy. We trust not in our faith but in the God who is the object of our faith.

The clearest Old Testament example of faith is found in Abraham. The patriarch, a very old man, is found in dialog with God. Abraham complains that God has given him no children of his own, despite an earlier promise (Gen. 12:2). God answers, expanding the promise. Not only will Abraham have children but his descendants will be as uncountable as the stars (Gen. 15:5). The next verse tells us that "Abraham believed God, and he credited it to him as righteousness" (Gen. 15:6). Romans says of the incident, "Against all hope, Abraham in hope believed. . . . He faced the fact that his body was as good as dead — since he was about a hundred years old — and that Sarah's womb was also dead. Yet he did not waver through unbelief regarding the promise of God, but was strengthened in his faith and gave glory to God, being fully persuaded that God has power to do what he promised" (Rom.

4:18–21). Abraham was fully aware of the circumstances. But despite everything Abraham dared to believe that God could be trusted to do what he promised. This is faith. Abraham put his trust in God and in God alone, and God accepted trust in him in place of a righteousness that Abraham did not possess.

The later history of Abraham's descendants helps us to understand more about belief and unbelief. After Abraham's family, now known as Israel, spent centuries in Egypt as slaves, God appeared to a hesitant Moses to announce that Moses would be the instrument of Israel's deliverance. Moses objects, "What if they do not believe me or listen to me?" (Exod. 4:1). God gives Moses power to perform three minor miracles as evidence that he has been sent by the Lord (Exod. 4:5–9). As the story unfolds, we see that the Egyptians also doubt God, and in ten miraculous judgments, God strips Egypt of its wealth and power. Israel is given proof after proof of God's greatness and his love for them. But even such great wonders as the bloody Nile, the plague of darkness, the destruction of Egypt's first-born, and the dividing of the Red Sea produce only momentary acknowledgment of the Lord.

Finally Israel is camped on the edge of the land that God promised to Abraham and his descendants. There the Word of God comes to them: Go up and take the land. But these people, who have witnessed miracle after miracle, refuse to respond to God's Word. Angrily God exclaims, "How long will these people treat me with contempt? How long will they refuse to believe in me, in spite of all the miraculous signs I have performed among them?" (Num. 14:11).

The Old Testament and the New Testament often look back on this incident. Moses later reminded a new generation, "You did not trust in the LORD your God" (Deut. 1:32). Hebrews warns against a hardened heart and looks back at Israel whose "evil heart of unbelief" was demonstrated by its refusal to obey.

The stories of trusting Abraham and disobedient Israel both illustrate the nature of faith. Faith does not rest on evidence; Israel had ample evidence of God's presence and his power. Faith rests on the confident conviction that God's Word is trustworthy. Israel had compelling evidence of God's wonder-working power but did not believe. Abraham, without such evidence, took God at his Word.

Faith in God engages the total person. Abraham recognized his own and Sarah's advanced age. But Abraham also recognized God as God. His view of God so changed his perspective that he easily accepted God's promise even though fathering a son was not humanly possible. Israel, camping on the edge of Palestine, could only see the strength of the inhabitants of that land. They "treated God with contempt" by refusing to consider the fact that he is real and greater than all.

In the Old Testament, then, faith is placed in the person of God who meets each generation in words of promise. When a generation or a person hears God's Word, trusts in him and acts on his Word, this is faith.

Faith viewed in the New Testament. In the New Testament the ideas of faith and belief are communicated by a single word group which speaks of relationships established by trust and maintained by trustworthiness. The range of meanings suggested in this word group are expressed by a number of English words that are used to translate its various forms: "to rely on," "to commit oneself to," "to trust," "faithfulness," "faithful," "reliable," "trusting," and "faith."

The New Testament focuses the faith on personal relationship with Jesus, for it is Jesus who is the focus of God's present message to humankind. As Jesus said, "I am the way, the truth and the life. No one comes to the Father except through me" (John 14:6). In the New Testament the particular response that constitutes faith is both the happy trust that you and I place in the person of Jesus and the allegiance that grows out of our personal commitment.

John distinguishes between a superficial belief and a true commitment. John 2:22–23 says that many who saw his signs "believed in him." But later, many of that same crowd "turned back and no longer followed" Jesus when his teachings became hard for them to accept (John 6:60–66). Superficial faith acknowledged that Jesus and his miracles were special, but this superficial faith died when Jesus communicated his message. Jesus' acts drew attention, but trust in his words was essential. Nicodemus illustrates this in his admission to Jesus that the leaders of Israel "know you are a teacher who has come from God. For no one could perform the miraculous signs you are doing were not God with him" (John 3:2). Yet the leaders would not believe in Jesus. True faith involves a heart response to the Word of God — a willingness to trust ourselves to Jesus.

Again and again John links this kind of faith with life. In John 3 we have Jesus' promise that the one who believes in him "shall not perish but have eternal life" (John 3:16). Through trust in Jesus, a person is born again, passing from death to life. John 5 announces that life is available only in Jesus: "Whoever hears my words and believes him who sent me has eternal life and will not be condemned; he has crossed over from death to life" (John 5:24). John 8 again focuses on the absolute necessity of a faith response to Jesus: "If you do not believe that I am the one I claim to be, you will indeed die in your sins" (John 8:24). Jesus' miracles could not be explained away even by his enemies. But faith is associated not with amazement at the miracles but with trust in the words Jesus spoke and in the claims Jesus made about himself.

In John's gospel believing is an active, continuing trust in Jesus. While mere belief acknowledges that there is something special about Jesus, Christian faith recognizes Jesus as the Son of God and trusts completely in his promise of eternal life.

Faith expressed in Romans. In the great theological letter, Romans, the apostle Paul carefully explains both the role that faith plays in Christianity and the nature of Christian faith. Faith words are clustered in this letter, so we can look at key chapters in which faith in Jesus is the subject.

Romans 3 explains the role of faith in salvation. In the first chapters of this great letter, Paul demonstrates the fact that all humanity is lost. No one has a shred of righteousness: All are sinners. Yet God must find a way to provide righteousness if he is to have a relationship with human beings. God's answer is seen in Jesus. Christ's death was a sacrifice of atonement. Through "faith in his blood," a person who believes is declared righteous. When we trust in Jesus who died for us, we are cloaked in his own righteousness, given to us as a free gift. ◗ RIGHT-EOUSNESS, ATONEMENT, SACRIFICE

Romans 4 explains the nature of faith. Here "faith" and "believe" are found fifteen times. Paul basically argues that faith is the same in the Christian era as it was in Old Testament times. Then, Abraham and David trusted God and were granted forgiveness of their sins. We, too, find forgiveness simply through trusting God. We hear his Word of promise, and like them, we "are fully persuaded that God has power to do what he had promised" (Rom. 4:21). God accepts this kind of confidence in him in place of the righteousness that no human being has.

The same chapter affirms the gospel promise that God, who has delivered Jesus up for our sins and has raised him to life again for our justification (John 4:25), will save us because of Jesus. Like Abraham, when we hear this Word, we look beyond our circumstances, consider who God is, and trust ourselves to him.

Romans 10 focuses on the word of faith. Paul contrasts human attempts to establish righteousness by good behavior with God's unique offer of a perfect righteousness, coming to us through faith in Jesus. Salvation is found only by trusting in the divine promise. Throughout history it has remained the same: Faith has always been trust in the God who has made promises. "Consequently," Paul says, "faith comes from hearing the message, and the message is heard through the word of Christ" (Rom. 10:17).

Faith expressed in the Book of James. Is there a conflict between Paul and James, as some have thought? In Romans, Paul explains the nature and the role of Christian faith. In James the author has a simpler and a different task. James writes to people who have faith, reminding them that trust in God necessarily leads to changes in behavior.

A person who trusts God will find guidance in prayer (James 1:2–7), will act on the Word rather than simply hear it (James 1:19–25), will have compassion for the powerless (James 1:26–27), will learn to control his or her tongue (James 3:1–12), will adopt God's peaceable wisdom rather than the argumentative wisdom of this world (James 3:13–18), will turn from worldly motives, which conflict with godliness (James 4:1–6), will find patience for suffering (James 5:7–11), and will find relief in prayer (James 5:13–18).

In chapter 2, James makes a distinction that is sometimes misunderstood. He asks what good it is "if a man claims to have faith but has no deeds?" (James 2:14). Here James is contrasting "belief about" and "belief in" God. He argues that "belief about" is meaningless: "even the demons believe [that there is one God] — and shudder" (James 2:19). So James looks back into history and selects persons who have the kind of faith he is concerned with, a faith that exists as trust in God. He selects Abraham and Rahab and notes that in each "faith and actions were working together" (James 2:22). Their claim to faith was justified (demonstrated to be valid) by what they did, not just by their words.

James is rightly concerned that you and I realize that trust in God will have a necessary impact on our lives. Biblical faith is a dynamic, transforming force. When trust brings us into personal relationship with God, that relationship will generate a change in our attitudes, values, and way of life. Belief *about* Jesus is an empty thing. Belief *in* Jesus brings us eternal life and leads to a fresh, new, and godly way of life here on earth.

All these Bible passages remind us of a central truth: Faith is something we place in a person, not just in a doctrine or an idea. Faith exists as trust in God (who speaks to us in his Word) and in Jesus (who is the focus of God's promises to humankind).

Christ's substitutionary death on Calvary provides the basis on which God can forgive human beings from every era. While the basis of saving faith remains the same, the object of faith has differed from age to age. Abraham believed God's promise of a son, and that faith was counted to him as righteousness. Today the object of faith and the basis of salvation are one and the same. We are given God's promise of forgiveness in Jesus, and we are called on to trust ourselves completely to the Lord. Now, as then, all we can do is simply trust ourselves to God, who has spoken in promise.

How does a biblical understanding of faith help those believers who fret and doubt the strength of their belief? It teaches us to look away from ourselves and realize that simple trust brings us into personal relationship with Jesus. Our salvation depends not on how strongly we believe but on how trustworthy God is. Christianity teaches us to abandon reliance on ourselves (even on our believing) and instead rely fully on God, who promises us salvation in Jesus.

How does a biblical understanding of faith answer the objection of outsiders who imagine that Christianity invites people to believe and then sin as much as they wish? It teaches us that faith launches the believer into a transforming relationship with the Lord. A faith that exists as trust in God produces a sure change in the believer as the new life and God's presence work within to make us persons who are truly good.

How important is faith? "Without faith," Hebrews 11:6 says, "it is impossible to please God, because anyone who comes to him must believe that he exists and that he rewards those who earnestly seek him." Faith looks beyond what can be touched and seen, listens to the promises that God gives us in Jesus, and trusts.

FALL

The Fall is described in Genesis 3. Adam and Eve lived happily in Eden, the beautiful garden God shaped for them. There the innocent pair enjoyed a rich life with each other and maintained daily fellowship with God. Then Satan stole into the Garden in the form of a serpent, and he tempted Eve.

God made human beings in his image and likeness. Because God is a moral person, human beings also must have a moral capacity. To permit Adam and Eve to exercise this capacity, God placed a tree called the "tree of the knowledge of good and evil" (Gen. 1:17) in the Garden, and he told the pair they must not eat its fruit. We don't know how long the two lived obediently in Eden. We only know that a day came when Satan found Eve alone and encouraged her to violate God's command.

The Genesis 3 story of the Fall, when Adam and Eve first distrusted and disobeyed God, is filled with significance. It is basic to a Christian understanding of the human condition.

The nature of sin is illustrated in Genesis 3. God spoke to Adam, warning against eating from the forbidden tree. Eve remembered the divine warning, but at Satan's prompting she distrusted God's motives, and relying on her own desires instead of the Lord's word, she disobeyed. Sin involves distrust of God issuing in disobedience.

The impact of sin is illustrated in Genesis 3 and 4. God warned

Adam that disobedience would lead to death. Here death means far more than the end of physical existence. ◆ DEATH

The evidences of death are awareness of guilt and shame (Gen. 3:7), alienation from God and a fear of him (Gen. 3:8–11), interpersonal conflict and blaming (Gen. 3:12–13), distortion of the husband/wife relationship (Gen. 3:16), a warping of nature itself so that our once-friendly planet resists human dominion (Gen. 3:17–18), and a deterioration of the body, leading finally to physical death (Gen. 3:19). Genesis 4 continues the story. Adam and Eve's sons were born marred by their parents' fall. The flaw was so great that Cain, flushed with anger, murdered his own brother (Gen. 4:1–8). A later descendant, Lamech, tore marriage from its intended shape as a lifelong union between two people and married two wives. How far the culture had strayed is illustrated by Lamech's justification of murder by arguing that the victim had injured him.

That first choice of sin warped our whole race, twisting God's original pattern for humanity and for nature itself. Romans 5 looks back and remembers: "Sin entered the world through one man, and death through sin, and in this way death came to all men." Deadened to God and insensitive to other human beings, our race rushed headlong to explore the depth of those selfish desires that first moved Eve to taste the forbidden fruit.

Some have boldly called the Fall a "fall up," arguing that in the Genesis tale human beings came to know good and evil. Their thought is that even tragic knowledge is better than innocent ignorance. But both God and Adam knew right and wrong. All that Adam and Eve lacked was experiential knowledge of the suffering and pain that doing wrong would bring.

No, the Fall that the Bible describes and that most Christians believe was an historic act, a fall from a state of original innocence and fellowship with God into a state of spiritual death. In this state, isolated from God and "gratifying the cravings of our sinful nature and following its desires and thoughts," humankind has become "by nature objects of [God's] wrath" (Eph. 2:3).

The story of the Fall has great personal significance to Christians. It helps us realize that we truly are trapped, without the possibility of self-reform. We need a special act of God to free us, to straighten what is warped in us, to counteract death by the infusion of life, to release us from our own cravings, and to set us back again on the path of obedience.
◆ DEATH, SIN, LIFE

How good that the Bible places alongside the story of this man, Adam, the story of another man, Jesus. Romans 5 sums up the great good news: "If the many died by the trespass of the one man, how much more did God's grace and the gift that came by the grace of the one man, Jesus Christ, overflow to the many! Again, the gift of God is not like the result of the one man's sin. The judgment followed one sin and brought condemnation, but the gift followed many trespasses and brought justification. For if, by the trespass of the one man, death reigned through that one man, how much more will those who receive God's abundant provision of grace and of the gift of righteousness reign in life through the one man, Jesus Christ" (Rom. 5:15–17). You and I have inherited Adam's flaw. How wonderful that we can receive God's abundant provision of grace and the gift of righteousness, not by inheritance but by simple trust in Jesus.

FEAR OF GOD

When we think about fear, we usually imagine terror or at least anxiety. Thus it is hard to realize that fear of God is a friend and not an enemy.

In the Old Testament fear of the Lord is deep reverence and awe of him. Fearing God is called the "beginning of knowledge" because recognizing God as the ultimate reality is the foundation of a holy life (Prov. 1:7). Fearing God (that is, recognizing who he is and taking him into account) means rejecting every other claim in order to serve only God (Exod. 20:3). When we fear the Lord, we love him, walk in his ways, and serve him with all our heart and soul (Deut. 10:12; Job 1:1; Ps. 128:1).

While the Old Testament closely links the fear of God with holy living and morality, the fear of God is also freeing. God's Old Testament people faced natural disasters and were surrounded by many enemies. But an awe of God frees believers from a terror of lesser foes. When dangers come, the person who fears God can joyfully say, "We wait in hope for the LORD; he is our help and our shield. In him our hearts rejoice, for we trust in his holy name. May your unfailing love rest upon us, O LORD, even as we put our hope in you" (Ps. 33:20–22).

The New Testament speaks of a different kind of religious fear. This was amazement and an initial fright, which struck those who observed some of Jesus' spectacular miracles. Once Jesus cast a horde of demons from a demented man. His neighbors later saw the man "sitting there, dressed and in his right mind" and "they were afraid" (Mark 5:15). They were so uncomfortable in the presence of God's work that they begged Jesus to leave their region, even though he had used his power only for good.

The New Testament suggests a possible source of such reactions. John writes in his gospel, "Light has come into the world, but men loved darkness rather than light, because their deeds were evil. Everyone who does evil hates the light, and will not come into the light for fear that his deeds will be exposed" (John 3:19–20). Even unacknowledged guilt creates a terror of exposure, and in some people, fear of God is transmuted from overjoyed awe into a guilty fright that drives the person away from the only source of healing and forgiveness.

The second kind of fear characterizes unbelief; it is the first kind of fear that is appropriate for believers. Aware of who God is, we are to live our "lives as strangers here in reverent fear" (1 Peter 1:17; 2:17). As for that terror that comes from a fear of punishment, John writes that "there is no fear in love. But perfect love drives out fear, because fear has to do with punishment. The man who fears is not made perfect in love" (1 John 4:18). His point is important.

Not only do we stand in awe of God, but we also have a personal relationship with him. We recognize the depth of his love in Jesus Christ, and we respond by loving him in return. In Jesus we learn that we can "rely on the love that God has for us" (1 John 4:9–16). We who experience the love of God are comfortable in our relationship with him, for we know the Lord has forgiven our sins. But though we no longer fear punishment, we still maintain a deep respect and awe for the Lord; out of respect for him we choose to do those things that will please him and will keep us safe within the sphere of his love.

FELLOWSHIP

Fellowship is basic to the Christian's experience. When we grasp the implications of this exciting biblical term, we can reach out and discover a new depth in our relationship with God and with each other.

Fellowship is a relational term. It is one translation of the Greek word *koinonia*, which is also translated as "sharing," "partnership," and "contribution." All too often we trivialize fellowship and drain it of its meaning by calling after-church chats or coffee-and-cookie hours "fellowship times." Biblical fellowship is far from trivial, superficial relationships.

In Greek culture *koinonia* was used to depict an ideal, harmonious society. That ideal society was to be marked by full participation and sharing of its members — a democratic Utopia. But Utopias have a way of floundering on the reality of human sinfulness, and the philosophers' dream remained a dream, leaving human beings hungering for intimacy.

Then, suddenly, a people whose lives and relationships were built around Jesus Christ burst on the first-century scene. Although far from perfect, this people experienced a shared life that awakened the wonder of outsiders.

Acts 2 gives us a picture of the church fellowship in Jerusalem, a growing communion that at last demonstrated the ideal of fellowship and sharing in a common life. When we read the passage today, we realize that although we are not called to duplicate the first church's experience, we are called to build relationships that are marked by mutual commitment and joy: "They devoted themselves to the apostle's teaching and to the fellowship, to the breaking of bread and to prayer. Everyone was filled with awe, and many wonders and miraculous signs were done by the apostles. All the believers were together and had everything in common. Selling their possessions and goods, they gave to everyone as he had need. Every day they continued to meet together in the temple courts. They broke bread together with glad and sincere hearts, praising God and enjoying the favor of all the people. And the Lord added to their number those who were being saved" (Acts 2:42–47).

In Paul's epistle the word *koinonia* is found only thirteen times (Rom. 15:26; 1 Cor. 1:9; 10:16; 2 Cor. 6:14; 8:4; 9:13; 13:14; Gal. 2:9; Eph. 3:9; Phil. 1:5; 2:1; 3:10). Paul uses "fellowship" to remind us of our union with Christ. God has called us "into fellowship with his Son Jesus Christ" (1 Cor. 1:9). We participate in all that Jesus is in the most intimate of family relationships because Christ has won the privilege of fellowship for us by his own blood (1 Cor. 10:16). The key to our relationships with other Christians is recognition that our union with Jesus overflows to make us family with all others who believe in him. In Jesus all Christians are brothers and sisters to whom we can reach out for mutual sharing (Gal. 2:9), sensing our common partnership in the gospel (Phil. 1:5). In Paul's letters, as in Acts 2, even what we call "giving" is placed in the context of fellowship and is called "sharing" (Rom. 15:26; 2 Cor. 8:4; 9:13; Heb. 13:16). New Testament giving is not to support institutions or buildings (which did not exist in that era of church history). The New Testament church gave to meet the basic needs of Christian brothers and sisters, and thus giving was a practical expression of the bond of fellowship, of that willingness to share in each other's experiences and needs.

In John's writings, like Paul's, fellowship with God precedes fellowship with other believers. Participating in Jesus and sharing in his love is key to the love that then can overflow to others. John teaches us specifically about how to live in fellowship with God (1 John 1:3, 6–7). He calls us to a common fellowship that "is with the Father and his Son

Jesus Christ." We experience this fellowship if we walk in the light rather than darkness. Here darkness is not sin but self-deceit, and light is honesty. If we acknowledge our sins, God forgives them and keeps on cleansing us, enabling us to stay close to him (1 John 1:9). ◆ CONFESSION Sharing everything with God, including our faults and weaknesses, enables us to stay in fellowship with him.

In a beautiful way the open and honest relationship that God calls us to maintain with him provides a pattern for our relationships with each other. Christians are to "put off falsehood and speak truthfully [each] to his neighbor, for we are all members of one body" (Eph. 4:25). Because we together are "God's chosen people, holy and dearly loved," we are to clothe ourselves "with compassion, kindness, humility, gentleness, and patience. Bear with one another and forgive whatever grievances you may have against one another. Forgive as the Lord forgave you. And over all these virtues put on love, which binds them all together in perfect unity" (Col. 3:12–14).

We believe, then, that we now have a basis for intimate relationship not only with God but also with each other. Because of Jesus we are linked with other Christians by unbreakable family bonds. Because of Jesus we are invited to love one another significantly. In the fellowship of his saints, we are to find acceptance and welcome. In the relationships we develop with other Christians, we can experience shared sorrows and shared joys, intimacy and honesty, forgiveness and encouragement, and that deep caring for each other for which we all yearn.

FLESH

How have Christians throughout the ages regarded the flesh? And what have they meant by this word? All too often this word, used in the New Testament to indicate the principle of sin in human experience, has colored our attitudes toward such healthy things as sexual desire in marriage. Some Christians, fearing every human emotion, have turned to self-denial and asceticism, struggling to extinguish their desires by refusing to give in even to the most common and normal desires. While such extremes have never reflected attitudes taught in the Bible, many Christians have been left with the vague feeling that flesh is bad and that daily life is tainted by its evil.

How can we develop a healthy Christian attitude toward ourselves, our bodies, and our desires? First, we need to look at how the term *flesh* is actually used in the Old Testament and the New Testament, and then we can apply what the Bible says to the issues that have troubled us.

"Flesh" in the Old Testament. The Hebrew word for flesh is found two hundred seventy-three times in our Old Testament. It has a number of meanings. *Flesh* may refer to our physical bodies, to the material we are made of, to living creatures in general, to intimate family relationships, and to the self — the individual person. When *flesh* is used to describe human beings, it has a particular emphasis. *Flesh* in the Old Testament views human beings in the framework of their life on earth, as mortal beings who live in a material universe. Thus when the Bible speaks of a man and woman becoming "one flesh" in marriage, it implies more than the marriage act. Yes, there will be sexual union. But that joining is a symbol of the fact that that couple will now live out a shared life in this world, partners who experience life's joys and sorrows together.

In the Old Testament flesh also emphasizes human frailty. Unlike our eternal, holy, all-powerful God, we human beings are mortal. We struggle with our weaknesses and have to look beyond ourselves when troubles come. Because of our inherent weakness, Scripture often warns human beings against relying on themselves or one another. As Jeremiah says, "Cursed is the one who trusts in man, who depends on flesh for his strength and whose heart turns away from the LORD." In contrast, Jeremiah adds, "But blessed is the man who trusts in the LORD, whose confidence is in him" (Jer. 17:5, 7).

The Old Testament's teachings on the flesh do not suggest that life on earth is intrinsically evil or that natural bodily functions are dirty or wrong. Human life on earth is limited, and human beings are frail creatures who must depend on God. But God is sensitive to our weaknesses and responds graciously to our needs, for "He remembers that they were but flesh, a passing breeze that does not return" (Ps. 78:39).

"Flesh" in the New Testament. The Greek words translated "flesh" occur many times in the New Testament, and the words are translated in a variety of ways: "unspiritual," "material," "worldly," "ancestry," and even as "sinful (desires)." The Greek word, like the Hebrew word, can mean "literal flesh," "the physical body," "all people," "family relationship," and "life in this present world." But in the New Testament the apostle Paul adds a special, theological use of flesh.

In Paul's letters flesh does more than affirm that human nature is frail compared to the divine. Here the word *flesh* is a theological word that captures the fact that human nature is twisted and tangled by sin. Here the human perspective, along with human understanding and will, is presented as actively hostile to God.

As a theological term "flesh" gives the following portrait of a lost humanity. Human beings are morally inadequate (Rom. 6:19; 7:7–11, 15–20; 8:3) and prone to rebellion against God and his standards (Rom. 13:14; Gal. 3:3; 5:13; Eph. 2:3; Col. 2:13–23). Such persons live "according to the flesh" rather than responsive to God's Spirit (Rom. 8:4–13; Gal. 5:16–26). Thus Paul says that "nothing good lives in me, that is in my flesh," meaning in his sinful human nature (Rom. 7:4–25); that sinful nature is motivated and energized by desires that run counter to God's will and result in all sorts of sinful actions (Gal. 5:16–26). Thus the limited human nature of the Old Testament is given a fresh examination and in Paul's analysis is shown to be not only weak but also corrupt. Thus even the good law of God, given to Israel, was unable to help humanity toward righteousness because the law's system was "weakened by our sinful nature [*sarx*]" (Rom. 8:3).

How does Paul apply this teaching? He further extends the Old Testament emphasis. Weak and fallible human beings had to depend on God to help them. In the same way corrupt and sinful human beings must depend on God to overcome the limitations placed on us by sin. This "God did by sending his own Son in the likeness of sinful man to be a sin offering," and so transformed our situation that "the righteous requirements of the law" can be fully met in us "who do not live according to the sinful nature but according to the Spirit" (Rom. 8:3–4). God's Spirit is able to work in us even in our mortality. So we have God's promise: "If the Spirit of him who raised Jesus from the dead is living in you, he who raised Christ from the dead will also give life to your mortal bodies through his Spirit, who lives in you" (Rom. 8:11).

The flesh and the Christian. What attitudes and notions about human beings are appropriate for Christians in view of what the Bible says about flesh? Both testaments remind us that we are limited and mortal and must depend not on ourselves but on God. The Old Testament emphasizes dependence on God for material needs and for protection from physical dangers. The New Testament stresses dependence on God for spiritual renewal and enablement.

But it is important to remember that both testaments encourage us to live good and righteous lives right here in our world. We are neither to reject ourselves as human beings nor to think of human thoughts, desires, and needs as evil in themselves. The people in Colosse made just this mistake. They adopted what came to be known as a Gnostic view of life, which labeled the material evil and the immaterial good. Taking this position, many people in the church of Colosse tried to find spiritual fulfillment by ascetic self-denial and rigorous, disciplined worship. In his letter to the Colossians, Paul corrects this misunderstanding. He writes,

"Since you died with Christ to the basic principles of this world, why, as though you still belonged to it, do you submit to its rules: 'Do not handle! Do not taste! Do not touch?' These are all destined to perish with use, because they are based on human commands and teaching. Such regulations indeed have the appearance of wisdom, with their self-imposed worship, their false humility and their harsh treatment of the body, but they lack any value in restraining sensual indulgence" (Col. 2:20–23).

In this letter Paul reminds Christians that God "has reconciled you by Christ's physical body through death to present you holy in his sight" (Col. 1:22). Just as Jesus did God's will and accomplished good in his physical body, so must you and I. The Christian life is not experienced by denying our natural desires or the significance of daily decisions in this world. The Christian life is experienced as we let God guide us to satisfy our natural desires in a holy, morally right way and as we let him guide us to those decisions that glorify him. The central reality of Christianity is that believers have been united to Christ, and in Christ we have died to evil so that we might live to do good. Paul puts it beautifully:

> Put to death, therefore, whatever belongs to your earthly nature: sexual immorality, impurity, lust, evil desires and greed which is idolatry. Because of these, the wrath of God is coming. You used to walk in these ways, in the life you once lived. But now you must rid yourselves of all such things as these: anger, rage, malice, slander, and filthy language from your lips. Do not lie to each other, since you have taken off your old self with its practices and have put on the new self, which is being renewed in knowledge in the image of its Creator. . . . Therefore, as God's chosen people, holy and dearly loved, clothe yourselves with compassion, kindness, humility, gentleness and patience. Bear with each other and forgive whatever grievances you may have against one another. Forgive as the Lord forgave you. And over all these virtues put on love, which binds them all together in perfect unity. (Col. 3:5–14)

The Christian is called not to a mean, miserable life of self-denial but to a rich and fulfilling life of warm, loving relationships. What the Bible's view of the flesh teaches us is to recognize those evils that spring up from sinful human nature and not to trust ourselves. When we recognize our need, we turn to Jesus. Then we experience an exciting renewal, and God gives us a new self, growing in the image of our Creator. Out of the new inner life that God gives us, strengthened by the Spirit who enables us, we are to live holy and loving lives here on earth. With every human relationship and every human desire purified by Jesus' touch, we need not be afraid to live active, involved lives. And we can welcome all those good things, which God gives us to make life on earth a joy.

FORGIVENESS

Forgiveness is important to Christians. But Christian forgiveness is very special. It is not passing off a hurt with an "Oh, it doesn't matter." Christian forgiveness recognizes that relationships of every kind can be spoiled by wrongdoing and that such hurts do matter. Christian forgiveness faces the challenge of restoring broken relationships, even though there is a high cost both to one who forgives and to one who is forgiven.

God's forgiveness in the Old Testament. In the Old Testament God is known as a forgiving person. Moses, begging God to forgive straying Israel, based his appeal on God's character as a loving person. "In accordance with your great love, forgive the sin of these people, just as you have pardoned them from the time they left Egypt until now" (Num. 14:19; Ps. 86:5; 130:3–4).

This vision of a God who recognizes human fault and yet forgives is basic to the Old Testament view of God. No wonder the psalmists celebrate him, praising, "If you, O LORD, kept a record of sins, O LORD, who could stand? But with you there is forgiveness; therefore you are feared. . . . O Israel, put your hope in the LORD, for with the LORD is unfailing love and with him is full redemption. He himself will redeem Israel from all their sins" (Ps. 130:3–4, 7–8).

Along with this picture of a loving God, the Old Testament presents the portrait of a penitent believer. Psalm 32 celebrates God's forgiveness and reveals the attitude of the psalmist. Burdened by a sense of guilt and an awareness that he had offended God, David resisted until finally he could say, "I acknowledged my sin to you and did not cover up my iniquity. I said, 'I will confess my transgressions to the LORD' — and you forgave the guilt of my sin" (Ps. 32:5). God's forgiveness was experienced only by those who acknowledged their sin and humbly came to him to receive forgiveness.

Forgiveness is offered freely by God. But forgiveness must be accepted by human beings who acknowledge their failures and openly confess their sins to the Lord.

The Old Testament does not fully explain how it is possible for a holy God to lovingly forgive his sinning creatures. But it does affirm that God is forgiving. And it celebrates the joys of those who are willing to abandon pride and beg, "According to your great compassion blot out my transgressions. Wash away all my iniquity and cleanse me from my sin" (Ps. 51:1–2).

Forgiveness in the New Testament. The Old Testament presents God as a forgiving person and relates forgiveness to the sacrifices of atonement that Old Testament law established. ▸ ATONEMENT To receive forgiveness, sinners must humble themselves, admit their sin, and demonstrate faith by bringing the appropriate sacrifice. Those who refused to admit their sins, or who rebelliously refused to approach God, could not receive the forgiveness God yearns to extend. This same pattern is seen in the New Testament, but here the great mystery of how God can forgive is solved.

We Christians too are convinced that God is a moral person. He is holy and just as well as loving. God can't just pass sin off as unimportant, for he has a moral obligation as judge of his universe to punish sin. So throughout the ages it remained a mystery how God could offer sinful human beings forgiveness of sins. That mystery was solved in the death and resurrection of Jesus. Romans puts it this way: "All have sinned and fall short of the glory of God, and are justified freely by his grace through the redemption that came by Christ Jesus. God presented him as a sacrifice of atonement through faith in his blood. He did this to demonstrate his justice, because in his forbearance he had left the sins committed beforehand unpunished — he did it to demonstrate his justice at the present time, so as to be just and the one who justifies the man who has faith in Jesus" (Rom. 3:23–26).

God extended forgiveness to Old Testament saints, even though no one could see justice in his offer of pardon. Then Jesus came and in his death offered himself as our substitute. The Bible says that "he himself bore our sins in his body on the tree, so that we might die to sins and live for righteousness" (1 Pet. 2:24). A holy God demands that sin be punished. But a loving God entered history to take that punishment on himself so that he might be free to forgive.

Jesus not only resolves the mystery of how God can forgive us and still retain his moral integrity, but Jesus is also the object of our faith. Like the Old Testament saints, we hear the offer of forgiveness. Like them, we humble ourselves. We admit our moral failure and desperate need. Stripped of pride, we throw ourselves on God's mercy, believing that he will forgive us for Jesus' sake. Then joyfully we rise again, aware that we have been accepted and forgiven by our God, for we have his Word: "Their sins and lawless acts I will remember no more" (Jer. 31:34; Heb. 10:17).

Experiencing forgiveness. Christians are a people called to enjoy forgiveness and live daily with its benefits. God's forgiveness is far more than a legal judgment of pardon and acquittal. Forgiveness is linked with love and freedom.

One day Jesus was eating at the home of a Pharisee who did not want to see Jesus as God's messenger. As they ate, a local prostitute slipped into the home, and weeping, she poured perfume over his feet. The Pharisee thought, "If this man were a prophet, he would know who is touching him and what kind of woman she is" (Luke 7:39). Jesus answered the Pharisee's unspoken criticism with a story about two debtors. One owed fifty denarii and the other owed five hundred denarii (a denarius was a coin worth one day's wage). If the lender canceled the debt, Jesus asked, which creditor would love him better? The Pharisee responded, "I suppose the one who had the bigger debt canceled" (Luke 7:43). Jesus looked toward the weeping prostitute and nodded agreement. The woman, whose sins were many, had recognized the wonder of forgiveness and had responded to Jesus with love. Similarly, as you and I remember how much we have been forgiven, our love for God deepens and grows.

Awareness of forgiveness is also freeing. The letter to the Hebrews looks at the impact of Jesus' self-sacrifice. There the writer calls the Old Testament sacrifices a shadowy illustration of the sacrifice that Jesus has made for us. While those Old Testament sacrifices spoke of God's promise, they "were not able to clear the conscience of the worshiper" (Heb. 9:9). Each repetition of those sacrifices reminded the worshipers that they remained sinners in continual need. But, the writer goes on, "the blood of Christ" cleanses "our consciences from acts that lead to death, so that we may serve the living God" (Heb. 9:14). The wonderful result of this "once for all" cleansing provided by Jesus is that Christians no longer have to feel guilty for sins (Heb. 10:2). We know that in Jesus our sins have been removed — removed so perfectly that God says, "Their sins and lawless acts I will remember no more" (Heb. 10:17).

Because we know our sins are forgiven, we can "draw near to God with a sincere heart in full assurance of faith" (Heb. 10:22). We need never cringe from our Lord or try to hide from him, for Jesus' death has won a full and complete forgiveness for us. We no longer need to carry the burden of our past failures, for in Jesus all our sins are forgiven and put away. Because of Jesus we can forget the past and look forward with hope to the future.

But true freedom is found not in removing the burdens of our past but in transforming our future. This also is linked with our continuing experience of forgiveness. Through forgiveness God promises us the freedom to become new and different persons.

In John's first letter he reminds us that we who are forgiven are not sinless. Despite our love for Jesus, we continue to sin. "If we claim to be without sin," John writes, "we deceive ourselves and the truth is not in us" (1 John 1:8). John goes on to explain that when we sin, we are to confess that sin to God, openly acknowledging our failure. We do this in the assurance that "God is faithful and just and will forgive us our sins" (1 John 1:9). Then that same verse adds an exciting promise. God will also "keep on cleansing us from all unrighteousness." Acknowledging our sins and accepting God's forgiveness opens up our hearts and lives to the transforming power of God's Spirit.

For Christians, then, forgiveness is the once-for-all pardon that we receive when we accept God's promise in Jesus, and forgiveness is also the way to maintain a close, living fellowship with our Lord. As we live humbly with God, acknowledging our failures and seeking his help for a fresh and better tomorrow, we experience his inner, transforming power.

Extending forgiveness to others. Forgiveness is a way of life for Christians. But forgiveness is not just something we receive from God. It is something we extend to and receive from each other.

In one sense, the sense of that Greek word *aphiemi* ("to send away"), only God can forgive sins. Only Jesus has such authority (Mark 2:1–12). But *charizomai*, meaning "to be gracious" and "to give freely," is possible for you and me. Thus Colossians 3:13 calls on us to "bear with each other, and forgive whatever grievances you have against one another. Forgive as the Lord forgave you" (see also Col. 2:13).

Mutual forgiveness is basic not only to truly Christian relationships but even to our experience of God's forgiveness. In Matthew 18, Jesus talks about greatness. He tells three stories, each of which is about forgiveness. First, Jesus compares us to sheep, who are prone to straying. When a person strays, we are to seek out that person and restore the relationship, letting forgiveness not only free us from bitterness or recrimination but also replace bitterness with joy. Second, Jesus compares the Christian community to a family, in which siblings sin against and hurt each other. When hurt, we are to take the initiative and seek reconciliation, forgiving freely when the other person apologizes. Peter asked Jesus how many times we must forgive. Jesus' answer ("seventy times seven") calls for unlimited forgiveness. Third, Jesus tells the story of a servant who was forgiven an unimaginable debt, mounting up to millions of dollars. That same servant then refuses to forgive another person who owes him mere hundreds. We who have been forgiven so much by God must be willing to forgive each other.

How important is mutual forgiveness to our Christian experience? Some New Testament verses introduce a conditional element. The unforgiving are not forgiven. For instance, "If you forgive men when they sin against you, your heavenly Father will also forgive you. But if you do not forgive men their sins, your Father will not forgive your sins" (Matt. 6:14–15). "And when you stand praying, if you hold anything against anyone, forgive him, so that your Father in heaven may forgive your sin" (Mark 11:25).

How are we to understand such passages? Do they conflict with other verses that promise us a full, free pardon and continuing cleansing as we confess our sins and trust him as our Savior?

The best answer seems to lie in the way forgiveness affects our inner selves. When we accept forgiveness from God, we become deeply aware of our own weakness and need. Pride is ruled out, and we are humbled before him. This attitude releases us from the tendency to judge others or become angry with them. We begin to realize that others, like us, are flawed by weaknesses. As this realization grows, you and I are freed to respond to others as God does to us, with love and forgiveness.

Forgiveness is like a coin; it has two sides. The one side of forgiveness is accepting it, the other side is extending it. The problem is not that God is unwilling to forgive the unforgiving. The problem is that the unforgiving lack that humility of spirit that permits them to receive it. The forgiven, freed of pride and self-righteousness, will learn to forgive.

Both testaments then portray God as a forgiving person. In the New Testament we discover that forgiveness is ours because of Jesus. We trust in him, confessing our need, and we find that accepting God's forgiveness opens up our lives to love for God and to personal transformation.

The Christian's experience of forgiveness changes our relationships with others. We who are forgiven develop a humility that enables us to treat other people compassionately. Because Jesus has forgiven us, we freely grant one another forgiveness, and we accept the forgiveness offered us by our brothers and sisters in the Lord.

FREEDOM

Christians are called to a joyous freedom. As our grasp of what Jesus has won for us deepens, the sense of release and of liberty grows.

In theology the emphasis has often been on free will rather than on freedom. Theologians ask, How free are those outside of Christ to do good or to cooperate in salvation? That issue is discussed in the next article. ♦ FREE WILL In this article I want to avoid that debate and simply explore the good news about the freedom that you and I can experience in Jesus Christ.

Secular notions of freedom. The New Testament words for freedom are drawn from Greek culture and originally reflected Greek ideas. Originally the word *freedom* expressed political ideals. A free person was a member of the community, a citizen with rights not possessed by slaves or outsiders. Freedom meant the right of political participation and the right to conduct one's affairs within the structure of laws that maintained social order. But history gradually taught the Greeks that this notion of freedom was flawed. Societies broke down. Laws were flawed. War, injustice, even crop failure demonstrated that human beings lack control over their destiny. Gradually the philosophers concluded that freedom could be found only within human personality. Some skeptics insisted that to be truly free, one must detach oneself from the external world and even from one's own emotions. Only then could a person be free from disappointment.

By the time our New Testament was written, the Greek words for freedom still carried the old political ideal, flavored by the skepticism of the philosopher. But the dominant notion was neither political nor philosophic. Like most people today, the ordinary person in the first-century world thought of freedom as the opportunity to do whatever one wants to do. To be truly free, a person would be released from all external restraints. To be free was to do whatever one wished, without limits imposed by others. So in the New Testament world freedom was thought of primarily as independence, and a "free" person was his or her own master.

But in the New Testament freedom takes on a totally new meaning. The New Testament gives no hint that freedom is political or that the way to freedom is the philosopher's path of self-denial. And there is direct contradiction of the common notion that freedom is license, the opportunity to do whatever one wants without hindrance or consequences. Christian freedom is something completely new, something outside the framework of first-century thought.

The background of bondage. We can only understand the biblical portrait of freedom when we understand Scripture's portrait of human bondage. Christians, impressed with the seriousness of sin, are convinced that human beings have never been truly free.

Our conviction grows out of a variety of biblical teachings. For instance the New Testament portrays persons outside of Christ as spiritually dead (Rom. 6:2–23; 8:21; Eph. 2:1–3). In the icy grip of death, human beings can glimpse the moral ideal set out in God's Law, but we can never be or do what is truly good (Rom. 7:3–6; 8:3; Gal. 2:4; 4:21–31; 5:1–13). ◆ GOOD Without the spiritual life, which God provides us in Jesus, we human beings are caught in the rushing tide of our own sinful passions and are mastered by them (Rom. 6:6; Eph. 4:22; Col. 3:9). Thus sin is an active force, carrying an all-too-willing humanity into acts that express the fallen human nature (Rom. 6:18–22; 8:2; 2 Peter 2:19).

None of this means that human beings can do *no* good. ◗ DEPRAVITY, DEATH It does mean that mankind lives in bondage to sin and inner death; all people live in a bondage that prevents them from being the persons they ought to be and may yearn to be. It means that choices that hurt others continue to be made, choices that spill over to victimize society with crime and injustice and war. As long as sin corrupts the human personality, the notion that freedom is license to do whatever one wishes is mockery.

Still, most of mankind persists in thinking of freedom as release from personal restraints. In fact false religious teachers use the promise of such a freedom to lure followers. Peter says that "by appealing to the lustful desires of sinful human nature, they entice people who are just escaping from those who live in error. They promise freedom, while they themselves are slaves of depravity — a man is slave to whatever has mastered him" (2 Peter 2:18–19).

Peter's point is compelling. Freedom, interpreted as the opportunity to do whatever one wishes, is empty indeed if what a person wishes to do is shaped by sinful impulses. The freedom human beings need is not a release from external restraints but release from domination by unhealthy and harmful desires.

True freedom. At times the New Testament uses the word *freedom* in very ordinary ways. It speaks of freedom to exercise personal rights (1 Cor. 9:1). The New Testament also contrasts free men with slaves (Gal. 4:22; Eph. 6:8). ◗ SLAVERY

But other New Testament passages explore what our Bible calls the "glorious freedom of the sons of God." This Christian freedom is found in release from those forces that keep mankind in bondage to sin and self and is found only in allegiance to a new master, Christ.

In the imagery of the New Testament, we who were slaves to sin have been purchased, that we might serve a new master. "You are not your own," the apostle Paul argues, "you were bought with a price" (1 Cor. 7:23). Only in submission to our new master can you and I find real freedom (Eph. 6:9; Col. 4:1). The reason is profound: Jesus purchased us as his own in order that he might make us truly free. "For freedom Christ has set us free," Paul says in Galatians 5:1, and he calls us a "people called to be free" (Gal. 5:13).

A number of New Testament passages focus on this unique freedom, which you and I can find only by choosing to be servants of Jesus Christ:

John 8:31–36. Jesus promises freedom to those who hold to (keep) his teaching. Those who obey him "will know the truth, and the truth will set you free." Jesus knows that humanity stumbles, lost in a world of illusion. Humanity's notions of what is healthy, good, and fulfilling is distorted by sin. Then Jesus comes with his words of truth, unveiling what is truly good and healthy and fulfilling. When we accept Jesus' view of reality and choose to live by his words, we come to know by personal experience what truly is good and good for us. We then "know the truth," and in this experience we find freedom.

Some who heard Jesus say this reacted angrily. "We have never been slaves," these people argued. How then could they be set free? But Jesus answered, "A person who sins is a slave to sin." The freedom Jesus promises is an inner release from the impulses of sin that lead to wicked acts, tragedy, and punishment. As we hear Jesus' words and obey him, we are led away from sin to a fresh, new, and happy path.

Romans 6:18–23. Here Paul builds on Jesus' statement that "you are slaves to the one whom you obey." Believers can choose to serve sin, "which leads to death," or God, "which leads to righteousness." Now that we belong to Jesus, we can choose to serve God and to become slaves to righteousness.

Paul warns us to consider the consequences of our choice. Sin pays a dreadful wage, in the coin of shame and death. Christian freedom is the freedom to do right and to win all the wonderful benefits of righteousness.

Romans 8:2–11. How is the believer able to do right? This is an important question because Christians, too, know the pull of the old sinful nature. The Bible's answer is not "try," but rather "rely." In salvation God gives his people the Holy Spirit. The Spirit provides the power to overcome our bent toward sin. When we rely on God the Spirit, who raised Jesus from the dead, he brings life to what is dead within us (Rom. 8:11). As 2 Corinthians 3:17 says, "Now the Lord is the Spirit, and where the Spirit of the Lord is, there is freedom." Relying on the Holy Spirit to guide and to enable us, we are released from our bondage to a sinful inner nature, which produces hatred, jealousy, fits of rage, envy, and other evils. Relying on the Holy Spirit, we are freed to be loving, patient, kind, faithful, and good. The secret power of a truly good life does not reside in an external law we struggle to keep, but in the indwelling Holy Spirit who prompts us toward good and enables us to be good.

Christian freedom is not license to do as we please; it is the freedom to choose between masters. All human beings must choose whom to serve: their sinful nature or God. Christian freedom is founded on the wonderful fact that because of Jesus, believers can be released from the forces that bind the unsaved. We can now choose to serve God.

The choice to serve God involves both a basic commitment and an endless series of daily decisions. In marriage a person makes a public, binding commitment to another person, then for the rest of his or her life that person makes daily choices that reflect the married state. The Christian is called to make a similar basic commitment to Jesus Christ as Lord. In dying for us, Christ purchased us, and we are his. Recognizing this, we commit ourselves to serve and obey him. Then, throughout our life, we are to make daily decisions that reflect allegiance to Jesus.

For Christians true freedom is the freedom to live out our commitment to Jesus in daily obedience. Because God has given us his Holy Spirit to guide and enable us, the freedom to live for Jesus truly is ours.

What are the implications of Christian freedom? First, when we submit to Jesus and live by his words, we experience true freedom. His words guide us away from what harms the human personality to what brings us fulfillment and joy. Second, when we submit to Jesus, we experience a surging power that carries us to goodness. What we could never do on our own becomes possible through the Holy Spirit. The freedom Jesus brings is a freedom to achieve beyond our ability and above our potential.

Christians believe in freedom, but not a freedom that exists as a license to do whatever we want. We believe in a disciplined freedom, which grows out of commitment to Jesus and is found by obedience to his Word. As creatures we have been shaped by God to love him, serve him, and enjoy him forever. Only in choosing to love and serve God can we become who we were created to be. Only in choosing to love and serve God can we find the joy that fellowship with the Lord brings. Only we who gladly submit to Jesus Christ as Lord can find that freedom, which is freedom indeed.

FREE WILL

The freedom Scripture promises is an exciting personal freedom. Because of Jesus the believer is not only freed from bondage to sin but also enabled by the Holy Spirit to reach out toward the very best. Christian freedom is found not in independence but in self-chosen submission to Jesus Christ as Lord. So the promise of freedom in

Scripture is an exciting, positive statement: We can achieve our fullest human potential through doing what is truly righteous and good in obedience to Christ. ◗ **FREEDOM**

When theologians speak of free will, however, they raise another issue. Essentially the question raised is, Just how and how much does the person participate in his or her salvation?

Christians know that salvation is from God and from God alone. Only because of Jesus can our sins be forgiven. Only because of Jesus can we be accepted as God's children and given a new life that is his own. ◗ **LIFE** But this salvation is received by faith. And so some have asked, Where does faith come from? Is it a response to the gospel of a person with the free will to choose, or does God so work within the human personality that the choice itself is from God?

In one significant way these questions are irrelevant. A person who believes in Jesus does so freely, without awareness of any inner coercion. A person who rejects the gospel also does so freely, never, in Luther's words, "as if he were taken by the neck and forced to it" (*Bondage of the Will*, XXV, p. 72). So from the viewpoint of human experience, each person, whether he or she accepts or rejects Christ, is aware that the choice is responsibly made. Whatever may happen or not happen beyond our consciousness is irrelevant to the person who is aware that the gospel calls him or her to make a conscious decision.

In other ways such questions are not irrelevant because they lead us to probe for a better understanding of God and of our human condition. In fact the historic differences in Christian views of free will often grow out of one's view of God, and the differences reflect attempts to guard what believers have felt honors God.

On one side, theologians have argued that only God has a free will. Only the Lord "does whatever pleases him, in the heavens and on the earth, in the seas and all their depths" (Ps. 135:6). Only God is truly free, able to operate without any restrictions other than those imposed by his own character. Human beings, on the other hand, are limited. Tied by the bonds of mortality to a limited space and time, weak in intellect compared to God and morally distorted by sin, human beings are in bondage to their creatureliness and to their own sin natures. Luther argues that the sinner does evil "spontaneously, and with a desirous willingness. And this willingness and desire of doing evil he cannot, by his own power, leave off, restrain, or change; but it goes on still desiring and craving. And even if he should be compelled by force to anything *outwardly* to the contrary, yet the craving will *within* remains averse to, and rises in indignation against that which forces or resists it" (*Bondage of the Will*, italics mine).

Luther's argument is cogent. The sinful human will cannot change itself. Thus to respond to the gospel, which calls us to a great change of mind about God, the human will must be changed by an outside agency. Thus "when God works in us, the will, being changed and sweetly breathed on by the Spirit of God, desires and acts, not from compulsion, but responsively, from pure willingness, inclination, and accord" (*Bondage of the Will*).

This argument has troubled some people, who feel that it is not as important to protect God's freedom as to safeguard his justice and his goodness. If it takes an act of God to free the human will to respond to the Lord, then some have no chance for salvation. This hardly seems fair or in keeping with the Christian conviction that God is both just and loving. In addition these theologians add that human beings simply must be free moral agents. Without free will human beings must be determined, like puppets. So both the fairness of God and his design of human beings as responsible moral agents, seems to demand that we have a truly free will.

A Contemporary Wesleyan Theology notes that "Freedom, as opposed to determinism in theological perspective, means that there is some dialogue with God, that human impact on God is significant, albeit not as significant as divine impact on the human; it also means that humans have a role to play in the process of salvation" (Vol. I, p. 718).

The problems that focus on the issue of free will seem to be like others that have divided Christians. Each side in the controversy is significantly right.

It is true that only God is truly free. It is true that human beings have been warped by sin so that the natural human will tends toward evil. It is true that human beings do not and cannot choose what is in full harmony with God's will. But it is also true that humans are morally responsible beings. It is true that human choices are not determined. It is true that the gospel offer is made to all and that "whosoever will may come."

In this and other cases in which each side in a theological dispute is right, despite the fact that logically only one side could be right, we enter the realm of paradox.

The notion of paradox, in which the apparently contradictory are equally true, is more easily resolved by Christians than by others. We simply emphasize the "apparently" or add that these seem contradictory "to us." Through Isaiah, God reminded Israel, "My thoughts are not your thoughts, neither are my ways your ways. . . . As the heavens are higher than the earth, so are my ways higher than your ways and my thoughts than your thoughts" (Isa. 55:8–9).

God is not limited by the capacity of our intellects or by our logical paradoxes. Where Scripture teaches that two apparently contradictory things are true, we abandon reliance on reason and rely instead on the trustworthy Word of the living God.

So what do we conclude about free will? Simply that the issues theologians raise cannot be resolved in a "right/wrong" dispute. Instead we confess that we do not understand how, but we believe the testimony of the Bible that we human beings are truly responsible for our own choices and at the same time are truly trapped in sin. We believe that God is totally free, and yet that we human beings are not determined. We believe the individual freely chooses to receive Christ and that God enables that choice. Perhaps most important, we know that we can freely share the gospel offer of a salvation that is for all human beings and will be accepted by any who choose to trust themselves to our God and Savior, Jesus Christ.

FUTURE

At times Christians become so involved in disputes about prophecy that they fail to remember what is so vitally and excitingly different about the Christian view of the future. It is not that prophecy is unimportant. ◆ **PROPHECY, MILLENIUM, RAPTURE** It is just that in our disputes about the differences between different Christian camps, we overlook the fact that Christians do look at the future in a common yet unique way.

If we look at non-Christians' attitude about the future, we make an interesting discovery. To them the future seems endless — until a final end. What I mean is this: The scientist speculates about humanity's continuing evolution. Humanity will stretch out, leaping from this solar system to explore the stars. Perhaps we will meet other alien races, but surely the future holds endless development and expansion — until the universe itself runs down. And then, as the stars dim and their atomic furnaces run down, a great shadow will settle over the universe. All life will go, and the last human forms will fall apart to dust the surface of empty planets spinning endlessly in the eternal dark.

Pessimists suggest the end may come sooner for humanity. They fear an atomic cataclysm, a burst of atomic fires that will purge earth of life or so blanket our world in radiation that only misshapen monsters born to the survivors will scramble in the ruins until the great dark comes for them, too.

What these and other variant views assume is that the universe extends endlessly in time as well as space. The future of the human race will be worked out within the confines of the material universe, for this is all there is. Whether the future for humanity is long or short, ultimately the great drama of life will end, and the last human being will lie down and die.

The Christian has a totally different view. We sense a reality beyond the material universe, and we hear God's Word that one day history will reach a culmination. On a day that God has planned, our earth, with all the heaven's starry host, will be set aside, and every person who has ever lived will be recalled to stand before our God. Christians may differ on the details of prophecy and on how God's final program will unfold, but Christians all look forward to God's final day. We know that Christ will appear to set things right, and he will welcome believers of every age into a fresh, new, and holy universe to spend eternity with him.

However optimistic unbelievers may seem to be about the centuries ahead, ultimately they believe that all life will come to an end. However optimistic unbelievers may seem about the future of the human race, ultimately they believe that individual lives end and the individual's personality dissolves with the body, forever lost.

At times Christians have been labeled pessimists. We discount notions of human moral evolution and expect both wars and rumors of wars. But in the end we are the world's true optimists. We know that God will step in long before the universe wears out. We know that in God, human beings will live again — forever. Because we look ahead and see God waiting at history's end to set all things right, we alone see a future filled with hope.

GOD

Like others we Christians struggle when we try to talk about God. It is not that we lack information about him. Ours is a faith that rests on revelation. Over the centuries and milleniums God has gradually unveiled more and more about who he is. No, our problem is that words are so inadequate. We can talk about God and describe him in many different ways. But God himself remains incomprehensible. He is great beyond our poor ability to grasp, awesome beyond our capacity to sense, beautiful beyond our ability to appreciate. The problem we have is that the wonder of God, and especially Jesus, simply cannot be compressed into our human speech or squeezed into our mental categories. Whatever we say about God, he is vast beyond our words. Our best descriptions provide us with only glimpses of his glory.

Given these inadequacies, how do Christians understand God? And how have we come to our understanding?

The second question probably should be answered first. Christianity is a *revealed* religion. That is, Christians have not reasoned their way to God. We have not take human qualities and projected the most noble "out there" to create God. We have not developed theories about the nature of the universe and reasoned back to some abstract "first cause." Instead we have heard a divine Word, a message from God to humanity. In that Word, written in Scripture and enfleshed in Jesus, God has shown himself to us. It is only because God has taken this initiative that we know about him and have heard his invitation to come to know him in a personal relationship. Our descriptions of God are found in his own self-revelation.

When Christians describe God, we are confident that what we say about God is correct. But we're also aware that no words can describe God adequately. What are the things that we are so sure of?

We believe that God is a living, eternal person. Each of these words is important. God is a person—a "you," not an "it." God has all those characteristics that mark human beings as persons, for we were made in his image. God is living, a present reality not only for us but also for every generation of all time. God is eternal; he always was and always will be.

When we look into Scripture, we learn many amazing things about this living, eternal person we call God. For example we learn that God has all the moral virtues in infinite degree. That is, God is good, loving, forgiving, truthful, righteous, compassionate, just, gracious, and he is all of these things beyond measure. Human beings have moral virtues, but our goodness and love are dim reflections of the goodness and love of God. While our goodness and love are limited, God is infinitely good and loving.

God also has qualities that we human beings do not share. He is omnipotent, omniscient, and omnipresent. That is, God has power without limit, wisdom without limit, and is everywhere present at all times. God also is absolute. By absolute we mean that God exists in himself, with no necessary relationship to other beings. We humans depend for our existence on our parents, and ultimately humanity itself depends on God who created us. But God is uncreated and has no source but himself. God also is Spirit. The Bible may picture God in anthropomorphic terms (giving God human characteristics) as seeing, hearing, and having a strong arm. But this is metaphorical and analogical language. God exists as a person, without his personality being bound to or expressed through a material form.

Two philosophical concepts are often used to describe the God of Scripture. We know him as both imminent and transcendent. In some religions God is so closely identified with the material universe that all things are thought of as parts of him (pantheism). In the Bible we discover a God who created the material universe but who is not of it. God transcends the material: He is completely distinct from it. So pantheistic notions of God are wrong. Yet at the same time God is everywhere present in his universe: He is here, in and through everything. So deistic ideas of God, which remove him so completely from the creation that he is unapproachable and unconcerned with human beings, are also wrong. We know God as both imminent and transcendent, two apparent opposites, which are both characteristic of our God.

The Bible and Christians use many other terms to describe God. We say that he is sovereign: He has ordained the past, controls the present, and will shape the future according to his will and plan. We call him Creator: He is the source of all that exists in the visible and the invisible realms. We call him Redeemer because he acts in time and space to deliver his people. We recognize him as judge because, as the ruler of the universe, he accepts responsibility to punish and to reward.

All in all we have a rich vocabulary with which to speak and to think of God. The words above (discussed in separate articles in this guide) are all words that help us sharpen our concept of God and help us to appreciate who he is. And yet all of them are inadequate. We wonder at God's power as we recall his mighty acts in history. We stand in awe of God's grace as we see him stoop to touch and redeem. We fall on our knees as we see his love shine so brilliantly from the cross. We cannot know all there is to know of God. But we can know God, and the glimpses we have of him in history and Scripture fill those three letters — GOD — full of meaning.

GOOD

We all have some feeling for what is good. *Good* is one of those words that everyone seems to understand but cannot adequately define. We know what people mean when they talk about good books, good deeds, and good looks. We can distinguish good from evil, and we generally agree on many characteristics of the "good life." Even so, philosophers have argued century after century about "the good," and ethicists have tried to organize lists of greater and lesser "goods" so we human beings might make decisions based on appropriate values.

Although the word *good* is full of ordinary meaning, it also can be used in such profound ways that it seems to defy definition. It is probably best for us to explore this word in a special way. We will best grasp what good is if we avoid the tortuous reasoning of the philosopher and simply see how *good* is used in Scripture.

The Old Testament's view of good. In the Old Testament the Hebrew for *good*, like our English word, draws together many different meanings. The good in the Old Testament is the beautiful and attractive, the useful or profitable, the pleasurable and desirable, and, of course, the morally right.

The common bond in all these uses is evaluation. To determine the good, we must compare. We place persons and things and actions beside other persons and things and actions. We set qualities beside qualities. We compare values and attitudes and patterns. The "good" then stands out as beneficial and right.

Good is introduced in the Creation story. There God shapes the world, and everything he makes is fresh and new. There God forms humans; Adam and Eve look around and at each other in innocent delight. God looks at all he has made and calls it "good." Like God's plan and even his own character, the creation is bright and beautiful.

But immediately the Bible's story turns. Genesis records the first pair's fall. Humanity is struck down, and nature screams under the crushing consequences of sin. The beautiful and beneficial are wrenched and twisted into other, tragic forms.

The Fall has two major consequences in relation to the good. First, sin destroys the harmony of the created order and introduces evil in its many shapes. Instead of the simplicity found in conforming to the will of God, life becomes complex, a confusing disorder reflecting the existence of many competing, contrary passions and desires. Choices are no longer as clear; the long-term consequences of choices are clouded and open to dispute. The good is harder to discern. The second consequence makes discernment even more difficult. Humankind is warped, and although we compare, we are often unable to tell just what in this now dark and tangled world is truly good.

Christians acknowledge the impact of sin on humanity's search for good — for the truly beneficial and right. We are convinced that because of sin's deadening and distorting influence, human beings are set adrift on a vast sea without sight of the stars and with no adequate inner compass. But we also believe there remains one who can accurately evaluate. This one, God, knows what is good and what is good for us. In his love, God has given us his Word as a beacon to guide us. By turning to God and trusting his evaluation, we can distinguish what will harm us and what will help. By following his Word, we can make the choices that benefit us and honor him — choices that bring a right fullness to life here and hereafter. As God said to Israel through Moses, "The LORD commanded us to obey all these decrees and to fear the LORD our God, so that we might always prosper and be kept alive" (Deut. 6:24). That which is right is beneficial: Following God's good (morally right) Word leads us to the good (beneficial) life.

This is basic to the Old Testament's view of good. That which is morally correct is truly beneficial to human beings, for God who ordains the right is a loving God. The Old Testament believer learned both to rely on God's evaluation of persons, actions, and things and to "do what is right and good in the LORD's sight, so that it may go well with you" (Deut. 6:18).

The New Testament's view of good. A single word in Hebrew is the basis for the Old Testament's rendering of "good." But the New Testament uses two Greek words, each used about the same number of times, to describe what is good.

One of them focuses our attention on what is useful or profitable. This word describes moral goodness. What is right is beneficial to all. The other emphasizes the aesthetic. The good is more than beneficial; it is beautiful. True beauty is found in the flawless and harmonious patterns that reflect God's will.

When the New Testament asserts that only God is good (Matt. 19:17; Mark 10:18), it means that only God's own actions are in full harmony with his nature and character. You and I may be good in a lesser sense. One person can be and do better than another; one action may be closer to the divine ideal. But no human action can be good in either absolute sense. Nothing we do is completely in harmony with God's will; nothing we do is beneficial to God.

Yet God does call us to live good lives. As we live in close relationship with Jesus, relying on his Holy Spirit and guided by his Word, our lives can be both beneficial and beautiful. We can pattern our lives after God the Father, whose love moves him to do good to the righteous and the unrighteous (Matt. 5:45). As we "do good to all," we discover the rewards, and all people will see the beauty of righteousness.

♦ GOOD WORKS, RIGHTEOUSNESS

Christians, then, accept the complex common meanings of the word *good*, and use the word in all the ordinary ways. But when asked about "the good," we probe deeper. We firmly believe that the good for humanity is expressed in God's Word and is experienced as human beings who believe in God put his revealed will into daily practice. Good is not primarily a subject for philosophic speculation. Good is essentially a lifestyle that harmonizes with the will of God, who desires only the best for human beings. How wonderful to realize that the truly good life is both beautiful and beneficial for us and our loved ones.

GOOD WORKS

Christians throughout the ages have debated the role of good works. None of us have crassly dismissed good works as unimportant in Christian experience. Instead the debate focuses on a definition of the relationship between faith and works.

The debate is a serious one. On the one hand, linking works with faith as a basis for salvation distorts the gospel message. On the other hand, isolating works from salvation just as seriously distorts our understanding of the dynamic nature of biblical faith.

As we sort out the issues involved, we should be impressed with one clear message: Christians have always been a people who affirm the importance of good works. Whatever our differences, we share the deep and common conviction that all who name Jesus as Savior are to be careful to do those things that honor God and benefit our fellow human beings. ♦ GOOD

Good works and salvation. In a sermon given in the first century, Clement argues that faith must issue in good works. One who serves God by keeping his laws will be saved, but one who transgresses Christ's commandments incurs eternal punishment. Nothing can save a person "if we shall not be found having holy and righteous works." This view is common in the apostolic fathers who lived in the late first and early second centuries. Good works are necessary if we are to become sure of forgiveness. Later, Tertullian taught that only if we "do not sin, but fulfill the law of God" can one remain in baptismal grace.

This strand of teaching is the seedbed of Catholicism's approach to salvation and was strongly rejected by the Reformers. They objected on biblical grounds (the early church fathers clearly misunderstood Paul), and they objected on other grounds as well. As the church became more and more hierarchical, good works became less and less (in Luther's term) "natural." That is, the good works the church encouraged focused on things like pilgrimages and building churches. Luther argued that it was more important to raise children well than to perform those legalistic religious duties the church of his day labeled "good works." Luther, like the other Reformers, also argued that so-called good works that involve any human effort to merit salvation as a deserved reward or recompense are detestable to God. Such works shift the focus of Christian faith from Jesus and his cross to our own efforts and to human righteousness.

The Reformers, and other earlier movements within Christianity, objected to the then dominant view that works were necessary as a basis for forgiveness. They looked back to Scripture, and there they found the strongest possible statements to support them:

> No one will be declared righteous in his [God's] sight by observing the law; rather, through the law we become conscious of sin. (Rom. 3:10)

> To the man who does not work but trusts God who justifies the wicked, his faith is credited to him as righteousness. (Rom. 4:5)

> Since they [the Jews] did not know the righteousness that comes from God and sought to establish their own, they did not submit to God's righteousness. Christ is the end of the law so that there may be righteousness for everyone who believes. (Rom. 10:3–4)

> All who rely on observing the law are under a curse, for it is written: "Cursed is everyone who does not continue to do everything written in the Book of the Law." Clearly no one is justified before God by the law, because, "The righteous will live by faith." The law is not based on faith; on the contrary. (Gal. 3:10–13)

> For it is by grace you have been saved, through faith — and this not from yourselves, it is the gift of God — not by works, so that no one can boast. (Eph. 2:8–9)

These and other passages stress the fact that the law, which defines good works for humanity, is no way of salvation. Rather, the law stands as a testimony to sin, convicting us of our failures. Anyone attempting to establish personal righteousness by "works of the law" must fail, for that kind of righteousness is not acceptable to God. Instead we must accept by faith a "righteousness that comes from God" and that is ours by faith, not by works. ◗ FAITH, RIGHTEOUSNESS

The Reformers reaffirmed Scripture's bold promise of a salvation that depends solely on the grace of God and that comes as a gift, "not by works, so that no one can boast" (Eph. 2:9). They rejected the notion that the forgiveness we have in Christ affects only past sins and strengthens us to do better in the future. It is not what we do, the emerging Protestant church trumpeted, it is what Jesus has done. With a renewed emphasis on Jesus and on the grace of God, Protestantism rejected the persistent notion that works are somehow necessary for the believer's salvation.

Certainly Christianity links salvation and good works. But good works are not a cause of salvation. In fact, it is more accurate to say that salvation is a cause of what the Bible calls good works!

Good works from salvation. Christians don't deny the importance of good works. How could we when our Scriptures are filled with sayings like, "as we have opportunity, let us do good to all people" (Gal. 6:9–10) and "our people must devote themselves to doing what is good" (Titus 3:14). Titus suggests Christ won us to himself so that we might be a people who are "zealous of good works" (Titus 2:14 KJV). What is distinctive in the Bible is the conviction that good works flow from salvation in a *necessary* way. That is, that a person who has come to a personal relationship with Jesus will surely do good.

Jesus made this point in a well-known illustration. He spoke of fruit and trees, pointing out that a good tree has good fruit. So one must "make a tree good and its fruit will be good" (Matt. 12:33). Applied, his figure means that "the good man brings good things out of the good stored up in him, and the evil man brings evil things out of the evil stored up in him" (Matt. 12:35). God's approach to good works is not to demand it from evil people but to make the evil person good by an act of his saving grace. And so Ephesians, reminding us we have been saved by grace through faith not works, goes on to say that, saved, "we are God's workmanship, created in Christ Jesus to do good works" (Eph. 2:10).

One of the most exciting themes in Scripture is that God's "divine power has given us everything we need for life and godliness through our knowledge of him" (2 Peter 1:3). Our relationship to Jesus is vital, dynamic, and transforming. In fact, our relationship to Jesus is so vital and life-giving that the apostle John writes that no believer "keeps on sinning. No one who continues in sin has either seen him or known him" (1 John 3:6). Why? "No one who is born of God will continue to sin, because God's seed remains in him; he cannot go on sinning, because he has been born of God" (1 John 3:9). In salvation, God forgives our sins and gives us his own life: We are truly born again. That vital principle of divine life within us does not mean we never fall. But it does guarantee that we will get up again and set out on the road that leads to righteousness. We do good works because Christ awakens us from within, and we are drawn to all that is beautiful and beneficial.

Salvation and good works, then, are related. Works do not provide a basis on which God accepts or rejects us, but good works flow out from relationship with Jesus, just as good fruit is produced by a good tree.

In James an often misunderstood passage makes just this point about faith and works (James 2:14–26). James looks at those who claim to have faith but do no subsequent good works. In disdain he dismisses that kind of faith. Why, the devils believe that God is one — and they shudder. A faith that exists only as belief about God (as distinct from faith in God) is worthless. Looking back in history, James points to

Abraham. God accepted his faith in place of righteousness (Gen. 15:6). But Abraham's life was marked by obedience to God. The visible obedience grew out of and demonstrated the reality of the invisible faith. In this way, faith and actions "were working together," and both God's statement and Abraham's own claim to believe in God were vindicated by Abraham's actions. Even Rahab, a harlot, showed she had a living faith by hiding Israeli spies. In every case, true faith will produce right action, and so works are necessarily associated with faith.

Luther argued that only salvation could bring a human being a positive desire to perform good works. One must be inwardly conquered by good for a person's works to be good. Any conformity to the external requirements of the law is meaningless; to be acceptable to the Lord, any action must flow from faith and be motivated by love.

We believe in good works, but we understand them as actions that flow from and express the reality of a salvation already worked within us by God. Nothing that you or I do can add to the salvation won for us by Jesus. But once we have been touched by God's grace and he has begun his work within, we will do good works.

What are good works? Works are actions, what we say and do. In Scripture the word *good* identifies what is right and beneficial. To do good works is to act in ways that will benefit others and glorify God.

How do we identify good works? In Old Testament times the law described a pattern of life to be lived by God's people. It contained both prohibitions and commands. In the New Testament we have the preeminent example of Jesus Christ, who reached out to the hurting and the needy. Jesus cared, and he acted to meet the needs of those around him. Ultimately Jesus sacrificed himself to meet our deepest need: our need of salvation. Christians find in Jesus' example a model of good works. We find models in believers like Dorcas, who was "always doing good and helping the poor" (Acts 9:36, 39). We also have explicit New Testament teaching about the honest, caring, serving life that God calls us to live here in this world. So we are not at a loss when it comes to defining good works. Instead we are excited and eager, realizing that every one of us finds daily opportunities to do good, to serve others, and so to honor our God.

Good works are important, not as a way to guarantee a salvation begun in faith and not as legalistic attendance to religious duty. The good works we know are the loving acts that benefit others and so transmit the touch of Jesus to all around us. The good works we know flow out of and express the reality of the relationship that we have with Jesus Christ. With all who know him, we too commit ourselves to "do good to all."

GOSPEL

Martin Luther, in his *Preface to the New Testament*, puts the gospel in clear focus. The good news Christians have to share "is nothing but the preaching about Christ, Son of God and David, true God and man, who by His death and resurrection has overcome all men's sin, and death and hell, for us who believe in Him. Thus the gospel can be either a brief or a lengthy message; one can describe it briefly, another at lengths. He describes it at length who describes many works and words of Christ, — as do the four Evangelists; he describes it briefly who does not tell of Christ's works, but indicates shortly how by His death and resurrection He has overcome sin, death, and hell for those who believe in Him, as do St. Peter and St. Paul."

"Gospel" is our translation of a Greek word meaning "good news," and all our good news is summed up in the person of Jesus Christ our Lord.

The word *Gospels* refers to the compilation of the good news about Jesus Christ in the first four books of the New Testament, which chronicle his life on earth.

GOVERNMENT

What is the relationship of the church and the state? Throughout the ages Christians' views have differed. Today issues of church and state are argued before our Supreme Court, and civil libertarians raise funds with TV clips designed to frighten viewers with the specter of the religious right gaining political power. The debate is clouded by differences over the most basic issues.

Perhaps the best way to explore this issue is to look at three ways in which Christians have experienced relationships between the church and the state and then to discuss contemporary church/state issues.

Church and state in conflict. In New Testament times and for several uncomfortable centuries, the church and the state existed in uneasy tension. Christians were often persecuted; even when believers were permitted freedom to worship, their individual freedoms were not guaranteed.

The statements in the New Testament about the Christian's relationship to the state are striking in view of the hostility of government to the Christian movement. Jesus laid down a basic principle, which was amplified by Paul and Peter. The believer is to "give to Caesar what is Caesar's, and to God what is God's" (Matt. 22:21).

The Old Testament provides a basis for the attitude of responsibility both to government and to God. While Israel was conceived to be a theocratic nation, whose ruler was God, Israel also had kings. Many kings, like Saul in his later days, were far from godly. Yet David acknowledged God's sovereign choice of Saul; even though David's life was threatened by Saul, David refused to touch "God's anointed." We sense the same principle in Daniel. Daniel wrote in Babylon, where Nebuchadnezzar had ruled. The pagan conqueror had overrun Palestine, radically changing political systems and national boundaries. Yet Daniel acknowledged God's sovereignty in it all and implied that people are to yield allegiance to existing governments: "the Most High is sovereign over the kingdoms of men and gives them to anyone he wishes and sets over them the lowliest of men" (Dan. 4:17, 25).

In the New Testament this implied allegiance is stated explicitly. Again, believers lived under an autocratic state that offered little legal protection to people who were not Roman citizens. Yet Paul taught that "everyone must submit himself to the governing authorities, for there is no authority except that which God has established. The authorities that exist have been established by God. Consequently he who rebels against the authority is rebelling against what God has instituted, and those who do so will bring judgment on themselves" (Rom. 13:1–2).

This judgment is not divine punishment, but it is imbedded in the secular powers of government itself. God has granted the power of the sword (of physical enforcement) to government so that it can carry out its ordained mission. What is that mission? Essentially the mission of government is to maintain social order, punishing whatever actions would destroy society, and thus providing a context in which human beings can live at peace. The only way that any government can carry out this mission is for its citizens to be obedient to its laws and responsive to its rulers. It follows that if you want to be free from fear of the one in authority, then "do what is right, and he will commend you. For he is God's servant to do you good. But if you do wrong, be afraid, for he does not bear the sword for nothing. He is God's servant, an agent of wrath to bring punishment on the wrongdoers. Therefore it is necessary to submit to the authorities, not only because of possible punishment but also because of conscience" (Rom. 13:1–5).

The point of this argument is that whatever form government may take, a governing authority is necessary for a stable society. The Christian submits to government, knowing that even antagonistic governments (like Rome) are God's gift and necessary to punish wrongdoers and thus promote the peace and security of citizens.

As persecutions grew and Christians suffered, it was harder to maintain this view of the government. Yet Peter, in a letter whose theme is suffering, calls on believers to "live such good lives among the pagans that, though they accuse you of doing wrong, they may see your good deeds and glorify God on the day he visits us" (1 Peter 2:12). Immediately Peter applies this principle to the believer's response to government: "Submit yourselves for the Lord's sake to every authority instituted among men, whether to the king, as the supreme authority, or to governors, who are sent by him to punish those who do wrong and to commend those who do right. . . . Show proper respect to everyone: Love the brotherhood of believers, fear God, honor the king" (1 Peter 2:13–14, 17).

Paul adds to Peter's call. Not only are Christians to submit to authority, but they also are to make "requests, prayers, intercession and thanksgiving" for everyone, especially "for kings and all those in authority that we may live peaceful and quiet lives in all godliness and holiness" (1 Tim. 2:1–2).

In a society where conflict exists between the church and the state, the Christian is to be a good citizen, submitting to the government in all things that do not conflict with duty to God. So the early Christians paid their taxes, honored their governors, but were willing to die when pagan rulers demanded they worship the emperor and deny Jesus Christ.

Church and state unified. The Christian church flourished under persecution. Then Christian emperors came to power. During this era, emperors tried to use the church as an instrument of public policy. These emperors believed that the society would be stronger if it were bound together by a common faith as well as common laws and rulers. So the emperors intruded in church affairs. They called councils to resolve doctrinal disputes, and they used their power to enforce the creeds the councils wrote. They expelled influential clergy and placed their own adherents in church offices.

Centuries later, as political power fragmented and church power was centralized in Rome, the situation was reversed. Pope Boniface issued his proclamation, *Unam Sanctum*, and announced that spiritual powers should direct the temporal. The church plunged into politics. Papal armies marched and papal legates intrigued in the affairs of nations.

Attempts to unify church and state were not limited to Catholicism. Reformers like Calvin and Zwingli held a common vision, calling on church and state to set out hand in hand to seek righteousness. Where did their vision come from, and how was it expressed?

The concept of a theocratic state was drawn from the Old Testament. There Israel is portrayed as a nation under God, with no distinction drawn in the law between the secular and the sacred. The governing authorities, like the citizens, are subject to the law of God, and the role of government is to lead the citizens to honor their common Lord. Klotsche describes the Reformers' ideas in his *History of Christian Doctrine:*

> Church and state though separate in organization cooperate closely to support each other. The church's authority is absolute in matters of doctrine. The discipline of the church is to be carried out by governmental agencies. "No government can be happily constituted, unless its first object be the promotion of piety," therefore Christian princes and magistrates "should employ their utmost efforts in asserting and defending the honor of him whose vice-regents they are and by whose favor they govern. . . . Their office extends to both tables of the law." The end in view in this theocracy is to produce a people of God by governmental agencies. God is the Lord whose will rules all. It is the duty of the church and state to carry out his will. Hence civil authority, in its service to God, is under obligation to exercise Christian discipline. (p. 240)

To Luther the marks of the true church were the preaching of the Word and the administration of the sacraments. Calvin and those in the Reformed tradition added the mark of discipline. Calvin writes,

> Civil government has as its appointed end, so long as we live among men, to cherish and protect the outward worship of God, to defend sound doctrine of piety and the position of the church, to adjust our life to the society of men, to form our social behavior to civil righteousness, to reconcile us with one another, and to promote general peace and tranquility. . . .
>
> Let no man be disturbed that I now commit to civil government the duty of rightly establishing religion, which I seem above to have put outside of human decision. For, when I approve of a civil administration that aims to prevent the true religion which is contained in God's law from being openly and with public sacrilege violated and defiled with impunity, I do not here, any more than before, allow men to make laws according to their own decision concerning religion and the worship of God.

In Calvin's ideal state, "the true religion" instructs the magistrates wherever civil issues may touch on doctrinal issues or matters of public piety.

This concept of church/state relationships is viable only if there is one church that can speak with a clear and unified voice and if those who govern acknowledge the right of church leaders to guide them in matters of doctrine and morality. It not only means that the agencies of the state will be used to prevent the development of religious pluralism, it also means inevitably that the leaders of the state will try to use the church to gain their end even as the church tries to use the state to reach its goals.

In practice, this approach to church/state relationships has led to persecution of minority religious groups. And it has led to the corruption of the church, as in Hitler's Germany where the state church was infiltrated and turned to promotion of Nazi ends.

Serious theological objections to this view of the church's relationship to government also arise. The model used by Calvin and others in the Reformed tradition is the Israel idealized in Old Testament law. That ideal was never achieved in history, and the divine agenda is clearly modified in the new covenant instituted by Christ. In the New Testament the church exists as communities of disciples who live in various cultures and under different forms of government. These Christians recognize Christ as Lord and seek to live as citizens of his kingdom. Part of that calling involves living submissively under whatever form the civil government may take. There is no hint here that the Christian's goal is to establish a godly government, although there is no reason to suppose that Christians who find themselves in government should not follow their own consciences, informed by Scripture, as they carry out their duties. There is no hint that the New Testament community, scattered as it was throughout the empire, was to seek establishment of a civil government whose conscience would be the church.

Church and state separated. In the sixth century Augustine argued that the kingdom of God and "kingdom of men" were of completely different orders. It would be error to suppose that God's purposes can be identified with any particular society or civilization.

While Martin Luther was forced to depend on the support of princes, whose motivations in supporting the Reformation may have been as much political as religious, his teaching tended toward the separation of church and state. Unlike Calvin, who added discipline to the visible marks of the true church, Luther was satisfied that the preaching of the Word and administration of the sacraments was enough. In one of his sermons Luther preached that "the two powers of government, God's and Caesar's, must be kept apart."

Luther stressed the responsibility of the believer to be obedient to the state, and he denied the individual any right of rebellion. He also urged rulers to exercise their God-given tasks responsibly. But ultimately Luther was convinced that the two powers, church and state, were so different in nature that it would be disastrous to confuse them. "There are two kingdoms," Luther writes in his *Open Letter against the Peasants:*

One [is] the kingdom of God, the other the kingdom of the world. I have written this so often that I am surprised that there is anyone who does not know it or note it. . . . God's kingdom is a kingdom of grace and mercy, not of wrath and punishment. In it there is only forgiveness, consideration for one another, love, service, the doing of good, peace, joy, etc. But the kingdom of the world is a kingdom of wrath and severity. In it there is only punishment, repression, judgment, and condemnation, for the suppressing of the wicked and the protection of the good. For this reason it has the sword, and a prince or lord is called in Scripture God's wrath, or God's rod (Isaiah xiv). . . . Now he who would confuse these two kingdoms — as our false fanatics do — would put wrath into God's kingdom and mercy into the world's kingdom; and that is the same thing as putting the devil in heaven and God in hell.

While Luther wrote this in support of the terrible persecution of rebelling peasants by their overlords, the basis of the argument is clear. Church and state are distinct, and the distinction must be preserved. The church, founded on grace, cannot enforce righteousness; the state can make no one good but is ordained to punish the ungodly.

The notion of separation of church and state has taken root in our country. Our Constitution prohibits the "establishment" of religion. In 1776, this prohibition was clearly understood: America should have no state church, no religion is to be established as *the* religion of the United States. Instead citizens are guaranteed freedom to choose and to practice their own religion without governmental interference.

Historically, then, we have seen three conditions: the state taking the role of enemy of the church; the state and the church in partnership, with one partner or the other seeking dominance; and the church and the state assigned separate spheres. In the United States the doctrine of separation of church and state rules. But the ways in which the doctrine is to be applied are still debated.

Contemporary church/state issues. What are some of the issues that we still debate, and are there any guidelines that can help us resolve them? Perhaps we need to think of guidelines first, and then see how they might apply.

First, every Christian is a citizen as well as a believer. As Christians we have an obligation to be good citizens. Citizenship responsibilities include paying taxes, obeying laws, and participating in the political processes established by law. Thus voting can rightly be seen as a citizen's obligation. In a democracy a believer may seek public office but not with the idea of "establishing" his or her religion. Second, Christians acting as citizens bring with them their moral standards and conscience.

While they are not to use state powers to impose their convictions on others, they will vote and act their convictions. This is understood in a pluralistic society. Those who have other moral standards have the same right to vote and act their convictions as well. Third, the wall established between church and state should protect religion from government intervention even as it protects against religious intervention in government. Finally, the Constitution is *not* anti-religion but pro-religion, for it provides positive guarantees for religion's free exercise. If we keep these guidelines in view, we can at least begin to see how to deal with troubling church/state issues.

Religious schools. Some people have established Christian schools for religious reasons. At times these come into conflict with the government. The school founders claim that the right of religious freedom releases them from state requirements governing teacher certification, curriculum, and the like. In such cases the state is not attempting to dictate doctrine, but rather it insists on conformity to laws governing the education of its citizens. Here it seems that the principle of a citizen's obligation to conform to law when no violation of God's law is involved should prevail.

Abortion. Some people cast abortion as a religious issue because Christians are in the forefront of the battle against abortion as a means of birth control. In fact, the issue is a constitutional one. The United States Constitution guarantees the right of human beings to "life, liberty, and the pursuit of happiness." The issue then hinges on one question: Is a fetus a living human being, or is a fetus simply a part of the mother's own body? Ultimately the Supreme Court will resolve this question and will recognize the rights of the unborn. As citizens, Christians who are against (or for) abortion are not only free to express their point of view, but in a free society they also are expected to attempt to influence the conscience of the community.

Use of public buildings. Recently, access to public buildings (such as public school classrooms) has been denied to groups who wish to use them after hours for non-partisan Bible studies. At the same time, access to such public buildings has been guaranteed to other groups, including homosexuals and communists. The establishment of religious doctrine has been broadly interpreted in such cases to mean government may do nothing that supports any religious activity. This broad interpretation goes beyond the intention of the framers of the Constitution and is likely to be reversed by the Supreme Court in the near future. In fact, we may soon come to the place where access to public buildings is guaranteed to religious groups on the grounds that while government is not to establish any one religion, it is to encourage the free exercise of religion by its citizens. (Current tax deductions granted for religious contributions and non-taxation of church properties and businesses are in fact designed to encourage the exercise of religion).

Prayer in schools. Prayer in public schools was common in the United States for nearly two hundred years. There seems to be no compelling reason to deny those who want it in practice, and there may well be no compelling reason to reinstate it either.

Religion in politics. The issue is usually confused. It is never wrong in a democracy for any group to seek to influence the political process. When one's convictions are based on religious values, it is clear that religion will necessarily be involved in a person's politics. Both the person voting and the person running for office will bring to that involvement his or her religious convictions and will express those convictions by the ballot and by the kind of laws he or she tries to shape. In a pluralistic society, attempts to influence the direction of a nation in democratic ways in no way violates the principle of separation of church and state. Instead the Christian's obligation to be a good citizen demands that he or she participate actively.

Christianizing America. The 1984 elections saw some people raise the specter of a country dominated by a fundamentalist minority that imposes its moral standards on dissenters through government. The adverse publicity about this issue distorted reality, for groups have often claimed a religious basis in seeking to influence the national conscience. The base and basis of Martin Luther King's vision of a racially unified America was religious, and ministers of every background called on citizens to put an end to discrimination. That essentially religious view of human beings was soon expressed in a variety of laws, and certainly some of them "violated" the conscience of racists. But those just laws were "imposed" because the moral vision of racial justice captured the majority in our nation. How then can anyone deny the right of "fundamentalists" to project their moral vision, hoping to likewise capture the conscience of the nation? What would be wrong if their moral vision — for instance, of the sanctity of the life of the unborn — also was to be reflected in laws enacted by the majority? Only if the moral vision of a minority were imposed by other than democratic means would political involvement by religiously motivated citizens violate the principle of separation of church and state.

It is clear from this brief review that Christians throughout the ages have had difficulty in working out the relationship between the church and state. Whether the state is to be seen as the enemy, the partner, or as an entity to be carefully separated from the church is a matter of dispute. Yet we agree that we are to live godly lives in this world, and this involves submission to the laws of the nation in which we live. American

Christians are especially fortunate, for implied in our citizenship is the privilege to exercise all the obligations that are ours in a democracy. While our church remains distinct from the state, as Christian citizens you and I are able to seek to influence the direction of our country, communicate our own moral vision, and incorporate it in our nation's laws.

GRACE

Grace is a vital biblical term, one that makes a basic statement about how God relates to human beings. To appreciate the message of the Bible, we must understand grace.

Grace also figures in theological debate. But there grace is always linked with other words, so the debates focus on phrases such as "prevenient grace," "common grace," and "efficacious grace." It is important to remember that the differences between the various theological traditions are not so much disagreements about grace itself as disagreements over the words that are associated with grace.

Since we are concerned in this book with the basics of what we Christians believe, we need to look first at the concept of grace itself. When we understand grace, we can turn to the words that theologians have added to express their special concerns about how grace operates in Christian experience.

Grace in Scripture. The concept of grace is given full expression in the New Testament. There is no exact parallel in the Old Testament. But one Hebrew concept comes close. One Hebrew word speaks of favor, of being merciful and gracious. The very first phrase in Psalm 51 clearly pictures the force of this beautiful Old Testament idea. David cries out, "Have mercy on me, O God, according to your unfailing love; according to your great compassion blot out all my transgressions." David's cry expresses his sense of helplessness. He turns away from self-reliance and relies only on the loving compassion of the Lord. God's nature as a loving, caring person provides the basis for David's appeal.

In the language of the New Testament, grace is *charis*. In Greek culture this word indicates a favor or benefit given and also is used of the appropriate response, gratitude. Paul fastens on *charis* and develops it as a technical theological term to sum up what Jesus has done and to sum up all that the gospel affirms about personal relationship with the Lord.

Human religions approach relationship to God from a common point of view. They assume that human beings are able to please God by their actions and that relationship with God depends to some extent on what a person does. This makes salvation a reward, something that a person merits or deserves.

Christianity approaches relationship to God in a totally different way. Human beings are viewed as lost, dead in trespasses and sins (Eph. 2:1). Unable to please God because sin is woven through and through our nature, it is only through God's free and spontaneous action in Jesus that salvation comes. Even the righteousness that increasingly marks the Christian's experience is a result of God's action in us and not a result of mere human effort.

Essentially, religion focuses on self, relies on works of the law, and results in condemnation. Essentially, Christianity focuses on Christ, relies on his work for us, and results in new life and personal righteousness. All of this is summed up in the New Testament concept of grace.

Ephesians 2:1-11 sums up grace. This passage.reveals a humanity that lies "dead in trespasses and sins" and follows "the ways of this world and the ruler of the kingdom of the air [Satan]" (Eph. 2:1-2). Humanity lies helpless. But moved by "his great love for us, God, who is rich in mercy, made us alive with Christ even when we were dead in transgressions — it is by grace you have been saved" (Eph. 2:4-5). God's grace is mediated to us "through faith — and this not of yourselves, it is the gift of God — not by works, so that no one can boast" (Eph. 2:9-10).

Grace views human beings as helpless. And grace affirms God as a loving, compassionate person who, moved solely by his great goodness, has acted in Christ Jesus to free all who believe from their bondage to sin and to give all who believe a new, eternal life as a foundation for practical righteousness.

While it is important to see the role of God's grace in salvation, it is just as important to realize that grace is the key to vital Christian experience. Perhaps the impact is most clearly seen in Paul's vision of a holy life, summed up in Romans 6-8. In Romans 6, Paul shows that the believer is united to Jesus in Christ's death and resurrection. That union frees us from a legalistic approach to the Christian life in which our own efforts are the key to pleasing God. Instead that union establishes us in the realm of grace. Now we can rely on God to enable us to do good and righteous acts. As we yield ourselves to God and trust him daily, God overcomes our innate helplessness and enables us to do his will.

In Romans 6, grace is not simply an orientation to relationship with God. Grace is a practical approach to living the Christian life. If we struggle to follow God's rules in our own strength, we will fail (Gal. 5:4). If we rely on Christ and the Holy Spirit, we will succeed in living a holy, loving life. Romans 7 applies this truth by describing Paul's own failure to achieve obedience by trying to follow God's law. In Romans 8, Paul describes the great release that comes as he learned to rely on grace and to count solely on the Holy Spirit within to move him to do good. Grace, then, is not only the way of salvation but also a way of life. Grace is a continuing reliance on God to make us holy even as we first relied on God to forgive our sins.

What does it mean for us to recognize and to rely on the grace of God? It means that we accept the impossibility of pleasing God by our own efforts. It means that we acknowledge God's great love expressed in Jesus and that we trust God to welcome us into his family for Jesus' sake. And it means that we continue to rely on Jesus as we live daily, counting on his strength to enable us to make those choices that are pleasing to our Lord. When we know God's great heart of love and the compassion that moved him to reach out to save us, we will "approach the throne of grace with confidence" (Heb. 4:16).

Theological debates. Christians throughout the centuries agree on grace. We recognize grace in God's actions taken for us, motivated by his great love, spontaneously reaching out to us in our need. But given this great common ground, there have been differences and disputes about how grace operates.

The doctrine of "common grace" is generally accepted by all Protestants. We all realize that non-Christians do good things and that few are as evil as they might be. Common grace views this as a result of God's loving concern for humanity, expressed in restraining evil passions and encouraging moral acts. Common grace is usually contrasted with "efficacious grace," which is involved with salvation. The distinction usually made is that common grace restrains or encourages natural human tendencies, while saving grace operates from within to change human nature.

Most Christians are comfortable with the concept of common grace, but the idea of efficacious grace has been troubling. Here the disagreement hinges on just how drastically sin has affected human nature. Has the impact been so great that a person is unable even to cooperate with grace in his salvation? Does God actually act within the will to change it so that a person freely believes? Calvinists, who hold this position, argue that saving grace is irresistible, in that those who receive this grace will always choose to believe. Others have argued that all human beings have been given sufficient grace to make their salvation a possibility, if only they accept rather than reject it.

An older theology book summarizes the different viewpoints in a brief paragraph:

A and B are alike sinners. A believes and B remains a reprobate. The Pelagian says, because A willed to believe and B to reject. The Semipelagian says, because A commenced to strive, and was helped, and B made no effort. The Arminian says, because A cooperated with common grace, and B did not. The Lutheran says, both were utterly unable to cooperate, but B persistently resisted grace, and A ultimately yielded. The Calvinist says, because A was regenerated by the new creative power of God's Spirit, and B was not. (A. A. Hodge, *Outlines of Theology*, Zondervan, p. 448)

There are reasons why exploring such differences are important to theologians and why the differing viewpoints should be examined. ▶ **PREDESTINATION** But there are times when we should *not* explore them.

This is one of those times *not* to explore the differences. Why? Because making grace a phrase, and then talking about "common grace" and "irresistible grace" and "cooperating with grace," draws our attention away from the wonder of that marvelous word, *grace*. You and I should meditate on grace, seen in splendid isolation as a testimony to the loving nature of our God. Rather than arguing over just how grace operates in relation to the human will, we should pause to contemplate the matchless compassion of God who, while we were yet sinners and powerless, gave his only Son to die for the ungodly. As we consider our own deep need, and how freely and spontaneously God acted to meet that need, our hearts truly are filled with wonder. God loved us, not because of ourselves but because he is love. And we love him in return, filled with gratitude for the incomprehensible favor he has done us in Jesus and for the continuing favor he shows us as we trust him daily.

In a very real sense, grace and grace alone puts our relationship with God in perspective. He owed us nothing, yet he chose to give us everything. We owe him everything, yet we can give him nothing that ever has or ever will merit his favor.

How wonderful, then, that God yet permits us to offer him, in thanksgiving but never in payment, all we have and all we are. Grace and grace alone enables us to live for the Lord. And grace alone moves us to want to please him.

GUILT

The word *guilt* is used in two distinct ways in our society, and the most common usage is not biblical.

Guilt feelings. In his outstanding book, *No Condemnation* (Zondervan, 1984), Bruce Narramore describes a discovery he made as a Christian counselor:

As I gained clinical experience, I began to recognize that more people were troubled by guilt than I had realized. Their guilt was hidden. I found that some people who were never able to "get their act together" and achieve academic, vocational, or marital success were troubled by guilt. Feeling undeserving of success (because of guilt), they repeatedly involved themselves in situations doomed to failure. Some sabotaged their consciously hoped-for success by selecting mates who repeated the neurotic relationship they had with their parents or previous spouse. Others set up a no-win situation with their employer. The woman who runs through two or three marriages with abusive husbands is a classic example. You would think she would be careful after a bad experience or two, but instead, she seems to have a desire to be mistreated and in fact she does. Since she does not believe she is deserving of a loving husband, she searches out men who make her suffer. (p. 16)

These discoveries led Narramore to rethink the common notion that guilt feelings are the voice of God, designed to lead us to repentance and constructive Christian living. Instead he discovered not only that guilt feelings were usually destructive but also that most guilt feelings are neurotic, with little relationship to what the Bible means by guilt.

What are guilt feelings? Essentially they are feelings of fault or failure that develop as others criticize or condemn us. A parent says, "You *never* go to bed when I tell you!" or "There, you've done it *again!*" Later a spouse complains, "You never spend any time with *me.*" The words, intended to make us change or at least to make us suffer, all too often take root in our conscience. A person who lives under a barrage of criticism for real or imagined failures may develop neurotic guilt feelings that rob him or her of self-esteem and self-acceptance. This neurotic guilt, which robs us of joy and fulfillment, is what most people in our society mean when they use the word *guilt*. Guilt is simply those unhappy feelings that are associated with failure and disappointing others.

Real guilt. The Bible does not use the word *guilt* in the sense of guilt feeling. Instead *guilt* is a word that focuses on a person's moral relationship to God as affected by specific acts of sin. Biblical guilt has three specific aspects: (1) the act of sin, (2) the resultant condition — one is guilty, (3) the punishment due. When we read the Old Testament, a particular use of the word *guilt* may focus on any of these three aspects. But in no verse is the issue how a person feels. Guilt is an objective thing: Each of us is responsible for his or her own actions and each of us will bear the consequences of wrong choices.

In the New Testament the Greek words used to speak of guilt are judicial in nature. Each insists that human beings have criminal responsibility for acts of sin. God himself holds the guilty person accountable for his or her actions (Rom. 3:19).

When the New Testament speaks of being guilty, it uses a word that implies conviction. And the convicted felon is liable for punishment (Matt. 5:22; Mark 3:29; 1 Cor. 11:27; James 2:10). Even in Hebrews 10, where some English translations suggest "feel guilty," the original emphasis is on our awareness of actual guilt.

Guilt in the Bible, then, is not a feeling. Guilt speaks of what happens when a human being sins. Because we are responsible for our choices and because God is the responsible moral governor and judge of his universe, acts of sin make us guilty before him, deserving of the punishment that a holy God must always decree for sin. ◗ SIN

God's remedy for real guilt. The Bible nowhere suggests that God forgives guilt. What God forgives is sin. This means that God looks back on our sinful acts, and because of Jesus, he forgives us. So the Bible promises, "in him we have redemption through his blood, the forgiveness of sins" (Eph. 1:7). God's forgiveness deals so fully with our sins that they are literally gone, washed away so completely that God can promise, "Their sins and lawless acts I will remember no more" (Heb. 10:17).

With our sins gone, we are neither guilty in God's sight nor liable for punishment. As forgiven people, guilt has no hold on us any more. We can rejoice in God's good word that "there is now no condemnation for those who are in Christ Jesus" (Rom. 8:1).

The biblical message of forgiveness brings release from the burden of our real guilt. And the biblical message provides the basis for our release from those false guilt feelings that plague Christians and non-Christians alike. ◗ FORGIVE

God's remedy for guilt feelings. All too often, Christians who know they have forgiveness through Christ continue to be plagued by guilt feelings. The neurotic guilt that Dr. Narramore writes about holds them in its grip. They feel unworthy, unacceptable. All too often they act in ways that bring the suffering and failure they sense they deserve. What is God's remedy for neurotic guilt feelings?

Here the whole gospel message is relevant. We human beings do sin and fall short of God's perfection. But God continues to love us. God continues to believe that you and I have worth and value. In fact, we are so important to God that he gave his only Son to die in our place so that we might live. The critical words we heard from our parents or spouses or friends, words that suggested we are not acceptable, do not reflect God's attitude at all. The fact is that you have infinite worth to God and are deeply loved. When we accept God's view as accurate and when we recognize the attacks of others as inaccurate views of who we really are, our sense of self-worth changes. So the gospel helps us feel good about ourselves, providing a solid basis for positive self-esteem.

The gospel is also a message of hope and expectation. Those messages that made us feel so guilty implied that we could never do anything right. We became convinced that we were doomed to failure, at least to failure in the things that are significant to us and to others. The gospel's good word is that, in Christ, we are invited to succeed. And now we can succeed! The Holy Spirit gives each of us a special gift that enables us to contribute to others. ♦ SPIRITUAL GIFTS

Each of us is given strength by Jesus to make right choices, to build a new and holy life. In place of the message of failure, we hear in the gospel a message of hope, a promise of a bright and new and meaningful tomorrow. ♦ HOLINESS

And what about the compulsion that so many with neurotic guilt feel to punish themselves? The gospel message is that Jesus has taken on himself the punishment we deserved. We no longer have any need to punish ourselves. The books have been balanced, and we are at peace with God and with ourselves.

The gospel message, then, invites us to look at ourselves again and to see ourselves as God sees us. In Christ we discover we are not the worthless failures that neurotic guilt suggests. No, we are the objects of God's love, cleansed by Jesus and made new in him. Because of Jesus, you and I are new creations (2 Cor. 5:17). We look forward to a life of goodness that God will enable us to live, and we confidently expect to experience the success and blessing that come to those who choose to live God's way.

Guilt and Christian experience. Too often Christians have wrongly taken guilt feelings to be a gift from God, intended to lead us to constructive Christian living. Parents who hold this view have tried to motivate their children by shaming, criticizing, and pointing out all they *should* have done but didn't. Pastors who hold this view have tried to shame their parishioners into witnessing, giving, and serving. But the gospel brings us release from guilt; it does not add to its burden. Guilt feelings do not move us to positive action, they crush us. Instead it is love and love alone that makes the Christian want to respond to God with obedience. Parents, pastors, and friends who want to help others grow can follow God's better way. We can reassure our loved ones that in Christ they are forgiven and that we also forgive their failures. We can reassure our loved ones that they are important to God and important to us. And we can reassure our loved ones about their future. In Jesus, and because of Jesus, we are confident that they will make those better choices that lead surely to a successful and a holy life.

HEAD

Christians usually add one of two phrases to this word *head*. We speak of the "head of the church" and the "head of the home." Each of these phrases is important.

The head of the church, according to Scripture, is Jesus himself. The word is linked to an analogy. According to the New Testament, the church itself should be thought of as a living body, an organism rather than an organization. ◗ BODY, CHURCH In this organism Jesus is the head, and we are all members (parts) of his body. We find this analogy in Ephesians 1:22; 4:15; 5:23; and in Colossians 1:18; 2:10; 2:19. Looking at these passages, we see that headship suggests Jesus' role as sustainer, protector, organizer, and source of his church's life.

It is important for Christians to recognize the central role that Jesus has in the ongoing life of his church today. Because Jesus is alive, we can look to him for guidance and find strength to do his will.

The head of the home image has often been distorted. In many cultures women are viewed as inferior, under the control of their husbands. The notion of control has often been read into passages that speak of the husband as head of the wife or the male as head of the female. Those who teach this kind of hierarchy fasten on Ephesians 5:22–24. There the husband is affirmed as the head of the wife, as Christ is the head of the church.

The explanation of the passage hinges on the *limits* that Paul places on the analogy. The husband's headship is to be modeled on Jesus who in his Savior role "gave himself up for" the church, in order "to make her holy, cleansing her by the washing with water through the word, and to present her to himself as a radiant church, without stain or wrinkle or any other blemish, but holy and blameless." Thus Paul tells us very clearly what he intends headship to involve. We may not be able, as mere human beings, to be the source of another's life in the same way that Jesus, the head of the church, is of our life. We may not be able, as mere human beings, to guide another's choices into God's will in the same way that Jesus, the head of the church, does for all of his people. But we are able to follow Jesus' example and give up ourselves for our wives, helping them realize their fullest potential, even as Jesus gave himself up for us, making us holy. Headship, then, has a limited application to the marital relationship. Headship is no blanket authorization to demand a wife's obedience. It is, instead, a broad admonition to the husband to put his wife's needs first and do whatever love can do to help his wife reach her potential as a person and as a Christian.

HEALING

Christians believe that God wants us to have eternal life forever and an abundant life now. To some Christians it seems clear that abundant life must include health. They are convinced that when Isaiah writes, "by his [Christ's] wounds we are healed" (Isa. 53:5), he promises physical healing now for believers. These Christians teach that all a believer has to do is to claim the promise of healing by faith, and healing will surely come.

Other Christians disagree. They point out that all believers surely will be healed of every physical infirmity, but such healing is only assured in our resurrection. And they argue that "abundant life" cannot be summed up in one's physical condition or economic standing. Abundant life is found in intimate relationship with Jesus. And the sick may have an especially close relationship with the Lord.

There have been other differences as well. Some Christians are sure that counting on God for healing means refusing any help from doctors. Faith alone is required. Other Christians have no hesitancy about getting medical help, sure that God uses various means in accomplishing his good purposes and that one can see a doctor and still rely fully on the Lord.

While these views differ significantly, they also hold common ground. Christians all believe in a God who is able to heal. We may differ in our understanding of when and how he chooses to act, but none of us doubts that God can act in our here and now. We all pray about our needs, sure that the God who hears us really does care.

Given the common ground, what does the Bible say about healing?

In the Old Testament sickness and disease are often used as pictures of sin (Isa. 1:4–6). Healing is thus related to forgiveness and to relationship with the Lord (2 Chron. 7:14; Hos. 6:1). It is true, too, that sickness is at times a punishment for sin, so that healing comes with forgiveness (Exod. 15:26). Still, sickness is not always a punishment, and while physical health comes from God, God's Old Testament people saw nothing inappropriate in the use of medication (Isa. 1:6; 38:21; Jer. 51:8). What the Old Testament does criticize is King Asa who sought help "only from the physicians" and not from the Lord (2 Chron. 16:12).

Healing was a very significant part of Jesus' ministry, and it also played a part in the early ministry of the apostles. In the Gospels healing is often associated with the sick person's faith (Matt. 8:1–3; 9:20–22; Acts 5:16; 14:9). Yet other miracles of healing never mention such faith (Matt. 9:23–26; Mark 6:5; Acts 3:1–10; 8:7; 28:8).

Surprisingly, we find almost nothing about healing in the New Testament letters. Hebrews 12:13 speaks of healing in an inner, spiritual sense. James calls on the sick to let the elders pray over them (James 5:14). And in 1 Corinthians 12, Paul lists healing as one of the spiritual gifts. But the idea that Christians can claim physical healing as a right is never taught explicitly in the New Testament.

Isaiah 53:5 speaks of healing by Jesus' wounds, and Matthew 8:17 says that was fulfilled in Jesus' acts of healing while on earth. While the primary focus in Isaiah is clearly on spiritual healing, the Matthew reference does indicate that spiritual and physical healing are linked. Does this pair of verses then indicate that physical healing is promised to God's people today as a right won by the blood of Jesus? If so, it is hard to explain what happened when New Testament believers became ill. Paul suffered from a serious disease (probably affecting his eyes). He "pleaded with the Lord to take it away" (2 Cor. 12:8). But God did not. Instead Paul was given grace to enable him to live with his disability. Timothy had chronic stomach trouble. Paul advises him to "use a little wine because of your stomach and your frequent illnesses" and stop drinking water only (1 Tim. 5:23). Epaphroditus, coming to Paul from Philippi, sickened and almost died. After the recovery of Epaphroditus, Paul writes, "Indeed he was ill and almost died. But God had mercy on him, and not on him only but also on me, to spare me sorrow upon sorrow" (Phil. 2:27).

What can we conclude? We see God as healer, and we depend on the Lord when we become ill. We bring this need to the Lord and pray with confidence. We know that God hears and that in his love he will do what is best for us. However, we pray realizing that we have no guarantee of healing in this world. All that Christianity guarantees is that there is healing in eternity and that in this world God will act in our lives for our good.

HEAVEN AND HELL

Christians share the conviction that humans are ever-living beings. Our lives and our significance cannot be summed up in the few brief years we spend on planet earth. Every person will exist, self-conscious, self-aware, uniquely himself or herself, forever and ever.

The question, "Where will you spend eternity?" makes poignant sense to Christians. Each human being has an eternity to spend.

The traditional Christian belief, rooted in Scripture's revelation of the future, is that human beings will spend eternity in either heaven or hell. Despite this common conviction, Christian images of heaven and hell are often uncertain and cloudy. We are sure that heaven is a place or state of blessedness and that hell is linked with torment, but few Christians have a clear idea of the meaning of biblical words linked with eternal destiny. To understand heaven and hell, we need to go back to Scripture and survey its teaching.

The Old Testament does not use "heaven" to indicate a place where the believing dead will go. But the Old Testament does look beyond time to eternity. Then this material creation will be dissolved and replaced by a new heaven and a new earth (Isa. 65:17). And God's people will share this fresh creation. "As the new heavens and the new earth that I will make will endure before me . . . so will your name and descendants endure" (Isa. 66:22). The Old Testament suggests a life that stretches out beyond history, a life that will endure forever.

Older English versions of the Old Testament do mention hell. Usually the Hebrew word so translated is a poetic term, a synonym for *grave.* So our Old Testament references to hell should be taken simply to mean the grave or death. Old Testament passages such as Psalm 86:13, which speaks of deliverance from *sheol,* mean rescue from deadly danger, not from eternal punishment.

Yet the Old Testament does forecast resurrection for the saved and the lost. In Daniel's words, "Multitudes who sleep in the dust of the earth will awake: some to everlasting life, others to shame and everlasting contempt" (Dan. 12:2). But the destiny of neither the saved nor the lost is described.

The New Testament like the Old speaks of "the heavens," meaning the created universe. But "heaven" is a timeless spiritual realm, existing even as does the physical realm. It is in this spiritual realm that our treasures lie (Matt. 6:20). It is in this spiritual realm that we will receive our rewards (Matt. 5:12; Luke 6:23); there our names are inscribed (Luke 10:20). Our true home is there (Heb. 12:22; Rev. 21:1), and one day Jesus will again break through every barrier when he comes again (1 Thess. 4:17; 2 Thess. 1:7). While we may not be inaccurate to think of heaven as the future abode of the saved or to think of going to heaven when we die, it is important for us to realize that heaven is a significant term in Scripture with far greater meaning that we sometimes give it.

The New Testament uses three different Greek words to refer to hell. *Gehenna* (Matt. 5:22, 29–30; 10:28; 18:9; 23:15, 33; Mark 9:43, 45, 47; Luke 12:5; James 3:6) is always translated "hell" in the New International Version. *Tartaros* is rendered "hell" in 2 Peter 2:4. This is the Greek word for the mythical abyss where rebellious gods were confined. *Hades* (Matt. 11:23; 16:18; Luke 10:15; 16:23; Acts 2:27, 31; 1 Cor. 15:55; Rev. 1:18; 6:8; 20:13–14) is sometimes translated as "death" or "the grave," and sometimes it is simply transliterated "hades."

How are we to understand these passages and the different words associated with hell? Hades (except where used in the sense of the grave in Matt. 11:23, Luke 10:15, and Acts 2:27, 31) indicates a temporary state, a residence for those awaiting final judgment. We see this clearly in Luke 16, where Jesus tells the story of a rich man and a beggar, Lazarus. Each died, and the rich man found himself in hades "where he was in torment" (Luke 16:23). The beggar was comforted in Abraham's arms. In the story Jesus uses powerful words to describe the condition of those awaiting judgment: They are "in agony in this fire" and in "torment." And between hades and the place of the blessed dead there lay an uncrossable gulf.

Many believe that when Jesus rose, he released the saved from their place of waiting and sent them directly into God's presence (Eph. 4:8–10; 1 Thess. 4:14). In Revelation's portrayal of that last judgment, condemnation awaits those who are in hades when the "dead were judged according to what they had done as recorded in the books" (Rev. 20:11–15).

As for *gehenna*, it was used both by the rabbis in New Testament times and by Jesus to indicate the place of final punishment. In Jesus' descriptions, it is often associated with fire (Matt. 5:22; 18:9; Mark 9:43). And Jesus speaks of a place of "eternal fire" where human beings will be punished with "the devil and his angels" for whom it was prepared (Matt. 25:41).

The most powerful portrait of eternal judgment is found in Revelation. There the lost are viewed in a "fiery lake of burning sulfur" (Rev. 19:20) where "they will be tormented day and night for ever and ever" (Rev. 20:10, 14).

However Christians may have viewed heaven and hell, it is clear from the Bible that each human being does have endless existence ahead. For those who know God and have responded to him with faith in the gospel, a place in heaven is reserved. For those who continue faithless, rejecting the testimony to God provided in creation as well as in the gospel, hell awaits.

HISTORY

Christianity is uniquely a historic faith. Other faiths rest on nature or on mystical experience or on human reason to discover God. Christianity insists that God has revealed himself in historical events and through an inspired book, which reports and interprets those events. In a unique way, Christian doctrines are historical events or historical interpretations.

When we say "history," most of us simply mean those past events that human beings have witnessed and reported. When we read history, we read not only bare reported facts but also certain facts selected and discussed by historians to provide us with an interpretation of the past. For most of our era Christians have maintained a simple view of history. We believe that God has acted in space and time. We believe that he actually spoke to Abraham. We believe that God intervened to bring plagues on Egypt and that a fiery, cloudy pillar led Israel across the wilderness. We believe that the eternal Son of God took on flesh, was born of a virgin, taught and worked miracles in Palestine, and after his death on the cross was raised from the dead. These events, the meanings of which are interpreted by Scripture, actually took place in space and time, and thus history itself provides a firm foundation for our faith.

In this century, some theologians have raised questions about the simple view of history expressed above. *Historie* was used by some theologians to describe objective, detached research into what actually happened. *Geschichte* was used to mean a study designed to discover the impact of the past on us today, that is, to determine its personal significance. The personal significance of the crucifixion of Jesus will be different for the Christian (who sees that death as a sacrifice for his sin) and the non-Christian (who may see it as nothing more than a miscarriage of justice). The two agree on the *historie*, but not on the *geschichte*. This approach has been both helpful and destructive. It is helpful because it reminds us that we cannot look back at the events on which Christian faith rests and view them simply as dead facts. These historic events call us to respond today, for in them we come face to face with God, and in them we hear his voice. You and I are to grasp the significance of what God has done for his people in the past and are to respond with faith and obedience.

The approach has been destructive because it has provided a wedge used by some to suggest that "salvation history" (*geschichte*) is different in nature from other history in that the events of salvation history need not actually have happened. Using this approach, some have tried to discard such basic Christian beliefs as the virgin birth and the literal resurrection of Jesus. Others have tried to rediscover a "historical Jesus" stripped of the New Testament's theological interpretations. Whatever we may say about this historical/theological school of thought, we have to note that its views differ completely from what Christians have believed through the ages.

What do we believe? Christians throughout the ages have believed that Scripture's report and interpretation of the past is trustworthy. The recorded events really did happen in our space and in our time. And the meaning of the recorded events is faithfully expressed so that we are able to understand the meaning of these events for you and me today as well as for the generation that witnessed them. Ours is a historic faith. In Scripture we have a trustworthy description of what really has happened. And in Scripture we have a reliable interpretation, explaining the meaning of God's actions and calling us to faith in the one who has revealed himself to us by his actions in our world.

HOLY SPIRIT

Christians honor and worship the Holy Spirit as God, the third Person of our Trinity. ◗ **TRINITY**

Christians differ in their understanding of some of the Holy Spirit's works, but we recognize him as God and affirm his importance in Christian experience. While our differences tend to attract attention, our areas of agreement are far greater and more significant.

The differences among us focus on two areas. One area is that of spiritual gifts. Some Christians believe that the visible gifts of the Spirit, such as tongues and healing, are given and operate today. Other Christians argue that the visible gifts were intended to authenticate early Christianity and ceased when the last book of our New Testament was written. The second area of difference is that of spirituality. Some Christians believe that after salvation, the Holy Spirit performs a second, special work that is important for personal holiness. Other Christians believe that the Holy Spirit enters fully into the life of the believer on conversion and that spiritual growth and personal holiness are simply matters of learning to "walk in the Spirit." The differences are explored in other articles in this book. ◗ **SPIRITUAL GIFTS, HOLINESS, SPIRITUAL-ITY** This article will focus on those things that Christians commonly understand about the unique and wonderful person, God's Holy Spirit.

The Holy Spirit, a divine person. Some people have suggested that the Holy Spirit should be understood simply as the "divine influence" or as God's "animating power." Such attempts to rob the biblical Holy Spirit of personhood and deity fail simply because they are so clearly contradicted by Scripture.

When Jesus spoke of the Holy Spirit, our Lord chose the personal pronoun "he," even though "spirit" in Greek is a neuter word (John 14:17, 26; 16:13–15). Christ promised to send his disciples "another Comforter" when he returned to heaven, and he identified the Spirit as the promised one. The word in Scripture for "another" is *allos*, a Greek term meaning "another *of the same kind*" in distinction to *hereros*, meaning "another of a different kind." Christ, the second person of the Godhead, was to send the Spirit, equally God, to live within those who believe.

There are many other indications that the Spirit is a Person and not a force or influence. The Holy Spirit knows and understands (Rom. 8:27; 1 Cor. 2:11). The Holy Spirit communicates in words (1 Cor. 2:13). The Holy Spirit acts and chooses (1 Cor. 12:11). The Spirit loves (Rom. 15:30), can be insulted (Heb. 10:29), can be lied to (Acts 5:3), can be resisted (Acts 7:51), and can be grieved (Eph. 4:30). The Holy Spirit teaches (John 14:26), intercedes (Rom. 8:26), convicts (John 16:7–8), bears witness (John 15:26), and guides (John 16:13). Each of these activities testifies to the fact that the Spirit is a person, not an impersonal influence.

The Holy Spirit is also a divine person. The Bible clearly identifies the Spirit as God by the titles it gives him. He is the eternal Spirit (Heb. 9:14), the Spirit of Christ (1 Peter 1:11), the Spirit of the Lord (Isa. 11:2), the Spirit of the Sovereign Lord (Isa. 61:1), the Spirit of the Father (Matt. 10:20) and the Spirit of the Son (Gal. 4:6). No other being apart from God bears such divine titles.

The deity of the Spirit is shown in other ways. He is omnipresent, as only God can be (Ps. 139:7; 1 Cor. 12:13). He is all powerful (Luke 1:35; Rom. 8:11). He was an agent in Creation (Gen. 1:2; Ps. 104:30) and has power to work miracles (Matt. 12:28; 1 Cor. 12:9–11). The Spirit is the one who brings us new birth (John 3:6; Titus 3:5). It was the Spirit who raised Jesus from the dead and who brings God's resurrection life to you and me (Rom. 8:11).

The Holy Spirit can be blasphemed (Matt. 12:31–32; Mark 3:28–29), and lying to the Holy Spirit is said to be lying to God (Acts 5:3–4).

The biblical testimony is clear. The Holy Spirit is a person. And the Holy Spirit is God.

The Holy Spirit through church history. The Bible presents the Holy Spirit as God. Yet despite the many passages that refer to him, all our questions about the Spirit's role and his relationships to the other members of the Trinity are not fully answered. ♦ **TRINITY**

While the Spirit was honored as God from the earliest days of the church, the doctrine of the Spirit developed gradually, as the first centuries of our era focused on attempts to define the divine/human nature of Jesus. It was not until A.D. 381 that the simple creedal statement, "I believe in the Holy Spirit," was more clearly defined by adding "the Lord and Giver of Life; who proceeds from the Father, who with the Father and Son together is worshiped; who spoke by the prophets."

In the Middle Ages the Catholic church developed the notion that God's grace was communicated to believers through the church, not directly through the working of the Spirit. The church's emphasis was on ritual and sacrament as the means through which God worked. This belief that God's grace was mediated through the clergy meant a de-emphasis on the Holy Spirit. The church even denied that the Spirit could teach Christians directly through the Word: Scripture had to be interpreted by an infallible church.

The Protestant Reformation placed little emphasis on the Holy Spirit. But in challenging many assumptions of contemporary Catholi-cism, it opened the door to dramatic changes in understanding of the Spirit's role. The Reformers denied that the clergy mediated between humans and God: The Spirit was recognized as one who works directly within our hearts. The Reformers denied that works bring salvation: It is the Spirit who regenerates and brings new life to those who believe. And the Reformers, insisting that the Scriptures are an infallible authority in faith and morals, honored the Spirit as the one who illuminates the Bible for the laity and clergy alike. Although the Protestant Reformers did not focus their attention on the Spirit, they acknowledged him as the one who draws people to God, who effects regeneration and sanctification, and who provides believers with power to live holy lives.

It was, however, the great revivals in England and the United States in the eighteenth century that drew concentrated attention to the Holy Spirit. First, God's power was manifested stunningly in these revivals, and the Spirit was recognized as the source. Second, the Wesleyan (holiness) movement emphasized the role of the Holy Spirit. In America the holiness movement spawned new denominations (such as the Church of the Nazarene), each of which stressed the working of the Holy Spirit. It was this revivalism and the holiness movement that drew the attention of theologians and scholars and led to reexamination of Christian beliefs about the Holy Spirit.

In the twentieth century the Pentecostal or charismatic movement further emphasized the Holy Spirit, often with an emphasis on visible gifts like speaking in tongues. Despite some excesses, the charismatic movement, which has touched all branches of Christianity including the Catholic church, should be understood primarily as a positive reemphasis on the power available to believers in the Holy Spirit. Often charismatic emphasis has resulted in spontaneous worship and enthusiastic evangelism.

So the Christian understanding of the Holy Spirit has grown and changed throughout the ages. Yet, as in the case of other Christian beliefs, our understanding of the Holy Spirit remains rooted in truths accepted by believers throughout the ages. Still, our appreciation for the Spirit and for all that he brings to us is perhaps greater today than in earlier times.

The cosmic role of the Holy Spirit. When we probe Scripture for the nature of the Holy Spirit's activities, we discover a complex and multifaceted ministry. While there are many ways these might be organized, we will simply consider both the Spirit's cosmic ministries as they relate to the context of God's plan and his personal ministries as they relate to the personal experience of human beings.

The Spirit's cosmic ministries focus on creation, revelation, and the Incarnation. Genesis 1 suggests that both Jesus and the Spirit are active in creation. Other passages link the Spirit to the origin of life (Job 33:4; Ps. 104:30) and to preservation of the created order (Ps. 104:29–30).

The Spirit often is linked to revelation. Old Testament passages such as 2 Samuel 23:2 and Micah 3:8 link the prophet's ministry as divine spokesperson to the Spirit of the Lord. The New Testament attributes a number of Old Testament verses to the Spirit (Matt. 22:43; Acts 1:16; 4:25), and Peter writes that "prophecy never had its origin in the will of man, but men spoke from God as they were carried along by the Holy Spirit" (2 Peter 1:21). Those who preached the New Testament gospel likewise did so "by the Holy Spirit sent from heaven" (1 Peter 1:12). ♦
REVELATION

The Spirit was intimately involved in the incarnation of Jesus and in the events of his life. Mary conceived by the Holy Spirit's act (Luke 1:35). The Spirit filled and led Jesus during his life on earth (Luke 4:1; John 3:34), and the Spirit's power was expressed in Christ's miracles (Matt. 12:28). Christ's death was a sacrifice offered to God by the Spirit (Heb. 9:14), and his resurrection was effected by the Spirit's power (Rom. 1:4; 8:11; 1 Peter 3:18).

As an active agent in creation, revelation, and the Incarnation, the

Holy Spirit has had a vital role in carrying out the cosmic plans and purposes of God the Father.

The interpersonal roles of the Holy Spirit. The ministries of the Spirit that have rightly drawn the most attention are interpersonal. The New Testament, and to some extent the Old Testament, shows that the Spirit is intimately involved in activities that vitally affect human beings. We perhaps can sum up these ministries under three headings. The Holy Spirit has ministries (1) that relate to the unsaved, (2) that are linked with initial salvation, and (3) that affect the experience of believers. Because most of these ministries are discussed elsewhere in this book, this discussion will simply survey the various interpersonal ministries.

Some ministries of the Spirit relate to the unsaved. Both testaments seem to suggest that the Holy Spirit operates in human society to restrain the full expression of sin (Gen. 6:3; 2 Thess. 2:6). Most important, however, is the work of the Spirit in convicting those who do not yet believe. Jesus defined this work in John 16:8-11, and it seems to involve presenting certain basic gospel truths in clear light. Whether or not people choose to believe, the Spirit confronts human beings with truth about sin, righteousness, and judgment.

Some ministries of the Spirit are linked with initial salvation. The Holy Spirit is the one who regenerates us (brings us new birth). While the Word of God provides the content of the message (James 1:18; 1 Peter 1:23), the Spirit gives life (Titus 3:5). At that time we are also baptized by the Spirit, as that term is defined in 1 Corinthians 12:13. While the word *baptize* is given a different meaning in some traditions, Paul uses it to define that act by which the Spirit of God unites believers to Jesus and to one another in Christ's mystical body. ◆ **BODY, BAPTIZE**

A number of passages speak of believers as sealed by the Spirit (2 Cor. 1:22; Eph. 1:13; 4:30). The seal is a mark of divine ownership and also suggests preservation and security. The Holy Spirit is the one who supervises our entrance into eternal life and who effects our union with Jesus.

Most of the personal ministries of the Holy Spirit focus on his work in the lives of believers. And, as *A Contemporary Wesleyan Theology* says, "It is evident in the teachings of Paul that the Holy Spirit is now present in every believer" (p. 427). Romans 8:9 and 1 Corinthians 6:19 make it plain that even unspiritual believers are no exception. The presence of the Spirit means that the source of our power and enablement is now available to us. The Old Testament speaks of the Spirit operating within believers (Gen. 41:38; Num. 27:18; Dan. 4:8) and falling upon them to give special enablement (Judg. 3:10; 1 Sam. 10:9–10; Judg. 14:6; 1 Sam. 16:13). But Jesus suggests that today our relationship with the Spirit is new and different (John 14:17; 7:39). Today the Spirit is with us as the source of overflowing spiritual life and joy (John 7:37–38), to be our helper in every need (John 14:15–17, 25–26; 15:26–27; 16:7–15). The Spirit opens our eyes to the meaning of what Jesus taught, and he leads us into truth (John 14:25–26; 16:12–13; 1 Cor. 2:10, 12–14). The Spirit guides our steps (Rom. 8:4–5), assists in prayer (Rom. 8:26), and is the one who transforms us toward Christlikeness (2 Cor. 3:18).

A number of biblical terms are associated with the overflowing presence and power of the Holy Spirit in the Christian. Some people take these terms as equivalent, and some argue for distinctions. But all of these terms (*baptism, filling, receiving, anointing,* and *pouring out of the Spirit*) communicate the exciting reality. God the Holy Spirit is present within us that he might be active in and through our personalities. It is our responsibility and opportunity to rely on the Holy Spirit, walking in step with him and responding to his promptings (Rom. 8:3–11; Gal. 5:16–18). ◆ SPIRITUALITY

Two biblical themes explore what the Spirit does in us and what he does through us. The fruit of the Spirit (Gal. 5:22–23) represent the transformation of the human personality in such qualities as love, peace, patience, and the like. We who are at birth corrupted by sin are progressively transformed as we remain close to Jesus and responsive to God's Spirit (John 15; 2 Cor. 3:18). The moral qualities and virtues indicated by fruit are the primary evidence of the influence and power of the Holy Spirit within us. ◆ TRANSFORMATION, SANCTIFICATION, HOLINESS

What the Holy Spirit does through us is expressed in the concept of spiritual gifts. The Spirit equips each believer with special enablements, which the New Testament calls "gifts." Not only do these various enablements make it possible for us to contribute to the spiritual welfare of others but they also may relate to our witness to non-Christians. ◆ SPIRITUAL GIFTS

We are convinced that the Spirit is the one who both produces the fruit of goodness in our lives and enables us to serve God and others. Because we rely on the Spirit to enable us, we understand God's commands as invitations to experience the Spirit's power and never as threatening demands. Because we know the Spirit is present to empower us, we respond to God's call to holiness with joy, sure that the Lord himself will lift us beyond our inadequacies.

Christians, then, recognize and honor the Holy Spirit as one of three persons of the Trinity. The Spirit had a role in those cosmic events represented by creation and the Incarnation, and he had a critical role in revelation. But most of what we know of the Spirit's work focuses on his interpersonal ministries. The Spirit restrains evil and enlightens everyone about basic gospel elements. The Spirit is the one who brings us God's new life and unites us to Jesus. And the Spirit is the one who ministers to believers. God's Spirit leads, guides, and empowers. God's Spirit works the inner transformation that produces moral fruit. And God's Spirit gifts believers with those enablements that make it possible for us to have a spiritual impact on each other's lives.

Although the differences about aspects of the Spirit's operation are important, they pale to insignificance when compared to those exciting truths that Christians hold in common. The Spirit *is* within each of us. Because the Spirit is present within us, you and I can live vital, victorious Christian lives. The presence of the Holy Spirit means that we can face our future with hope and confidence. The Spirit will lift us as we rely on him, and he will help us reach our full potential in Jesus.

HOLINESS

It becomes God's people to be holy, for God is holy. This message fills both testaments and is succinctly stated in passages like 1 Peter 1:14–16. Peter calls on us "as obedient children" not to "conform to the evil desires you had when you lived in ignorance. But just as he who called you is holy, so be holy in all you do; for it is written: 'Be holy, because I am holy.'"

In view of the Bible's emphasis, it is not surprising that Christians of all traditions have a concern for holiness. True, we don't all agree on how Christians reach out toward holiness. ◗ SANCTIFICATION, PERFECTION We do agree that we are to *be* holy. What are the characteristics of the holy life that we are called to?

Holiness in the Old Testament. Hebrew words that are translated "holy" and "holiness" in the Old Testament have a common root, meaning "set apart." Anything that is holy is removed from the realm of the common and moved to the sphere of the sacred.

God himself is holy, and he is the focus of all that is sacred. Thus in the Old Testament *holy* is a technical religious term used to describe persons, places, times, and things that are considered sacred because they are consecrated to the Lord. The seventh day was holy (Gen. 2:3; Exod. 20:8–11). Mount Sinai, where God appeared in fire to give the Ten Commandments, was holy (Exod. 19:23). Everything associated with worship and sacrifice was holy. Indeed, because Israel had been chosen by God and set apart as his own special possession, the nation and the Jewish people were considered holy (Deut. 7:6; 14:2, 21).

A central aspect of Old Testament holiness is the separation of the consecrated from the common. Nothing holy is ever to be used in a secular way. The holy was reserved for God's use alone — forever.

Holiness in Israel was both cultic and moral. The cultic included all religious rituals and all the morally neutral practices prescribed in biblical law. For instance, "Do not cook a young goat in its mother's milk" is a morally neutral command. Yet the godly Jew carefully observed such laws and saw them as a holiness issue. The person who lived a life set apart to God kept the cultic as well as moral rules taught in Old Testament law. And Old Testament priests were to "distinguish between the holy and the profane, between the unclean and the clean" in order to "teach the Israelites all the decrees the LORD has given them through Moses" (Lev. 10:10).

While a number of Mosaic statutes are cultic, many Old Testament commands display moral content. Such commands are directly linked with God's holiness. It is because "I, the LORD your God, am holy" (Lev. 19:2) that Israel is to be cleansed of idolatry, theft, lying, fraud, slander, and revenge. It is because God is holy that the community is to be marked by love for neighbors.

All this is essential because Israel's God is morally perfect. He is always faithful in his own commitment to good. So God's moral demands on his people mirror his own character as a righteous person. It is because God is holy that we who are his people *must* be holy, remembering that the Lord will demonstrate his holiness by judgment on sinners. "The LORD Almighty will be exalted by his justice, and the holy God will show himself holy by his righteousness" (Isa. 5:16).

In obedience to the cultic demands of the law, Israel demonstrated her identity as a sacred people, set apart from all others to be God's own. In obedience to the moral demands of the law, Israel mirrored the character of the God who had made her his own. It was unthinkable that those who claim relationship with a holy God should be anything but holy in their own moral behavior.

Holiness in the New Testament. One frequent use of the word *holy* in the New Testament is to identify God's people as his "saints," literally his "holy ones." The name reflects our standing: In Jesus we are set apart to God. But the name also describes our calling: We are to live lives of love and moral purity. We are to *be* holy, for he is holy. The most frequent use of the word *holy* in the New Testament is to identify God's Spirit as the Holy Spirit. This is only in part because the Spirit is by nature holy.

Perhaps more important, the name reminds us that God's Spirit is the source of our transformation; his is the energy that enables the Christian to live a holy life. ◗ **HOLY SPIRIT, TRANSFORMATION, SANCTIFICATION**

When we look through the New Testament to discover the nature of the holy life to which we are called, we find a significant difference exists between the testaments. Holiness in the Old Testament called for a strict separation between the secular and sacred. The clean can never come in contact with the unclean, and Israel must fiercely guard its differences from surrounding nations. Cultic practices undoubtedly were designed in part to stress Israel's uniqueness as a people set apart from all other nations on the earth.

But Christians today find themselves in a very different setting. We believers are not in a separate nation; we are scattered in tiny communities throughout human society. We live *in* the world and yet are not of it. Paul even wrote to the Corinthians to say, "I have written you in my letter not to associate with sexually immoral people — not at all meaning the people of this world who are immoral, or the greedy and swindlers, or idolators. In that case you would have to leave this world" (1 Cor. 5:9–10). The holiness to which we are called is not found in isolating ourselves from contact with the secular or unclean.

In fact, New Testament holiness is a dynamic concept. It is a moral and spiritual purity, a vibrant love that is lived out in contact with the present evil world and with the people who populate it. Our holiness is modeled on Jesus' holiness, for our Lord maintained his purity even when his association with "publicans and sinners" stimulated the criticism of his isolationist religious opponents.

We sense the nature of this dynamic holiness in many New Testament passages. When Peter calls us to "be holy in all you do" (1 Peter 1:15), he goes on to explain. In chapter 2, he shows how those who are "a chosen people, a royal priesthood, a holy nation, a people belonging to God" are to live to glorify our Lord. We are "as strangers and aliens in the world, to abstain from sinful desires, which war against your souls. Live such good lives among the pagans that, although they accuse you of doing wrong, they may see your good deeds and glorify God on the day he visits us" (1 Peter 2:9–12). We fulfill our calling to holiness by good lives and good deeds, ruled not by sinful desires but by the will of God.

Paul's epistles reveal the same emphasis. In Colossians, Paul dismisses ritualistic and ascetic practices as having no value in the Christian life (Col. 2:20–23). Holiness is found in the inner life, in putting aside our earthly nature and old self to put on that new self, which is renewed in the Creator's image (Col. 3:5–11). Our holiness is expressed in the "compassion, kindness, humility, gentleness and patience," in the forgiveness and the love that Christ makes possible as we follow him (Col. 3:12–14).

The conclusion we draw is significant. New Testament holiness does not call for a rigid isolation of the sacred from the secular. Instead the New Testament's call to holiness is a call to express our relationship with God, and indeed the Lord's own character, in the ordinary processes of life.

There is another shift in emphasis between Old Testament and New Testament views of holiness. In the Old Testament cultic holiness labeled special persons (priests), places (the temple), things (the altar, temple furniture), and times (the Sabbath, the festivals) as the holy. In the New Testament the holy is intensely personal. "Don't you know," Paul writes powerfully, "that you yourselves are God's temple and that God's Spirit lives in you?" (1 Cor. 3:16). In the New Testament holiness is concerned with what God's Spirit does in and through believers. Thus in the New Testament holiness is always rooted in personal relationship with Jesus and in relationship with the Spirit whom Jesus has sent to be within us.

Conclusions. In both testaments holiness is a matter of consecration to the Lord. In the Old Testament holiness was both cultic and moral. The cultic was expressed by strict separation of the sacred from the secular, while the moral was a matter of personal commitment to God's moral will.

In the New Testament the cultic is set aside, and teaching about holiness focuses on personal character. Also in the New Testament holiness is not expressed by isolation from the secular or profane. Instead holiness is a dynamic love and goodness to be lived out in the ordinary life of believers, expressed in every daily activity and relationship.

In both testaments what is holy is set apart to God for his sole use. But in the New Testament it is only persons — you and I — who are so honored. You and I have been united to Jesus now, and God's Holy Spirit is planted within us. As we respond to the Spirit and rely on him, the Spirit acts within us to make us more Christlike, better able to *be* holy, although holiness can only be represented fully in God's own person and character.

What is holiness for you and me? Simply to be fully committed to doing God's will and to express his love as the Holy Spirit of God fills our lives, enabling us to live as Jesus lived in this world.

HOPE

Hope belongs uniquely to Christians. Our hope is not a desperate wish or romantic dream; our hope is a settled confidence, a sure expectation.

Hope in the Old Testament. In the Old Testament the Hebrew words for "hope" not only call us to look ahead eagerly, but also to be patient. In fact, "wait" is one way to translate *yahal*, a word for hope that dominates the Psalms and later prophets. The fulfillment of our hope lies in the future. We, as believers, look forward with confidence, yet we realize that, for a time, we are simply to wait.

The Old Testament does not clearly spell out just what believers are waiting for. It focuses our attention on the basis for our confidence about the future. That basis is our personal relationship with God. As the psalmist says, "LORD, what do I look for? My hope is in you" (Ps. 39:7).

The Old Testament witnesses constantly to a God who is our Deliverer. We believe that God will act to save those who hope in him. Because God is who he is, we can wait in him. No matter what our circumstances, "I will always have hope" (Ps. 71:14). Because "the LORD preserves the faithful," we who hope in him can "be strong and take heart" (Ps. 31:24).

In the Old Testament, then, "hope" is essentially a word about God and our relationship with him. Hope is a word overflowing with trust. We never know what is ahead for us, but we do know the Lord. That is enough. "Put your hope in the LORD," the Scriptures invite us, "for with the LORD is unfailing love, and with him is full redemption" (Ps. 130:7).

Hope in the New Testament. The core of Christian confidence is in our relationship with God. We are convinced that God is a faithful person who loves us deeply and who guards our future. But the New Testament takes us a step beyond the Old Testament in explaining our hope. In both testaments "hope" is something good that we must wait for. But in the letters of the apostles, the mystery of what God has in store for us is unveiled. It is a sudden burst of light; the good things God has planned for us are brightly illumined.

Resurrection is foremost among the good things we confidently expect and hope for. The Book of Acts glows with the promise of bodily resurrection (cf. Acts 2:26; 23:6; 24:15; 26:6–7). Since it is our destiny to be raised with the Lord, Christians do not have to "grieve like the rest of men who have no hope" when death takes a loved one (1 Thess. 4:13).

Many exciting truths are linked with the hope that resurrection gives us. Jesus himself someday will appear or "resurrect," in all his now-hidden glory (Rom. 5:2, 4, 5; Titus 2:13). This, Jesus' return, is often called our "blessed hope." Our bodies, and creation itself, will be released from their bondage to decay (Rom. 8:20, 24). When Jesus comes, we will experience fully all it means to have eternal life. We will enter into the inheritance that God now guards for us, his children (Titus 1:1; 3:7; 1 Pet. 1:3; 1 John 3:2, 3).

But our hope is not limited to what will happen at history's end. The New Testament speaks of a present, progressive growth in holiness. We are being transformed even now, increasingly taking on Jesus' likeness (2 Cor. 3:18). Because God the Holy Spirit is at work in our lives, we as Christians have a "righteousness for which we [can] hope" (Gal. 5:5). Because Jesus is in our lives, we "hope for all the glorious things to come" to us because of him (Col. 1:27). A relationship with God, through Jesus, has the power to transform our tomorrows as well as our eternity.

Hope in our lives and character. John called attention to the fact that our destiny is to be like Jesus. John writes that "everyone who has this hope in him purifies himself, even as he [Jesus] is pure" (1 John 3:3). We're told that "faith and love spring from the hope that is stored up for you in heaven" (Col. 1:5) and that they rest "on the hope of eternal life, which God, who does not lie, promised" (Titus 1:2).

Peter gives us a beautiful picture of the impact of hope in our lives. He pictures the situation in which suffering and difficulties come, and then he reminds us to be "prepared to give an answer to everyone who asks you to give the reason for the hope that you have" (1 Peter 3:15). The image of a quiet confidence that transcends circumstances (and thus stuns the unbelieving observers) gives us a deep insight into the nature of Christian hope. Because our hope — our confidence, our expectation of good things ahead — is anchored solidly in our relationship with Jesus, we have a deep sense of joy and a positive outlook even when personal tragedies come (Rom. 12:12; 1 Thess. 1:3).

So you can see why hope "belongs uniquely to us Christians." Hope, as a quiet confidence and assurance about the future and as a positive outlook that helps us wait out our troubles patiently, is possible only because we know and believe that God is and that he loves us. Only our relationship with God, a God who cares, who saves, and who has good things in store for us, enables us to have hope.

HUMANITY

It has been said that the most important questions anyone can ask are these three: "Who are we? Where did we come from? Where are we going?" The answers that you and I give to these questions, the beliefs we hold about them, will surely shape our lives and our destinies. Yet today there is a growing gap between the answers given by Christians and the answers given by non-believers.

Naturalistic answers. Naturalists believe that everything must be explained as the result of some natural process that has taken place within the material universe. Naturalistic answers to our three questions (whether given by "scientific" humanists or ideological humanists) ultimately downgrade humankind. At best they view human beings as animals with rationality added — animals whose evolutionary source was some chance blending of amino acids and whose emergence was made possible only by further chance changes in genes and chromosomes. Struggling mindlessly upward through the evolutionary chain, the first human finally emerged when a spark of self-conscious intelligence flared in some shambling brute. Man the animal. His source is primeval muck and his destiny is in doubt, endangered by his power to bring about an atomic holocaust. But whether or not man the animal destroys himself, he will sooner or later die out as the universe exhausts itself and everything fades to endless dark.

This is the naturalistic view of humanity. And in this scheme only mankind counts. Human beings live for a brief moment; humans laugh, hope, rejoice, and suffer, and then they are forever gone. Whatever destiny the naturalists may see for humankind, all they can see for the individual is the sure death of awareness, the certain loss of personal identity in the grave.

However glowingly naturalists may describe their view of humankind, stripped of poetic phrases, humans are merely intelligent animals and the individual is nothing at all.

The Christian view of humanity challenges the chilling position of the naturalist at every point. We see a nobility in human beings, and we affirm the significance of every person. Our convictions about who we are, where we came from, and where we are going are rooted in the belief that the material universe is not all there is. We believe in a God who lies beyond what we can see and touch and feel, and we are sure that he has given us answers to our ultimate questions in Scripture. With such a starting point, we give completely different answers to questions about mankind.

Christian answers: Our origin is in the direct creative act of God. Genesis presents God as the creative source of the whole material universe. But most striking about the Creation story is the unique place given to humanity. According to Genesis, both the earth, with its rich vegetation and teeming animal life, and the star-filled heavens seem shaped simply to provide a place for human beings to live and work out their destiny. Human beings seem to be not only the crown of creation but also the focus of God's special concern. Looking back, the psalmist is filled with wonder at God's concern for humanity: "When I consider your heavens, the work of your fingers, the moon and the stars, which you have set in place, what is man that you are mindful of him, the son of man that you care for him? You made him a little lower than the heavenly beings and crowned him with glory and honor. You made him ruler over the works of your hands; you put everything under his feet" (Ps. 8:3–6).

Creation displays God's power and his complex mind. Yet God's heart is seen in his care for human beings, whom he shaped to be special and whom he has destined to rule.

Looking back into Genesis 1 and 2, we can see clues to our human identity. Some of the vital teachings of these chapters, which shape the Christian's view of humanity, are:

We are created beings. As creatures we must understand ourselves in relation to God. Mankind is not the measure of all things: We are measured by and against God. Human beings can never find fulfillment by rejecting the fact of our total dependence on God or the necessity of orienting our lives to him.

We are unique creations. A number of things underline this fact. God states his intention to create humanity "in our own image, in our likeness" (Gen. 1:28). All other things were fashioned with a spoken word. Genesis portrays God stooping to carefully blend earth's dust and then to breathe life into the shape he formed (Gen. 2:7). As special and unique, God determined to "let them [human beings] rule over" the rest of his creation (Gen. 1:26). ◆ DOMINION

So many wonders are implied in mankind's special creation. Clearly, human beings differ from the animals in kind, not in degree. As G. K. Chesterton once pointed out, it seems a truism to say that the most primitive men drew pictures of monkeys, while it seems a joke to suggest that the most intelligent of monkeys might draw a picture of a man. From the beginning human beings have been set apart, distinct and special.

Christians have differed about the exact meaning of the "image and likeness" that human beings share with God. But clearly implied are conscious selfhood, moral purity, and every quality of personhood that enables us to relate to each other and to God. ◆ IMAGE AND LIKENESS

Also implied in the Genesis account is a dual nature. We are of the earth, physical beings. And yet we have been touched by the breath of God, infused with the eternal. The eternal is, in fact, so firmly established in us that each human being has an eternal destiny: Physical death is not the end of our existence. This mixed mortal and spiritual identity, along with various terms used in Scripture to describe different human capacities, has led to debates about a supposed two-part (body/soul) or three-part (body/soul/spirit) human nature. ◆ SOUL AND SPIRIT, FLESH

But Christian differences over such issues are minor in view of those things on which we all agree. We believe human beings are special. Our origin is a direct creative act of God; everything about us is special because we are God's distinctive handiwork. The wonderful and the admirable in humankind can be traced back to God's gifts at our origin. It is here we find the explanation for artistic sensitivity, for civilization's accomplishments, and for human moral vision. We are who we are because we have been wonderfully made by the Creator of all.

Christian answers: Our natures have been distorted by the Fall.
Martin Luther looked back to Eden and sketched his vision of humanity fresh from the hand of God. His description of Adam underlines dark aspects of the human condition that you and I know today:

> That image of God in which Adam was created was a workmanship the most beautiful, the most excellent, and the most noble, while as yet no leprosy of sin adhered either to his reason or to his will. Then all his senses, both internal and external, were the most perfect and the most pure. His intellect was most clear, his memory most complete, and his will the most sincere, and accompanied with the most charming security, without any fear of death and without any care or anxiety whatsoever. To these internal perfections of Adam was added a power of body, and of all his limbs, so beautiful and so excellent, that therein he surpassed all other animate natural creatures. For I fully believe that, before his sin, the eyes of Adam were so clear and their sight so acute, that his powers of vision exceeded those of the lynx. Adam, I believe, being stronger than they, handled lions and bears, whose strength is so great, as we handle the young of any animal. I believe also that to Adam the sweetness and the virtue of the fruits which he ate were far beyond our enjoyment of them now. (*Commentary on Genesis*)

Genesis presents a bright picture of human origin and early existence. But Genesis also holds a dark vision. Genesis 3 describes a choice made by the first pair, a choice that has had a shattering impact on us all. Adam and Eve sinned, willfully violating God's command. As a result creation itself was cursed, and every human being born into our world was tainted. To some Christians that taint seems so deep that nothing human beings can do has value or merit. To others the effect of the first sin seems indirect: Human beings are born with moral potential, but they are born into cultures so warped by evil that even though they make their own free choice, they follow the pattern of Adam's failure. Whatever our differences in defining sin, Christians agree that sin infests our world. We can only understand ourselves and the human condition when we take sin into account and when we recognize it as the villain that has stolen our heritage and that brings each of us in danger of eternal loss. ▶ SIN

Naturalists look at human failings and see a remnant of the animal that mankind is struggling to leave behind. This is their explanation for evil; they have no explanation for good. Christians recognize the good in humanity as a reflection of the divine image. We realistically call the evil that distorts even our best efforts "sin," an inheritance from our first parents, expressed in our own willing choice to follow Adam in wandering from God's way.

Christian answers: We are the focus of God's purposes and love. Christians understand humanity by looking back at origins and by looking ahead at destiny. When we do look ahead, we see a redeemed humanity that will live in eternal fellowship with the Lord. God's original intention, to give human beings dominion, will be realized then. Hebrews notes that "at present we do not see everything subject to him [human beings]. But we see Jesus, who was made a little lower than the angels, now crowned with glory and honor" (Heb. 2:8–9).

God did not abandon humanity when Adam turned from him. God has not abandoned us now, even though every person who ever lived has retraced Adam's footsteps. Instead God has chosen to intervene. In Christ, God stepped into our world not only to unveil himself fully but also to die so that in Jesus' resurrection, you and I might be raised — perfected — to everlasting life.

Christians pause in wonder when we consider the purposes of God. We know that although God loves us, we are creatures. The Creator, not the creature, is the most important being in the universe. We realize that in caring for us, God has additional deep and wonderful goals in mind. Through the drama of Creation, Fall, and Redemption, we who are saved will be "for the praise of his glory" (Eph. 1:12). Through that "eternal purpose which God accomplished in Christ Jesus our Lord," he is making "known to the rulers and authorities in the heavenly realms" God's "manifold [multifaceted] wisdom" (Eph. 3:10–12). We know that God loves us immeasurably. Yet we also know that in stooping to redeem humanity, he is achieving in us vast and wonderful purposes. Our destiny is to enjoy and glorify God forever.

Thus Christians are convinced that both human origins and human destiny testify to mankind's significance, for both are linked eternally to

God. God is the center of all, and humankind finds meaning, purpose, and identity only by acknowledging that relationship with the Lord.

Christian answers: Each person has worth and value. So far we have looked at humanity: at the origins of our race and at its destiny. Only in understanding ourselves as the product of divine creation and as the focus of God's love and purpose can we have an adequate view of humankind. But Christians believe that the individual as well as the human race is important.

While our lives are transmitted to us by our parents, the Bible suggests that God is personally involved in the shaping process. David expresses his conviction that God shapes the individual and not just the race: "For you created my inmost being; you knit me together in my mother's womb. I praise you because I am fearfully and wonderfully made; your works are wonderful, I know that full well. My frame was not hidden from you when I was made in the secret place. When I was woven together in the depths of the earth, your eyes saw my unformed body. All the days ordained for me were written in your book before one of them came to be" (Ps. 139:13–16).

Jesus also emphasized the value of the individual. Human beings are free to seek God's kingdom and his righteousness simply because we are sure that our heavenly Father knows our needs and that we are valuable to him (Matt. 6:25–34). The whole created universe cannot be weighed against the value of an individual life (see Matt. 16:26; Luke 9:25).

One reason that the individual is so important is that each of us has an immortal nature. Life does not consist in plentiful possessions (Luke 12:15), for after the material universe flares out of existence, the individual will remain, aware and self-conscious. Thus each of us has an eternal destiny — an eternity to spend in fellowship with God (Matt. 19:29; 25:46; Luke 16:9; 18:30) or alienated from him (Matt. 7:13; 18:8; 19:29; 25:46; Luke 16:9; 18:30). ◗ HEAVEN AND HELL

This view of the significance of individuals realistically blends every aspect of our revealed identity. Humans, flesh and spirit, were created by God. We fell. The Fall distorted but did not destroy the image of himself that God had granted us. Fallen, we remain creatures of destiny, for God intends even now to lift human beings up to himself so that through Christ, God's purposes in us might be achieved and his love satisfied. So the individual is of central importance. Each person is lost but may be found; each is dead but may be made alive. Each person is deadly ill but still attracts the loving attention of Christ, our Great Physician. Jesus is the ultimate proof of individual significance, for Christ willingly gave his life so that we can have new life in him.

Summary. We cannot sum up everything significant about humanity in a few brief paragraphs. In some ways, half the articles in this book add insights about humanity in the image of God or humanity in the grip of sin. ♦ MIND, FLESH, SOUL AND SPIRIT, LOVE, SIN, DEPRAVITY While such topics may fascinate us and lead to fresh speculations about human nature, we must never lose sight of the central issues and the great, towering truths that Scripture unveils.

Ultimately, human beings are the product of either mindless chance or God's purposive creation. Ultimately, life is either meaningless or infused with a meaning to be found in God's purposes and goals. And ultimately, either each person lives for only a brief hour before his or her identity is swallowed up in death or each of us lives forever, endlessly aware of joy or torment.

For Christians the choice is clear. Where did humanity come from? From God, who created Adam and Eve. Who are we? We are flawed but still precious individuals, loved by God and shaped for his own good purposes. Where are we going? Into eternity where each of us will exist forever — in God's presence or banished from it — forever ourselves and by faith forever his own.

ILLUMINATION

Even our theology books sometimes fail to list this concept, but illumination is an important conviction, shared by Christians through the ages. Simply put, illumination refers to the work of the Holy Spirit in those who read, hear, or study the Bible. Illumination is God operating within us to show us the true or personal meaning of his Word.

Paul explains illumination quite simply in 1 Corinthians. He writes that the Spirit has unveiled even the deep things of God in human speech, in "words taught by the Spirit," and as for "the man without the Spirit [who] does not accept the things that come from the Spirit of God . . . he cannot understand them, because they are spiritually discerned" (1 Cor. 2:13–14).

This special work of the Holy Spirit isn't just for the theologian, struggling to master some deep concept. Actually, illumination is most often linked in the Bible to what we might call "heart understanding." Jonathan Edwards, an early-American preacher, links illumination with the application of God's truth to our lives: "This light and this only has its fruit in an universal holiness of life. No merely notional or speculative understanding of the doctrine of religion will ever bring us to this. But this light, as it reaches the bottom of the heart, changes the nature, so it will effectually dispose to an universal holiness" (Sermon on "Divine and Supernatural Life").

Because the Holy Spirit's illumination of our hearts through the Scripture is so important, Paul often prays for Christian growth in understanding and knowledge (1 Cor. 2; 2 Cor. 4:4–15; Eph. 1:17–19; Phil. 1:9–11; Col. 1:9–14).

In one sense illumination applies to the community of faith: The church through the ages has shared a common understanding of who God is and of what our relationship is to him. But in another, exciting sense illumination applies to you and to me. God guides us by his Word and Spirit. Wesley, England's great evangelist and founder of the Methodist movement, speaks of the joy he found in the Scriptures, opened to him through his relationship with Jesus:

> At any price, give me the book of God! I have it: here is knowledge enough for me. . . . I sit down alone: only God is here. In His presence I open, I read His book; for this end, to find the way to heaven. Is there a doubt about the meaning of what I read? Does anything appear dark or intricate? I lift up my heart to the Father of Lights: Lord, is it not thy word, "if any man lack wisdom, let him ask of God"? Thou has said, "If any be willing to do Thy will, he shall know. I am willing to do, let me know, Thy will." Then I search after and consider parallel passages of Scripture, comparing spiritual things with spiritual. I meditate thereon with all the attention and earnestness of which my mind is capable. If any doubt still remains, I consult those who are experienced in the things of God; and then the writings whereby, being dead, they yet speak. And what I thus learn, I do.

You and I, too, can open the book, commit ourselves to do what we discover there, and be sure of God's inner guidance in our lives. As Paul closes his thoughts, he gives us this unique assurance: "The spiritual man makes judgments about all things." You and I can face life with confidence, for "we have the mind of Christ" in the Word of God, unveiled within by his own Holy Spirit (1 Cor. 2:15–16).

As Augustine writes, "Behold, brethren, this great mystery: the sound of our words strike the ear, but the teacher is within."

IMAGE OF GOD

Luther despaired of understanding the image of God. Yet the conviction that humanity has been created in the image of God underlies the Christian's conviction that every human being has unique worth and value.

What the Bible teaches. The concept of humanity being created in God's image is certainly biblical. We are introduced to it in Genesis 1:26, as God says, "Let us make man in our image, in our likeness, and let them rule over the fish of the sea and the birds of the air, over the livestock, over all the earth." And the passage continues, "So God created man in his own image, in the image of God he created him: male and female he created them" (Gen. 1:27).

Whatever this image was, and however much it was distorted by Adam's sin, it persists after the Fall. Genesis 9 decrees the death penalty for murder, "for in the image of God has God made man." And James warns us against cursing others, for all "have been made in God's likeness" (James 3:9).

At the same time it is clear that whatever the image of God in human beings was and is, that image was damaged by the Fall. One of the wonderful benefits that Christians experience in our relationship with God is that our new selves "are being renewed in knowledge in the image of [our] Creator" (Col. 3:10). The Bible says these new selves were, "[re]created to be like God in true righteousness and holiness" (Eph. 4:24).

While the Bible thus suggests a moral aspect to the image of God, one that is being renewed in us as we grow in Christ, it also looks ahead to full restoration of all that the image of God implies. In Paul's great affirmation of our resurrection, he presents Jesus not only as the one who perfectly bears the image of God but also as the one who is himself the model for our ultimate transformation. "Just as we have borne the likeness of the earthly man," Paul promises, "so shall we bear the likeness of the man from heaven" (1 Cor. 15:49).

Each person has worth and value, for each is human. We belong to a race created in the image of God himself, and each of us still shares enough of that image to make murder an unthinkable crime and even bitter words inappropriate. Individually, too, each one of us has the potential for a full reconstruction of God's image within us, as we live out the new lives given us in Christ. And finally each believer is destined to perfectly reflect the image of God eternally, for in our resurrection we will be like Jesus, bearing the wondrous likeness of the "man from heaven" (see John 3:1–15).

What is the image of God? Christians throughout the centuries have studied the Bible's teaching about what it means that we are made in God's image. But Christians still debate just exactly what that image is. Many of the church fathers argued that image indicates those capacities that make us, like God, persons. (Luther observed that if this were all image and likeness intends, then Satan would have to be considered made in God's image, too. This the Bible never suggests.) Others have thought the image involves our imperishability: the fact that, like God, every person will remain self-consciously aware through eternity. Still others have noted the association in Genesis of the image of God with our responsibility of dominion. Others, like Wesley, have fastened on our moral nature and capacity as the key to understanding God's image. Wesley writes that God created human beings, "not merely in His *natural image*, a picture of His own immortality; a spiritual being, endowed with understanding, freedom of will, and various affections; — nor merely in his *political image*, the governor of this lower world, — but chiefly in His *moral image*, which according to the Apostle, is "righteousness and true holiness" (Eph. 4:24) (italics mine).

To Wesley, then, the chief mark of the image of God is seen in moral character. In the original creation, mankind "was full of love; which was the sole principle of all his tempers, thoughts, words, and actions. God is full of justice, mercy, and truth; so was man as he came from the hands of his Creator. God is spotless purity; and so man was in the beginning pure from every sinful blot; otherwise God would not have pronounced him "very good" (Gen. 1:31).

But still the mystery remains. In the Fall humanity lost that spotless purity and perfect love of which Wesley writes, and yet humanity has retained some semblance of the divine image. So what can the image of God in us really be?

It is no wonder that Luther considered all the options and writes, "When we now attempt to speak of that image, we speak of a thing unknown; . . . Of this image therefore all we now possess are the mere terms — the image of God. These naked words, are all we now hear, and all we know."

But Luther's conclusion was wrong. We may not understand all that the image of God means. We may not be able to determine everything Adam was before the Fall or what remnants we now possess. But those words, *the image of God*, are rich in affirmation and promise. What we do know is that humanity is special, unique in all creation through God's gift to mankind of his image. We know that each human being has worth and value. Life is to be respected and preserved because even as sinners, we retain something of God's own image. And we know that in Jesus Christ, God is now at work refashioning our personalities. God is rebuilding the image restored to us when we believed, bringing out the new potential that relationship with Jesus implies. And we know, too, that one day soon, Jesus will come. Then all that we are potentially will be fully realized, and we truly will be like him.

IMMORTALITY

The same Greek word translated "immortal" in our New International Version is also rendered "imperishable." These words are used with a special and wonderful emphasis. They affirm that God is not subject to the corruption and decay that infect our universe (Rom. 1:23; 1 Tim. 1:17), but he is forever immune to the forces associated with death. And these words promise that you and I, who have been given new life by response to his incorruptible seed (1 Peter 1:25), are released from these forces also, assured of a resurrection in which we will be "clothed" with immortality (1 Cor. 15:42).

Some have thought of immortality simply as endless personal existence. But every human being will exist forever, self-conscious and self-aware. No, immortality means that we will exist forever free from the grip of sin on our nature, released to live with God and to be like Jesus in his freedom from every flaw.

IMPUTATION

A. A. Hodge defines imputation simply as "the charging or crediting to one's account as the ground of judicial treatment." The definition sounds dry and technical, and certainly "imputation" is a technical theological term. But imputation touches the very heart of what Christians believe about God and our relationship with him.

The Greek and Hebrew words used to express the idea of imputation are usually translated by words like "reckoning," "considering," or "crediting." For instance, Romans 4:3 says, "Abraham believed God, and it was credited to him as righteousness," while Romans 4:8 quotes one of David's psalms, "Blessed is the man whose sin the LORD will never count against him."

God, the universal judge, chooses to treat the person who believes in Jesus as if he or she actually were righteous, and he chooses not to impute (hold judicially responsible, hold legally guilty for) their sin.

The concept of imputation occurs in three primary contexts. First, every human being is charged with the guilt of Adam's sin as well as his or her own personal sins. Romans 5:12 puts it this way: "Sin entered the world through one man, and death through sin, and in this way death came to all men, because all sinned." In some sense Adam's failure was our failure, too. Not only have we inherited Adam's sin nature but we are also justly charged with guilt for his original act of disobedience.

But the Scriptures focus on something else entirely when exploring imputation. They focus on what might be called a grand exchange. God, in his love and grace, has chosen to charge Jesus with our guilt and to credit his death on the cross to our account. Jesus took our sin and gave us his own righteousness.

While the terminology of reckoning to one's account is not used of Christ's death, many passages make clear what has happened. "The LORD has laid on him the iniquity of us all," Isaiah 53:6 affirms, and 1 Peter 2:24 agrees: "He himself bore our sins in his body on the tree." Jesus was without sin, and yet, "God made him who had no sin to be sin for us, so that in him we might become the righteousness of God" (2 Cor. 5:21). Jesus was made judicially responsible for our sins, and he took our punishment when he died on the cross.

The grand exchange unveiled in Scripture is the imputation now of Jesus' righteousness to you and me. God imputes righteousness to us, freeing him to give us all those good things that only the righteous deserve. He forgives our sins and cloaks us in a perfection that belongs to Jesus alone, drawing us into his family, making us joint heirs with Jesus of the riches of his grace. Imputation means that in God's sight, we who believe are considered righteous, like Abraham, even though we fall short. Our relationship with God does not rest on our own merits or efforts but on the merits of Jesus himself.

Imputation, then, is a way of explaining what happens when we trust Jesus Christ as Savior. It is not the only way of talking about salvation, and it does not sum up everything involved in salvation, but it is basic to true Christianity. We are guilty of sin — our own personal sins and Adam's guilt as well. Yet God has made a way for us to find release. Jesus died, bearing our sin and taking our punishment. When we trust him, our sins are charged to his account. When we trust him, he credits us with his own righteousness. Clothed in Jesus, we stand confident before God; we are sure of his acceptance because in Jesus, God sees and welcomes us as truly good. ◗ RIGHTEOUSNESS, SUBSTITUTION, SALVATION

INCARNATION

The Old Testament foretold the Incarnation in a name. The promised Messiah/deliverer of the Jewish people was to be called Immanuel. The name, capturing the emphasis of the Hebrew structure, means *"With us is God."*

It was hard even for some early Christians to grasp. And the idea has been ridiculed by ancient and modern skeptics. Yet it is clearly taught in the Bible and is basic to our faith. In the person of Jesus Christ, God has come to us in the flesh. This is the Christian doctrine of incarnation. We believe that God has pierced the barrier between the seen and the unseen, and in history's greatest miracle, God became a true human being.

The Bible does not attempt to explain this reality, but it clearly and forcefully teaches the Incarnation. We can look, for instance, at four New Testament passages. John's gospel begins by identifying Jesus as the Word who "was with God, and the Word was God" (John 1:1). ▶ WORD This Word "became flesh and lived for a while among us . . . the one and only Son, who came from the Father, full of grace and truth" (John 1:1–14). The eternally existing Word took on flesh, becoming a true human being, who for a few brief years lived among other human beings on planet earth.

Galatians 4:4–5 picks up the theme of preexistence — the fact that the one who came was Son with Father from eternity. "When the time had fully come," the Bible says, "God sent his Son, born of a woman, born under the law, to redeem those under law, that we might receive the full rights of sons."

Philippians 2 is one of the clearest and most powerful biblical expressions of incarnation. It presents Jesus Christ "who, being in very nature of God" yet "made himself nothing, taking on the very nature of a servant, being made in human likeness." As a human being the Son of God "humbled himself and became obedient to death — even death on a cross." Exalted now, Jesus has been given "the name that is above every name" and will hear "every tongue confess that Jesus Christ is Lord" (Phil. 2:5–11).

A fourth passage is found in Colossians. There Jesus is described as the "[express] image [the exact representation] of the invisible God." It was "by him all things were created: things in heaven and on earth, visible and invisible. . . . He is before all things and in him all things hold together," for "God was pleased to have all his fullness dwell in him [Jesus]" (Col. 1:15–19). It was Jesus Christ whom God invested with humanity and who is the agent of salvation. Through Jesus, God chose to "reconcile to himself all things . . . by making peace through his blood, shed on the cross" (Col. 1:20). And the same passage emphasizes the fact that the Incarnation was no mere illusion: God has reconciled us "by Christ's physical body through death" (Col. 1:22).

Given the fact that the Bible teaches the Incarnation, why make an issue of it? Why view the incarnation of Christ as central to Christian faith? Simply because so much hinges on it.

Before the first century A.D., philosophers despaired of ever really knowing God. He was so wholly "other." Whoever or whatever "God" might be, whether Aristotle's "unmoved mover" or Neoplatonism's "pure spirit," God was so removed from mankind's universe that he was unknowable. And then, in an obscure little country on the fringe of the mighty Roman Empire, this unknowable God arrived. He came not in majesty but as an infant. He lived as a real human being, not among the political movers but among the common people. And he died, not a victim but the Victor. Because God the Creator entered his own universe, the hidden God that humanity despaired of knowing was fully unveiled. And because God acted to free humanity from bondage to sin, the distant God that humanity feared was discovered to be lovingly near, inviting each of us to truly know him in an intimate, personal relationship.

This is, of course, the real reason for and necessity of the Incarnation. Sin's ruin had devastated our whole race, alienating us from God, and so warping our outlook that we were actually "enemies in your minds because of your evil behavior" (Col. 1:21). Only God's personal intervention could deal finally with sin, reveal the full extent of his love for us, and transform us from enemies into children. No one could do for us what Jesus did, and so Jesus had to come, impelled by the necessity imposed by God's deep love.

Yes, Christians believe in the Incarnation. We believe that God loved us enough to enter the universe and take on human nature. We believe that God loved us enough to live among us and die for us. And because we do believe, we acknowledge Jesus of Nazareth as fully God, and we worship him. ▶ **JESUS CHRIST**

INSPIRATION

Is our Bible really trustworthy? Is it a record of human speculation and experience, or is it a revelation given to us by God himself? Christians agree: the Bible is special, an unveiling of truth by God. ▶ **TRUTH, REVELATION**

What is inspiration? When speaking of their message, the Old Testament prophets often identified it as the "word of God." The words they spoke could be counted on to accurately convey God's intention. As David affirmed, "The Spirit of the LORD spoke through me; his word was on my tongue" (2 Sam. 23:2).

The New Testament describes the process, saying simply that "all Scripture" is "God-breathed" (2 Tim. 3:16). Inspiration pictures the breath or wind of God filling the writer and carrying him or her along so that the product, the words, convey just what God intended.

From the beginning the Christian community has agreed that the

Bible is inspired, its words the trustworthy expression of God's thoughts. Clement of Alexandria calls the Scriptures "true, given through the Holy Ghost; and ye know that there is nothing unrighteous or counterfeit in them." Justin Martyr spoke of them as the product of the "energy of the Divine Spirit . . . using men as an instrument like a harp or lyre" to "reveal to us the knowledge of things divine and heavenly." Irenaeus called the Scripture "perfect, since they were spoken by the Word of God and His Spirit." Origen writes that "the sacred books are not the compositions of men, but they were composed by inspiration of the Holy Spirit." Even those who challenge the doctrine today admit that from the beginning of time to the eighteenth century, Christians remained convinced that God exercised a supernatural influence on the writers of the Scripture, enabling them to communicate his truth without error, giving us a trustworthy and authoritative Word on which we can rely.

The necessity for inspiration. By the time Jesus was born, the most astute philosophers had agreed there was no way to know God. He was too distant, too different, too divorced from the material universe. Most doubted that a God really existed, but if one did, there was no way for humans to know him.

Those same philosophers had long ago despaired of gaining knowledge of reality. Empedocles, who lived in the fifth century B.C., writes: "Weak and narrow are the powers implanted in the limbs of man; many the woes that fall on them and blunt the edges of thought; short is the measure of the life in death through which they toil. Then are they borne away; like smoke they vanish into air; and what they dream they know is but the little that each hath stumbled upon in wandering about the world. Yet boast they all that they have learned the whole. Vain fools! For what that is, no eye hath seen, no ear hath heard, nor can it be conceived by the mind of man."

The apostle Paul picks up Empedocles' words as he speaks of the necessity of a divine revelation. "'No eye has seen, no ear has heard, no mind has conceived what God has prepared for those who love him'—but God has revealed it to us by his Spirit" (1 Cor. 2:9–10).

Paul goes on to point out that only the spirit of a person knows his or her inmost thoughts. Only the Spirit of God knows the thoughts of God. Weak and narrow as our powers are, we could never penetrate the thoughts of God or discover the nature of reality unless God communicated it to us. And so we have the wonder unveiled. God has chosen to communicate, speaking to us through the prophets and apostles, "not in words taught us by human wisdom but in words taught by the Spirit" (1 Cor. 2:13).

Apart from divine revelation we have no way to know God or to understand the nature of our universe, that "whole" that a few "vain fools" of Empedocles' day imagined they had learned. Our Christian belief in inspiration simply means that we believe God *has* spoken and that he so guided those who wrote the words of Scripture that those words truly are the Word of God, his trustworthy and reliable message to humankind.

Contemporary challenges. To insist that our Bible expresses the inspired Word of God doesn't deny human influence. Kenneth Kantzer, a modern theologian, explains this in an article on "The Communication of Revelation":

> All of Scripture was produced by human authors whose writings reflect through the individual personality and linguistic habits of each particular Biblical author. At the same time the Spirit of God so worked upon the Biblical author that what he wrote is also exactly the words which God wishes to convey to man. Biblical inspiration may be defined, therefore, as that work of the Holy Spirit by which, without setting aside their personalities and literary or human faculties, God so guided the authors of Scripture as to enable them to write exactly the words which convey His truth to men, and in so doing preserved their judgments from error in the original manuscripts.

Kantzer expresses the conviction of Christians throughout the ages when he says inspiration means that God's written Word carries "divine authority and [is] without error in faith (what we ought to believe) and practice (what we ought to do)."

Some theologians have used the terms "verbal inspiration" and "plenary inspiration." Others prefer to speak of "dynamic" inspiration. Both groups would agree with Laird Harris, who explains "that God superintended the process of writing so that the whole is true — the historical, the doctrinal, the mundane, the minor, and the major!" So Christians believe that the original writings are inspired and should be considered God's words as well as Hosea's words or Paul's words.

The challenge to the Christian's belief in inspiration has come as people have charged the Bible with historical and scientific errors. The argument is focused on an idea associated with inspiration: If the Bible really is verbally or dynamically inspired, shouldn't it be without error? Those who think they have found historic and scientific errors in the Bible have taken this as evidence that what is expressed in such places is simply the mistaken notion of the writer who lived in an unscientific age or who included errors of historic fact, either purposely or by mistake.

In fact, some people argue about the supposed "errors" that raise the challenge. Some modern Christians want to argue that the Bible is, in fact, without error of any kind. Others aren't disturbed by the notion that the humanity of the authors might be expressed in the inclusion of a few errors on mundane matters. A leading Wesleyan theologian, A. M. Hills, asks in his *Fundamental Christian Theology* (Vol. IV, p. 1–13:16): "What is the infallibility we claim for the Bible? It is infallible as regards the purpose for which it was written. It is infallible as a revelation of God's saving love in Christ to a wicked world. It infallibly guides all honest and willing and seeking souls to Christ, to holiness, and to heaven."

Whatever our view of the "how" of inspiration, and whatever our view of whether inspiration guarantees the inerrancy of the Bible, all who are true believers are convinced that our Bible, the Word of God, has been touched by God himself and that it is a trustworthy guide to all who seek to know the Lord and walk in his ways.

ISRAEL

We've lost something of the wonder of Israel. But when the nation Israel came into existence in 1948, in the ancient Jewish homeland, a political entity that had not existed for two thousand years was then re-established. Many Christians look on re-establishment of the nation as a step that set the stage for the prophesied return of Jesus.

But not everyone holds that view. One of the problems we face when we ask what Christians believe about Israel is the fact that the term is used in so many ways in the Bible. We can best sort it out by looking at Israel in history, prophecy, and hermeneutics.

Israel in history. We first meet Israel as a personal name given to Jacob, the son of Isaac and grandson of Abraham. Like other Hebrew names, this one has meaning. It is composed by linking words meaning "prince with God" (Gen. 32:28; 47:31).

The name is quickly extended in the Old Testament for use as a tribal name. The descendants of this man are called "Israel," emphasizing the family identity and the special place this family plays in God's plan. Often in the Old Testament, the word *Israel* is used simply to affirm and identify the Jewish people as the people of God (see, for example, Exod. 1:1; 3:16; 12:3; Deut. 1:38).

The people of Israel were slaves in Egypt until God sent Moses as their deliverer. After a time of wandering, the people entered Palestine, a land promised centuries before to Abraham and a land promised to be a permanent Jewish possession. The nation Israel was established there, governed by the Mosaic law. A number of changes in national structure took place under David and the later monarchy, but from entrance of the people of Israel into Palestine, Israel has had a national aspect as well as a personal and tribal one. Many times the word *Israel* in our Old Testament stands simply for the nation, that political entity formed by the people of God (see Judg. 19:1; 2 Sam. 1:12; 1 Kings 9:5).

The political unity of the Jewish people was shattered after the death of David's son, Solomon. Two kingdoms emerged in the divided land: the southern kingdom, identified as Judah, and the northern kingdom, identified as Israel. As the centuries passed, people and nations strayed from God's ways. As a result the land was devastated by powerful pagan enemies. First the northern kingdom was defeated and her people taken captive; then a century and a half later the southern kingdom was overtaken. Often in the Old Testament, Israel is used in the sense of the splinter northern kingdom.

It is clear from this brief survey that the word *Israel* is a multifaceted one. At times in the Bible, especially in the later books of the Old Testament and in the Gospels, Israel may be used in all of the common senses: as a family, a religious community (the people of God), as a national entity, and often simply as the land claimed by the people as their national homeland.

Israel in prophecy. Much of our Old Testament is prophetic in nature: The writers look to the future and offer predictions and promises. Often Israel is prominent in these prophecies. At times prophecy seems to focus on the descendants of Jacob and their bright prospects as the people of God. Taken literally Old Testament prophecies tell of a universal religious conversion for Israel, re-establishment of a lost national identity, reoccupation of the promised land, and many associated blessings (see Isaiah 44:21–23; 45:17; Jer. 31:21–27; Amos 9:11–15). But in prophecy, too, Israel has varied meanings; thus we need to determine what aspect of Israel is foremost in the writer's mind.

Israel in hermeneutics. But how Christians understand Israel is even more complicated. In the New Testament Paul notes that many who are physical progeny of Israel have no vital relationship with God. "Not all who are descended from Israel are Israel," he writes in Romans. "It is not the natural children who are God's children, but it is the children of the promise [who believe in God's promises and trust him] who are regarded as Abraham's offspring" (Rom. 9:6, 8). The concept is found in the Old Testament as well, where the prophets often speak of a "remnant." This term indicates Israelite believers who are preserved to experience the blessings that God promises his people. The New Testament also affirms that even Gentiles, who had no share in the Old Testament promises to Israel, are brought through faith into covenant relationship with God and, in a sense, become the spiritual heirs of Abraham, Isaac, and Israel. In at least a limited sense, it is clear that *all* believers (Christians as well as Old Testament Jews) are part of Israel and are Abraham's spiritual descendants. ◗ **COVENANT**

We have traced the complicated ways that the word *Israel* is used in the Bible for a simple reason. The many different meanings have led to differences in the way Christians understand and apply a number of Old Testament passages. To many Christians the Old Testament's promises to Israel and its prophecies about Israel's future are spiritualized: they are taken as metaphors and symbols of Christian experience. Promised blessings of wealth and national security for Israel in Palestine are interpreted to mean heavenly possessions and inner peace for the modern Christian. On the other hand, many Christians insist that we are to take prophetic references to Israel in the Old Testament in a literal sense, unless the context clearly suggests otherwise. To these Christians promises of national restoration, wealth, and blessing are to be fulfilled literally. Israel and the church, while both the people of God, are not identical and should not be confused. That God has guarded the separate identity of the Jewish people for thousands of years and that recent history has seen the re-establishment of a Jewish state, seems evidence that he still has a purpose for them as a people.

One reason that the definition of Israel is significant is that the position Christians take on the meaning of Israel tends to reflect, if not to shape, many aspects of their theology — particularly their interpretation of prophecy. ◗ **PROPHECY**

But clearly, the differences Christians hold are overwhelmed by the understandings we share. We all see God at work in his ancient people. Through Israel, God's revelation came. From Israel's race, Jesus was born. The Messiah of the Old Testament is the Savior of the New Testament, and that faith in God that won Abraham's salvation is the key to our own. Spiritually, you and I, with the saints of the Old Testament, acknowledge Abraham as our forefather and look forward to a shared eternity in God's presence. In these most significant of ways, God's people of every age truly are one. We can affirm significant differences between the church and Israel if we choose, but we can never lose sight of the essential unity of God's people.

JEHOVAH

Probably, if uttered in the Hebrew tongue during biblical times, the name sounded more like "Jahweh." But it is not the pronunciation of the name that is important. It is the meaning.

Jahweh is significant because it is not so much a descriptive name, like "Prince of Peace," or "God of Hosts [Armies]," but rather it is the personal name that God revealed to his people through Moses. Jahweh is not so much a description of God's character or actions as an unveiling of his essential nature. This special name is rendered "LORD" in our English versions of the Old Testament.

Exodus 3 is key to our understanding. God appears to Moses and sends him to deliver his people from Egyptian servitude. When Moses asks how to explain to the Israelites who has sent him, God replies, "Say to the Israelites, 'I AM has sent me to you.'" The Lord goes on to explain, "Say to the Israelites, 'The LORD [Jahweh], the God of your fathers — the God of Abraham, the God of Isaac, and the God of Jacob — has sent me to you.' This is my name forever, the name by which I am to be remembered from generation to generation" (Exod. 3:14–15). Later, in Egypt, God tells Moses that though he appeared to Abraham, Isaac, and Jacob, he did not make himself known to them as Jahweh (Exod. 6:2). It was in the mighty acts and unmistakable miracles of the Exodus that Israel came to know her God as Jahweh.

What then does the name mean? Most agree the name is based on the Hebrew verb "to be," and means "He who is" or "the One who is always present." This is what God wants his people to grasp. He is not simply the God of Abraham, who lived in ancient times. He is not only God of the covenant, who promises his people a bright future. God is essentially a living, active person, one who is always present with his people. God is real *today*, and we are to experience him and his power in the present time.

Of all the Near Eastern peoples, Israel alone possessed this unique name of God. The Jews regarded this name as so holy that it was not spoken aloud, and scribes took a ritual bath whenever they penned it on a biblical manuscript they were copying.

Jahweh, the most intimate of the Old Testament's names for God, is the name most closely connected with his self-revelation in history and in Scripture. It is the name most intimately associated with redemption, the name linked with the power displayed in those terrifying plagues that forced Egypt's Pharaoh to let God's people go.

The Old Testament's consistent association of Jahweh with revelation and redemption has led many Christians to the conviction that the

Jahweh of the Old Testament is none other than the Jesus of the New Testament. Surely Jesus is the ultimate revelation of God. Surely he is the true agent of our salvation. And we also have God's promise that Jesus, like Jahweh, is always present with his people, for he has promised, "Never will I leave you; never will I forsake you" (Heb. 13:5; see also Matt. 28:20).

JESUS CHRIST

Commenting on the *Earliest Christian Creeds*, Martin Luther expressed the common conviction of all Christians: "He who steadfastly holds to the doctrine that Jesus Christ is true God and true man, who died and rose again for us, will acquiesce in and heartily assent to all the other articles of the Christian faith. Paul's saying in Ephesians 1:22 is true — that Christ is the chief treasure, the basis, the foundation, the sum total to whom all are drawn and under whom all are gathered. And in him are hidden all the treasures of wisdom and knowledge, Colossians 2:3."

Jesus is central. He is the heart, the soul, the beauty, and the being of our faith.

Who is Jesus? It is important that when we speak of Jesus, we mean the real Jesus. Some theologians, in attempting to discover what they call a "historical Jesus," have challenged the Bible's teaching about him. They have assumed that after Jesus' death, his followers gradually ascribed deity to the simple carpenter of Nazareth. Jesus, the Jewish prophet whose moral and spiritual vision was so exalted, is to be honored, they say, but simply as a man. These scholars taught that even though Jesus was even the best of men, he was never any more than what any of us can aspire to become.

This Jesus of the critics, stripped of majesty and robbed of essential deity, is not the Jesus of Christian faith. The Jesus of faith is the Jesus the Bible proclaims, the Jesus whom Luther identifies as "true God, and true man, who died and rose again for us."

Rather than mimic the uncounted books that have been written on the Bible's picture of Jesus, I want to simply list key passages and the central truths they teach. And then I want to share something of who Jesus is *for us*. This is what is so exciting about our Lord. He is God, but he is God bent low, stooping to bond himself to you and me, that in him we might be lifted high. Only the Jesus of the Bible, he who is God and man in one, could be everything for us that he is.

Who is the Jesus of the Bible? In a helpful *Handbook of Basic Bible Texts* (Zondervan), John Jefferson Davis lists the following key passages that identify the biblical Jesus. According to Scripture, Jesus is:

Co-equal with God, the second person of the Trinity, who existed from all eternity	Isa. 9:6; Mic. 5:2; John 1:1–3; 6:38; 8:56–58; 17:4–5; Gal. 4:4–5; Phil. 2:5–7; Rev. 22:12–13, 16.
Virgin born, conceived by the Holy Spirit	Isa. 7:14; Matt. 1:18–25; Luke 1:26–38.
Without a sinful nature, clear of acts of sin	Luke 1:35; John 8:29, 46; 14:30–32; Acts 3:14; 2 Cor. 5:21; Heb. 4:15, 26–28; 9:14; 1 Peter 1:18–19; 2:22–23; 1 John 3:4–5.
Truly and fully human	Matt. 4:1–2; 8:23–24; Luke 2:52; 24:39; John 1:14; 4:5–6; 11:35; 19:28, 34; Rom. 1:2–3; Heb. 2:14, 17–18; 4:15.
Truly and fully God, the possessor of divine titles:	Isa. 9:6; Mark 1:2–3; Luke 1:17; 3:1; Acts 2:21; Matt. 26:63–65.
possessor of divine attributes:	John 1:1; 17:5; Phil. 2:5–7; Rev. 22:13; Matt. 28:20; Eph. 1:22–23.
possessor of divine power:	John 1:3, 14; 5:21, 26; 11:25; Col. 1:16, 17; Heb. 1:2.
possessor of divine prerogatives:	Matt. 25:31–32; Mark 2:5–7; John 5:22, 27; Acts 7:59.
Equal in every way with the Father	John 1:1; 20:28; Titus 2:13; Heb. 1:8; 1 Peter 1:1.
Willing sacrifice, who laid down his life to win us salvation	Isa. 53:4–5; Mark 10:33–34, 45; John 10:14–15, 17–18; Acts 2:23; Rom. 3:25; 5:10; 2 Cor. 18–19; Gal. 3:13; Eph. 2:15–16; 5:2; Col. 1:19–20; 2:15; 1 Tim. 2:5–6; Heb. 9:14; 1 Peter 1:18–19; 2:24; 1 John 2:2; Rev. 5:9.
Resurrected in the body and taken into heaven to guide and empower his church	Matt. 28:9; Luke 24:36–39, 50–51; John 20:19; Acts 1:1–2, 9–11; Rom. 1:2–4; 15:3–6, 17, 20; 1 Cor. 2:32–33; Eph. 1:19–21; Phil. 2:9–11; Heb. 4:14; 7:26; Rev. 1:5.

Christians joyfully confess that Jesus is who the Bible states he is, and this Jesus of Scripture is the focus of our worship and our hope.

Who Jesus is for us. *Jesus is our prophet.* A prophet speaks for God. Jesus is the ultimate spokesperson, the ultimate revelation of the Father and of his will. We pay careful attention to all that Jesus taught, confident that his words are completely trustworthy. We acknowledge the miracles that authenticated his message, but most important we rely on the Spirit's inner testimony, which enables us to recognize his voice. We trust Jesus' portrait of the Father, we rely on his promises, and we respond obediently to his commands. We yearn to experience the kingdom of heaven he described, and we expect to experience the perfect love and holiness he promises. Jesus is our prophet, the source of truth about God, the trustworthy spokesperson, whose words guide and shape our lives (see Matt. 5:1–7:29; John 10:1–4; 14:15–22; Heb. 1:1–3; 2:1–4). ♦ REVELATION, PROPHET, OBEDIENCE, HOLINESS, LOVE

Jesus is our High Priest. A priest is a mediator, representing God to the people and the people to God. Jesus, our High Priest, offered himself as the perfect sacrifice to God. That one sacrifice "made perfect forever those who are being made holy." As our High Priest, the living Jesus stands today by the Father's throne. He represents us there, praying for us and hearing our petitions. His intercession guarantees continuing forgiveness when we fall short of God's will or stray from his paths. Jesus understands and sympathizes with our weaknesses. His presence in heaven gives us the confidence to freely approach God's throne whenever we need mercy or help (Heb. 3:1–4:16; 1 John 1:8–2:2). ♦ PRIESTHOOD, SACRIFICE

Jesus is our coming King. We recognize Jesus as the ultimate authority and power in the universe. He, the source of all, is also ruler of all. The kingship of Jesus is real in our lives, for we acknowledge him as Lord and obey him. But we look forward to Jesus' return. Then he will exercise his power openly, and then every knee will bow to Jesus. In the age to come, Jesus will be acknowledged by the universe as King of Kings and Lord of Lords. He will rule over all, instituting his golden age of righteousness and peace (Rev. 11:15–19; 19:11–16). ♦ KINGDOM, LORD

Jesus is our example. We view the life that Jesus lived on earth as the perfect life. His lifestyle reveals true spirituality, that close fellowship with and obedience to God that finds expression in compassion for human beings. Jesus' walk on earth expresses the values that we profess. His outlook on what is important in life is the outlook we struggle to share. We look to Jesus to learn how to respond to hurts and injustice, to opposition and hatred. We look to Jesus to see how we are to react to suffering. From Jesus we learn how to trust ourselves to the Father, whatever the circumstances. We see in Jesus the perfect love that he commands in his disciples. In confessing Jesus to be our model, we agree with the apostles that we who claim him are to love as he loved, to walk as he walked. Jesus is our example, and we delight to walk in his steps (Matt. 5:43–48; Luke 6:40; 1 John 2:6; 3:16). ♦ HOLINESS, LOVE

Jesus is our life. Jesus is the source of all that is good in us. The new life that God gave us when we trusted Christ as Savior is his. He is the vine, and all the power to produce fruit comes from his vitality flowing into us. The life we live on earth now is in the most significant sense his life—eternal and enriching, expressing itself in love, joy, peace, patience, kindness, goodness, faithfulness, gentleness, and self-control. All that is good and beautiful in our lives is an expression of Jesus, springing directly from our relationship with him. Because Jesus lives in us, our bodies can become instruments of righteousness and our hearts the home of love. We depend on Jesus not only for forgiveness but also for everything. He truly is the food we eat, the air we breathe, the life we live (John 15:1–8; Gal. 2:20; 5:22–25; Eph. 2:4–10; 2 Cor. 12:9–10). ◗ LIFE, UNION WITH JESUS

Jesus is our risen Lord. In his resurrection, Jesus was given the name above every name: Lord. His is the authority, his the power, his the right to rule. He is head over the church, his body, and he is Lord of every person. Acknowledging the lordship of Jesus means that we confess his right to set our standards, establish our priorities, and guide our choices. We respond to Jesus as he speaks to us in his written Word, and we open our lives to his special, supernatural guidance. We acknowledge Jesus' lordship over other Christians and extend them the freedom to follow their own convictions, fully responsible to Christ. We pray to our Lord about our decisions, and we depend on him to shape our circumstances. Because we believe that Jesus as Lord has all power in heaven and on earth, we face even suffering with hope, sure that "in all things God works for the good of those who love him." Because Jesus is Lord, he merits our total allegiance, and we commit ourselves fully to him and to his will (Matt. 28:18; Rom. 8:28–29; 14:1–13; Eph. 1:18–23; Phil. 2:9–11; 1 Peter 3:14–15). ◗ LORD, HEAD, SOVEREIGNTY

In every way Jesus truly is the heart, the center, the beauty, and the glory of our faith. Christianity is no mere philosophy. It is not simply a higher ethical vision. Christianity is Jesus Christ, foretold in the Old Testament, unveiled in the New Testament. Christianity rests entirely on the conviction that in Jesus of Nazareth, God became flesh to dwell among us. Jesus lived, taught, died, was raised again, and even now is at the Father's right hand, ready at any moment to return.

But Christianity offers more than God enfleshed. Christianity offers us a transforming, personal relationship with this God. Through faith Jesus becomes ours: our Savior, our Prophet, our High Priest, our coming King, our Example, our Life, our risen Lord. Everything that we have and are is ours through Jesus Christ alone.

Christianity is Christ. We rejoice, for we are his and he is ours.

JUDGE

What does it mean to affirm that God is judge? Most of us suppose the title is judicial, that God evaluates human beings and acts to punish sins. Certainly such judgment is involved in the title. But the Old Testament's use of the word is even more powerful. The Hebrew root word *shapat* and its various derivatives imply every function of government. To say that God is judge means that we acknowledge his rule over the universe. As judge, God has and exercises the right to determine what is right and good. As judge, God has and exercises the right to evaluate our actions. As judge, God has and exercises the right to act as he chooses in the universe and to execute any punishments his righteousness demands.

We believe that God is judge in this full, biblical sense. We acknowledge his right, and we worship him as sovereign Lord. ◗ SOVEREIGNTY, JUSTICE, LAW

JUDGMENT DAY

The New Testament Greek words translated "judge" or "judgment" mean "evaluate" or "distinguish." At times these words are used in a legal sense, with God cast as judge on the bench and with humankind the criminals before the bar.

Christians believe that God is the only one truly qualified to judge us, for he alone is able to evaluate all things accurately. And we have complete trust that his judgment is fair.

But we also believe that God has already reached his verdict. The Bible unveils not only the standards by which God evaluates but also the conclusions he has drawn. Bluntly, God's evaluation is that "there is no one righteous, not even one" (Rom. 3:10), for "all have sinned and fallen short of the glory of God" (Rom. 3:23).

All that is left is for these conclusions to be expressed in an act of judgment, which Christians are convinced lies ahead. Paul spoke of it to mocking skeptics in Athens: God "has set a day when he will judge the world with justice by the man he has appointed" (Acts 17:31). Jesus, who lived history's only perfect life, has been granted authority to judge (John 5:22, 27), and Jesus' verdict has already been announced. The world is "condemned already" (John 3:18). When judgment day comes, all who find themselves standing before the divine bar, to be evaluated on the basis of what they have done, will be cast into what the Bible calls "the lake of fire" (Rev. 20:11–15).

Christians take this revelation of human failures and peril as one of God's greatest gifts. Why? God has announced his judgment and our sentence long before that sentence is to be executed. According to Romans 2–11, execution is delayed; it is withheld by God's kindness and tolerance in order to give human beings an opportunity to repent and believe. Until the day of judgment does come, human beings are invited to acknowledge their sin and turn to Jesus Christ for forgiveness. For those who believe in Jesus, there is no condemnation, for Jesus has already taken our punishment and offers us eternal life in him (John 5:21–30).

A judgment day is coming. But for Christians judgment day is past. Judgment day occurred two thousand years ago when the Son of God died for our sins at Calvary. All that is waiting ahead for us now is life, an eternity to be spent with our Redeemer and Lord.

JUSTICE

Typically when religious people talk about justice, they mean "social justice." All too often such talk takes the form of a debate. Should Christians seek to bring about a just society? Is doing justice simply a personal matter? Are human cultures so warped that only the return of Jesus can make social progress possible?

If we are to talk and think about "social justice," we surely need to have an understanding of the biblical idea of justice.

Hebrew words for justice. Two sets of Hebrew words are translated in our Old Testament as "just" and "justice." Where the Old Testament speaks of doing justice or of doing what is just, the root is usually *mishpat*, a term encompassing all aspects of government. Here justice suggests a fair judicial decision, or even the fair code against which actions can be judged. In this sense justice involves human rights and duties under law.

When words from the root *tsedek* are rendered "just" or "justice," the emphasis is on the existence of ethical norms. What is just is in harmony with the norms; unjust acts are those that violate the norms.

The Old Testament's idea of justice is never abstract or philosophical. Justice is always intimately related to God, for God himself established and revealed the standards by which we are to measure right actions. We believe that God has given us "regulations and laws which are just and right" (Neh. 9:13). We are convinced that the norms God has revealed are, in fact, expressions of his own character, trustworthy guides provided by "a faithful God who does no wrong," who is "upright and just" (Deut. 32:4). When we speak of justice, then, we are not involving ourselves in a debate over human standards. Instead we are concerned with doing what is right in God's eyes, for he is the true measure of right and wrong.

Doing justice. In the Old Testament God's prophets call Israel back to a just lifestyle. Israel has strayed from the pathway marked out by God's law, and as a result, her society is marked by injustice. The prophets' messages richly illustrate what constitute justice in individuals and in society. Isaiah's powerful words, and Jeremiah's echo, give us a clear sense of justice and injustice from God's perspective.

> Is this not the kind of fasting I have chosen:
>   to loose the chains of injustice
>   and untie the cords of the yoke,
> to set the oppressed free
>   and break every yoke?
> Is it not to share your food with the hungry
>   and to provide the poor wanderer with shelter —
> when you see the naked, to clothe him,
>   and not to turn away from your own flesh and blood?
> if you . . . spend yourselves on behalf of the hungry
>   and satisfy the needs of the oppressed,
> then your light will rise in the darkness,
>   and your night will become like the noonday.
> (Isa. 58:6–7, 10)

Of the godly, Jeremiah says,

> He did what was right and just,
>   so all went well.
> He defended the cause of the poor and needy,
>   and so all went well with him.
> Is this not what it means to know me?
> But your eyes and your heart
>   are set only on dishonest gain,
> on shedding innocent blood
>   and on oppression and extortion
> (Jer. 22:15–17)

In passages like these, we discern the principle that underlies God's law and thus underlies justice. God, who is just and loving, gave Israel a law that showed human beings how to express love for neighbors. "Doing justice" is at heart doing good to all others. It is showing a loving concern for the well-being of the weak and powerless as well as for our friends.

Justice is essentially interpersonal: It governs how we treat other individuals as well as how we respond to society. God's laws about fairness in treating others touch on both individual behavior and the structure of social institutions. These laws convince us that God calls Christians to "do good to all," not only to those who are part of the family of faith.

How do we do justice? All Christians agree that we are to be just and fair in our personal feelings with others. Christians differ about whether or not we should become involved in attempts to shape or change social institutions. Even greater debate focuses on whether or not the Christian community, as the organized church, should seek to influence economic and social conditions.

On the one hand, Christians do not expect to push and pummel a resisting secular society into the shape of God's kingdom. When Jesus returns, he will bring true peace and justice. But peace and justice will not come until then. Christians who emphasize Jesus' return tend to focus on personal morality and on personal redemption. They may reach out to help hurting people, but they are willing to abandon the world to run its course.

Other Christians are dissatisfied with this approach. Why just offer sympathy to the family whose member was killed by a drunk driver when we can get involved in MADD (Mothers Against Drunk Drivers) and pass laws that will help keep drunk drivers off the road? Why just tutor the minority child who has been forced into inferior schools when church influence may be used to improve education for all?

For Christians who reason like this, God's call to justice, to loving concern for all, is clearly a call to become socially involved. It is a call to take a stand based on Christian convictions, to struggle to influence the conscience of society so that just laws can be passed and injustices can be exposed.

But even if we decide that a Christian understanding of justice calls believers to social involvement, Christians still do and will continue to differ. Does involvement mean we should picket abortion clinics? Or sell the stock of companies that invest in countries whose governments are slack in upholding human rights? Or raise money to influence the outcome of political elections? Or boycott the produce of farmers who underpay labor? Just stating a few of the issues in which activist Christians are involved in the name of social justice demonstrates it. Even those convinced that God's call to do justice is a demand for social action as well as for personal sensitivity to the needs of others are sure to disagree about just what our involvement should be.

But perhaps this is all right. Jesus is Lord, and each Christian should be free to respond to those issues of justice and injustice that he or she senses are closest to God's heart.

And what of those who hold back, insisting that involvement is not implicit in God's call to justice? Jesus is Lord in their lives, too, and they are responsible for that conviction only to him.

But perhaps just because we are responsible to Jesus, each of us should think again about justice. Perhaps we should read the prophets and sense the Lord's pain as he sees individuals and society acting in ways that crush and hurt the powerless. Perhaps we should listen and sense in their passionate words the heart of our God, calling us to care.

JUSTICE OF GOD

When the Old Testament speaks of justice, the subject usually is human action. Justice is concerned with how we live with others individually and in society according to the loving pattern laid down in God's law. ◆ JUSTICE But now and then the Old Testament affirms the conviction that lies at the heart of the concept of justice. God himself is just, the core and model of justice, and all the works of God's hands are "faithful and just" (Ps. 111:7). In most of the New Testament, references to justice underline this conviction, arguing forcefully that God truly is just.

But why argue so strongly for the justice of God? Perhaps because to unconverted humanity, the gospel seems terribly unfair. The philosophers curl their lip at the idea of one dying for the sins of others. How could that be fair? And why would anyone ever think it was necessary? Ordinary sinners, hearing that others (whose feelings are just as bad as their own) claim to be forgiven merely because they "believe," react as well. How is that fair? If one is forgiven, surely everyone should be. If one is punished, why should others whose acts are also evil be let off?

The New Testament answers such arguments simply by affirming that God is just. In fact, God's justice is demonstrated in Jesus' death (Rom. 3:21–26; 1 John 1:9). God does not "let off" sinners. God demands that the full penalty for sin be paid. But God's love impelled him to pay that penalty himself. Because the penalty was paid by Jesus, God, with perfect fairness, can offer a free salvation to all who simply trust themselves to the Lord. ◆ FAITH

God's justice is demonstrated both in forgiveness and condemnation. "God is just," the New Testament says, and will "pay back trouble to those who trouble you," when Jesus comes to "punish those who do not know God and do not obey the gospel of our Lord Jesus" (2 Thess. 1:6–8; Rev. 15–16).

So the New Testament affirms that God's treatment of people, both in the forgiveness of those who believe and in the punishment of those who do not, is totally just and completely fair.

Still, many people who examine Christian teaching don't like it. Somehow the gospel violates *their* sense of fairness.

It is here that Christians since the beginning of our era have stopped to challenge the critics. You see, Christians insist that God, not humanity, is the measure of all things. It is the Creator alone who is the moral governor of his universe. It is his moral judgments that are fair, for only his moral vision is clear and only his moral commitment to righteousness is complete. How foolish for human beings, warped as we all are by sin, to claim that our clouded moral vision is sharper than his or that our commitment to righteousness is greater than his.

For Christians God is God, and we gladly subject our judgment to his. We are neither surprised nor upset by the argument that God is unjust or that the gospel is unfair. Instead we remain confident and sure. On Resurrection Day, when our eyes are clear and the last residue of our sin is purged, we will understand fully the justice of God. Until then, in faith, we agree with God's Word. God is just in forgiving sinners who believe in Jesus. And God is just in ordaining the coming punishment of those who do not believe.

God is just. And we are perfectly willing to honor him by subjecting our moral judgment to his own.

JUSTIFICATION

Justification and *justify* are key theological terms, lying close to the heart of the gospel. By tracing these concepts in the Old and New Testaments, we gain a better understanding of God's plan of salvation.

Justification in the Old Testament. The Hebrew root expressing this concept is often translated "righteous," but it has important judicial meaning. In law a person's actions are called into question and examined. The person will be justified if found innocent, and his or her actions thus will be vindicated.

The theological meaning of the word *justification* rests on the judicial meaning. God is the judge who evaluates human actions. He does not clear the guilty. Yet David, in Psalm 51, calls on God for forgiveness. Although David is aware of his guilt (Ps. 51:4–5), he still relies on God's mercy (Ps. 51:1–2). David expresses the conviction that God can free him of guilt and restore his joy (Ps. 51:7–14). David asks God to justify him — to declare him innocent — despite the fact that he is guilty.

Passages like this prefigure the promise of justification that is so beautifully developed in our New Testament. In Isaiah 53, the Old Testament also prefigures the basis on which God can and will justify sinners. In this vital passage, Isaiah looks ahead to speak of Jesus' suffering and sacrificial death. The prophet describes Calvary in stunning detail, and concludes: "After the suffering of his [Jesus'] soul, he will see the light of life, and be satisfied; by his knowledge my righteous servant will justify many, and he will bear their iniquities. Therefore I will give him a portion among the great, and he will divide the spoils with the strong, because he has poured out his life unto death, and was numbered with the transgressors. For he bore the sin of many, and made intercession for the transgressors" (Isa. 53:11–12). On the basis of that poured-out life, God will declare many to be righteous, in spite of their many sins and failures.

Justification in Paul's letters. The Greek word translated "justify" is also a legal term. It, too, means "to acquit," "to vindicate," or "to pronounce righteous." The conviction that Christians are justified by faith in Jesus is expressed in the earliest New Testament preaching (Acts 4:12). But the apostle Paul is the one who develops this doctrine, especially in Romans and Galatians.

Paul begins Romans by showing that no human being can be righteous in God's sight (Rom. 1–3). Because all people are sinners, salvation can come if God chooses to pronounce sinners righteous. Romans 3:21–31 announces a "righteousness from God" that God freely gives to those who have faith in Jesus Christ. Paul shows that Jesus' substitutionary death provides a basis on which God is now free to make this judicial pronouncement. Since all human beings fall short of the divine standard, our daily hope is for a righteousness that comes to us apart from our own actions.

Paul moves on in Romans 4 to review history. The ancient greats, Abraham and David, were judicially credited with a righteousness they did not possess. They were reckoned righteous, not on the basis of their actions but on the basis of their faith.

Romans 5:2 emphasizes that we who believe "have been" justified. We *now* "have peace with God through our Lord Jesus Christ." God, the judge, has announced his verdict, and the person who has faith in Jesus stands acquitted.

Galatians adds that a "man is not justified by observing the law, but by faith in Christ Jesus" (Gal. 2:16). No one who relies on the merits of his or her own actions can win a favorable verdict from God. "By observing the law no one will be justified" (Gal. 2:16).

While justification is a declarative act by which God pronounces a person righteous, our justification involves more than this. The person God declares to be innocent by his sight in virtue of faith has entered a personal relationship with Jesus through that same faith. In Galatians 3, Paul shows that we can live by faith and go on to *be* righteous. Justification is a dynamic principle as well as a judicial one in Christianity. We rely on God to declare us innocent despite our sins, and then we rely on him to work in us to make us truly good.

Justification in the Book of James. At first glance, the Book of James seems to be out of harmony with the Pauline letters. Luther, unable to reconcile the two, dismissed James as an "Epistle of Straw." What troubled Luther was James' insistence that "a person is justified by what he does and not by faith alone" (James 2:24). But there is no real conflict, for while Paul was comparing faith with works, James compares "faith" with faith. James dismisses a faith that is mere mental assent to the truth of a set of facts. Of that kind of faith, James asks, "What good is it?"

To James, Christian faith is commitment to God. When we commit ourselves to God, our lives change. God does more than declare us righteous: He goes on to *make* us righteous. So James points to Abraham and Rahab as examples of men and women whose claim to "believe" in God was vindicated by the fact that they acted on their belief (see James 2:14). The Scripture that pronounced them righteous was fulfilled when their faith found expression in their actions (James 2:21–23).

In this, James is in complete harmony with Paul's letters and with the Old Testament record. Faith that trusts itself to God is the kind of faith that justifies.

God justifies the believing sinner on the basis of Jesus' death for mankind. Most excitingly, God works within the justified sinner to make righteousness a reality. So the gospel offer of justification by faith offers not simply pardon but also transformation. God will declare us righteous, innocent in his sight. And God will make us into the kind of persons he has declared us to be.

If we look through the records of church history, we discover that this powerful concept of justification was all too quickly mislaid. The Catholicism of the Middle Ages used the word *justification* to indicate an infusion of divine power which was supposed to enable the person who cooperated with it to make right choices and thus to merit salvation. It was in the Reformation, as Luther, Calvin, and the others rediscovered the grace of God, that the biblical doctrine of justification by faith alone was rediscovered.

Today this great truth, so central to the nature of the believer's relationship with God and to our thinking about his grace, is commonly understood by Christians. God declares you and me to be innocent. We are vindicated in his eyes, not because of what we do but because we trust in Jesus who died for us. How wonderful to discover, as we experience our renewing relationship with Jesus, that what God says we *are* is also what we are becoming. ⟩ ATONEMENT

KINGDOM

The kingdom of God is important to Christians. It must be. Jesus tells us that the search for God and his kingdom is to have first priority in our lives (Matt. 6:33). No sacrifice is too great to enter it (Mark 9:43–47). The kingdom, brought so near in Jesus (Matt. 4:17; Luke 17:21), calls for a unique lifestyle that Jesus describes in his Sermon on the Mount (Matt. 5–7).

Even though Christians agree that the kingdom is important, we haven't all agreed on exactly what God's kingdom is or how it is expressed. Too often this is because the church in a particular age or a particular church group has taken one aspect of a complex biblical concept and emphasized it at the expense of other aspects.

What is the kingdom, and how have Christians understood it? How do we understand the kingdom today, and what does it mean for us to be citizens of "the kingdom of the Son he [God] loves" (Col. 1:14)?

Kingdom in the Old Testament. The words translated "kingdom" in our Old Testament are derived from the Hebrew word for king, *melek*. This word simply means "a ruler," but it refers to a ruler who combines in his person all the functions of modern government: the legislative, executive, and judicial. In modern thought, a kingdom is a geographic area, with its own boundaries and laws. But the biblical concept is best expressed by the idea of reign or sovereignty. A ruler's kingdom is made up of the persons or things over which the ruler has authority and over which the ruler exercises control.

In the Old Testament kingdom is often the sphere of authority of human rulers. But the Old Testament also speaks of God's kingdom in two significant forms. On the one hand, the universe itself is God's kingdom, for he exercises sovereign, though hidden, control over all things. As Psalm 103:19 affirms, "The LORD has established his throne in heaven, and his kingdom rules over all."

This over-arching rule of God is sometimes expressed in mighty acts in history (see Ps. 145:11–13), but it typically operates quietly, unnoticed. The Old Testament affirms that God is in control, however those who oppose him may struggle (see 2 Chron. 13; Dan. 1:4; 6:26–27).

On the other hand, the Old Testament looks forward to a visible expression of the divine rule, an expression in which his sovereignty will be undisguised. Daniel tells of a coming age when "the God of heaven will set up a kingdom that will never be destroyed, nor will it be left to another people. It will crush all those kingdoms and bring them to an end, but it will itself endure forever" (Dan. 2:44).

Much of the Old Testament's prophecy is focused on this future age, when the earth will be ruled by Israel's Messiah, and "the kingdom will be the LORD'S" (Obad. 21).

Kingdom in the New Testament. The root concept of kingdom in our New Testament is drawn from the Old Testament rather than from Greek culture. A kingdom is a realm in which a king acts freely, exercising his control and authority over and through his subjects. Thus the kingdom of God is not a place, but it is that timeless realm in which God is free to act and exercise his control.

The Old Testament affirms God as king of the created universe and reveals that he is always at work here, actively shaping history's flow. The Old Testament looks forward to and promises a messianic age, when with raw power God will openly establish his rule over the earth.

In Jesus' time, Palestine was under the control of Rome, just the latest of a series of foreign conquerors. In this situation the second aspect of the Old Testament kingdom concept was particularly attractive. It is not surprising that when Jesus appeared and was associated with the Old Testament's Messiah, that he was expected to establish the visible, powerful Jewish state of prophecy (see, for example, Matt. 20:21–23; Acts 1:6–7).

But then Jesus unveiled yet another aspect of the kingdom — yet another aspect of God's rule. In essence, Jesus introduced a new avenue through which God would work in human affairs.

John the Baptist announced Jesus by warning, "Repent, for the kingdom of heaven is near" (Matt. 3:2). This message was also the theme of Jesus' early ministry (see Matt. 4:17; Mark 1:15), as he announced the "good news of the kingdom." Jesus' miracles are integral to his kingdom message. Once Jesus said, "If I drive out demons by the finger of God, then the kingdom of God has come to you" (Luke 11:20; Matt. 12:28). Jesus' point is that his miracles demonstrate his kingly authority. Every realm, material and spiritual, was subject to the power of our Lord.

Along with his miracles, Jesus taught. He showed his listeners that if they had faith in him, they could step into that realm where he would exercise his power for them. Those who commit themselves to Jesus, to trust him and to do his will, find themselves living in Jesus' kingdom — the kingdom where Jesus actively works in human lives to guide, to guard, and to transform (see Matt. 3:2; 4:17; 9:35; 10:7; Mark 1:15; Luke 4:43; 8:1; 9:2, 60; 10:9).

Jesus' references to a kingdom in which believers can live now does not replace earlier visions of the kingdom of God or make them obsolete. Unfortunately, some Christians have emphasized one view of the kingdom and have ignored or denied the others. The universal form of the kingdom and the future earthly kingdom to be ruled by Christ find biblical expression in both testaments. But it is very clear that the New Testament emphasizes the current rule of Jesus and what this means for his people.

In teaching his disciples to pray, Jesus began, "Your kingdom come, your will be done on earth as it is in heaven" (Matt. 6:10).

We experience the kingdom today by submitting to the will of God, doing it on earth. Living in an obedient relationship with Jesus, our Lord and king, we find the kingdom realized in our lives. As you and I do the will of God, we will experience his power in our own lives. His power will change us and will be exercised to fit our circumstances to his purposes for us.

The kingdom in church history. In the early centuries of the church, the future aspect of Jesus' kingdom was emphasized. Judgment day was fast approaching, and believers expected the kingdom promised Israel by the prophets. Reinhold Seeberg, who discounts this form of the kingdom, nevertheless notes in his *History of Doctrines* that "the more ancient the document examined, the more fervent is the expression of longing for this kingdom" (Vol. 1, p. 81).

Saint Augustine, in the fourth century, saw the kingdom of God as the true church (meaning the saints of God) but also as the *organized* church. Later Luther and the other Reformers challenged part of this identification. There will always be counterfeits and hypocrisy in the visible church on earth. But the church invisible, composed of those who experience faith and forgiveness through God's rule in their hearts, are the true kingdom of our Lord.

Martin Luther taught that the kingdom of God "comes to us in two different ways: first, in time, through the Word and faith; and secondly, it shall be revealed in eternity."

The present kingdom cannot be identified with in any temporal way or form, for it is, "an eternal, imperishable kingdom, which begins on earth through faith, and in which we receive and possess those eternal riches, forgiveness of sins, comfort, strength, renewal of the Holy Spirit, victory and triumph over the power of Satan, death and hell, and finally eternal life of body and soul, that is, eternal fellowship and blessedness with God."

The kingdom has present expression not only in the forgiveness that operates as its basic principle but also in the character of its citizens. Luther writes that "the kingdom of God is nothing else than to be pious, orderly, pure, kind, gentle, benevolent and full of all virtue and graces; also, that God have his being within us and that he alone be, live, and reign in us. This we should first of all and most earnestly desire."

In later activist times, some have thought of the kingdom as a righteousness to be expressed in contemporary society. The kingdom will be established as the gospel message wins the hearts of humanity and reshapes individuals and social institutions to reflect the ethics of God. This idealistic view of the kingdom has few biblical roots because the transformation of society in Scripture is consistently associated with the coming of the messianic King.

The kingdom of God for us. If there is anything we can safely say about the kingdom of God, it is that Christians haven't really exhausted or grasped its full import. Christians who see Jesus' kingdom primarily as Christ's future rule on earth miss the wonder of the power that Jesus exerts in and for us now. Even those who emphasize the fact that God's kingdom can be seen now have historically missed the full power of this teaching.

Kingdom emphasizes the exercise of a ruler's power. Kingdom is a personal and dynamic concept. When Jesus was on earth, he demonstrated his personal authority by miracles that showed his power over every material and spiritual force that binds humankind. Jesus as king acted not only in human hearts but in the physical universe as well. This Jesus invites us to trust him and through the new birth that faith provides, to become citizens of his kingdom (see John 3:3, 5). We are to enter that realm in which Jesus even now exercises his complete authority.

When we establish our relationship with Jesus, we become citizens of his kingdom. Here Jesus is king, and we are to obey him. As we obey, doing his will on earth as it is done in heaven, we find that Jesus exercises his sovereign power in us and for us.

This is why you and I can seek the kingdom of God and his righteousness without concern for those material needs that trouble pagans. We know that our Father cares for us and that our Lord can and will act for us. When, like the early church, we face persecution or opposition, we can turn to our sovereign Lord. We can appeal to him, certain that he will act for us (see Acts 4:23–30).

The Bible's teaching on the kingdom of God is an exciting call to understand who God is and just what it means to have a relationship with him. God is sovereign in our universe. His is the hidden, universal rule. God will be sovereign in our world. His is the coming glory and power. But God is sovereign now, and we can experience the wonder-working power of Jesus our Lord. As we obey him and acknowledge his rule, we enter the wondrous realm in which all things in this world continue subject to his power, and we see him working within our hearts and in every circumstance of our lives.

LAITY ◆ PRIESTHOOD

LAST DAYS

Christians look at this world as temporary. We're convinced that Jesus will return, that judgment day will come, and that eternity lies ahead.

Some Christians tend to think that these events will not happen soon but off somewhere in the distance, well beyond their own expected lifetime. But others of us have a sense that Christ's return is just around the corner. We expect that Jesus' return, not death, will mark the end of our own days on earth.

Christians haven't always pointed to the best evidence for their conviction that their own generation may be the last. For instance, Martin Luther once wrote, "I do not wish to force any one to believe as I do; neither will I permit anyone to deny me the right to believe that the last day is near at hand. These words and signs of Christ (Luke 21:25–36) compel me to believe that such is the case. For the history of the centuries that have passed since the birth of Christ nowhere reveals conditions like the present."

In a personal letter, Luther shared: "The world runs and hastens so diligently to its end that it often occurs to me forcibly that the last day will break before we can completely turn the Holy Scriptures into German. For it is certain from the Holy Scriptures that we have no more temporal things to expect. All is done and fulfilled."

Christians of earlier generations haven't been right in their convictions that theirs were the last days and that Jesus would return in their lifetime. But the attitude of expectation is often a positive influence in the Christian life. When we expect Jesus at any moment, we are less likely to settle down comfortably forgetting that our treasures are in heaven. Fixing our hope in Jesus and the transformation to be ours when Jesus comes is a purifying force (see 1 John 2:2–3).

Besides, Luther was right about one thing. We do have no more temporal things to expect. Jesus may come, tomorrow. And certainly during our lifetime. ◆ **SECOND COMING, MILLENIUM, PROPH-ECY/PROPHET**

LAW

What do Christians believe about law? There is no simple answer to that question, largely because we often have different meanings in mind. The Bible itself uses the word *law* in a number of ways. So it is not surprising if some confusion and disagreements exist.

When we understand some of the issues that our faith raises about the nature of law — and here I mean the divine law rather than human law — it is not all that complicated. Christianity has a unique and exciting message for humankind.

Law throughout church history. Whatever the intended role of law in biblical Judaism, the Judaism of the first century supposed that the law of God possessed a living power that stimulates human beings to do good. The good that they do is then accepted by God as a basis for justification. The gospel immediately confronted this notion, and the early church recognized the law of Moses as a yoke human beings were unable to bear (Acts 15:11); the law of Moses was a burden that would only "make it difficult for the Gentiles who are turning to God" (Acts 15:19).

In the ages following the completion of the New Testament, the gospel focus on forgiveness of sins by faith in Christ was clouded. Good works were held to be essential for the assurance of eternal life. Marcion, around A.D. 140, attempted a reform that included (with a number of heretical concepts) an insistence on separation of the law and gospel. Marcionite congregations persisted for several centuries. But in the developing Catholic church, the attitude toward the law of God paralleled that of Judaism. God was thought to give grace to help the Christian resist sin and keep the law of God. To this extent, salvation, or at least Christian experience, depends on keeping the law.

Most of our modern thinking about the law reflects the Reformation, which reaffirmed the doctrine of salvation by faith alone and the nature of Christ's death on the cross as providing full satisfaction for our sins. But this reaffirmation of salvation by faith forced a fresh rethinking of the role of God's law.

Martin Luther made a strict division between law and gospel. Law, God's revelation of his requirements and rules, tells us what we ought to do and what we have not done. While the moral law expressed in the commandments is a permanent requirement binding on all, it has a deadly impact. Law does not give life, rather law always slays, for it has no capacity to renew us inwardly. Instead, law only condemns, for it confronts us with our sin and awakens in us a terror of God.

Luther believed that the law should be preached in the churches, for a knowledge of sin awakens the conscience and stimulates repentance and conversions. But Christians are not under law and are not to look to law. The law might reveal what we must do, but the gospel brings us the power to do it. The law diagnoses the sickness, but the gospel is the medicine. To Luther, then, the law had a severely limited function. Law confronts us with our failure and condemns us so that we can be led from reliance on our own effort to rely instead on Christ.

Luther was not always consistent in the way he wrote about law and its place in the church. But Luther did consistently see Christ as fulfillment of the law in every sense. In Jesus we see the complete and most positive expression of God and his will. We are to trust Christ completely for salvation and trust that God who has sent us the Holy Spirit will enable us to follow our Lord Jesus' reign in our lives.

John Calvin established another Reformation tradition, one that gives a prominent role to the law of God. Luther and Calvin agree that the law is at heart a revelation of our God. In the law's commandments and statutes, we see a reflection of the moral character of God.

The law also has the important function that Luther emphasized: It establishes our sinfulness and our need for salvation. In the pure light of divine obligation, we discover what we should have done, and we grasp the extent of our failure.

But Calvin adds a "third use" of the law, which he thinks of as "principle one." This reflects the continuing need believers have for norms in the Christian life. The rationale is that God's commandments express positive principles of righteousness that are valid for all peoples of all times. Everyone, and especially Christians who want to do the will of God, needs the commandments for moral direction. Calvin writes that "unless [God] prescribes to us what his will is and regulates all the actions of our life according to a certain rule, we would be perpetually going astray."

This "third use" does not imply a strict legalism or a life lived by following rigid rules, although it is all too easy for believers to fall prey to legalism. For Calvin, Jesus embodies all the law calls for, and Jesus "has been set before us as an example whose image we ought to express in our life." Calvin did not expect Christians to be able to keep the law of God unaided. In a sermon on Ephesians 4, Calvin taught, "that our Lord Jesus Christ is given us for an example and pattern, and moreover, that it is his office so to reform us by the Spirit of God his Father, that we may walk in newness of life." We may not live by the spirit of Moses and the older Testament, but we are to enflesh the universal moral principles expressed there as we live in Christ, by his Spirit.

In this review, we sense a closer harmony between the viewpoints of Luther and Calvin than many have recognized. But we have hardly provided a basis on which to resolve other nagging questions. For instance, why does the Bible relate the Christian's freedom to serve God with freedom from law (Rom. 6:11–14)? What does Paul mean when he calls law the power of sin (1 Cor. 15:56)? How is freedom from a law that Paul calls "powerless" related to the fact that in Christ, God expects the "righteous requirements of the law to be fully met in us" (Rom. 8:3–4)? For answers to these questions, and to sort through the varying ways in which the word *law* is used in the Bible, we have to turn directly to Scripture.

Law in Old Testament use and life. The Old Testament term for the word *law* is *torah*, meaning "teaching" or "instructions." In the Old Testament these instructions were focused on how one should live rather than on the academic. The Old Testament view of law is a rich and positive one. A fatherly God has stooped lovingly to share with his people words that show Israel how to live in his love and how to live lovingly with each other. Moses tells Israel, "Observe them [God's instructions] carefully, for this will show your wisdom and understanding to the nations, who will hear about all these decrees and say, 'Surely this great nation is a wise and understanding people.' What other nation is so great as to have their gods near them the way the Lord our God is near us whenever we pray to him? And what other nation is so great as to have such righteous decrees and laws as this body of laws I am setting before you today?" (Deut. 4:6–8).

In this quote we see a developed meaning to *torah*. God's instructions were binding instructions. And they regulated the social, ceremonial, and religious life of his people.

In time the word *law* came to indicate everything that God had revealed to Israel through Moses, and the word *law* was used of the Pentateuch itself. So in the Old Testament the word *law* may refer to divine revelation in general, to a specific set of instructions, to written moral or ceremonial requirements, or to the writings of Moses. Whichever of these meanings is in view, *torah* is at heart divine instruction, provided by God as a gift to his people.

The law was a historically necessary gift. God established a covenant relationship with Abraham and with his descendants. After God delivered those descendants from slavery in Egypt, Israel's continuing unresponsiveness to God demonstrated the people's need for guidance and discipline (see Exod. 15:22–17:7). God provided that guidance in the law given at Sinai, explaining at the same time the consequences of disobedience and obedience. The person or generation that wandered from the law would meet disaster, and the person or generation that lived by it would be blessed. So law was a great gift to ancient Israel, a well-marked road sign pointing the way to an experience of God's very best and greatest blessings.

But we need to remember that the Old Testament law was not simply the great moral code expressed in the Ten Commandments. Law provided an overall structure for Israel's life. It guided individual acts and worship. It structured social life and laid down criminal law. It provided the constitution for Israel as a nation, and it designed Israel's worship system. In short, everything in the life of the Old Testament believer and in Jewish society was governed and regulated by the divine law.

The godly Israelite did not see this law as a set of rigid, burdensome regulations. Two of David's psalms reflect the true believer's attitude during the Old Testament era. To one who senses a personal relationship with the Lord, law is God's loving voice of instruction.

> The ordinances of the LORD are sure
>   and altogether righteous.
> They are more precious than gold,
>   than much pure gold;
> they are sweeter than honey,
>   than honey from the comb.
> By them is your servant warned;
>   in keeping them there is great reward.
>
> (Ps. 19:10–11)

> I rejoice in following your statutes
>   as one rejoices in great riches.
> I meditate on your precepts
>   and consider your ways.
> I delight in your decrees;
>   I will not neglect your word.
>
> (Ps. 119:15–16)

But while the true believer responded to the God whose voice was recognized in the law, law as a system failed to make Israel righteous. The nation and individuals fell short of justice and righteousness, and despite the fact that Israel knew what was good, generation after generation failed to do good. The prophets recognized this flaw in law and looked ahead to a day when God would take another approach to righteousness. Jeremiah predicted a day when the Mosaic law would no longer be relevant, and God would supplant the Mosaic covenant with a new covenant. Then he would put his "law in their minds and write it on their hearts" (Jer. 31:32–33).

We, who study the Old Testament today as God's revelation for us as well as for Israel, must be careful in our thinking about the law. We must not jump to the conclusion that the law was less than just and good. It was given to God's people to bless them. On the other hand, we must not jump to the conclusion that the law is essential if God is to produce righteousness in humanity. The Old Testament itself speaks of the inadequacy of the law; the Old Testament promises that God will one day introduce a better way to produce righteousness. What we need to understand is that God's better way has been introduced in Jesus Christ. God's ultimate approach to making humanity good is to operate in you and me today.

Law in the New Testament. The Greek word rendered "law" is *nomos*. It is used in the New Testament with even more meanings than *torah* has in the Old Testament. In Greek culture, law assumes a social process by which a custom or tradition becomes a norm, a way in which a society's members define their duties and obligations. By the fifth century B.C., *nomoi* were written laws, which brought punishment if they were not obeyed.

The Greek philosophers were troubled by the shifting and uncertain nature of human laws. They looked for some ground outside of society for universal laws or principles that reflect the nature of the universe. Many philosophers felt life could be meaningful only if it were lived in harmony with such universal principles.

At times the word *law* is used in the New Testament in the sense of universal principle, as when Paul in Romans 7 describes his own struggle with the principle of sin in his human nature (his flesh). Finally Paul realized that only another universal principle, "the law of the Spirit of life in Christ Jesus," could lift him out of his spiritual powerlessness (Rom. 8:2).

Most often, however, the use of the word *law* in the New Testament is shaped by Old Testament thought. In the New Testament as in the Old Testament, the word *law* is used to refer to instruction from God, the Mosaic code, the whole body of Mosaic revelation, and revelation itself.

But what is the attitude of the New Testament toward law? In

Jesus' day the rabbis, those teachers of the law, felt that each person could and must keep the regulations God had laid down for his people. The rabbis made the same assumption as did the rich young ruler who met Jesus. To them the law was the source of life, and the central question of religion was, "What must I do to inherit eternal life?" (Luke 18:18).

Jesus never attacked, denied, or sought to overthrow the law. But he did challenge the understanding of law on which contemporary Jewish belief was based. In a vital statement, Jesus confronted his critics, "Do not think that I have come to abolish the Law or the Prophets; I have not come to abolish them but to fulfill them. I tell you the truth, until heaven and earth disappear, not even the smallest letter, not the least stroke of a pen, will by any means disappear from the Law until everything is accomplished" (Matt. 5:17–18).

Jesus' stated intention to "fulfill" the Law and Prophets has usually been taken as a reference to his own perfect life. But his listeners would have heard "fulfill" in another sense. It was every rabbi's desire to fulfill the law in the sense of explaining it accurately, of exposing its true and deepest meaning. So in Matthew 5 we see Jesus go on to do just this.

Jesus taught that the commands of the older revelation are to be practiced, but he warns that a person's righteousness must surpass that of Pharisee and teacher, who had committed themselves to do each detail of every biblical injunction, and even the additions and traditions that had grown up around the law over the centuries. Christ, in a series of illustrations, pointed out that the Old Testament law regulates behavior, but God is concerned with the heart. Murder is forbidden by the law, but God judges the anger and hatred that lead to murder. The law forbids adultery, but God condemns the attitude that looks at a person of the opposite sex as an object to be used. The law speaks only to what we *do*, but God evaluates what we *are*.

What is it that God seeks in human beings? When Jesus was asked what was the law's greatest commandment, he responded, "Love the Lord your God with all your heart and with all your soul and with all your mind. This is the first and greatest commandment. And the second is like it: Love your neighbor as yourself. All the Law and the Prophets hang on these two commandments." Where there is a controlling love for God and a controlling love for others, those good actions defined by the law flow naturally and spontaneously.

Often the New Testament indicates that the day of the Mosaic law had ended with the death and resurrection of Jesus (see, for example, Matt. 11:13; Luke 16:16–17; John 1:17; Heb. 7:11–12). This in no way suggests that God is no longer concerned with righteousness. It does suggest that in Jesus, God has brought us a way to achieve a righteousness that is greater than any law implied or made possible.

Part of our difficulty with the approach to law expressed in the Epistles is that many Christians have failed to realize that the writers have introduced yet another meaning in their discussion of law.

Paul and the writer of Hebrews look at law and write about it as a *system*.

In Hebrews the word *law* indicates the perfectly balanced Old Testament system that has as its elements commands, sacrifices, priesthood, and tabernacle worship. This system is so intimately interrelated that a change in any one part necessitates a change in the others. And in Jesus, God introduces a new priesthood and a new covenant. For the writer of Hebrews, it follows that there must "also be change of the law" (Heb. 7:11–12). The old, obsolete Mosaic approach, in which God's expectations for humanity were engraved in stones, is to be done away with, as God now intends to take the righteousness expressed there and "put in their minds," so that his desires for men and women will be "written on their hearts" (see Heb. 8).

Often when Paul uses the word *law*, he too has in mind a system. However, his system includes as its elements God's moral code, human beings, and the interaction between them. If we view the Mosaic code objectively, looking at it in isolation from its impact on human beings, it is "holy, righteous, and good" (Rom. 7:12). But when we look at law as it functions within the system, the word *law* is a harbinger of death and destruction (Rom. 7:9–10). In fact, law is the strength of sin (1 Cor. 15:56), for it stirs up the evil in the flesh to acts of rebellion (see Rom. 7:4–6). While there is nothing wrong or imperfect in the objective law of God, the system that calls on human beings to relate to God through the law is "powerless" in that "it was weakened by the sinful nature" (Rom. 8:3).

When Paul insists that "we are not under the law but under grace," he teaches us that we must relate to God in any way that places no reliance on human effort to achieve the moral standards that are expressed in and as law.

At this point we can return to the various functions of the law suggested by the Reformers. Yes, law does reveal God's character, and by setting up a standard against which to measure our actions, law does reveal human sinfulness. As Paul points out, "I would not have known what sin was except through the law. For I would not have known what it was to covet had the law not said, 'Do not covet'" (Rom. 7:7).

In Romans 3:31, Paul argues that the gospel actually "upholds" God's law. Paul means that by shifting the focus of religion to faith and to justification by grace, law is given its proper place in religion. That place is to destroy human pretentions and to display to each person his or her sin.

What then about the "third function" of the law? Is the law intended to guide believers into a holy life?

We must admit that this was one of the uses in Old Testament times. But too many specific passages in the New Testament contradict the notion for us. Paul insists that believers are not under law (Rom. 6:14). According to Romans 7:1–4, believers died to the law with Christ. We are released so that we might serve God in a new way and live for Christ (Rom. 7:6; Gal. 2:19). We are redeemed from under the law (Gal. 4:5), which is not for good people but for evil (1 Tim. 1:9).

But if we do not admit the third function of law, how can we become truly good persons? How can "the righteous requirements of the law" be "fully met in us, who do not live according to the sinful nature but according to the Spirit" (Rom. 8:4)?

The answer comes when we realize that the gospel changes the focus of thinking about righteousness. We no longer are primarily concerned with what we do, but with who we are.

In Christ, God gives us a new life, and he personally enters our personality to energize and guide us. Paul explains that if we are led by the Spirit, we are not under law, for the Spirit produces such fruit as love, joy, peace, patience, kindness, and goodness in our personalities. And Paul observes, "against such there is no law" (see Gal. 5:16–25).

The point is vital. Law by its very nature stands *against* evil. Where there is no evil, law is irrelevant. By working within our personalities to make us truly good, God short-circuits law and makes it irrelevant to us.

This does not mean that Scripture is irrelevant. It does not mean that by reading the Bible and by seeing God's values and concerns expressed there we cannot learn more of him and more of the persons he is calling us to be. It does not mean that God's commandments no longer stand in judgment over our actions when we sin. Freedom from the law means that we no longer rely on the law system to make us righteous. Instead we rely on a new system. We rely on the inner working of God's Spirit, who guides and energizes and changes us from within, so that the righteousness that law describes will flow spontaneously from our transformed selves.

Summary. It is no wonder that our talking and thinking about law seems confusing at times. It is a complex subject because the word *law* has many different meanings. In the Old Testament law is the divine revelation — those statutes and commands that provide the foundation for Israel's national life. This law was a gift, for it showed God's people how to live in harmony with him and with one another. But law was never the focus of Old Testament religion. That focus was faith in God himself. Tragically, too many people in Israel took the law as a way of salvation and attempted to keep the law in order to be justified in God's sight.

When Jesus came, the original focus was restored. Christ called on his hearers to believe in and commit themselves to him. He taught about the law, showing that God must demand an inner and not simply an outer righteousness. Then Jesus died so that all who fail to keep the law might have eternal life and forgiveness by faith in him.

The Epistles not only use *law* in all the old senses but also add another. Paul and the writer of Hebrews use *law* to describe systems — basic approaches to faith and life. Paul shows that even God's revelation of righteousness in the Mosaic code cannot help the believer to become good. We are enabled to live a righteous life by relying on the Spirit, not by struggling to keep the law. You and I can look at Scripture's codes and regulations to sense the holiness of God and to glimpse the persons God intends us to be. But when the issue is becoming this kind of person, we are to look away from the "do's and don'ts" of law and instead rely on the Spirit within.

LIBERTY ◆ FREEDOM

LIFE

Life is a great gift; life is worth living, whatever our circumstances. Life is precious and is to be protected. Human life has unique value.

These statements capture something of the Christian's attitude toward life. But many more expressions would be required to sum up the wonder of the earthly and eternal life God has given us.

Perhaps the best way to explore what life means to us is to look at what the Old and New Testaments say about the meaning, the purpose, and the possession of God's gift of life.

The Old Testament's view of life. The Old Testament's perspective of life concentrates on human experience in this world. One of the Hebrew words rendered "life" simply means "having life," "to be living." Another speaks of "individual being," "of the unique living 'I.'"

In the Old Testament each person's existence is traced back to God, the source of life for our race (Gen. 2:7). Because the life we human beings have can be traced to the Lord and has been stamped with his image, each person has unique value. No person's life is to be snatched away by another (Gen. 9:5–6; Exod. 21:23; Deut. 19:21).

Life in the Old Testament is no abstract concept. Living is a vital, practical thing: It is using all the powers and capacities God has given us in a fulfilling way. Living life on earth is a gift and a blessing.

Both our existence and the quality of our life on earth is important in the Old Testament. Those who follow God's ways are to experience a fulfilling life, not merely to have existence. Moses captures this thought as he exhorts Israel to keep God's commands. "See," he says, "I set before you today life and prosperity, death and destruction" (Deut. 30:15). Obedience to God brings an enriched life, but disobedience shades our experience toward suffering and death, and results in the loss of our human potential.

While eternal life is hinted at in the Old Testament (see Ps. 30:5; Prov. 12:28; 15:24; Dan. 12:2 as well as Ps. 16:11; 21:4–6), the focus is on life here and now. Our present life is precious. It is to be accepted as a wondrous gift and is to be experienced in a rich, fulfilling way.

The New Testament's view of life. In the New Testament the focus shifts away from our biological life to our spiritual life. Now, too, death is viewed in its aspect as alienation from God, as being cut off from the source of all life and being.

There are several words in the Greek language for life. *Bios* focuses on the externals: on a person's lifestyle, his or her wealth and possessions. This word is seldom used in the New Testament, and when it is, it is used negatively (Luke 8:14; 1 John 2:16). *Psuche* stands for conscious life and often means the inner person or the personality. Jesus gave his life (his very self) as a ransom for us (Matt. 20:28). And Jesus warns that to save one's life (*psuche*, the inner, true self), a person must lose himself or herself for the Lord. Only by surrendering ourselves to Jesus can our full potential be realized, can we become the person we can be.

The third Greek word is *zoe*, which in the New Testament is a theological term. It shifts our vision from this earth to the life that spans time and eternity. This is the distinctive word with which Christians are most concerned as we explore what the Bible teaches about spiritual life and death.

In the New Testament this life is everywhere contrasted with death. Adam and Eve sinned and brought on our race death — alienation from God and a corruption of human capacities and powers. With that curse came biological death as well. But Jesus brings us life in every sense of the term. He restores us to relationship with God, he frees us to find fulfillment, and ultimately he will release us from corruptibility through a glorious resurrection. As Jesus said, "I tell you the truth, whoever hears my words and believes on him who sent me has eternal life and will not be condemned: he has crossed over from death to life. I tell you the truth, the time is coming and now is when the dead will hear the voice of the Son of God and those who hear will live. For as the Father has life in himself, so he has granted the Son to have life in himself" (John 5:24–26). Relationship with Jesus releases the vitality of a fresh, spiritual life which the Bible calls eternal.

The Bible's vision of eternal life contains a promise of endless personal existence of fellowship with God. Dying Christians can face death in the assurance that their biological end is nothing less than a new beginning. Ahead, too, is resurrection, when the promise comes true that "death has been swallowed up in victory" (1 Cor. 15:53–55). ▸

HEAVEN AND HELL

But eternal life means even more to us than this. God's gift of life in Christ means that "the old has gone, the new has come." We have within us now the vitalizing power of God, which can lift us beyond our moral limitations and enable us to actually "bear fruit to God" (Rom. 7:4). We can experience fulfillment through being what humanity was originally created to be: creatures who glorify God and who enjoy him now and forever.

A number of key New Testament passages explore God's gift of eternal life. Among them are John 3:15–36; 5:21–26; 6:27–68; 10:10–28; 11:1–44; 1 John 2–3; 5:10–12; Romans 5:9–10, 12–21; 6:1–10; 8:1–11; 2 Corinthians 4:1–12; 3:12–18.

The Christian's outlook on life. Christians have a perspective on life that is shaped by Scripture. First, we acknowledge God as the source of both biological life and the human personality. Because life is his gift to each of us, life is precious and to be protected. Because life includes all the potentials that God has structured into human nature, a fulfilling life will involve the exercise of our potentials. So Christians are concerned that people have the opportunity for self-development. We are concerned with the quality of human life as well as with its continuation.

We are also convinced that a self-centered life, lived in the grip of sinful passions, can never be a fulfilling life. We look to God to renew our personalities, to transform us from within through a fresh infusion of spiritual life by Jesus. In Jesus we are given God's own eternal life, and once again we can enjoy relationship with the Lord and obey him. In obedience we become the persons we were intended to be, and we find the fulfillment that God intends his people to know.

Yes, we believe that this life is a gift from God. We believe every person has worth and value and that the quality of personal life on earth is a matter for our concern. Yet we believe that the most important concern of human beings is eternal life. Each human being will exist forever, and only when we exist in relationship with God can existence truly be called life. In Christ each person can have eternal life now. While eternal life will be known in fullest only in our resurrection, it can be experienced today as we who know Jesus respond to him and shape our lives by his Word.

LOGOS ♦ WORD

LORD

Lord is a particularly significant word for Christians, who confidently assert that Jesus is Lord. As with other vital terms of faith, those who so acknowledge Jesus may not realize just how significant this title is. It is, as Paul says in Philippians 2, "the name that is above every name." And to call Jesus Lord involves one of the most significant of Christian commitments.

Lord in the Old Testament. Where our English versions use the word "Lord," the Hebrew original has "Jehovah," or "Jahweh." Where "Lord" is found, there is another Hebrew word meaning "a superior," "a master," or "owner." Jahweh is the more significant name, for it is the personal name of God, a name that affirms that our God is "the one who is always present." God's personal name, Jahweh, is found over 5,300 times in the Old Testament. It is the name intimately associated with both revelation and redemption and thus with God's personal involvement in his creation and with his people.

When the translators of the Hebrew Scripture translated "Jahweh" into Greek, they chose *kurios*, the term that English also translates as "Lord." So when you and I acknowledge Jesus as Lord, we are identifying him with the Jahweh of the Old Testament. Jesus is, and forever has been, the God of the Bible: the God who is always present in and before and after history itself.

Lord in the New Testament. The Greek word *kurios* was used in ordinary speech in New Testament times as a term of respect or form of address, something like our "sir." In the Gospels some people who addressed Jesus of Nazareth as Lord had nothing more in mind than this. Yet when Jesus spoke of himself as Lord, he often referred to the Old Testament emphasis on his deity (see Matt. 12:8; Luke 20:42–44). In the vocabulary of faith, calling Jesus Lord is like Thomas' confession, "My Lord and my God" (John 20:28).

Acts and the Epistles show that the church immediately following the resurrection recognized Jesus as Lord. In Philippians, Paul traces the process by which Jesus, "being in very nature God," emptied himself and took on a servant's nature. Thus to acknowledge Jesus as Lord is to acknowledge his full deity: to worship and obey him as God.

The New Testament not only affirms the lordship of Jesus, it also explains what it means to you and to me to acknowledge him as Lord.

First, the fact that Jesus is Lord means that he holds all authority. Everything is subject to him, for he is God (see Eph. 1:21; 1 Peter 3:22). Second, the fact that Jesus is Lord also means that he exercises personal authority over believers. In Romans 14, Paul points out that the lordship of Jesus over "every man" means that each of us is responsible directly to Jesus for our actions and convictions. We are not to judge each other but to acknowledge that Christ alone exercises authority over our brothers and sisters. The fact that Jesus is Lord also means that he exercises pervasive authority over his church. We live "in" and "under" and "through" our Lord. These phrases occur repeatedly in the New Testament, reminding us that the presence and power of Jesus are central in our experience. And at history's end Christ's lordship will be obvious to all as it is demonstrated by his return and his final victory over sin.

God calls on you and me to acknowledge Jesus as Lord. We are to honor him as God. But more, we are to willingly submit ourselves to him and to his will. The key to vital Christian experience is not found simply in agreeing that Christ is Lord but in fully submitting ourselves to his will so that he might work out all that his lordship means in our very lives.

LORD'S DAY ◗ SABBATH

LORD'S SUPPER

Christians remember Christ's suffering and death in a ceremony which the Scripture calls the Lord's Supper (much later it is called Communion or the Eucharist). The meaning of this ceremony has been understood differently by different Christian traditions. But for all of us, the Lord's Supper holds deep significance.

Most biblical texts describe the Lord's Supper (Matt. 26:26–29; Mark 14:22–25; Luke 22:14–20). Only one passage in the New Testament letters speaks of the Lord's Supper at any length (1 Cor. 11:23–26).

The Supper instituted. Christ met with his disciples just before his death for a last meal, a meal that many believe to have been the Passover meal. ◗ PASSOVER Christ shared much during that evening together (see

John 13-17). But its most significant moments came when Jesus took bread and wine and with these symbols taught the twelve disciples the meaning of his death. His action instituted a practice that has been followed by Christians for nearly two thousand years.

If we combine the reports of the event, we hear again what our Lord said during one of history's most solemn moments. Of the bread, which Jesus took and tore apart with his hands, Christ said, "Take, eat, this is my body, which is given for you. Do this for my remembrance." And of the common cup containing wine, he said, "All of you drink from it, for this cup is the new covenant in my blood, which is poured out for many for the remission of sins. Do this as often as you drink it for my remembrance."

The meaning of Jesus' words. The symbolic significance of the Passover time and of Jesus' words help us establish the meaning of Christ's death as well as of the Lord's Supper. The Jewish Passover recalled how God spared his people from the death that struck the Egyptians, who had refused to release the Israelites from slavery in the time of Moses. Through the body and blood of Jesus, all who believe are about to be released from spiritual death and from the slavery to sin, which grips humankind. The words of Jesus make it clear that Christ's death (his blood and broken body) instituted the "new covenant" promised by Jeremiah. The inauguration of this covenant of blood, the most binding of Old Testament commitments, means the replacement of the older Mosaic covenant and the dawning of the new day in which God will forgive sins and plant his law within the hearts (personalities) of believers (Jer. 31). Jesus' words about forgiveness recall Isaiah's description of God's Servant, destined to pour out his life for transgressors (Isa. 53). These words and images make perfectly clear the meaning of Christ's approaching substitutionary death. But what about the meaning of the phrase "in remembrance"?

Paul recalls the words of Jesus on this evening, and the apostle emphasizes three things. First, the Lord's Supper is a memorial feast. Biblically a memorial or memorial event calls for a special kind of "remembrance." It calls on believers not to recall history, but to visualize themselves present in an event that has a continuing impact on their relationship with God. Just as members of each generation of Israelites were to visualize their present freedom as a result of God's ancient deliverance from Egypt, so we are to visualize ourselves present in Jesus' death. Our forgiveness and present freedom from sin's power flow directly from our identification with him on Calvary.

Second, the Lord's Supper is a way in which Christians "proclaim the Lord's death" (1 Cor. 11:26). In Augustine's words, this ceremony puts the gospel forward in a "visible word." Jesus' death for us is vividly portrayed in the Lord's Supper. In this special service, Christ is present in the same way he is always present when God's Word is proclaimed.

Finally, the Lord's Supper is an event in which the communion or fellowship of God's people, united by our common faith in Jesus, is affirmed. Because cup and bread are "a participation in" the blood and body of Christ and "because there is one loaf, we who are many, are one body, for we all partake of the one loaf" (1 Cor. 10:16–17). It is Christ himself, the center of our common faith, who makes fellowship possible, and this remembrance of his death affirms our union with other believers.

Over the centuries Christians have disagreed over the exact nature of the Lord's Supper. Early in our era Christian writers began to speak of the Lord's Supper as a sacrifice. The Catholic church developed the view that, in the Eucharist, Christ's sacrifice is offered again and again to God. The developed doctrine supposes a "real presence" of Christ in the wafer, which is shared with the faithful, and in the wine, which is drunk only by the offering priest. The Reformers rejected this view, finding no basis for it in the New Testament and noting the Bible's clear statement that "Christ was sacrificed once to take away the sins of many people" (Heb. 9:28). It was "by one sacrifice [that] he has made perfect forever those who are being made holy" (Heb. 10:14). But even the Reformers did not agree about the nature of the presence of Christ in the Lord's Supper, and their debates brought division.

So what is our view of this special service, faithfully conducted by believers throughout the centuries?

Christians, and particularly Protestants, recognize the Lord's Supper as a special and holy ceremony. Some of us call it an ordinance, and some call it a sacrament (that is, a means by which God's grace is given to us). In some of our churches the Lord's Supper is conducted weekly, in others once a quarter. But whatever the distinguishing features of our tradition's view of the Lord's Supper, it continues to offer us a special moment to remember Jesus' death and our participation in it. It offers us a way to publicly present the gospel in a visible Word, and it also reminds us that in Christ and because of Christ, we who know Jesus are a single people, the people of God.

LOVE

When the church has been most faithful to Christ, it has been marked by its love. That shouldn't be surprising. Jesus identified love for

God and for neighbor as the greatest of the commandments (Matt. 22:37–39). Paul emphasizes faith, hope, and love, but calls love the "greatest" (1 Cor. 13:1–7). And the first-named fruit of the Spirit, perhaps one in which all the others are implied, is love (Gal. 5:22).

What does love mean to Christians, and how does love function in our faith? A survey of the two testaments gives us the insights we need to tune our own hearts to the Lord.

Love in the Old Testament. One Old Testament word for love expresses a number of relationships, from general liking, to the welcome and respect extended to neighbors (Lev. 19:18) and strangers (Lev. 19:33), on to the deep family affection. This word is also used to express our love for God and his commands and is often used of God's love for humankind. A different word, translated "love" or "lovingkindness" in our modern English versions, has special theological implications. This word describes a bond of loyalty, a choice to remain committed to another. This word is central in the Old Testament's portrait of God, who has made a covenant commitment to his people and who expresses his love for them by his faithfulness. As Moses cries out, "The LORD, the LORD, the compassionate and gracious God, slow to anger, abounding in love and faithfulness, maintaining love to thousands, and forgiving wickedness, rebellion and sin" (Deut. 34:6–7).

How is love expressed in the Old Testament? God's deep affection is given as the motive for God's choice of Israel. Again the words of Moses: "Because he loved your forefathers and chose their descendants after them, he brought you out of Egypt by his Presence and his great strength" (Deut. 4:37).

It continues to be love that motivates God's blessing of his obedient people (Deut. 7:13–15). Even God's discipline of Israel is an expression of fatherly love (Prov. 3:12). God's love reaches the individual, especially the righteous poor and the oppressed (Ps. 146:8–9). One day salvation will come, and God will then be free to love Israel fully (see Isa. 43:1–7; Hos. 14:11).

The other love, commitment love, is fixed uniquely on those whom God has redeemed. Moved by this love, God provides guidance and leading (Gen. 24; Exod. 15:13). He calls people to worship him (Ps. 5:7; 26:3), delivers them from enemies (Ps. 6:4; 17:7), protects (Ps. 21:7; 32:10), forgives (Ps. 25:7; 51:1), answers prayer (Ps. 66:20), and remains faithful for his purpose for them (Ps. 138:8). God's affection has moved him to make a commitment to his people, and within the framework of that commitment, he pours out his love on Israel.

The Old Testament also speaks of human love for God. But only in one place (Jer. 2:2) does the Bible use the commitment-love word for Israel's devotion to the Lord. But the other word shows us clearly how affection for God is expressed.

The Old Testament people expressed their love for God through their obedience to him. Moses' great call to "love the LORD your God with all your heart and with all your soul and with all your strength" focuses immediately on "these commands that I give you this day," which are to be "upon your heart" (Deut. 6:5–6). Later Deuteronomy adds, "What does the LORD your God ask of you but to fear the LORD your God, to walk in all his ways, to love him, to serve the LORD your God with all your heart and soul, and to observe the LORD'S commands and decrees that I am giving you today for your own good?" (Deut. 10:12–13). Again and again the Old Testament links love for God and obedience and sees the love we give him as a fitting response to God's own initial saving acts.

We should also note that love for others is a central requirement of God's Old Testament law (see Lev. 19:18; Matt. 22:37–39). Loving God is the key that opens the door to our ability to love one another.

Love in the New Testament. Just as the Hebrew uses different words for love, the Greek also uses different words for love. One common Greek word for love, *eros* (which focuses on sexual desires), is not found in our New Testament. Even the most common word, *philia* (which indicates fondness in and outside of family bonds), is used infrequently. Instead the New Testament writers picked an overlooked and weak word for love, *agape*, and transformed it by infusing it with unique meaning. It is this word, adopted into Christianity, that stands today as the measure of love's deepest and fullest meaning.

First of all, *agape* is the word used to express God's wonderful love for us. The New Testament says that "God is love" (1 John 4:16) and that all he does is an expression of love. We realize the extent of God's love only in Jesus' self-sacrifice. John writes, "This is how God showed his love among us: He sent his one and only Son into the world that we might live through him. This is love: not that we loved God, but that he loved us and sent his Son as an atoning sacrifice for our sins" (1 John 4:9–10).

That sacrifice was made not for friends but for enemies. "God demonstrated his own love for us in this: While we were still sinners, Christ died for us" (Rom. 5:8). The incarnation and crucifixion of Jesus are the universe's ultimate expression of love, convincing us beyond a doubt that God is committed to us, fully and forever.

In the New Testament *agape* is used to speak of the believer's love for the Lord. By nature humanity is at odds with God; we are his enemies (see Col. 1:21; Eph. 2:3). But the vision of Christ's love expressed in Calvary and faith in the God who offers us salvation in him can transform our attitude toward God. When we respond to his love with faith, our love for God is awakened. As John writes, "We love because he first loved us" (1 John 4:19). Faith creates a channel through which God's own love pours into our life.

God's outpouring of love into our hearts is the key to understanding the power of Christianity. That love is the sanctifying power that transforms us, enabling us to please God and to reflect Jesus in this world. What does the Bible link with this love?

Love prompts obedience. As the Old Testament shows, the one who loves God is the person who will be moved to obey him. Jesus said, "Whoever has my commands and obeys them, he is the one who loves me" (John 14:21; see 14:23; 1 John 5:3).

Love creates community. It is this love that enables us not only to love each other as Christ has loved us (John 13:14) but also to build the intimate caring fellowship that is the mark of discipleship. Every Epistle reemphasizes the importance of Christians loving one another (see, for example, Rom. 12:9–10; 1 Cor. 13; 2 Cor. 8:24; Gal. 5:13; Eph. 5:2).

Love provides our motivation. In 2 Corinthians 5, Paul explains the basis for his confidence that even carnal Christians will choose to live for the Lord. "Christ's love compels us," the apostle writes (2 Cor. 5:14). We do not motivate change in others by threats or loading on guilt. We must rely on the inner power of the love of Jesus to move others —and ourselves.

Love brings transformation. Many New Testament passages promise that we who believe in Jesus will become more and more like him. It is love that brings about this change, moving us to be righteous in every relationship. In Romans 13:10, Paul writes that "love does no harm to its neighbor" and explains that "therefore love is the fulfillment of the law" (see Gal. 5:21–23).

Love provides purpose. Desire for material things is an inadequate goal for life (see 1 Tim. 6:10). Only by loving God and our neighbors can we take hold of that wonderful purpose for which we were created and redeemed (see 1 Thess. 4:9–10; 2 Thess. 3:5; Heb. 10:24; 1 Peter 4:8).

Love stabilizes our relationships. Unity is maintained in the Christian community as love makes it possible for us to differ, even on important matters, without destructive antagonism (1 Cor. 8:1–13; Phil. 2:2; Col. 2:2).

Love compels mutual concern. Love moves us to share freely, to help meet the material and spiritual needs of others (1 John 3:16–18).

Even a brief survey of the New Testament helps us to sense that love is the key. Love is the key to understanding Jesus' willingness to die on the cross for us. The love that God awakens in us when we trust Jesus is the key to that obedience to God which moves us toward righteousness. And the love that God pours into our hearts is the key to a vital Christian life. Love transforms our desires, our motives, our values, our relationships, our very selves.

Christianity best reflects Christ when Christians grow in love and live out the love that is the one infallible mark of Christ's presence among his people.

MERCY

Christians tend to have high standards for themselves and others. At our best, we remember a vital, balancing reality: that all of us fall short. So it is no wonder that mercy is a valued quality, in God and in us as well.

But what is mercy? And how is mercy to be experienced and expressed in our Christian lives?

Mercy in the Old Testament. If you glance through a concordance of a modern English version of the Bible, you will discover that the word *mercy* is hardly mentioned in the Old Testament. Actually, it is there. It is just that the Hebrew words meaning "mercy" can be translated by several different English terms. One word conveys the love of a superior for an inferior, seen in deep feelings that move the superior to act and help. Usually our versions express this as "love" or as "compassion." Another Hebrew word focuses on the act of one who is able to help another person who is in need. Again the sense is that the one who helps is moved by deep feelings and that the person who is helped has no right to expect aid. This root is often translated "grace" in our versions.

However these words may be translated in our versions, the basic meaning does shine through. Mercy is love, reaching out to help the helpless without considering the merit of the person who receives aid.

Mercy in the New Testament. A single Greek root is rendered "mercy" in our New Testament. Mercy here, too, is a compassionate response: being moved to give help to an afflicted or powerless person.

In the Gospels we often see Jesus respond to cries for mercy as persons with needs call on him for help (see Matt. 15:22; 17:15). Jesus' compassionate response to such persons assures us of God's attitude toward you and me in our needs. The Gospels also report Jesus' many calls for his hearers to have mercy. Jesus' disciples are to "be merciful, just as your Father is merciful" (Luke 6:36). The religious officials of Jesus' day are confronted because they have "neglected the more important matters of the law — justice, mercy and faithfulness" (Matt. 23:23). We are closest to the heart of God when we identify with the needy and reach out to help them (see Matt. 9:9–13; 12:1–7; 18:21–33).

The Epistles also emphasize mercy. In Romans 9 and 11, Paul identifies God's mercy as the basis for his saving action. God responds to the need of the helpless, not to any supposed merit in those he chooses to love. It is because God is "rich in mercy" that he has "made us alive with Christ even when we were dead in transgressions" (Eph. 2:4–5). His saving action was "not because of righteous things we had done, but because of his mercy" (Titus 3:5). The Epistles assure us that God continues to deal with us in mercy. They often link mercy and peace (see 1 Tim. 1:2; 2 Tim. 1:2; 2 John 2; Jude 2). Remembering that God is merciful is a source of inner peace for you and me. Hebrews 4:16 is most significant. Jesus remembers how weak we are, how easily trapped by our humanness. Because he stands always at God's right hand to represent us, we can come boldly, with total confidence, to the very throne of grace "to receive mercy, and grace to help in time of need." Our failures do not cut us off from our God, for God is ever ready to have mercy on us.

Paul calls on us "in view of God's mercy" to offer our bodies "as living sacrifices, holy and pleasing to God" (Rom. 12:1). God's mercy does make us careless, but it also fills us with a special wonder and love. When we truly understand how God stooped to love us in our helplessness, and loves us still, we can do nothing less than gratefully offer ourselves to him. As God's mercy makes us sensitive to the fact that our own failures move the Lord to compassion rather than anger, we become more willing to deal gently with others. As we show mercy to others, we provide a living witness to the compassionate love of our God.

MESSIAH

Christians believe that Jesus is the Messiah for whom Israel has hoped for centuries. The word *messiah* comes from a Hebrew root meaning "to anoint." The Messiah, then, is the anointed one.

In Old Testament times persons set aside for special office like the priesthood or kingship were anointed with oil (see Lev. 8:30; Exod. 40:15; 1 Sam. 10:1; 16:1). This act of consecration had religious as well as social significance: Such a person was *God's* anointed, and the appointment to the office was considered to be made by the Lord (see

1 Sam. 12:3, 5). Many Old Testament passages look forward to God's appointment of an ideal king for Israel: One from King David's line is to be anointed by God to be the perfect ruler. Some of the passages that have been identified as messianic are Deuteronomy 18:18–22; Psalms 8, 22, 45, 69, and 72; Isaiah 4:2; 7:10–17; 9:1–7; 32:1–8; 55:3–4; Jeremiah 23:5–6; 31–33; Ezekiel 17:22–24; 34:22, 24; Micah 5:1–4; Zechariah 9:9–10.

In view of the extensive body of Old Testament prophecy that not only portrays God's ideal ruler but also promises that he will rule over a world-wide kingdom, it is not surprising that most Jews in first-century Israel had preconceived ideas about what their Messiah would be like. But there is also an extensive body of Old Testament prophecy that portrays God's anointed as a suffering servant (see Isa. 53), and anointing suggests priesthood as well as kingly authority. For Christians who still take the Old Testament's prophecies in a literal way, the resolution seems simple. Jesus came to suffer and, performing the function of a priest, to offer himself up for our sins. Jesus was resurrected and is coming again. When Jesus returns, all the promises made by the prophets will be kept, and Jesus will then be revealed as God's promised king. In both offices, priest and king, Jesus and Jesus alone serves as God's anointed.

The first chapters of Matthew's Gospel refer to a number of Old Testament messianic texts. Matthew wrote to demonstrate to the Jewish people that Jesus truly is the one God anointed to be king of his present and coming kingdom. ▶ KINGDOM

As for us, every time we identify our Lord as "Jesus Christ," we acknowledge him to be God's anointed, for the name Christ is the Greek translation of the Hebrew word *messiah*, meaning "the anointed one."

MILLENNIUM

Millennium is a Latin word meaning "a thousand." This much-debated word is used six times in the Book of Revelation to identify a specific future time. At the beginning of the thousand years, Satan is to be bound. Then those people killed because of their testimony to Jesus are raised to reign with Christ for the period. At the end of the thousand years, Satan is released from his imprisonment to stimulate a final rebellion against God (Rev. 20:1–10).

The early church families took this description of the future literally. They saw the thousand years as the period of time during which the Old Testament promises of an earthly kingdom would be fulfilled. Christ's coming would usher in an age of righteousness and peace.

After a few centuries this view was dismissed. Since then some Christians have envisioned the final thousand years before Christ's return as an era of peace. A. A. Hodge, in his *Outlines of Theology*, describes the "Scriptural doctrine" of the millennium, saying, "Both the Old and the New Testament clearly reveal that the gospel is to exercise an influence over all branches of the human family, immeasurably more extensive and more thoroughly transforming than any it has ever realized in time past. This end is to be gradually attained through the spiritual presence of Christ in the ordinary dispensation of Providence and ministrations of the church.... The period of this general prevalency of the gospel will continue for a thousand years, and is hence designated the millennium" (pp. 568–569).

Other Christians have discarded the idea of a millennium entirely. They argue that the language and imagery of Revelation is symbolic and that whatever the reference to a thousand years may mean, it should not be taken literally.

A third view, premillennialism, takes the thousand years literally and like the early church, expects Christ to return before the millennium begins. As one critic notes, premillennialism "has to its credit the astounding readiness to take the Old Testament Scriptures in a realistic manner, with simple faith, not asking whether the fulfillment of these things is even logically conceivable, offering as its sole basis the conviction that to God all things are possible" (Geerhardus Vos, *The Pauline Eschatology*, Baker, p. 227). While Vos considers this a "naïve faith," many Christians today consider such literalism basic to correct interpretation of prophetic Scriptures. These Christians argue that the teaching of both Testaments is in complete harmony with a premillennial view. ◆ SCRIPTURE, PROPHECY/PROPHET

What, then, do Christians believe about the millennium? Is the thousand-year reference in Revelation symbolic? Does it refer to the first thousand years of our era? Or does it refer to a reign by Christ on earth after his second coming? Simply put, we are divided in our answer. But there is one thing that we agree on: History moves now toward a great culmination. Jesus will return, and when he does come again, our Lord's intervention will utterly transform the future of every human being, living or dead. Today we may not agree on everything that Christ's return will involve, but we do trust the shape of the future to God. We are sure that when the future unfolds, while it may not be the particular future our view leads us to expect, it will surely be the one that God has planned.

MINISTRY ♦ PRIESTHOOD, ORDINATION, MISSION

MIRACLE

Miracles don't particularly trouble us. Christians are sure that God is able to perform them. But we are divided on whether God performs miracles today — at least, as some of us understand *miracle.*

What is a miracle? In the Old Testament three Hebrew words are closely linked with miracles. The first, *pala*, means to be "wonderful" or "marvelous." It is used to describe God's acts in creation or in history, and it expresses the wonder and awe that his acts stimulate in us. The second, *mopet*, also means "wonder," "miracle," or "sign." It is used most often of God's acts when delivering Israel from Egypt and in caring for his people afterward. The third, *'ot*, is used most widely and means "a miraculous sign" in about eighty of its Old Testament uses.

Looking at the Old Testament's use of these words, we see that miracles are obvious and clear acts of God in time and space, and they have a special impact on the observer. For instance, the plagues on Egypt were intended to deepen Israel's faith (Exod. 6:6–7), to confront the Egyptians with the reality of Jahweh (Exod. 7:5), and to show the powerlessness of Egypt's gods by revealing the power of the true and living God (Exod. 12:12). In miracles God reveals something of his nature and power so that the false image of believer and unbeliever are shattered; both the believer and the unbeliever better understand who God truly is. No wonder David calls on God's worshipers to "tell of all his wonderful acts" and "remember the wonders he has done, his miracles" (1 Chron. 16:9, 12).

In the New Testament the Greek words used to speak of miracles reflect the Old Testament viewpoint. *Dunamis*, often translated "miracle," emphasizes an act as an expression of divine power. *Semeion* means "sign," in the sense of an authenticating mark or token. Miracles in the New Testament were understood to indicate that the doer of the miracle was God's messenger. *Teras* (meaning "wonder") and *erga* (meaning "work") are also used in the sense of miracle. Another group of words describes the reaction of observers to Jesus' miracles; they express the wonder, awe, or fear that his supernatural acts created.

What then is a miracle? In the biblical sense it is a direct intervention by God in our world of space and time; it is God clearly and unmistakably setting aside natural law so that the supernatural source is recognized by observers.

Why miracles? When we read the Bible, we are struck by the fact that the miracles described are never purposeless explosions of raw power. Typically miracles are expressions of God's power exercised to aid his people. We see this especially in Jesus' miracles. He moves no mountains and destroys no enemies. Instead Jesus quiets the storm that threatens his disciples' life. Jesus heals the sick, feeds the hungry, releases the demon-possessed, and he even recalls the dead. His miracles demonstrate God's power over all the forces that tyrannize human beings and show clearly that God chooses to use his power to aid human beings, not to harm them.

We sense the same thing in the Old Testament. We see miracles in Exodus as God unleashes his power to release Israel from captivity, showing himself faithful to his ancient promises to Abraham. Even when God's power is used to punish a disobedient Israel, the purpose is to guide his people back to obedience so that he can bless them.

Biblical miracles not only unveil God's power but also reveal God's intention to use his power for his people rather than against them.

Miracles created a sense of wonder or fear. This reaction is associated with the function of miracles as "signs," intended to authenticate the person who prays for or performs the miracle. God gave Moses such signs to show the elders of Israel and Pharaoh that God indeed had sent him (see Exod. 4:1–9). Jesus' miracles were proof that he spoke and taught with authority. Even Jesus' enemies were forced to confess, "No one could perform the miraculous signs you are doing if God were not with him" (John 3:2).

This particular function of miracles is related to an often-ignored fact. The history of God's Old Testament and New Testament people is not marked by a *continuous* flow of miracles. Instead miracles are associated with very specific and limited times in Bible history. One of these times is the Exodus period. Another is the day of the prophets Elijah and Elisha. Another is the time of Jesus and the earliest years of the New Testament church. Only in these limited and theologically significant periods do we find numerous miracles performed.

The Bible foretells one other time when miracles will be common. It is the time of the Antichrist, when Satan will exercise his supernatural powers to deceive those who have not trusted Christ (see 2 Thess. 2:9–12).

Why miracles then? First of all, miracles reveal something of God's power and his goodness. Second, at critical times in sacred history, miracles authenticate God's messengers and their message.

But the fact is that miracles in this biblical sense are uncommon rather than common and are linked with critical turning points in Bible history. They have not been a part of the "normal" experience of God's people.

Do miracles happen today? Often when Christians today talk about miracles, they are not using *miracle* in the distinctive biblical sense. Instead we may hear a Christian tell of a serious illness: "The doctors gave me six months. But I prayed and God answered! When I went back for the next examination, the disease was cured. It is a miracle." Or we may hear a Christian say: "There we were, our car broken down, a blizzard coming, and on a back road nobody traveled. And suddenly a jeep drives up and the driver tells us he never takes this road, but today he just felt he should. It was a real miracle."

Such stories do express an important Christian conviction. We believe that God intervenes today as he has in the past and that he intervenes to help us. God isn't locked in to the "normal course of events." God can and does shape events to his will. Our sicknesses are subject to God's power, and he can heal. Our situations are never hopeless, for God remains able to change them. The doctor might look at a cure and note that it is unusual or beyond his ability to explain. The driver of that jeep may wonder about the impulse that led him to turn down a road he seldom uses. But others who hear the stories can dismiss the "miracles" as a "spontaneous remission of the disease" or as a "happy coincidence."

No one who observed Jesus' miracles could dismiss what they saw. In the case of Jesus' miracles and the other biblical miracles there was a clear, *public* setting aside of the normal — an unmistakable intrusion of the supernatural.

The fact that God has acted does not make something a miracle. What makes a miracle is when God's action is clearly, publicly, unmistakably a supernatural event.

In the biblical sense, miracles remain uncommon. This does not mean that God cannot or will not perform miracles in the biblical sense today. It simply means that most Christians don't find the miraculous a part of their normal Christian lives. But in the sense in which most Christians use the word *miracle,* the miraculous is more common than most might think.

We sense God's hand in all that happens in our life. We pray and fully expect God to answer our prayers. We are sick, we become well, and we gratefully attribute our recovery to the Lord. We have financial and other needs, and when these needs are met, we praise God for his loving care. Christians are firmly convinced that the God who at times has set aside the normal course of events is fully able to work through everyday circumstances.

In the strict sense we do not expect miracles. In the broader and perhaps more significant sense, we count on the miraculous every day.

How glad we are to have a God who is totally free to exercise his power, in natural process as well as in the miraculous, and who continues to use that power for you and me.

MISSION

One thing that sets Christianity apart is that it provides us with a sense of purpose. The naturalist's scheme of things offers human beings only a few brief years of life without real purpose or meaning. Each person will die, and death is the end. Ultimately even the universe will wear out and cool to a frigid darkness. Set against this stark view of reality, nothing in life offers us any real meaning or purpose.

Christians have a completely different outlook. We see the material universe as only one facet of reality. Yes, this universe will end, and most of the human family will die, but this is not the end. Each person will exist endlessly, and a new universe will replace the one we have outgrown. In giving us endless existence, God has also given life meaning and purpose. The life we live now will affect us and others for eternity.

It is this conviction that gives Christians and the church our sense of mission. Christianity holds out goals and purposes that have ultimate — not just temporary and passing — meaning.

Christians have agreed on the basic shape of our mission here on earth. In broad outline that mission is to share the gospel with all people, to express God's love for others in our relationships with them, and to glorify God by the quality of our lives. You and I can live meaningful and fulfilling lives as we commit ourselves to these purposes.

In one sense, these basics are self-evident to Christians. We are sure that humanity is lost apart from Jesus. It is urgent, then, that others have the opportunity to hear and respond to the message of salvation. Where people spend eternity is of utmost importance. Throughout church history Christian missions and evangelism have grown out of the conviction that Christ died for all people and that all must hear God's good news.

At our best, Christians have also been convinced that the quality of human life in this world is also our concern. It was Christians in England who led the crusade to ban the slave trade. It was Christians who spearheaded the hospital movement. Christians have mounted the efforts that brought education, modern medicine, and practical help to poor and disadvantaged nations and continents. Jesus' own compassion for the poor and helpless, reflecting the call of the Old Testament prophets, has often been reflected in Christian concern for people's present needs as well as their eternal destiny.

Christians have also been aware of our need for personal moral transformation. Jesus, who lived history's only perfect life, set us an example, and our goal is to be "like our teacher" (see Luke 6:40). Paul's call to be "imitators of God, as dearly loved children, and live a life of love, just as Christ loved us and gave himself up for us," sets the challenge before us. Just as Jesus glorified God by his life on earth, so we are to glorify our Lord by a life of Christlikeness.

At times Christians tend to lose a sense of mission. Too often we think of mission only in terms of a professional ministry — of foreign missionaries or pastors or evangelists. But the mission of the church of Jesus Christ is not just for selected people. Every one of us has a spiritual gifting, enabling us to contribute to the growth of others in Christ's church. Every one of us can pray for and share the gospel with friends and neighbors. Every one of us can show compassion, reaching out to people in need or becoming involved with efforts to correct injustices in our society.

In a significant way our sense of mission and of the meaningfulness of our own lives is summed up in an old hymn: We are to live "with eternity's values in view." The better we understand and are shaped by God's values (what is important to him), the more we will find ourselves meaningfully involved in the mission of the church.

MORAL RESPONSIBILITY

We first see moral responsibility in the Genesis story of Adam. Adam and Eve are placed in a beautiful garden and are given wide freedoms. Yet within that garden they are not to eat of one tree. Only when such a choice existed could Adam and Eve be persons in a complete sense, fully responsible rather than puppets lacking the right of individual choice.

Historically there are two bases on which the idea of moral responsibility has been attacked. The naturalist sometimes argues that individuals are not responsible because their heredity and/or environment make them act as they do. That is, people do not make true choices, but what they decide has already been predetermined.

The classic formulation suggests that a person steals because he or she comes from a poor environment. But determination theories break down because the choices of individuals clearly are *not* determined. Many poor people are responsible citizens, while other people with great advantages commit crimes. An ideal childhood is no guarantee of good character, and many with tragic childhoods become loving, caring people. Without discounting the influence of circumstances, it is clear that determinism does not really explain personal decisions. Each person makes his or her own choices and is responsible for them.

The second basis on which moral responsibility is questioned is religious. Since human beings are corrupted by sin, can they have true freedom of choice? Won't they make wrong choices because the corrupting power of sin makes such choices necessary? But if our choices are necessary, we don't really have freedom of choice. If we lack freedom of choice, how can we be morally responsible?

This is a classic objection to belief in moral responsibility. But it, too, has an answer directly from Scripture. In Ezekiel 18, God answers those of his people who shrug off their own responsibility and blame past generations for current troubles. In this powerful chapter the prophet declares God's message: "'I will judge you, each one according to his ways,' declares the sovereign LORD" (v. 30). The same message is repeated in Romans 2:6: "God will give to each person according to what he has done" (see also Ps. 62:12; Prov. 24:12). We are not only responsible for our choices, we are responsible for them to God.

Human beings are tainted by sin, and our choices are going to be affected by our sinful human nature. ◗ **DEPRAVITY, SIN** But it is very clear from Scripture that whatever the extent of sin's impact on us, we still make those decisions that affect the direction of our lives.

MYTH

Myths are seldom mentioned in our Bible, and when they are, it is in strong negative terms (see 1 Tim. 1:4; 4:7; 2 Tim. 4:4; Titus 1:14; 2 Peter 1:16). In each case myths are contrasted to sound, historical truth.

In modern religious language a myth is not necessarily true or false. Instead a myth is a narrative or story by which a community or group of people express their basic beliefs about themselves and their place in the universe. In this special sense the Old Testament story of the Creation and even the Gospel narrative about the death and resurrection of Jesus are myths. They are stories that express Christians' most basic beliefs; they sum up the Christian understanding of who human beings are in God's universe, and they sum up our beliefs about relationship with God.

What is confusing is that in most modern uses of the term, myth implies fairy tale. That is, the story may contain "truth" in the sense of accurately expressing a people's view of the world, but the events themselves are not historical. Some who have attempted to demythologize Christianity have gone about it by denying that biblical events actually took place in time and space. The demythologizers say that Old Testament and Gospel stories do express what the storytellers believed, but they do not express what actually happened.

It is here that Christianity stands in sharp contrast to the myths of the ancient world and to the myths that express the world view of other religions. Christians firmly believe that the stories told in our Scriptures are historical. The events reported really happened. Our stories express our basic outlook on life. But the validity of that outlook rests on the factuality of the events reported. It is because God made Adam and Eve in his own image that human beings have unique worth and value. It is because God's own Son was born of a virgin, died on a cross, and was raised from the dead that we hope for our own resurrection.

Are the stories in the Bible myth? In the sense that they present Scripture's world view in narrative form, yes. But in the sense that Scripture represents historical reality, no. The Bible's stories are unique, for those stories accurately report what happened on planet earth. ◗ HISTORY

NAMES OF GOD

In the Old Testament as in other ancient cultures, a name is more than a label. In those days names were intended to sum up the essence of the person named: Names revealed character and personality. A person who "knows the name" of another has a significant knowledge of what that person is like.

This distinctive characteristic of names in the Old Testament era underlies the promise of Psalm 91:14: "I will protect him, for he acknowledges my name." To acknowledge the name of God means to recognize the attributes revealed by his name and to respond to him as that kind of person.

No single name could sum up all that God is. Therefore, God revealed himself to Israel through a number of significant names. These names remain significant to Christians today, for the names continue to speak of who God is, calling on us to acknowledge his character and put our trust in him.

What are some of these special, revealing names of God? The most important is certainly Jehovah (or Jahweh). The name means "the one who is always present," and emphasizes God's redemptive involvement in the lives of his people of every age. ◗ JEHOVAH

Books have been written about the other names of God and what they express about him. The following list describes several of God's other significant names. By acknowledging these names, we can develop a closer relationship with our Lord.

El was the basic name for God in ancient Middle Eastern cultures. The name emphasized God's power, greatness, and authority. In essence it recognized God as supreme (see Gen. 17:1; Josh. 3:10; Isa. 9:6; Ezek. 10:5). The Old Testament uses this name in the plural, *Elohim.* This form, which appears over two thousand times in the Bible, has been called the "plural of majesty." *Elohim* beautifully expresses our Scripture's conviction that ours is the one true God, supreme over all other gods named by humanity. You and I acknowledge God by remembering that he truly is supreme. We submit to his authority and fear no other, lesser powers.

Adonai means "Lord" or "Master." The Bible presents God as the master of the world (see Josh. 3:11). Most often, however, this name is linked to God's personal relationship with his people. It emphasizes the mutual obligations and responsibilities of that relationship. As master, he is responsible for our well-being, and because he is Master, it is our responsibility to honor and obey him. We acknowledge God as Lord today by obeying him gladly, sure that as we do his will, he will meet our every need. ◗ **LORD**

El Shaddai means "God Almighty." It is a name that suggests strength, stability, and permanence. The name occurs often in the Psalms, poetically affirming God as unmovable, a reliable refuge for his people. This name is closely associated with the covenant promises given to Abraham (see Gen. 17). We acknowledge God as God Almighty when we turn to him in our fears and find comfort in the assurance that our all-powerful God remains faithful to those who trust in him.

El Olam means "God of Eternity" or "Everlasting Lord." The emphasis seems to rest on God's unchangeable character. Our times are at best uncertain. World and personal circumstances constantly shift and change. But God remains unaffected, stable, certain, sure. We acknowledge God as *El Olam* by resting our hopes in him and remaining sure that whatever our situation, his love is unchangeable and his plan for us is good.

El Elyon means "God Most High" (see Ps. 18:13). This name affirms God as omnipotent and supreme. But the name also does more. It insists that God alone has a claim to deity. Only he is to be worshiped; only he is to be feared. We acknowledge God as *El Elyon* by giving our Lord our full allegiance.

Elohim sebhaoth identifies God as "God of hosts" or "God of armies" (see Jer. 11:20). The name affirms his control over all agencies and powers in the spiritual and material universe. He controls not only his armies of angels but also the hosts of all the nations. We acknowledge God as Lord of armies when we rest in his sovereignty, letting our awareness of his control of all things quiet our fears and give us confidence to face our future.

God is called our "Rock" (see Deut. 32 and many of the Psalms). The image is one of security, of God as the believer's fortress and shield. Because he is ours and we are his, we truly are safe from all who would harm us.

God is called the "Righteous One" (see Ps. 7:9; 129:4; 145:17). This name is closely linked with the Old Testament covenants that God made with Israel. Because God is an upright person, he remains true to his commitments to judge as well as to bless. How wonderful for us to acknowledge God's righteousness and remember that he will faithfully keep every promise.

God is also called Israel's "Holy One" (see Ps. 71:22). This name is found throughout Scripture and is used over thirty times in Isaiah. The name emphasizes God's transcendence and his separation from all that is unworthy or sinful. We acknowledge God as holy not only when we honor him by living holy and righteous lives but also when we seek to do what pleases him.

The Old Testament includes other significant names: the Mighty One (Ps. 50:1), Light Giver (Gen. 1:16), Father (Ps. 89:26), Judge (Gen. 18:25), Redeemer (Job 19:25), Savior (Isa. 43:3), Deliverer (Ps. 18:2), Shield (Ps. 3:3), and Strength (Ps. 22:19).

As we study the Bible passages in which these names appear, we meet the Lord in his names. We appreciate even more the greatness, faithfulness, and power of our God.

NATURE/NATURAL LAW

It is common these days to separate the material and the spiritual. The processes that we observe within the material universe are the "natural laws," and the beings and things in the material universe together constitute "nature." For many people, only those things existing or operating in the material universe are real.

Christians have different outlooks on nature and natural law. When we stop to think about our belief, their impact is greater than most of us may suppose.

Is God limited by nature? Christians believe that nature and natural law are subject to God. But most human beings assume that if there is a God, he really has little to do with the world of here and now. God may have created the universe long ago, but even those who accept the idea that there must have been a first cause tend to think that now God is limited to the spiritual realm.

One of the major arguments raised against miracles says that a miracle can't happen because it would "violate natural law." The argument seems particularly foolish to Christians. If God is great and wise enough to create a universe and establish, for instance, the law of gravity, by what reasoning can the law of gravity be thought of as greater than God?

This, then, is one of our basic beliefs about nature and natural law. We believe firmly that nature is subject to God and that natural laws do not limit his freedom to act.

This conviction is expressed every time we pray about our own material needs or the needs of others. We bring everything to the Lord, convinced that he remains in control of events in this world. We believe that God can and will act to shape the circumstances of our lives.

Can moral choices be justified by nature? It is not unusual to hear a person justify his or her decisions by arguing that a particular course of action is "natural." Usually the argument is applied to sexual ethics. It is natural when one is hungry to eat; it is natural when one is aroused to have sex. Because it is natural, it is assumed to be good and right.

It is true that the idea of being natural does have ethical implications. In Romans 1:26–27, Paul calls homosexuality a great sin because it is "against nature." But Paul's argument has a different core than does the excuse of the promiscuous person.

Paul argues that homosexuality is a terrible sin because God created human beings male and female, and he intends intercourse to take place between the sexes. The ethical core is the intention (that is, the will of God) and not the feelings or desires that surge in sinful human beings.

For this reason the mere fact that sexual intercourse is intended "by nature" to take place between male and female cannot be extended to mean that sex can take place between any male and any female at their whim. God intends sex, by its nature, to bind a husband and wife together in that lifelong commitment we call marriage. The nature of the act as God intends it to be places strict limits on the choices we are free to make. It is not our feelings or urges that are to control us but the revealed will of God. Strikingly, many things God asks us to do demand that we make decisions against our natural desires rather than in accord with them. It is God, not nature, who defines what is the measure of right and wrong. It is God, not nature, who defines what is good.

What is the relationship between humanity and nature? Christians believe that God is not limited by, but is in control of, nature and natural law. We also believe that God's will rather than what seems "natural" is to guide our ethical choices. But does God's revealed will suggest any special relationship between human beings and the world in which we live?

For our answer we have to return to the Creation story and to a striking statement made by God. There God expresses his intention to create humanity in his own image and to "let them rule over the fish of the sea and the birds of the air, over the livestock, over all the earth, and over all the creatures that move along the ground" (Gen. 1:26–28).

It is important for us to understand the word "rule." That term implies both authority and responsibility. Rule does not imply a raw power that enables humanity to misuse the earth's resources, but it does imply an authority that is to be used to manage those resources wisely.

Recent scientific advances have given us the power to understand and broadly affect nature. Now that those powers are ours, we are not only to appreciate God's revelation of himself in nature but also to accept responsibility for the way our actions affect our community and our planet.

The Christian view of nature and natural law has other implications: it highlights the fact that what we believe does dramatically affect how we view nature and natural law. ◗ **REVELATION** Because we believe that God is sovereign over nature, we bring every need to him in prayer, confident that he can and will answer us. ◗ **PRAYER** Because we believe that God's will rules over and in nature, we look to him for guidance and not to those urges and desires that seem natural to humankind. And because we believe that God has chosen to make humanity responsible to him for his creation, we are beginning to take more seriously our obligation to make decisions that affect ecology.

NEIGHBOR

An embarrassed legalist once asked Jesus, "Who is my neighbor?" (see Luke 10). Jesus identified the basic message of God's law by saying to the young man: love God fully and love your neighbor as yourself. Confronted by Jesus' answer and aware of falling short of it, the legalist hoped to excuse himself by defining neighbor in a way that limited his responsibility. Jesus' response established a definition of neighbor that has stunning implications for us Christians.

Jesus told the story of a traveler who was robbed, beaten, and left lying beside the road. Two of the traveler's fellow countrymen passed him by, fearing the robbers might still be near. And then a Samaritan, a citizen of a neighboring nation whom the Jews absolutely despised, came by. He stopped, helped the injured traveler to an inn, and even provided the funds to care for the man until he recovered. Jesus finished the story and asked, "Which of these three do you think was a neighbor to the man who fell into the hands of robbers?" There was only one possible answer: The neighbor was "the one who had mercy on him."

In the story Jesus immediately establishes a new definition of neighbor. A neighbor is not a fellow citizen or one who lives nearby. A neighbor is any human being in need or any person who acts to meet another's need.

What is important about this definition? Both testaments speak of the believer's obligation to love our neighbors as ourselves (Lev. 19:18; Luke 10:27). Jesus has established once and for all who that neighbor is. The hungry, the unemployed, the sick, the divorced person, the abandoned child—anyone with a need is our neighbor. To act as a neighbor is to reach out to such as these to help and to care.

So Christians are called to be neighbors. We are called to overlook racial differences, social position, and educational levels of others and simply to respond lovingly to human need.

NEW COVENANT ◀ COVENANT

OBEDIENCE

Obedience is not something Christians resent. For us obedience is not restrictive or a burden. In the language of faith, *obedience* is a word that breathes love, intimacy, and security. But obedience is a complicated concept. It involves far more than conforming to God's moral rules and revealed will. In our faith, obedience grows out of a deep understanding of who God is. Obedience can exist only when it wells up as an expression of honest love.

Who God is. Christians know God as the Creator and judge of the universe. We live in his universe, totally dependent on him. This reality immediately begins to put obedience in perspective. Surely the one who ordained the natural laws that govern the material world has every right to ordain moral laws to govern the relationships that exist between his creatures. So to begin with, obedience to this person is utterly appropriate: It is fitting for God to be God and for him to command. It is fitting for us to honor and obey him. We resent it if another person orders us about, insisting that his or her will is superior to ours. But we cannot resent God, who truly *is* superior and whose will rightly should govern our own.

But what really frees us from resentment is our awareness of God's motive for sharing his moral standards. Our relationship to God goes far beyond that of creatures with a Creator. We have a personal relationship with God, which makes his call to obey something more than a demand that we honor him.

The Old Testament makes it clear that God reached out to renew his relationship with fallen human beings because of love. Moses puts it this way in Deuteronomy: it was "because he loved your forefathers and chose their descendants after them, he brought you forth out of Egypt by his Presence and his great strength" (Deut. 4:37).

God's great love for his Old Testament people was the motive that led him to give them his law. God revealed his standards so that his people could always live in his presence and so that he would be free to bless them rather than forced to punish them. Again from Deuteronomy: "The LORD commanded us to obey all these decrees and to fear the LORD our God, so that we might always prosper and be kept alive, as is the case today" (Deut. 6:24).

The Old Testament constantly links God's loving concern for the well-being of his people with law and obedience. God yearns to bless those he loves, and so he urges, "Follow my decrees and be careful to obey my laws, and you will live safely in the land. Then the land will yield its fruit, and you will eat your fill and live there in safety" (Lev. 25:18–19).

Today, too, the Christian's attitude toward obedience is shaped by the belief that God's will is "good, pleasing, and perfect" (Rom. 12:2). Obedience is not burdensome because the God who commands us to do his will speaks lovingly, eager to guide us away from what might harm to what can only help. We recognize God's right to demand our obedience, but we also know that God's demands express the depth of his love. Only by living in obedience can we be truly secure. Only by living in obedience can we experience the wonderful blessings that God intends for us.

Obedience and love. The Bible assures us that God's commands are loving. The Bible also makes it clear, however, that obedience is beyond us. Israel had God's commands and his promises, but the people of Israel repeatedly disobeyed. Even self-interest, based on the promise of blessings to follow obedience, failed to move God's people to respond to the Lord.

The Old Testament teaches that love is a necessary condition for obedience. The believer is to "Love the LORD your God with all your heart" and then "these commandments that I give you today are to be upon your hearts" (Deut. 6:5–6). In fact, love is clearly the key to obedience, for "What does the LORD your God ask of you but to fear the LORD your God, to walk in all his ways, to love him, to serve the LORD your God with all your heart and with all your soul, and to observe the LORD'S commands and decrees" (Deut. 10:12–13).

God gives us his commands for our "own good" (Deut. 10:13). But only when we respect and love God for himself will we actually be moved to obey.

But it is Jesus who puts the case most strongly. Jesus taught that obedience can only flow out of a personal relationship. Obedience must come into existence as an expression of love.

> Whoever has my commands and obeys them, he is the one who loves me and will be loved by my Father, and I too will love him and show myself to him. (John 14:21)
>
> If anyone loves me, he will obey my teaching. (John 14:23)
>
> He who does not love me will not obey my teaching. (John 14:24)
>
> If you obey my commands, you will remain in my love, just as I have obeyed my Father's commands and remain in his love. (John 15:10)

Only a love for God can move human beings to be truly obedient to him. Terror may force a semblance of outward conformity, but that wholehearted responsiveness to the will of God, that joyous *desire* to do what God wants, can come only from love.

So obedience truly is not burdensome to Christians. We may fail the Lord at times. But as we grow in our relationship with Jesus, we better understand the deep love that has motivated God to communicate his will to us. And as we grow in our relationship with Jesus, our own flowering love for him makes us want to honor him with an obedience that comes from the heart. We who trust and love God find that obedience is joy.

ORDINATION

Ordination means being installed into a specific office. We are most likely to use it of pastors, men or women set aside to preach and teach in our churches, or lay leaders of our local congregations. For most of us ordination is no problem because we assume that the way things are is the way things should be. For other Christians, however, the idea of ordination raises unsettling questions.

We find ordination practiced in the Old Testament as people were installed into various offices (see Num. 27:18–21). Also the Levites as a family were inducted into their special post of service in Israel's worship, although later generations held office by family right (Num. 8).

The New Testament apostles publicly and officially recognized elders in various local churches (Acts 14:23). The practices of the church of the first few centuries, however, were based on Old Testament models of ministry, and church offices were thought to parallel the priestly and prophetic offices of that era. By A.D. 350, the division between laity and leadership was so great that the *Apostolic Constitutions* insists, "Neither do we permit the laity to perform any of the offices belonging to the priesthood as for instance neither the sacrifices, nor baptism, nor the laying on of hands, nor the blessing whether the smaller or greater. . . . For such sacred offices are conferred by the laying on of hands of the bishop" (III:10.6–7).

It is this implication of ordination that bothers some Christians today and, in fact, bothered the Reformers. We read in the New Testament of a priesthood for all believers. On what basis then are some "ordained" for special service not open to others?

Luther recognized the tension but still believed in a specially trained and ordained leadership. He writes, "Everyone who has been baptized may claim that he already has been consecrated priest, bishop, or pope, even though it is not seemly for any particular person arbitrarily to exercise the office. . . . Only by the consent and command of the community should any individual person claim for himself what equally belongs to all."

To Luther ordination related only to ministers of the Word. He writes that "The public ministry of the Word, I hold, by which the mysteries of God are made known ought to be established by holy ordination as the highest and greatest of the functions of the church on which the whole power of the church depends."

John Calvin, too, wanted some form of official recognition for the preacher, that he might "be received by the common consent of the company of the faithful."

On the other hand, George Fox, the Quaker, insisted later that there should be "no outward Law to hinder or restrain any People from hearing any whom they believe is a minister of the Gospel, nor yet to compel any to hear any one they believe is not a minister of the Gospel; for an outward Law can but restrain or compel to the Good, but the Law and Power of God only in the heart: therefore let there be free Liberty for all people to meet concerning their worship."

On the one hand, the practice of ordination was distorted in the early centuries of the church, leading to the Roman Catholic version of a priesthood that rigidly isolates the average Christian from significant ministry. In the Reformation the biblical vision of a priesthood for all believers was recaptured. But the Reformers' concern that the preaching office be protected led them to continue ordination of their preachers and teachers. Today in most Protestant churches, the practice of ordination may be one of the major factors that continues to keep the average Christian from recognizing and responding to his or her own calling by God to significant ministry. ◆ PRIESTHOOD, SPIRITUAL GIFTS

It is typical that Christians who are particularly sensitive these days to the full priesthood of every believer are least comfortable with ordination. But ultimately ordination is one of those things that is neither explicitly taught nor denied to the church in the Bible (unless Matthew 20:25–26, Ephesians 4, and Matthew 28:8–12 are taken to rule it out). What seems most important for us is to resist the tendency to see ministry in the church as the responsibility of the few. Whatever view we may hold about ordination, it is certain that a ceremony that installs people into a particular office does not free the rest of us from responsibility to actively serve as God's ministers in his church. ◆ MISSION

ORIGINAL SIN

Original sin is a technical term in Christian theology. It points us back to Adam's willful disobedience, the first human sin, and to an examination of that sin's impact.

If we were to give a theological definition of original sin, we might speak with Wesleyan theologian Orton Wiley of "the corruption of the nature of all the offspring of Adam, by reason of which everyone is very far gone from original righteousness or the pure state of our first parents at the time of their creation, is averse to God, is without spiritual life, and is inclined to evil, and that continually" (quoted in *A Contemporary Wesleyan Theology*, Vol. I, p. 266).

In more ordinary terms we use the term *original sin* to explain the shattered relationships that mar every life. We look around us and realize that human beings are not naturally comfortable with God but fear or resent him. We look around and see persons who are not at peace with themselves but are burdened with guilt, failures, and flaws. We see strained and shattered relationships in families, communities, and nations. Crime and injustice, jealousy and anger, hatred and war—all are commonplace human experiences. The pride that hardens us, the lovelessness that hurts us, the rebelliousness that isolates us, the ingratitude that embitters us all must have some source. Somehow we cannot believe that humanity came so misshapen from the creative hand of our good and loving God.

When we are asked to explain the failures and tragedies that mark the human condition, Christians open the Bible to Genesis 3. There we read about Adam who came pure from the hand of God. But Adam made a tragic choice. God had warned that death in all its various forms must come if Adam disobeyed. From that original act of Adam, which broke his relationship with God, distorted his relationship with Eve, corrupted his character, and destroyed his harmony with creation, all other sins flow. Sin, as a destructive and corrupting power, was released into God's world and has tainted the personality of every human being ever born. ◆

DEATH, DEPRAVITY, SIN

What difference does our belief in original sin make? Probably the most important difference is to locate the cause of human sin and failure in Adam's shattered relationship with God. Any hope for humankind depends on restoring relationship with the Lord. How good to know that just as death swept over us because of the act of one man, Adam, so life springs up through the act of another, Jesus Christ. Through Jesus and through Jesus alone our harmony with God, ourselves, and others can finally be restored (see Rom. 5:12–21).

PARABLE

We Christians are particularly comfortable with our Bible. We don't see it as an obscure book at all. Some parts may be harder to interpret than others, but generally we believe that the plain sense of what we read is the intended sense. After all, God's purpose in Scripture is communicating with us, not providing us with some code we have to struggle to break. ◆ **SCRIPTURE**

Parables are a special and different way of communicating. They are simply stories or sayings drawn from common situations and used by a speaker to illustrate or emphasize a point. For instance, Jesus told about a shepherd who left his ninety-nine sheep to search for the one who strayed. The search and the shepherd's joy at finding the lost sheep powerfully illustrate God's joy when a lost human being is restored to relationship with him.

But not all parables are intended to explain. Some of Jesus' parables were actually intended to obscure. Jesus explained to his disciples that his parables of the kingdom of heaven (Matt. 13) were to be understood by them and not by the crowds. Here Jesus spoke in parables so that "Though seeing, they do not see; though hearing, they do not hear or understand" (Matt. 13:13).

Understandably, all Christians have not agreed about the exact meaning of these mystery parables, and many different applications have been drawn from them.

For the most part, however, the Bible's parables do clarify rather than puzzle. The striking yet everyday character of these simple illustrations stay with us and help us to remember basic principles of our life with God.

PARACLETE

This name for the Holy Spirit is found only in the writings of the apostle John (John 14:16, 26; 15:26; 16:7; 1 John 2:1). In the Gospels, the name is usually translated as "Comforter," "Counselor," or "Helper," and in John's first letter, it is translated as "Advocate." This designation always emphasizes the Spirit's interpersonal ministry — what the Spirit does for us or in us. While Bible students still argue about the exact meaning of the word *Paraclete*, the words of Phillips in his paraphrase of the New Testament express its meaning for you and me. Jesus told his disciples that when he left, he would send "someone else to stand by you." That someone else is the Holy Spirit, who is with us today and stands by us always to comfort and to guide. ◆ HOLY SPIRIT

PEACE

We all yearn for peace. Some of us actively try to promote world peace. Others are sure that war and rumors of wars will exist until Jesus comes. Many of us think of peace as a subjective experience: It is inner peace, unshaken by tragedies, that is important.

What do Christians believe about peace? To explore that, we have to first understand what the Bible says about peace. Then we can examine the prospects for world peace and inner peace.

Peace in the Bible. In the Old Testament peace is a powerful theological term. The Hebrew word *shalom* means "wholeness," "harmony," "that which is complete and sound." *Shalom* also suggests the happy condition of health, prosperity, and fulfillment. Most often *shalom* is a relational term used to describe the harmony between persons and nations that releases us to find fulfillment without the destructive impact of strife.

In the Psalms and the writings of the prophets, *shalom* is especially significant. Here we find nearly two-thirds of the Bible's use of this concept, and here it expresses the fulfillment that comes to human beings when we experience God's presence. That fulfillment is available to the individual and to the nation. When David is forced to flee from his rebellious son Absalom, he is under life-threatening pressure. David turns his thoughts to God and finds comfort in him. "I will lie down and sleep in peace," David says, "for you alone, O LORD, make me dwell in safety" (Ps. 4:8).

Peace for individuals is consistently portrayed as the result of a right relationship with God. In another Psalm, David says, "Great peace have they who love your law" (Ps. 119:165). As for those who reject God and his ways, Isaiah 57:20–21 warns: "The wicked are like the tossing sea, which cannot rest, whose waves cast up mire and mud. 'There is no peace,' says my God, 'for the wicked.'"

The Old Testament also speaks powerfully of peace for the nations. This, too, is seen to hinge on the presence of the Lord. A day is coming when God's "Prince of peace" will appear and "of the increase of his government and peace there will be no end" (Isa. 9:6–7). When God's Spirit is poured out and his kingdom is established, "The fruit of righteousness will be peace; the effect of righteousness will be quietness and confidence forever. My people will live in peaceful dwelling places, in secure homes, in undisturbed places of rest" (Isa. 32:17–18).

In the Old Testament peace is the internal and external harmony that comes to human beings and nations who live in intimate relationship with God.

In the New Testament the word for peace is *eirene*. In Greek culture it was first used to describe an orderly, prosperous society. Later philosophers applied the concept to inner, personal peace. But when *eirene* is used in the New Testament, it draws its deepest meanings from *shalom* and not from Greek culture. In every theologically significant passage in the New Testament, peace is rooted in the relationship that rests on restored harmony with God. Inner harmony and harmony between persons are possible only when our shattered selves have been made whole again through a personal relationship with Jesus Christ.

The link between relationship with God and peace is seen in many greetings and farewells in the New Testament letters. Peace is "from God our Father and from the Lord Jesus Christ" (Rom. 1:7), for God is "the God of peace," its bringer and its source (Rom. 15:33; Heb. 13:20). While peace is an inner experience, the wholeness suggested by *shalom/eirene* is visibly expressed in the believing community. The gift of God's peace means that among Christians, hostility gives way to unity (Eph. 2:14–17), and commitment to unity matches our commitment to holiness (see Heb. 12:14; 2 Tim. 2:22). Colossians 3:12–15 provides a picture of the interpersonal peace that God brings to the community of faith: "As God's chosen people, holy and dearly loved, clothe yourselves with compassion, kindness, humility, gentleness and patience. Bear with each other and forgive whatever grievances you may have against one another. Forgive as the Lord forgave you. And over all these virtues put on love, which brings them all together in perfect unity. Let the peace of Christ rule in your hearts, since as members of one body you were called to peace. And be thankful."

In the New Testament, then, peace is most often the well-being and wholeness that Jesus restores to relationship with God and others. Even when circumstances bring tension and personal suffering, this inner peace is ours; it is rooted in relationship with God and not with external conditions. As Jesus said, "Peace I leave with you; my peace I give you. I do not give to you as the world gives. Do not let your hearts be troubled, and do not be afraid" (John 14:27). The inner presence of Jesus brings peace, fulfillment, and harmony to our lives.

Prospects for world peace. Christians have yearned for peace on earth. At times, various Christian movements have imagined that world peace was just around the corner, and they have worked enthusiastically to promote it. The peaceable kingdom, when wolf and lamb will feed together and "will neither harm nor destroy in all my holy mountain" (Isa. 65:25), surely seems worth working for.

But throughout the Old Testament, *shalom* on earth is associated with the presence of God. In the prophets' vision, world peace can come only with the appearance of God's promised ruler, the Messiah. It is his righteous reign that makes peace possible. ◗ MESSIAH, PROPH-ECY/PROPHET

The emphasis on God's personal presence is maintained in key prophecies about the Messiah. For instance, Isaiah calls the child to be born "Wonderful Counselor, Mighty God, [and] Everlasting Father" as well as "Prince of Peace" (Isa. 9:6). How clear the old prophecies become in Christ. How certain we are that when our Lord returns, God *will* be personally present on earth. Then world peace can and will become a reality, for God will rule.

This association of world peace with Jesus' return shouldn't make us withdraw from contemporary concerns. We do not know how long it will be until Jesus returns. But we do know that God cares about human suffering today. While nothing we can do will bring world peace, anything that we do to lessen the pain of war and strife is close to our Lord's heart and is a valid witness to the One who yearns with us to bring human beings the blessings of peace.

Prospects for inner peace. The prospect for world-wide peace hinges on the return and personal presence of Jesus. The prospect for personal, inner peace also hinges on the personal presence of Jesus, but that personal presence is available to everyone now.

Inner peace and harmony begins when our broken relationship with God is restored. And the key to restored relationship with God is faith, a deep yet simple trust in Jesus as Savior. ◗ FAITH Romans 5:1 says to all who have believed, "Since we have been justified through faith, we have peace with God through our Lord Jesus Christ." Peace is the present possession of God's people.

Out of our relationship with Jesus comes the fullest experience of everything implied in *shalom/eirene*. We experience a growing wholeness as sin's shattering impact on us gradually heals. We experience an increasing harmony with God as his motives and values gradually become ours. We experience deepening unity with other Christians, whom we learn to accept and love as brothers and sisters. As Christ's presence reduces our tensions and restores us to spiritual health, we discover that building our lives around Jesus brings us increasing fulfillment. There is a prosperity of soul that nothing can replace or destroy. And this restoration, this fulfillment is the overflow of the healing peace that comes through personal relationship with our Lord.

Christians have a very special view of peace. We see peace not in terms of external circumstances but in terms of harmony with God, inner harmony, and harmony in our relationships with others. This harmony is possible only as we live in relationship with Jesus, for it is his presence that brings peace. Secure in our relationship with God and finding fulfillment in doing his will, we experience a prosperity of soul that outweighs material prosperity.

But God's peace brings more than inner blessings. God's restoration of harmony and wholeness is expressed today in our relationships with others, especially Christians. Where his peace rules, love and harmony characterize the church. The vital living presence of God in his church is witnessed in this love and peace.

One day God's visible presence on earth will bring true peace to our world. Until then we will experience wars and rumors of wars, for mankind refuses to live in God's presence. We will live in a world torn by strife, and sometimes we will suffer because of the actions of others. Yet wherever we go, we can witness to the peace that God gives, not only by our changed lives but also by our willingness to do whatever we can to reduce strife in our own portion of the world.

PENTECOST

The Day of Pentecost was one of history's great days. All previous celebrations of the Festival of Pentecost, stretching out across centuries, merely foreshadowed the Pentecost that followed Jesus' resurrection. For many Christians the events of that one day seem to set the tone for the normal Christian life.

The Festival of Pentecost was one of three important Jewish celebrations, which called the people of Israel to Jerusalem. It is known by several Old Testament names: the Feast of Ingathering, the Feast of Harvest, the Feast of First Fruits, and the Feast of Weeks. Pentecost was essentially a harvest festival held at the end of Israel's seven-week grain harvest. It was a joyous occasion, marked by offering God the first products of the harvest with which he had blessed his people.

Pentecost is mentioned only three times in the New Testament. Two of these times the writers refer to Pentecost simply as a calendar event, as we might speak of visiting someone at Thanksgiving (Acts 20:16; 1 Cor. 16:8). The other reference, Acts 2, describes that day when the Holy Spirit came on the disciples as Christ had promised them he would (John 16:7, 13; Acts 1:4–5).

The Book of Acts tells of a sudden violent wind, visible flames resting on Jesus' followers, and a filling with the Spirit of God, which enabled the gathered believers to speak words that were heard by foreign visitors as their own native tongues (languages) (Acts 2:4, 11). Peter explains these stunning events as a fulfillment of prophecy: What had happened was the mark of God's promise to one day "pour out my Spirit on all people" (Acts 2:17; Joel 2:28–32). Empowered by the Spirit, Peter announced that in this new day of the Spirit, "everyone who calls on the name of the Lord will be saved" (Acts 2:21). He went on to demonstrate that the crucified and resurrected Jesus is both Lord and Christ (Acts 2:36). Most Christians agree that this moment marks the birth of the church as an institution. ◆ **CHURCH, BODY OF CHRIST**

But a number of Christians today see Pentecost as far more than a historical turning point. Not only was it the beginning of the church but it also was the beginning of an age in which the Holy Spirit is poured out on all God's people. For such Christians the bursting power evidenced at Pentecost is the heritage of the church of every age. Christians who abandon themselves to God's Spirit and who trust him completely can experience continual filling, a filling that transforms their inner lives and provides power for effective witness. For many, the critical sign that Christians truly have been touched and filled with the Spirit is to speak in tongues, as the disciples did that first day. ◆ **SPIRITUAL GIFTS, TONGUES**

This is not the place to argue for or against what has become known as the Pentecostal movement. But one thing is very clear and very important: Any of us who look back to Pentecost must take very seriously the significance of the promised Holy Spirit who began a special work in Jesus' people on that day. The Spirit is the source of every spiritual endowment and spiritual power. When we take the Spirit's presence in our lives as a reality, when we count on him to work in and through us, we open our lives to a deeper, more powerful working of God. Our confidence that the Spirit is present with us is a key to the trust that enables us to act in faith. As we act in faith, responsive to God's Word, the Spirit's power is unleashed. ◗ HOLY SPIRIT

Whether or not we believe that the presence of the Holy Spirit is witnessed by some special sign, it is vital that we recognize the reality of the Spirit's work. Through Jesus we are given the Spirit of God. With God's Spirit in our lives, you and I can face every challenge with quiet confidence, knowing that the Spirit truly is the source of power.

PERFECTION

Sometimes the word is part of a phrase, "sinless perfection." The phrase conjures up an exciting ideal. How wonderful it would be to be free of the nagging tug of sin within. How wonderful it would be to be free of the sense of guilt that accompanies failure. It is no wonder that the idea of perfection, whatever that word may mean, has been attractive to Christians.

Today we hear less talk about perfection. But there are theological traditions that insist an exciting kind of perfection is available to us Christians.

Scriptural view of perfection. Often the meaning of words in theological systems differs from the meaning of those same words as they are used in the Bible. So before we look at the theological positions that suggest a Christian perfection, it is helpful to look at the way the word *perfect* is used in the Old and New Testaments.

The Old Testament word for *perfect* comes from two Hebrew words: *Kalil* means "completeness," "wholeness," or "perfect beauty," which offers no protection against the choice of sin (see Ezek. 16:14; 28:12); *tamim* means "complete," suggesting uprightness or blamelessness. While God is completely perfect (Deut. 32:4), human beings are perfect in a limited sense, and this is true only when they are armed with divine strength (2 Sam. 22:33). Both David and Job, whom the Bible identifies as *tamim*, were men who could and who did sin.

In the New Testament a single word group is rendered by the words "perfect" and "perfection." Again the basic idea is completeness or wholeness. When used in a biological sense, *perfect* means "mature." A perfect thing or person is whole, complete, with nothing essential left out. To call a believer perfect, in this sense, can indicate he or she fulfills God's expectations for a mature believer, without implying sinlessness.

A special use of *perfect* is found in Hebrews. There the writer argues that the Old Testament system was unable to bring to completion the task set for its sacrifices. That system "made nothing perfect." On the other hand the sacrifice of Jesus made believers "perfect forever" (Heb. 7:28; 10:1, 14). Jesus' one sacrifice on Calvary accomplished its purpose, cleansing us so completely that we are now able to stand in God's presence.

Neither the Old Testament or New Testament use of *perfect* implies sinlessness. In fact, the biblical evidence suggests that "we all stumble in many ways" (James 3:2). John says very plainly that "if we claim to be without sin, we deceive ourselves and the truth is not in us" (1 John 1:8). Although perfection is not sinlessness, there is a sense in which we are called to be perfect. As Jesus said, "Be perfect, as your heavenly Father is perfect" (Matt. 5:43–48). Our potential as Christians can be realized. We can become mature — all that God intends believers to be — and when we are, we will act and love as God does.

Christian theology's view of perfection. In theologies that stress the importance of perfection, that term means more than maturity. Perhaps the best representative of this strand of Christian hope and thought is found in Wesleyanism.

Wesley believed that God could work in the heart of believers so that we are purged of our inner disposition toward sin, so that every desire and every conscious choice will always be to respond obediently to God. Thus a Christian who has been overtaken by what Wesley thought of as "perfect love" will not sin, in the sense of willfully choosing what he or she knows to be wrong.

Wesley did not believe that it is possible to be free from "involuntary transgressions" in this life. Such acts are a consequence of our mortality and our ignorance. Thus even perfected Christians must continue to rely on Jesus' atoning blood and must continually say, "Forgive us our trespasses."

Christian perfection, then, focuses on the will and on the conviction that God's Spirit can purge us of evil desires. The perfected Christian will be so controlled by love for God that he or she will consistently choose to do God's known will. Since in this system only acts of willful disobedience to God are considered sin, the believer who has reached perfection does not and will not sin. ▶ SIN

Is this Wesleyan position right? On that, Christians differ. Many cannot accept the idea of the eradication of the tendency toward sin this system seems to imply. Others argue that sin involves more than conscious, willful acts and insist that what the Wesleyan calls "mistakes" or "infirmities" are nothing less than mislabeled sins. Still others insist that the teaching runs counter to Christian experience. Even the best of us are aware of failures that we feel are sins, and even the best are troubled by temptations.

And yet it is also true that Christians remain eager for holiness. Most of us honestly desire to please God. The yearnings we feel may very well be the calling of God's Spirit to a deeper spiritual life than we have yet experienced. Whether or not a particular theological expression of that desire is right on every point may be less important than the realization that in Jesus, our deepest spiritual hungers can be satisfied. There is a perfection to which God calls us, a maturity that tunes our hearts to God and motivates us to choose his will. We may not agree in our descriptions of what happens within our personalities or about the specific ways in which God's Spirit works to transform us. But we do agree that God calls us to a deeper experience with him and to a quality of life that can only come from loving him. ▶ HOLINESS, SANCTIFICATION

PRAISE

The Book of Revelation describes John's vision of heaven. There he saw God on his throne, surrounded by creatures who cried out in worship and praise, eager to "give glory, honor, and thanks to him who sits on the throne." They sang, "You are worthy, our Lord and God, to receive glory and honor and power, for you created all things, and by your will they were created and have their being" (Rev. 4:9, 11).

What does the Bible tell us about praise? A number of Hebrew words are used to express the concept of praise. Each is linked, however, by common elements. First, praise is addressed to God or to his "name." ▶ NAMES OF GOD His qualities are the content of praise, and he is the one to whom praise is addressed. Second, praise in the Old Testament is essentially corporate. It is the joy-filled response of the believing community to the person of the Lord. People can praise God in private, of course. But most often praise in the Old Testament is a congregational expression. Third, praise always exalts the Lord. Praise acknowledges our creaturehood and our dependence on God and explicitly acknowledges his goodness. Psalm 145:3–7 captures the power and wonder of the praise God deserves and receives from his people: "Great is the LORD and most worthy of praise; his greatness no one can fathom. One generation will commend your works to another; they will tell of your mighty acts. They will speak of the glorious splendor of your majesty, and I will meditate on your wonderful works. They will tell of the power of your awesome works, and I will proclaim your great deeds. They will celebrate your abundant goodness and joyfully sing of your righteousness."

The essential nature of praise is established in the Old Testament. The New Testament echoes the message with a variety of words that express the believer's awareness of and response to God's greatness. Their meanings include "to commend," "to bless," "to speak well of," "to give glory."

In each testament praise is a response to God's revelation of himself. As God shows us who he is, we first acknowledge him and then learn to take delight in him. As we come to know him better, our love wells up and overflows. With overflowing hearts, with growing appreciation of and love for God, the joy of knowing God wells up as praise.

Praise is important because God is worthy of our praise. But praise is also important because as we praise God, focusing our attention on who he is, our own faith is deepened and our lives are enriched. As we lift up our hearts in praise, we link our hearts with believers through the ages who have expressed their love for the Lord by praising him, reveling in remembrance of his wonderful acts and of his wonderful self.

PRAYER

Most of us don't probe the mysteries implicit in prayer. We simply pray. Even the greatest theologians ultimately abandon themselves to prayer's simplicity. They echo Luther's personal testimony as, setting aside the theological questions, the great Reformer simply shared, "None can believe how powerful prayer is, and what it is able to effect, but those who have learned it by experience." Luther goes on, "It is a great matter when in extreme need, to take hold on prayer. I know, whenever I have earnestly prayed, I have been amply heard, and have obtained more than I prayed for; indeed, sometimes delayed, but at last he came."

The mysteries do trouble some of us. How can prayer "change" the mind of God? Does it modify events? If we didn't pray, would things still work out the same? How does prayer relate to God's sovereignty and foreknowledge? But these questions are speculative. When we turn to our Bible, we discover that Scripture hardly notices such issues. Instead the Bible emphasizes the simplicity of prayer. And believers through the ages have learned by experience that simplicity is the key. We believe that God is a person who loves us, who hears and answers our prayers. We freely bring everything to the Lord, certain that he will act. As we pray earnestly, we find that we are "amply heard."

Prayer in the Old Testament. Our Old Testament is filled with references to prayer. God's people speak to him, call on him, cry out to him. The language of faith is rich with words like *request, petition,* and *intercede.* What do the Hebrew words for prayer teach us?

Palal is widely used of personal and corporate prayer. The word itself indicates an appeal to God, the call of a dependent begging God to examine a personal need and act to meet it. *'Atar* emphasizes both the intense feelings of the person praying and the deep need stimulating the appeal to God. *Sha'al* means "to ask about something" or "to ask for something." It is closely associated with divine guidance, and many of our versions render it "inquire." The use of this word in the Old Testament reminds us that showing dependence and relying on God's guidance is especially important to the Lord (see Isa. 30:1–2). *Paga'* suggests intercession, using one's influence to entreat God for another person. *Halal* is a cry for mercy or help when in danger. *Hanan* is supplication, addressed to one we are sure is able to meet our needs. This cry expresses reliance on God's essential kindness and sometimes is translated "be gracious to me."

Studying these words and how they are used enables us to understand the foundations of prayer. In the Old Testament, prayer is an expression of personal relationship. The believer acknowledges God as Creator, as Redeemer, and as God of the covenant. As Creator, God has limitless power. He is able to meet every and any need. As Redeemer, God has acted in history to deliver Israel. He has shown that he is a God who saves, who will intervene for his own. As God of the covenant, the Lord has made a basic commitment to his people expressed in unbreakable promises. When we are faithful to God, we can be sure that he will remain faithful to us. Even when we have been unfaithful, confession and recommitment restore us to relationship and assure his blessing. Trusting God as Creator, Redeemer, and Covenant Maker establishes a personal relationship on the basis of which we can appeal to the Lord in prayer.

Old Testament prayer is rooted in more than knowledge of who God is. It is also rooted in awareness of human limitations. Compared with God, the greatest of us is no more than a humble supplicant. In reality every human being is completely dependent on God; ultimately every issue of life hinges on God's goodness and grace. Prayer flows out and expresses an appropriate dependence on the Lord. At heart, prayer is the appeal of a little child, who depends for everything on a loving Father.

Most prayers recorded in the Old Testament are beautiful in their warmth and simplicity. They express the worshipers' sense of need and their confidence that God is approachable. The Old Testament contains very little prayer liturgy. Instead, there is that spontaneous expression of needs and desires that reveals how deeply prayer is rooted in a very personal relationship with the Lord. Psalm 55 illustrates the intensity of felt need and the comfort that is found in dependence on a God who cares:

> My thoughts trouble me and I am distraught at the
> voice of the enemy. . . .
> My heart is in anguish within me;
> the terrors of death assail me.
> Fear and trembling have beset me;
> horror has overwhelmed me. . . .
>
> (Ps. 55:2–5)
>
> Evening, morning and noon
> I cry out in distress. . . .
>
> (Ps. 55:17)
>
> Cast your cares on the LORD
> and he will sustain you;
> he will never let the righteous fall.
>
> (Ps. 55:22)

Other model prayers in the Old Testament are found in Genesis 18:16–33; Exodus 32:5–14; 1 Samuel 2:1–10; 2 Samuel 7:8–29; 12:13–23; 1 Kings 8:22–53; 2 Kings 19:14–19; 2 Chronicles 20:5–12; and Ezra 9.

Prayer in the New Testament. The New Testament uses a number of different Greek words for prayer. These words tend to be used interchangeably, though they may have slightly different emphases. The basic word *proseuchomai* was originally a technical and formal term for calling on a deity. In the New Testament the classical stiffness is transformed, and prayer takes on characteristics of conversational intimacy and warmth. *Alteo* means "to express a desire," "to express a want," or "to make a request." *Deomai* also means "to ask" or "to request" but suggests an overwhelming sense of need. It is a cry for specific and definite help. *Erotao* can mean "ask a question" but also is used of asking in prayer for someone else. Also words like *seek* and *knock* suggest a prayerful approach to the Lord. The way these words are used in our New Testament reinforces the Old Testament perspective. Prayer is an expression of relationship and can only be understood in the context of intimate relationship with the Lord.

And relationship brings us to a special aspect of New Testament prayer. Prayer now is associated with relationship to each person of the Godhead. Jesus taught that when we pray, we are to come to God as "our Father" (see Matt. 6:5–8). As Father, God knows our needs and intends to meet them, for we are more important to God than the birds he feeds and the flowers he clothes so beautifully (Matt. 6:25–34). As the Son, Jesus died to establish the relationship that we believers now enjoy with God. Jesus is the way and "no one comes to the Father except through" Jesus (John 14:6). Because we do know Jesus as Savior, we "approach the throne of grace with confidence," certain that we will "receive mercy and find grace to help in time of need" (Heb. 4:16). Remaining close to Jesus and responsive to him maintains the intimacy of relationship that assures us our prayers are heard (see John 15:7; 16:23–24). As Holy Spirit, God lives within each of us to facilitate the intimate exchange we know as prayer. The Bible says that "the Spirit helps us in our weakness. We do not know what we ought to pray, but the Spirit himself intercedes for us with groans that words cannot express" (Rom. 8:26–27) so that with his aid, we can pray "in accordance with God's will."

Again we see the emphasis. Prayer calls us into intimate relationship with God, even with each person of the Trinity. Because our relationship with God is continuous, we can speak spontaneously to the Lord at any time (see Acts 2:4; 1 Thess. 5:17; 1 Tim. 5:5). Strikingly, a survey of the Epistles shows us that most New Testament prayer is intercessory. As we come to know and love other believers intimately, their needs become our concern, and we express that concern by praying for them.

But is prayer as simple as it seems? Doesn't the Bible speak of conditions we must fulfill if our prayers are to be answered? Some people have thought so. But prayer is no obstacle course we have to negotiate successfully to win God's answer as if his concern were a prize. The conditions that some speak of are best understood as promises, reassuring us of God's constant love.

The Old Testament warns that disobedience (Deut. 1:43–45; Isa. 1:15–17), lovelessness (Isa. 58:3–10), and injustice (Mic. 3:1–4) all prevent God from hearing and answering prayer. Prayer has always been relational, and sin cuts off human beings from intimate relationship with God.

The New Testament promises that when we agree with others in our prayers, we will be heard (Matt. 18:19). It speaks of believing, for prayer has always been an expression of trust in God (Matt. 21:22). It tells us that when we are responsive to Jesus' words (John 15:7, 16) and obey him (1 John 3:22), our prayers will be answered, for responsiveness to God is always a characteristic of an intimate relationship with the Lord. And we can know that as our requests conform to God's will, "we have what we asked for" (1 John 5:14). Are these restrictive clauses? Not at all. Instead each provides us with encouragement. In each case we are reassured that relationship is all-important. God answers our prayers, not because we deserve his help but because he loves us and we love him. All true prayer flows out of relationship, expresses relationship, and rests on relationship. As you and I live close to the Lord, trusting him, depending on him, obeying him, we experience an assurance that comes from knowing that as we call out to him, our God is bending near, eager to respond and meet our every need.

PREDESTINATION

Probably no other doctrine has caused more dispute between Christians or more concern in individual hearts. Does God sovereignly choose individual Christians for salvation? Is the rest of humankind utterly without hope? If individuals are so chosen, how can you and I know if we are among that select company?

On the one hand, those who believe in predestination insist that only this doctrine guards the freedom and sovereignty of God and makes salvation something that is truly of grace. On the other hand, those who deny predestination insist that the doctrine robs human beings of freedom, casts God in the role of an unjust monster, and makes the gospel offer of salvation for "whosoever will" come a mockery.

The doctrine of predestination is closely linked with other beliefs that characterize differing theological systems. Because the links are so complex, it is impossible in a brief overview to offer a harmonizing position. So in this article I want to sketch the linked beliefs in two representative Christian understandings of what the Bible teaches and then to explore the Bible's use of the words *predestination* and *election.* ▶ SIN, DEPRAVITY, FREE WILL, GRACE, MORAL RESPONSIBILITY

Predestination and election in Calvinism. Calvinism is a major Protestant theological tradition, represented by Reformed and Presbyterian churches. Calvinism emphasizes both the sovereignty of God and human ruin by sin. A Christian understanding of God must begin with the recognition that he truly is God, in total control of all events in the universe. God has planned the whole from before the Creation itself, and his power guarantees that his every purpose will be realized. In it all, God made his choices freely, moved only by his love and his grace and not at all affected by the choices that he foresaw human beings would make. The fact that salvation rests completely on God's action in carrying out his purpose is demonstrated by the Bible's teaching on sin. Adam's fall ruined the race, making it impossible for any human being to choose to obey or respond to God. Human choices are made freely, but sin has so warped human beings that the free choices of unsaved persons will never be in true harmony with God's will. Thus both the sovereignty of God and the depravity of humanity make it clear that an active work of God, changing people within so that they will choose to believe and thus be saved, is utterly necessary. Predestination is the simple confession that personal salvation is a result of God's purpose and of his action in us.

It is important to note that while God chooses those destined for salvation and acts to move them to an irresistible faith, he does not predestine the unsaved in the same sense. That is, God does not actively choose those who will be lost for damnation, nor does God act to move them to unbelief. His activity is focused on salvation. It is only human sinfulness and unwillingness to respond to God that result in condemnation.

Predestination and election in Wesleyanism. Wesleyanism, represented by historic Methodism and Wesleyan Methodist churches, reflects an Arminian position. God is sovereign, and his purposes will be worked out in our universe. But while God knew from eternity the people who would be saved, he did not predestine them in the active, irresistible, Calvinistic sense. Instead God provided humanity sufficient grace that, despite the impact of sin, any person may choose to respond to the gospel. It follows that sin has not had as drastic an impact on human beings as is supposed by Calvinists. Although the person's free will must be exercised in cooperation with God's grace, the choice of the individual neither initiates nor merits salvation. Salvation is still completely by grace. God has been able to structure all things in the universe according to his plan, not because he acts to make some believe but because he knew from the beginning who would choose to believe.

Predestination in Scripture. The Greek word for "predestine" occurs only six times in the New Testament (Acts 4:28; Rom. 8:29–30; 1 Cor. 2:7; Eph. 1:5, 11). It means "to mark out ahead of time," "to predetermine." In each biblical reference just what has been predetermined by God is carefully identified. In Acts 4:28, it is the events culminating in Jesus' crucifixion, which unfolded as God's "power and will had decided beforehand what should happen." In Romans 8:29, those who love God are "predestined to be conformed to the likeness of his Son." The Corinthians 2 passage looks at God's plan of redemption, calling it "destined for our glory before time began." And Ephesians 1:5 focuses again on believers, affirming that in love God "predestined us to be adopted as his sons through Jesus Christ, in accordance with his pleasure and will." Verse 11 of the same chapter adds that "in him we were chosen, having been predestined according to the plan of him who works out everything in conformity to his will." Calvinists see these verses as proof of their position. Wesleyans note that none of the passages says anything about the role of the human will in believing. Instead it is those who do believe who are predestined, not to salvation but to adoption as heirs and to conformity to Jesus' likeness.

While "predestine" appears only a half dozen times, other words that are translated "appointed," "determined," or "destined" affirm God's final control over all things.

Election in Scripture. Both testaments frequently portray God making choices. Words from the Greek word group meaning "to choose" are used to express the idea of election. The word *election* is used in the Bible and theology to affirm God's sovereign choice of places and especially of persons.

The Old Testament shows God making a number of significant choices. For instance, God chose Jerusalem, where his temple would be erected. More importantly, God chose Israel from all the peoples of the world (see, for example, Deut. 7:6; Gen. 18:5; Ps. 33:12; Isa. 14:1; 45:4). God also chose individuals. He chose Abraham (Gen. 18:19; Neh. 9:7), Moses (Ps. 106:23), and David (1 Kings 8:16; 1 Chron. 28:4). In each case, these choices were free, motivated only by God's own love and purposes. We see it clearly in Deuteronomy 7: "The LORD did not set his affection on you and choose you because you were more numerous than other peoples, for you were the fewest of all peoples. But it was because the LORD loved you and kept the oath he swore to your forefathers" (Deut. 7:7–8).

The apostle Paul picks up this theme in Romans 9 and argues against those who try to find a reason for God's choice in some supposed human merit or inherited right. God chose Isaac but rejected Ishmael. Jacob and Esau were twins, yet before their birth, before either "had done anything good or bad — in order that God's purpose in election might stand: not by works but by him who calls," their mother was informed that God had chosen the younger to receive the covenant promises (Rom. 9:6–13). Paul's point is that "it does not depend on man's desire or effort, but on

God's mercy" (Rom. 9:16). All rests on grace, and grace, flowing solely from the character and the love of God, is expressed in God's free and sovereign choice.

When the references that deal with God's choices are traced through the New Testament, it is clear that in eternity past, the Lord determined to provide the salvation that his church now enjoys. But Christians still disagree as to whether these passages indicate that he has chosen some for salvation and neglected to choose others. It is clear, however, that in most New Testament contexts, God's choices are linked with the believing community rather than individual Christians.

How do we explain these different points of view about election and predestination? It seems that each camp has chosen to emphasize different strands of biblical teaching. The Calvinist emphasizes the sovereignty of God and the sinfulness of human beings. The Wesleyan emphasizes the gospel offer of salvation to all who believe, and the love of God for lost human beings. Wesleyans do not believe that sin has had the totally destructive impact on the human will that the Calvinists do. Neither group denies God sovereignty. Neither denies the role of faith. Neither denies human beings are sinful and lost. Neither denies the transforming power of the gospel. But the differences in emphasis have led to the disagreement about predestination and election sketched above.

So which position is right? In the New Testament two logically contradictory things are both taught. First, everything related to salvation is ascribed to God's free and sovereign choice. Salvation isn't a joint enterprise, part from God and part from human beings. But second, human beings are responsible persons, invited and called to make a real decision about the gospel.

While these two may seem logically contradictory, there is no biblical contradiction. God chooses and human beings are invited to choose. Many are convinced that God's choice overrides every other consideration, that only predestination can adequately express that reality. Others are convinced that a person's choice is free, yet made without violating the ultimate freedom of God to accomplish every purpose and plan of his own.

The personal impact of predestination. Predestination is a doctrine that has troubled many people since its first clear articulation. Some are upset because they feel predestination implies unfairness on God's part. Others have been deeply troubled, fearing that they are not among the elect. Every momentary uncertainty convinces them that they do not really believe or that their belief is something less than saving faith. Probably as long as a person's focus is on the doctrine of predestination rather than on Christ, he or she is bound to be troubled.

Martin Luther does point a way out: "When a man begins to discuss predestination, the temptation is like an inextinguishable fire; the more he disputes, the more he despairs. Our Lord God is opposed to this disputation and accordingly has provided against it baptism, the Word, the sacraments and various signs. In these we should trust and say: 'I am baptized, I believe in Jesus Christ; what does it concern me, whether or not I am predestined?' He has given us ground to stand on, that is, Jesus Christ, and through him we may climb to heaven. He is the one way and the gate to the Father."

How wise Luther was. Salvation does not hinge on belief in or rejection of predestination. It is Jesus that God sets before us, promising all who believe in him forgiveness of sins. You and I may discover when we meet the Lord in glory that our salvation was predestined in the fullest sense of that word. Or we may discover that our response to the gospel was simply foreknown. But what will count then, and what counts now, is that our faith is placed in Jesus and in Jesus alone. Whether or not our faith was predestined, our faith has saved us.

Without dismissing the doctrine or the important issues with which it deals, Christians may still say, with Luther, "I believe in Jesus Christ; what does it concern me, whether or not I am predestined?" I believe. Jesus is mine, and I am his—forever.

PRIESTHOOD

Protestants have been uncomfortable with the idea of priesthood. The Old Testament certainly held to the office of priest, and the Reformers reaffirm the New Testament belief in a priesthood of all believers. But the notion of a priesthood seems foreign to us, and we are not quite sure just what priests do. Most Christians aren't sure what their own priesthood involves; they are equally unclear about the priesthood of Jesus.

To understand what Christians believe about priesthood, we need to look at the Old Testament priesthood, Jesus' high priesthood, the priesthood in church history, and then our own priesthood.

The Old Testament priesthood. In the Old Testament the tribe of Levi was set aside for ritual religious service. From this tribe, Aaron's family was designated for the priesthood. Deuteronomy 33:8–10 describes the priests' ministry as watching over the covenant, teaching God's precepts and law, and making the sacrifices and offerings ordained by the law.

As representatives of God, the priests called God's people to holiness and taught them the law, interpreting and applying it (see Lev. 13–15).

As representatives of a people who constantly fell short, the priests made the blood sacrifices prescribed by the law and then made the joy-filled offerings that testified to the fellowship with God that the sacrifices reestablished.

In the Old Testament priesthood there was one high priest. The high priest had two religious functions that were distinct yet express the role of the whole priesthood. Once each year on the Day of Atonement, the high priest entered the holiest place in the temple, the place of God's presence, to offer blood sacrifice for all the sins of the whole people (see Lev. 16).

◗ ATONEMENT The high priest alone could provide this central sacrificial ministry. Second, the high priest wore on his robes the Urim and Thummim, "the means of making decisions for the Israelites," by which God's people could seek his will (Exod. 28:30).

Why is the priesthood so significant in the Old Testament? Because the faith of Israel is essentially relational. It is rooted in personal relationship between God and humanity. The priests mediated this relationship. The law with its teaching functions expressed the holiness of the God whom Israel was to know and to serve. The sacrificial function expressed the seriousness of sin and the willingness of God to accept the sinner on the basis of blood sacrifice. The priests served an altar where sinful people and a holy God met, and fellowship was restored.

Jesus' high priesthood. The Book of Hebrews presents Jesus as our High Priest. He made the sacrifice that establishes our relationship with God and provides the basis on which that relationship can be maintained. He lives always to make intercession for us (Heb. 7:1–25). Everything implied in the Old Testament priesthood is fulfilled in Jesus, who is the one mediator able to bring human beings into a full and complete relationship with God.

What is more, Christ is the ultimate communicator of God's will. Through his sacrifice, Jesus instituted a new covenant by which the word once written in stone is "put . . . in their minds and written on their hearts" (Heb. 8:10). Every mediatorial role of the Old Testament priesthood not only has been taken over by Jesus but also has been completely fulfilled by him.

The priesthood in church history. The New Testament speaks of an unlimited priesthood shared by all believers. This priesthood of all was understood and practiced by the church for several centuries. While those with clerical responsibility were given special respect, all believers were seen as priests. Church historian Reinhold Seeberg notes that there is "the fullest recognition also of the free activity of all believers in spiritual things." But gradually Christians began to view the Lord's

Supper as a sacrifice rather than a remembrance, and they saw their clergy in the role of the Old Testament priest. Around A.D. 250, Cyprian became the first to argue an actual priesthood for the clergy. His view predominated and was a major factor in the development of Catholicism. ◆ LORD'S SUPPER

The Reformers of the seventeenth century returned to Scripture and to the view of the early church. The Lord's Supper is not a sacrifice but a remembrance. Jesus' one sacrifice on Calvary fully reconciles us to God. There is not room in Christianity for a priesthood that mediates between God and his people, for there is "one mediator between God and men, the man Christ Jesus" (1 Tim. 2:5). Whatever Christian priesthood involves, it is not mediatorial in the sense that the Old Testament priesthood and Jesus' high priesthood were mediatorial.

While calling for a priesthood of all believers, the Reformers felt a need to maintain an ordained clergy. ◆ ORDINATION Luther writes, "Let every one, therefore, who knows himself to be a Christian be assured of this, and apply it to himself, — that we are all priests, and there is no difference between us; that is to say, we have the same power in respect to the Word and all the sacraments." But Luther adds, speaking of the church's ordained ministry, "However, no one may make use of this power except by the consent of the community or by the call of a superior."

The tension suggested here persists. The priesthood, many Christians say, is for all. And yet only those recognized by the congregation or spiritual authority may exercise the priesthood. And what *is* the priesthood? According to Luther it is "properly nothing but the ministry of the Word," with its attendant exercise of prayer, and administration of the ministry of the Christian community to the poor.

The priesthood of believers. One reason why Christians remain uncertain about the priesthood of believers is that we have no more resolved the tension between clergy and laity than Luther was able to do. As a result we don't really understand the spiritual ministries to which we are called as priests — and those ministries that are not priestly.

First, because Jesus is the one mediator in Christianity, our priesthood does not mean that we offer atoning sacrifices to God. Second, there are only two New Testament references to Christian priesthood. In 1 Peter 2:9, Christians are called a "chosen people, a royal priesthood, a holy nation." These titles are applied with the comment that our new identity in Christ enables us to "declare the praises of him who called you out of darkness into this wonderful light." The reference is likely to worship, for we are called in context to offer "spiritual sacrifices acceptable to God through Jesus Christ" (1 Peter 2:5). The other Scripture is Revelation 1:6, which shows that as a "kingdom of priests," with direct access to God through Christ, we "serve his [Jesus'] God and Father." This priesthood reference, too, focuses on worship rather than on any public ministry.

Third, while New Testament references to our priesthood focus on worship, the New Testament pictures Christians functioning in ways similar to some functions of Old Testament priests. Under the new covenant God has planted his Word in all our hearts, and we are all to minister to each other and encourage spiritual growth (see 1 Cor. 12:7–11; Eph. 4:11–16). We also are to pray for one another, representing our brothers and sisters to God.

Worship, serving others with our spiritual gifts, and praying for others are ways that every believer can and is expected to minister. These priestly ministries are not the tasks for which Christians ordained a clergy.

What do we believe about priesthood? Christians agree that the Old Testament priesthood was mediatorial; the sacrifices offered then were essential for Israel's fellowship with God. We believe that Jesus completely fulfilled the ministry of the priest when he offered himself as a sacrifice for our sins. In that sacrifice he established himself as the one mediator humanity needs; in that sacrifice he has perfected forever all who trust in him. There is no more need for a priesthood that offers such sacrifices to God.

But Old Testament sacrifices also were worship. Old Testament priests instructed God's people and made offerings on their behalf. Like that ancient priesthood, every Christian worships God, serves others, and prays for others. In these ministries we, too, are a priesthood—a priesthood that has nothing to do with public ministry or with sacrifice but that remains significant for the people of God.

PROPHECY/PROPHET

Christianity is a revealed religion. Christians believe that God has communicated with humanity in clear words that express truths about him and his plans. The prophets we meet in the Old and New Testaments were God's spokespersons, agents through whom his revelation came. We often think of prophecy in the narrow sense of foretelling the future. But prophecy is properly a broader term, and the prophet of Scripture has a wider, more significant role. What is prophecy, and what is the role of the prophets? And what do we mean when we speak of a "prophetic" ministry today?

Prophecy and prophets in the Old Testament. The basic Hebrew word for prophet means "spokesperson," or "speaker." Essentially a prophet is a person authorized to speak for another, as Moses and the Old Testament prophets were authorized to speak in the name of the Lord (Exod. 7:1–2; Num. 12:1–8). Prophets are also called "messengers," "seers," and "men of God" in the Old Testament. Their messages are called "prophecy," "visions," "oracles," "burdens," or simply "the word of the Lord."

The men and women who served as God's spokespersons had the primary task of providing supernatural guidance to God's people. They came from every walk of life. Their ministries took them to kings and priests, to foreign lands, to the common people. Most often the prophet's message was moral; it confronted Israel with sin and called her back to the holy ways established in God's law. But prophets also gave military advice, made promises to Israel about her future, and warned against various courses of political action.

The prophet's mission was, first of all, to the people of his or her own time. The predictive gift focused primarily on near events. By identifying correctly what would happen in the near future, the prophet's claim to be God's spokesperson was authenticated. God alone can "make known the end from the beginning" and bring about what he has planned (Isa. 46:9–11). Foretelling future events without mistake was compelling evidence of the prophet's call to be God's spokesperson.

But the predictive prophecy found in the Old Testament often shifts from the near future to reach far beyond the prophet's own lifetime. In powerful images, Old Testament prophets express visions that share God's plans for Israel and the world. Much of our Old Testament is prophecy in this sweeping, majestic sense.

Christians have disagreed on how to interpret much of this sweeping Old Testament prophecy. For one thing, prophecy is rich in figurative language and is filled with images that can be difficult to visualize. Prophecies are often fragmentary, giving some details of future events, but not enough for us to understand the full future and its context. Also prophecy can have multiple references, portraying not just one but a series of similar events that foreshadow a culminating event at history's end. The problem of interpretation is further complicated by the fact that some prophecy is conditional; for instance, Jonah warned Nineveh that God would destroy them because of their wickedness, but when the people repented, the city was not destroyed. Still, if we take Old Testament prophecy literally, as portraying events that will actually take place, Scripture provides a powerful vision of the future. The timing and the exact sequence of events may be blurred, but the major elements are clear.

But should we interpret prophecy in a literal way? Some people believe we should, and they point to a striking fact. The prophecy that has been fulfilled, even though it was spoken hundreds of years before the foretold events, has been fulfilled in a concrete, literal way. For example, Daniel outlined the course of pagan empires spanning hundreds of years of history now past. Centuries before Jesus was born, the Old Testament described his appearance from David's line (Isa. 9:6–7; 11:1). It told of his supernatural birth (Isa. 7:14) in Bethlehem (Micah 5:2) and of his early years in Nazareth (Isa. 9:1–2; 11:1). The Old Testament prophets told of Jesus' death with criminals (Isa. 53:9, 12), his burial with the rich (Isa. 53:9), of the offer of vinegar while he hung on the cross (Ps. 69:21), and of soldiers gambling for his clothing (Ps. 22:18). The prophets recorded Christ's dying words (Ps. 22:1; 31:5) and said that though his side would be pierced (Zech. 12:10), his bones would remain unbroken (Ps. 34:20). While the Old Testament never explained how these events would fit together (in a single life and in the span of a few brief years), each prophecy was fulfilled in a literal, historic way.

Then what picture of the future does unfulfilled Old Testament prophecy provide? Even Christians who believe that most prophetic visions are symbolic of Christian experiences and blessings agree. If Old Testament prophecy were to be literally fulfilled, the future would include a final gathering of Israel to her ancient land, a great world conflict with worldwide tribulation, and the intervention of God to put down evil and establish his own glorious kingdom. These elements are found over and over again in the writings of the Old Testament prophets.

Prophecy and prophets in the New Testament. What about visions of the future found in the Gospels and the Epistles? Like Old Testament prophetic visions these are fragmentary, incomplete images of vast events, indefinite about times and sequences. What future does the New Testament envision? Again, if we take the predictions in a literal sense, the New Testament foretells a time of worldwide tribulation and trouble (Matt. 24), promises Jesus' personal return (1 Thess. 4:13–18) to rule on earth (Rev. 20:1–6), and foresees the re-creation of the universe after final judgment (2 Peter 2; Rev. 21). In this there is no essential conflict between Old Testament and New Testament visions of the future. But Christians who take such prophecy very seriously debate how the details fit together and what will be the actual sequence of these future events.

Some Christians today are attracted to the detailed pictures some Bible teachers offer of the future. These pictures feature a step-by-step presentation of events as they are supposed to unfold. Other Christians pay no attention to prophecy at all. Whatever our orientation, we should all remember that the essential ministry of the prophets was to their own generation, exhorting, challenging, comforting, and confronting. Their prophetic visions of the future, whether of judgment or blessing, are directly linked to their messages for their own times. So when we look back at the prophets, we want to attend to their visions. But we must not overlook the way the prophets' visions were related to the historical situation and the needs of the generation in which they ministered. When we read prophecies, we should focus first on the message that visions of the future were intended to underline and only then on the future they portray.

Despite our different emphases, there is one area of clear agreement. The words of the Old Testament and New Testament prophets were often written down and have come to us as Scripture. No prophets of our era can add to the canon of Scripture, for God's special revelation is now complete. ◆ **REVELATION**

Prophecy today? The New Testament also describes prophets and prophecy in the early church. People who were moved by the Spirit gave special messages to local congregations (Acts 11:27–30; 21:10–11). Prophecy is named as a spiritual gift in 1 Corinthians 12 (see also 1 Cor. 14:29–32). But what is the prophetic gift? Some Christians believe this indicates a continuation of Old Testament prophetic ministry, that even today some believers can give special guidance from God to congregations and individuals. Other Christians take the New Testament references to prophets in a weaker sense. Prophets are still God's spokespersons, but they speak for him through teaching and preaching. Still others see the prophetic ministry as confrontational. Like the Old Testament prophets, some believers are specially called to confront their brothers and sisters and their society. In confrontation, the prophets among us are God's spokespersons, calling us to live by God's standards of justice and mercy.

What similar points of view about prophets and prophecy do Christians hold? First, we agree that God has had spokespersons who delivered his message to the men and women of their own generation. Through their writings, these Old Testament and New Testament prophets speak to us as well.

Today the ancient prophets minister to us in two ways. First, they call us to a holy and righteous life. Second, the prophets of Scripture portray a future that is firmly in God's control, a future in which his plans and purposes will be fulfilled. We differ in the way we interpret biblical passages envisioning the future, but we agree completely that history is marching toward a divine denouement, when God will put all things right.

PROPITIATION

Is God really angry with human beings over sin? This is the issue raised by the Christian doctrine of propitiation. The word speaks of a change of attitude, of an offering that sets wrath aside and permits God to deal favorably with the offender.

Some Christians have argued that a loving God has no need to be propitiated. But the Bible speaks plainly about God's holiness and his wrath. ▶ WRATH, HOLINESS

The New Testament also calls Jesus' death on the cross for us a *hilasmos*, a Greek word that certainly meant propitiation in that culture. Romans 3:21–26 argues that God, who offers sinners righteousness as a gift, demonstrated his justice by punishing sins in Jesus, whom he presented as a "sacrifice of atonement" (literally, "propitiation"). The same powerful word is used in Hebrews 2:17, 1 John 2:1–2, and 1 John 4:10.

Historically, Christians have seen Jesus' death as more than a symbolic act. Jesus gave himself as a sacrifice for us, paying for our sins on the cross, and he thereby removed every ground of our holy God's righteous anger.

But what about the supposed conflict between our understanding of God as a loving person and the need for this person to be propitiated? Most simply, we believe in a God who is both holy and loving, a God who is both committed to do right and committed to forgive. We see in Jesus' death the divine solution to the dilemma. Jesus died to satisfy the inner demand for justice that God's holiness imposed on him, for he cannot act or feel against his character. But the fact that Jesus died in our place is the universe's ultimate demonstration of the depth of God's love.

In the cross love and justice meet, and both triumph in the propitiation Jesus offered there.

PROVIDENCE

Although the word *providence* is not found in the Bible, it sums up basic biblical teachings about God's relationship to his world. What is providence? Providence indicates God's care for and supervision of all things, from the moment of creation on into eternity.

Christians are convinced that God truly is in control of all things. This doesn't mean that human beings are like puppets on his string. In fact, we are convinced that humans act responsibly and make decisions freely. We are also convinced that cause and effect operate in the natural universe. But our God is so great that he weaves together the free choices of myriad human beings and the waves of cause and effect that sweep through history and bends them to his own purposes. God is in firm control. Rather than depending solely on direct action, he uses "natural processes" to accomplish his purposes. His influence is usually hidden; he does not violate our freedoms. Yet he sovereignly guides and shapes all things according to his will.

Two passages clearly illustrate providence. In the Old Testament the Book of Esther tells the story of a terrible threat to the Jewish people. In 476 B.C. an influential confidant of the Persian ruler, Xerxes, felt slighted by the Jew Mordecai and determined to destroy his whole people. But Mordecai's niece, Esther, had recently been installed as Xerxes' queen. Although Esther was a Jew, she had concealed her racial origin to everyone in the court. Urged by Mordecai, Esther spoke to Xerxes about the threat to her fellow Jews. In a series of what appear to be coincidences, Xerxes is disposed toward Mordecai and against the Jews' enemy, Haman. In the end it is Haman who is hung and those hostile to the Jews who are killed. In the whole Book of Esther, God's name is never mentioned. But the unfolding of coincidental events illustrate God's control and his commitment to his ancient people.

In the New Testament Jesus' death is the prime example of providence. Looking back on that death, Peter relates how the leaders of the Jewish people conspired against Jesus. While they acted freely and responsibly, still "they did what your power and will had decided beforehand should happen" (Acts 4:27–28). Even the willful actions of God's enemies unwittingly harmonize with what God has purposed.

What does belief in providence mean for you and me? It means that we can never be victims of chance, and we have no need to fear the future. The ancient pagans lived with the grim conviction that chance, or the fates, rule human experience. Christians know that chance has no role in this universe. God exercises control of the events that affect individuals as well as nations. Because God is in control, we do not fear the future. We look in everything to discover what he is teaching us, what good gift he intends to give us. We look ahead with hope and never with despair. While we accept responsibility for our personal choices, we remain convinced that "in all things God works for the good of those who love him" (Rom. 8:28).

RAPTURE

The apostle Paul describes it: "For the Lord himself will come down from heaven, with a loud command, with the voice of the archangel and with the trumpet call of God, and the dead in Christ will rise first. After that, we who are still alive and are left will be caught up with them in the clouds to meet the Lord in the air. And so we will be with the Lord forever" (1 Thess. 4:16–17). And for those who had been shaken by the death of their loved ones, Paul adds, "Therefore comfort each other with these words" (1 Thess. 4:18).

The imagery is powerful and clear. So is the purpose of this particular passage. We know that death is not the end, that Jesus is coming, and that through him our resurrection is coming, too. It is this, the catching up of the living to be resurrected with the dead in Christ, that Christians call the Rapture.

While Christians rejoice with Paul at this prospect, they have also debated the Rapture. The arguments focus not on the event itself but on its relationship to other still-future events. *When* will this resurrection of Christians take place?

Some Christians believe that Jesus will come to earth to establish a thousand-year kingdom. They believe that just before the kingdom is established, the earth will experience a period of terrible upheavals. World war and natural disasters will make this a time of unmatched tribulation. This terrible period is expected to span seven years, to be ended only by the personal appearance of Jesus. ◆ **TRIBULATION** But people holding this belief differ on just when Christians will be caught up into the clouds. Will it be at the beginning of the seven-year period so that believers can be spared the terrors of that time? Will it be in the middle or at the end of the seven-year period? The "Rapture question" expresses no doubt that Jesus will come or that we will be caught up. It does express Christians' uncertainty about the relationship of the Rapture to other prophesied events. ◆ **PROPHECY**

Other Christians believe that the world will grow better gradually as the preaching of the gospel influences every society. In this view, Jesus will come after a thousand-year peace. The Rapture is one of many foretold events that occur simultaneously at history's end. Again the question is not whether the Rapture will happen, but when?

If we were to ask the question, "Who is right?" I suspect that many would volunteer, "I am!" But a better answer may be, "None of us!" Why? Because the prophetic visions of Scripture simply are not neatly organized, with times and sequences spelled out. Instead glimpses of the future are provided, and they are given for a purpose.

The purpose in the vision of the Rapture is to comfort grieving Christians with the certainty of a coming reunion with loved ones. Somehow the question of just how this event fits in with other prophesied events doesn't seem too important to Paul or to the other writers of Scripture. Rather than seeking to satisfy our curiosity, they use prophecy to satisfy the most heartfelt of human needs.

What, then, do Christians believe about the Rapture? We disagree about times and sequences, but we agree that a great day is coming. When Jesus returns, we who believe will be united with him and with our loved ones.

We find comfort in this assurance, for we live in a tormented world. We are each subject to suffering and tragedy. But in our darkest hours we can look ahead with Paul and sense life's clouds dispelled by the bright vision of Jesus' coming. When Jesus comes, we will be caught up together, and we will forever be with him.

REASON

Many Christians are uncomfortable with reason. One cause of the discomfort is the fact that reason failed to lead history's great philosophers to God. Another cause is that modern appeals to reason dispute Christian doctrine. Probably the major cause of our discomfort is that *reason* is a slippery word, and we need to define what we mean when we argue about it. We certainly do not mean that Christianity is an *un*reasonable faith. But neither do we mean that reason can take the place of faith or can lead a person to faith.

Reliance on reason. What happened in Great Britain in the eighteenth century illustrates why Christians hesitate to emphasize reason. Developments in science and philosophy led to a movement called the Enlightenment, which was marked by the conviction that there were no limits to what human beings could achieve through reason. Every social and scientific problem seemed capable of solution. It is not surprising that confidence in reason influenced religion. At first, it was assumed that reason would lead a person to Christian convictions, and revelation was to be little more than an aid to reason. Then Christianity was reinterpreted as one of many natural religions, compatible with other faiths that also conform to the natural order of things. Finally there developed sharp opposition to the supernatural in Christianity. Miracles were declared impossible because they were unreasonable, and the Bible's claim to be revelation was rejected. By relying on reason as a trustworthy religious authority, in the span of a century and a half, the

Church of England broke radically with historic, orthodox Christian faith. It was at this point that God raised up Wesley, a bold minister whose evangelistic movement swept the British Isles.

So Christians are rightly suspicious of an over-reliance on reason. Christianity is a revealed religion. Commitment to the authority of Scripture rather than the authority of reason is essential to our faith. ◗ REVELATION

Rejection of reason? For some the only alternative to reliance on reason is to reject its role entirely. Christianity is appropriated by faith. Faith, not reason, has the central role in Christian experience. But to assign a central role to faith doesn't rule out the use of reason, though it may help us to define appropriate roles for reason.

Martin Luther described reason as carnal, stupid, and an enemy of God. But his attack was directed against reason invading faith's domain. Luther believed that our natural reason is used properly in its own domain, that is, applied to issues where the source of information is the natural universe. And Luther believed that the Christian can use reason to explore spiritual issues, guided by and subject to the Word of God. But reason cannot be relied on as an authority, and reason cannot replace revelation as a source of information about God.

The Bible also seems to downgrade human reason, but again the focus is on wisdom operating in the religious realm. "In the wisdom of God," Paul writes, "the world through its wisdom did not know him" (1 Cor. 1:21). The way of salvation God chose seems foolish and unreasonable to human beings and thus demonstrates that "the foolishness of God is wiser than man's wisdom" (1 Cor. 1:25). Only by turning from human reasoning to submit to the gospel's revelation of God's love and power can human beings know truth or know God (1 Cor. 1:18–2:16).

In Romans 1, Paul argues that God is unveiled in nature as well as in Scripture's special revelation. He says, "What may be known about God is plain to them, because God has made it plain to them. For since the creation of the world God's invisible qualities — his eternal power and divine nature — have been clearly seen, being understood from what has been made, so that men are without excuse" (Rom. 1:19–20).

We have evidence, proof of God's existence, and the evidence is clearly seen despite sin's impact on our natural capacities. But Paul argues that the very capacity of reason people rely on leaves them without excuse, for "although they knew God, they neither glorified him as God nor gave thanks to him, but their thinking became futile and their foolish hearts were darkened" (Rom. 1:21). Reason does bring human beings to confrontation with God. It is a person's choice *not* to accept reasonable evidence of God's existence, demonstrating how lost humanity is. Refusing to submit to God or to respond appropriately to him, humanity misuses reason and sharpens it as a weapon to use against the Lord. By misusing reason in this way, and refusing to "accept the things that come from the Spirit of God," all ability to reason spiritually has been lost. Now even revealed truths "are foolishness to" the unsaved, and they "cannot understand them, because they are spiritually discerned" (1 Cor. 2:14).

It is clear, then, that the reasoning of unbelievers cannot be relied on in spiritual matters. Even revealed truth cannot be grasped without a faith commitment that abandons human reasoning about religion to embrace salvation by faith in a crucified and risen Jesus.

What, then, can Christians say about reason? First, we rejoice in every capacity God has given us, and we use every capacity joyfully. We can rejoice in our reason, too, and use it to expand the horizons of our knowledge of the world. Second, we also joyfully use our reason to better understand what God has revealed about himself. We study to show ourselves approved by God so that we can teach each other and gently instruct those who oppose us, relying on God to give them that change of heart that alone can lead to a knowledge of the truth (2 Tim. 2:25). Third, we insist that human reasoning about religion is necessarily faulty until faith in Jesus makes a person sensitive to the Spirit of God. Aided by God's Spirit, we can understand the meaning of truth revealed in nature and in Scripture. But even the Christian's reasoning about spiritual things must always be subject to Scripture, for the Word of God and not our reason is the authority in our faith.

RECONCILIATION

The idea of reconciliation is basic to Christian thinking. It describes the necessary restoration of broken relationships.

Restoring relationship with God. Christians recognize sin as a terrible barrier to personal relationships. One impact of sin is to destroy harmony with God, creating both fear and hostility. Despite God's continuing love for us, sin creates in the human heart a deep antagonism toward the Lord.

In Romans 5, Paul links reconciliation to Jesus' death. On the basis of Jesus' death, God declares innocent those who believe. ◗ JUSTIFICA-TION That death demonstrates God's unquenchable love, and it frees us from all threat of punishment. The barriers that sin erects, objective and subjective, are all done away with in Jesus. So the Bible says, "When we were God's enemies, we were reconciled to him through the death of his Son" (Rom. 5:10). Another key passage says that "God, who reconciled us to himself through Christ" also "gave to us the ministry of reconciliation: that God was reconciling the world to himself in Christ, not counting their sins against them" (2 Cor. 5:18–19).

Several important truths about reconciliation are expressed in these passages. First, we are the ones who are reconciled to God. His attitude toward us has always been one of love; it is our orientation to him that must change. Second, God has acted in Christ to reconcile us. The cross confirms it: Our sins are no longer counted against us. Third, the objective work of reconciliation has been accomplished. When we take the step of faith, we experience a psychological change as our attitude toward God is brought into harmony with reality. Once enemies of God, we now "rejoice in God through our Lord Jesus Christ." Only because Jesus truly has paid for our sins can our hostility and fears be transformed into joyful love.

Restoring relationships with each other. Sin does more than distort relationship with God; it also distorts our relationships with each other. Humanity is a divided race, marked by hostilities that are justified by race, sex, social status, economic advantage, cultural background, and the like. In Ephesians, Paul points to the deep hostilities that divided Jew and Gentile in the New Testament world. Yet those who were "strangers and foreigners" have been joined "in this one body," now "fellow citizens" and "members of God's household." The same blood of Christ that brought both groups near to God also brought them into harmony with each other, "for he himself is our peace, who has made the two one and has destroyed the barrier, the dividing wall of hostility" (Eph. 2:11–18).

One of the exciting realities of our faith is that Christians recognize others as brothers and sisters and love them despite differences. Our common relationship with God through Jesus makes us family. Not all Christians experience this reality, but the reality is there. A basis has been laid by Jesus for harmonious and loving personal relationships between Christians.

It is important that Christians live out the reality of reconciliation. Every Epistle stresses the importance of love for our brothers and sisters.
 ♦ LOVE And Jesus taught, "If you are offering your gift [to God] at the altar and there remember that your brother has something against you, leave your gift there in front of the altar. First go and be reconciled to your brother; then come and offer your gift" (Matt. 5:23–24). Certainly this is one of the most important gifts you and I can give to the Lord. We

can live in harmony and at peace with each other, treating one another with the love that God has showered out on us in Jesus Christ.

REDEMPTION

The roots of this important theological word are planted deeply in our Old Testament. But the full meaning of what God intended from all eternity is only realized in the New Testament. In each testament there is a doctrine of redemption. In each testament there is hope for a helpless humankind.

Redemption in the Old Testament. Three Hebrew words are translated "redeem" or "ransom." Each comes into play only when the objects of redemption are trapped by forces they are helpless to overcome. Freedom can be found only when another, powerful party intervenes.

One word was originally a commercial term indicating a transfer of ownership through a payment or equivalent consideration. Looking back on Israel enslaved in Egypt until released by God's intervention, Deuteronomy 15:15 says, "Remember that you were slaves in Egypt and the LORD your God redeemed you." Israel was released so that the people might be God's possession. Remembering this relationship with the God who unleashed his power to win Israel's freedom, God's Old Testament people had a basis for hope that the Lord would continue to intervene and deliver.

Another Hebrew word means to take a kinsman's role and to act to help a relative in trouble or danger. The word and its derivatives, which occur over a hundred times in the Old Testament, always imply a victim who is helpless in the grip of another until a third party appears to win release. In Old Testament law a person always retained the right to redeem personal property and a relative also had the right to aid. How significant it is that Jesus was born a true human being, establishing a relationship with our race that enabled him to redeem you and me.

Finally, the third Hebrew word means "to ransom," "to make an exchange that wins the freedom of another."

Together these words and the way they are used in the Bible develop a clear doctrine of redemption. In our Old Testament redemption is an action by one who is able to win the release of another who is in danger or bondage. The words are used in common ways, referring to business and legal transactions. But they are extended to explain the meaning of God's actions on Israel's behalf. God has taken the role of a family member, acting out of love to meet the needs of the helpless.

Redemption in the New Testament. As is so often the case, the meaning of the Greek words for redemption used in the New Testament are shaped by Old Testament images. The basic redemptive concepts developed in the Old Testament are retained.

The Greek word *lutroo* focuses attention on a release won by a payment made. The New Testament makes it clear that Jesus' life was the price of our redemption from sin's bondage. Only the "precious blood of Christ, a lamb without blemish or defect," could release us from the "empty way of life" received from our forefathers, and free us from "all wickedness" (1 Peter 1:18–19; Titus 2:14; Matt. 20:28; Mark 10:45). Redemption by God results in a new relationship in which we are freed to "serve the living God" (Heb 9:12–14).

The word *exagorazo* is found four times in the New Testament. It is a strong word, picturing a purchase that takes the thing purchased off the market. We who were slaves to sin have been selected by God to become his sons and daughters (Gal. 3:26–29; Eph. 4:17–5:2; Col. 3:5–10).

The New Testament takes the Old Testament concept of redemption by God and focuses it on the issue of individual salvation. In the New Testament we see every human being helpless in the grip of sin. Only Christ's blood can break the hold of sin and win the believer a place in God's family. Purchased by Christ, we belong to God and are called to live a life that honors him.

Redemption, then, speaks to the deepest of our needs. It proclaims God's commitment to a helpless humanity. And it explains the cross as the price Jesus had to pay to free us. Jesus has paid that price. When we trust in him, we truly do become free.

REGENERATION ♦ BORN AGAIN

RELIGION

Christianity is considered to be one of the great religions of the world. But perhaps it shouldn't be. Religion is hardly ever mentioned in the New Testament. When it is, religion is seldom linked with Christ.

In some of our English versions "religion" is found in Acts 25:19 and 17:22, which actually have a Greek word that suggests a superstition. Another Greek word rendered "religion" in the New Testament indicates the rituals and trappings of ceremonial faiths (Acts 26:5; Col. 2:16; James 1:26–27). A third word, sometimes translated "religion," means "piety" but is usually translated "godly" in modern versions.

The dictionary defines religion as "the service and worship of God," "a set of attitudes, beliefs, and practices about the supernatural." Both worship and beliefs are part of Christianity. But the heart of our faith is relationship. Only in Christianity does the Creator of the universe reveal himself and explain the ruin sin has made of our race. Only in Christianity does God step into history as a human being to offer himself in payment for our sins. Only in Christianity and in Jesus Christ does God both invite us to accept forgiveness as a free gift and then welcome all who trust him as children in his family. Only in Christianity is an endless life of fellowship with God assured.

Like the religions of the world, Christianity does have its own distinctive beliefs. And like the religions of the world, Christianity has its worship of God. But unlike all the rest, Christianity is a personal relationship with the one true God. In Christianity alone can human beings come to know him. Christian faith is not a religion. It is a living, vital relationship with God.

REPENTANCE

Is repentance the same as being sorry? Perhaps in the vocabulary of common speech, but in the vocabulary of faith, the word *repentance* has a far deeper meaning.

The Hebrew word expressing the idea of repentance occurs over a thousand times in the Old Testament, with a wide range of meanings. Over a hundred and fifty of these uses are linked with Israel's covenant relationship to God. Repentance invariably indicates a turn from false gods to the Lord or a turn from evil ways to God's ways. Repentance is a commitment to God and to his way of life.

It is clear that repentance represents a change, for repentance is a return, the reversal of an earlier wrong choice. At times the change may be preceded by deep sorrow and conviction of sin. But at the heart of the matter, repentance is not sorrow but a change of life-direction.

In the New Testament the word translated "repentance" is *metanoia*. Other words (like *conversion*) are linked with the fact that faith in Jesus sets life on a new course. The word *metanoia* emphasizes the fact that faith involves a decision to abandon the errors of the past and turn to God and his ways. To repent is to make a decision that changes the total spiritual and moral direction of life.

The moral impact of repentance is illustrated in the preaching of John the Baptist who, in the tradition of the Old Testament prophets, demanded that his listeners make a decision to turn from their ways to holiness (Matt. 3:2; Mark 1:15). Jesus' early preaching concentrated on the same theme (Matt. 4:17; Mark 6:12). Later, when Jesus himself had become the issue, repentance meant to change one's mind about him. Repentance involves a decision about Jesus, a change that can only be represented in a personal commitment to him as Savior and Lord (Luke 13; Acts 2:38; 3:19).

Repentance today. Repentance remains a vital concept in Christian faith. Our faith calls for more than mental agreement to a set of doctrines or a casual acknowledgment of Christ. Our faith calls for a deep commitment to Jesus and for holiness of life. To know Jesus means confronting those areas in our own life that are out of harmony with our calling; to know Jesus means deciding to turn from wrong thoughts and ways to a deep commitment of all we are to the Lord.

At times Christians have felt that repentance must be added to faith if a person is to be saved. The truth is more significant. Faith and repentance are linked, for biblical faith is itself an act of commitment. It is out of faith and through faith that the change and the commitment of true repentance grows. Where faith is real, the decision to change and a life that displays change will surely come.

RESURRECTION

We look ahead to resurrection with confidence. One day the dead will rise, and we who believe will be given bodies that are fresh and new, as perfect as Jesus' own resurrection body.

Resurrection in the Old Testament. Although resurrection is suggested in the Old Testament, it does not seem to be a major element in Old Testament faith. Old Testament saints looked beyond this life, but for the most part they trusted God without clear information about his ultimate plan. Thirteen hundred years after Abraham, Isaiah revealed that God would "swallow up death forever" (Isa. 25:8). In the future "your dead will live; their bodies will rise" (Isa. 26:19). The clearest statement about resurrection is found in the prophet Daniel, one of the last of the Old Testament prophets: "Multitudes who sleep in the dust of the earth will awake: some to everlasting life, others to shame and everlasting contempt" (Dan. 12:2). So death was not thought of as the end. But the doctrine of resurrection, though taught, is not developed in our Old Testament.

The resurrection of Jesus. It was only with Jesus' resurrection that we catch a glimpse of the glory awaiting us. The fact of Jesus' resurrection is central to our faith. Jesus "was declared with power to be the Son of God by his resurrection from the dead" (Rom. 1:4). Every claim Jesus made during his life is confirmed by his resurrection. Jesus is also called the "firstfruits of those who have fallen asleep" (1 Cor. 15:20). His resurrection is the guarantee that death has been conquered and that endless life is now our destiny. And the resurrection means that "because Jesus lives forever, he has a permanent priesthood. Therefore he is able to save completely those who come to God by him, because he always lives to intercede for them" (Heb. 7:24–25). No wonder the resurrection of Jesus was a keystone in early preaching of the gospel (Acts 2:24; 3:15; 4:10; 5:30; 10:40; 13:34–37; 17:18–32).

Appearances of Jesus

To Peter, later the same day	Luke 24:34; 1 Cor. 15:5
To the disciples on Emmaus Road	Luke 24:13–31
To the apostles (Thomas absent)	Luke 24:36–45; John 20:19–24
To the apostles (Thomas present)	John 20:24–29
To seven by the Lake of Tiberius	John 21:1–23
To some five hundred in Galilee	1 Cor. 15:6
To James in Jerusalem and Bethany	1 Cor. 15:7
To many at the ascension	Acts 1:3–11
To Paul near Damascus	Acts 9:3–6; 1 Cor. 15:8
To Stephen when he is stoned	Acts 7:55
To Paul in the temple	Acts 22:17–19; 23:11
To John on Patmos	Rev. 1:10–19

The resurrection of the believer. All the dead will one day appear before God for judgment (Rev. 20:11–15). But this recall is not what the Bible means by resurrection. Resurrection is a transformation to a new state of being; resurrection is reserved for believers.

John looks forward to this transformation and says, "What we will be has not yet been made known." What we do know is that when Jesus "appears we shall be like him" (1 John 3:2). We find more details in 1 Corinthians 15. Our resurrected bodies will correspond to our present bodies but will be imperishable, glorious, infused with power, and be spiritual rather than natural (1 Cor. 15:42–44). Those bodies will be in "the likeness of the man from heaven" (1 Cor. 15:49).

It is fascinating to note that our resurrected bodies will be like Jesus' own. For instance, Jesus' raised body was "flesh and bones" (Luke 24:39) but not "flesh and blood" (Lev. 17:11). Jesus could appear among his disciples in a locked room. Does the resurrected body move between the atoms of the material universe? We do not know, but we know that when resurrection comes, unimaginable powers will be ours.

Resurrection and the Christian life. The New Testament presents an exciting prospect that is linked to resurrection and also available to us today. Paul writes that "if the Spirit of him who raised Jesus from the dead is living in you, he who raised Christ from the dead will also give life to your mortal bodies through his Spirit, who lives in you" (Rom. 8:11). Paul's point is that the Holy Spirit, whose power affected Jesus' resurrection, lives in believers today. Although our bodies are "dead" in their mortality and are corrupted by sin, the Holy Spirit who raised Jesus can infuse life into us today. By the Spirit's power, we can be lifted beyond the limitations imposed by our mortality and live righteous lives that honor the Lord.

Any Christian can yearn with Paul to "know Christ and the power of his resurrection" and so "attain to the resurrection from the dead" (Phil. 3:10–11). That yearning can be satisfied, as the "power of his [Jesus'] resurrection" works within our personalities to make us more and more like him.

Conclusions. In pagan thought there might be a life after death, some continuation of being, but resurrection seemed utterly ridiculous. In our world today many assume that death is the end. The Christian message is bold in its contrast. We believe not only in a "continuation of being" but also in endless, personal, self-conscious existence for all human beings. But we know from Scripture that there is a terrible division in humanity. For some people endless existence will mean endless alienation from God; they will experience a reunion of body and personality, but to "shame and contempt." For believers, however, resurrection means a total transformation; our resurrection will mean a full restoration, not just of innocence but of the full glory that God intended for humanity. Because of what Jesus has done for us, you and I look forward to a time when we will be like him, bright images of his holiness and his love. We look forward to a resurrection that is resurrection indeed.

REVELATION

Christians have been convinced that only God can make God known. And we are just as firmly convinced that God has made himself known.

This conviction is expressed in our belief in revelation. The word *revelation* simply means "to unveil something hidden," "to make something known for what it is." Some people sum up revelation by saying it is knowledge *about* God that comes *from* God.

Christians focus on two avenues of revelation. The first is usually called general revelation. General revelation includes those wordless ways God expresses truth about himself to all humanity. The second is special revelation. Special revelation includes God's unveiling of himself to individuals or groups in a variety of ways. Our Bible comes to us by special revelation, and Jesus himself is the ultimate special unveiling of the person of God.

General revelation. Most Christians see two primary avenues of general revelation. The first is the Creation itself. The psalmist says, "The heavens declare the glory of God; the skies proclaim the work of his hands. Day after day they pour forth speech; night after night they display knowledge. There is no speech or language where their voice is not heard. Their voice goes out into all the earth, their words to the ends of the world" (Ps. 19:1–4).

The apostle Paul says of creation's silent witness, "What may be known about God is plain to them, because God has made it plain to them. For since the creation of the world God's invisible qualities — his eternal power and divine nature — have been clearly seen" (Rom. 1:18–19).

Paul argues elsewhere in Romans that God has implanted another witness to himself in human nature. This witness is conscience, which bears witness that we live in a moral universe. While the specific actions different cultures define as wrong may differ, every culture identifies some actions as morally right and others as wrong. And everywhere there is the inner judge, conscience, expressed as we judge or excuse ourselves for actions that make us feel guilty.

What can human beings know about God from general revelation? We can know that God exists. We can know the Creator is not only greater than his creation but also distinct from it. We can know something of his intelligence. We can also sense his moral nature and realize that he will judge human actions. Because so much knowledge about God is accessible to us in general revelation, Paul concludes that "men are without excuse" (Rom. 1:20) for their failure to acknowledge God and respond to him with praise and thanks.

What may be most striking in the New Testament's treatment of general revelation is just this fact. Human beings meet and come to know truth about God in general revelation. But humanity has always reacted negatively to this knowledge. Warped by sin, our race has failed to glorify or thank the God we meet in nature; instead humans have foolishly "exchanged the glory of the immortal God for images made to look like mortal man and birds and animals and reptiles" (Rom. 1:23). More than information about God is needed. There must be an inner transformation of humanity's attitude toward God. There must be faith, which historically has been stimulated only by very special revelation from God.

Special revelation. The Book of Hebrews begins, "In the past God spoke to our forefathers through the prophets at many times and in various ways, but in these last days he has spoken to us by his Son" (Heb. 1:1–2). Special revelation has come through dreams, waking visions, and by "face-to-face" communication with God. This revelation has been shared in stories passed down verbally, expressed in ritual and sacrifice, and recorded in Scripture. Separate revelations, unfolding over the centuries, have been gathered into a harmonious whole, together giving us in our Scriptures a clear portrait of God and his purposes. ▸

INSPIRATION, SCRIPTURE

What is so exciting about special revelation is that it does more than show us God from a distance. Special revelation takes us inside the heart and mind of God, showing us his deepest motives and purposes. In special revelation, the meaning of his actions in our world is explained. Why did God create? Who are human beings? What is God's attitude toward sin and sinners? Why did God choose Israel as his people and miraculously free this people from slavery in Egypt? As God reveals more and more of himself and his purposes, we come to realize that all special revelation is gospel; all is good news, for all portrays a God who cares deeply about human beings and who reaches out to establish a personal relationship with any who will trust him. Through general revelation we know that God is. Through special revelation we know who he is and what he is like.

Christians view the Bible as special revelation, a reliable record of all that God intends to unveil to us until Jesus returns. But we also recognize Jesus himself as the ultimate unveiling of God. In the words, actions, and character of Jesus Christ, we have "the exact representation of his [God's] being" (Heb. 1:3). As Jesus said, "Anyone who has seen me has seen the Father" (John 14:9).

Special revelation takes us beyond the evidence that God exists to help us know God as a person. We trace his thoughts as they are unveiled in Scripture, and in Jesus we sense the fervor of his love and the depth of his commitment to us. As we come to know the God who unveils himself so fully, our fears dissolve, and we joyfully respond by trusting him with everything we have and are.

REVIVAL

We read about revivals in the Old Testament. And we know about them from church history.

For fifty-five years, Israel had been corrupted by evil King Manassah. His successor, Josiah, led a return to the Lord. When workmen found a copy of the lost Scriptures in the Jerusalem temple, a stunned Josiah recognized the extent of Israel's wickedness. He determined to turn wholeheartedly to God's way. God commended Josiah, because "your heart was responsive and you humbled yourself before the LORD when you heard what I had spoken" (2 Kings 22:19). Josiah's inner response to the Lord was expressed in action. He burned the groves where idols were worshiped, and he tore down the pagan altars. Eager to fulfill all the written law, Josiah reinstituted the Passover festival, got rid of mediums and spiritists, and committed himself to God "with all his heart and with all his soul and with all his strength, in accordance with all the law of Moses" (2 Kings 23:25).

Revivals are characterized by the things we see in Josiah: a responsive and humble heart and a commitment to do God's will, resulting in obedience. But revival is more than a personal thing. Revival affects a generation.

Revivals are not limited to Old Testament days. Our own era has known times when God has moved in a special way. Wesley's ministry stimulated revival in England. A cold, rationalistic Church of England had abandoned supernaturalism, and the society was marked by increasing wickedness. In the fifty years of his ministry, Wesley and his followers won hundreds of thousands to Christ and holiness, and in the process, Wesley reestablished the moral conscience of his nation.

Our own country has known a number of revivals. Often they were stimulated by a few people meeting to pray, committed to obey God. Revivals have started in haystack prayer meetings, in home Bible studies, in camp meetings, and in churches. At times they have been associated with a powerful preacher like Wesley; at other times no single leader can be identified. Revivals have touched every continent and most countries.

What happens in a revival? Revival starts in the hearts of believers. It starts when believers are moved to deep commitment and responsiveness to God. Then it spills over to affect others. The great revivals of the Christian era have seen thousands of new believers won to Christ. Often the great revivals have led to significant changes in society as sin has been exposed and the conscience of a people has been reawakened.

Revivals are a special moving of the Spirit of God. While it is important for us to pray for the kind of massive movement that takes place in a revival, we must remember that God alone can flame the fire that springs up to change a whole nation.

REWARDS

Does it "pay" to be a Christian? It seems so. Jesus once answered a disciple who asked, "We have left everything to follow you! What then will there be for us?" Jesus responded, "At the renewal of all things when the Son of Man sits on his glorious throne . . . everyone who has left houses or brothers or sisters or fathers or mothers or children or fields for my sake will receive a hundred times as much and will inherit eternal life" (Matt. 19:27–29).

It seems amazing. God not only sacrificed his Son to bring us life when we were helplessly lost, but God also rewards the believer who follows him.

There are two senses in which following Jesus leads to rewards. The first is because God has established a moral universe. Peter quotes Psalm 34, "Whoever would love life and see good days must keep his tongue from evil and his lips from deceitful speech. He must turn from evil and do good; he must seek peace and pursue it" (1 Peter 3:10–11). A moral life brings blessing (Deut. 28:1–14), and sinful choices bring disasters (Deut. 28:15–68). Doing good brings its own rewards to all who choose God's ways.

The other sense reflects Jesus' response to his questioning disciple. Our salvation (or acceptance by God as members of his family) is ours freely through faith in Christ. Salvation is not a reward for believing. Salvation is a gift that anyone who believes receives. ◆ FAITH But all of us who do believe will one day appear before God and our works will be evaluated. Paul compares the quality of the Christian's life to gold, silver, and costly stones (or on the other hand, to wood, hay, and straw). We each will be rewarded, Paul says, "according to his own labor" (1 Cor. 3:10–15).

We are not sure just what these rewards involve, but we trust Jesus' promise that his rewards are a hundred times more than anything we might give up now. And we know that the Bible calls our rewards "crowns." In the Old Testament one word for *crown* suggested position or authority. The other Hebrew word is used figuratively to symbolize honor or blessing. In the New Testament the crowns that are symbolic of rewards are *stephanos*, garlands of wreaths awarded the victors in athletic contests like the Olympic games. Although the crowns had no intrinsic value, they symbolized the honor and glory the victors won for their home city. (In fact, Olympic victors were awarded a lifetime pension from their home city, typically about one hundred times the earnings of an ordinary laborer!)

The crowns of Scripture remind us that God has graciously chosen to honor his faithful saints and reward us with crowns — crowns of life (1 Cor. 9:25; 2 Tim. 2:5; James 1:12; Rev. 2:10), crowns of righteousness (1 Tim. 4:8), and crowns of glory (1 Peter 5:4).

RIGHTEOUSNESS

Christians believe in a righteous God. We also believe that God calls us to live righteous lives. But the righteousness we believe in isn't some drab existence of following endless sets of rules. The righteousness we believe in is dynamic, positive, and exciting.

Our understanding of righteousness and how we become righteous comes directly from Scripture; righteousness is a theme that echoes throughout both Old and New Testaments.

Righteousness in the Old Testament. The Hebrew words translated "righteous" are also translated in our English versions as "just" and "justice." The underlying idea is that of conformity to a norm. A person is "righteous" when his or her actions are in harmony with established standards.

As far as believers are concerned, the only valid standard by which righteousness can be measured is the revealed will of God. In Old Testament times God's will was expressed most clearly in the Mosaic law. Righteousness is not at all abstract in the Old Testament. The person who meets the obligations that the law establishes is righteous.

In a deeper sense, the Old Testament often calls God "righteous" (Ps. 4:1; Isa. 45:21). What God does is "always righteous" (Ps. 71:24; Jer. 12:1). Simply put, all that God does is in harmony with his character, and God's character is the ultimate standard by which all actions are to be measured.

According to the Old Testament God's actions express his righteousness in two special ways. First, "He will judge the world in righteousness" (Ps. 9:8). God's acts of judgment express his righteous character and his commitment to do what is right. Second, God will "deliver me in [his] righteousness" (Ps. 31:1; 119:40). God's saving work is also in harmony with commitment to all that is right and good.

The Old Testament speaks frequently of righteous men and women, despite the fact that "no one living is righteous before you" (Ps. 143:2). No one is righteous in the absolute sense of bearing God's full moral image. But in the Old Testament, righteousness is seldom used in an absolute sense. People who are responsive to God can behave righteously without being sinless, since righteousness is a matter of behaving in conformity with standards. And righteousness can be comparative: Saul admitted to David "you are more righteous than I" (1 Sam. 24:17).

It is important to remember: Righteousness in the Old Testament involves behavioral conformity to God's laws. As Moses taught Israel, "If we are careful to obey all this law before the LORD our God, as he has commanded us, that will be our righteousness" (Deut. 6:25).

But even the righteousness that is measured by observing behavior is intimately associated with a warm personal relationship with the Lord. The righteous are "those who serve God" (Mal. 3:18), who rejoice in him (Ps. 64:10), and who praise his name (Ps. 140:13).

The righteousness that consists in obeying God brings many blessings. The people who live by God's standards will be blessed and rewarded (Ps. 5:12; 112:6). God will help them in all their troubles (Ps. 34:19). The righteous can be sure that God will listen to their prayers (Ps. 7:8; 119:121). Isaiah, in his warning of judgment against Israel, pauses to say, "Tell the righteous it will be well with them, for they will enjoy the fruit of their deeds" (Isa. 3:10).

Ultimately, though, no human righteousness can merit God's favor. The Old Testament warns Israel, "After the LORD your God has driven them [your enemies] out before you, do not say to yourself, 'The LORD has brought me here because of my righteousness.' . . . It is not because of your righteousness or your integrity that you are going in to take possession of their land; . . . the LORD your God will drive them out before you to establish what he swore to your fathers, to Abraham, Isaac, and Jacob. Understand, then, that it is not because of your righteousness that the LORD your God is giving you this good land to possess" (Deut. 9:4–6).

God's love and his faithfulness to his promises, rather than any supposed human goodness, is the basis for every good thing he provides.

Righteousness in the New Testament. Some New Testament passages use "righteous" with its basic Old Testament meaning of "one whose behavior conforms to the law" (Matt. 1:19; 5:45; Mark 6:20). But the Old Testament concept of righteousness is expanded and transformed in Christianity.

In Matthew 5, Jesus explores the relationship between the law and righteousness. Jesus assures his listeners that his teaching does not make the law null or void. He insists that their righteousness must "surpass that of the Pharisees and teachers of the law" (Matt. 5:17–20). This stunned his listeners, for these Pharisees had committed themselves to obey every detail of the Mosaic code and the thousands of traditional interpretations of that code. But Jesus went on to explain, "You have heard that it was said . . . 'Do not murder. . . .' But I tell you that anyone who is angry with his brother will be subject to judgment. . . . You have heard that it was said, 'Do not commit adultery.' But I tell you that anyone who looks at a woman lustfully has already committed adultery with her in his heart." Jesus' sayings shift the focus from behavior to a person's inner thoughts and desires. The person who is angry with another person is guilty, for murder springs from anger. The person who lusts is guilty, for adultery springs from lust. Righteousness is a matter not of behavior but of the heart, and God ultimately is concerned with inner righteousness. Without that, Jesus says, "you will certainly not enter the kingdom of heaven" (Matt. 5:20).

In Romans, Paul explains a righteousness that is "by faith from first to last" (Rom. 1:16–17). He shows righteousness as something that God must impute to those who have faith before anyone can actually become righteous.

The Book of Romans is about righteousness. In Romans 2 and 3 the writer shows that neither Jew nor Gentile has any righteousness at all. All human beings sin and fall short. Whether measured by the law of Moses or by the law of conscience, everyone sins. Thus "no one will be declared righteous in his [God's] sight by observing the law; rather, through the law we become conscious of sin" (Rom. 3:20).

In Romans 3:21–4:25, Paul shows that the righteousness God demands has always been linked with faith. He says that the Old Testament itself speaks of a "righteousness from God, apart from law" (Rom. 3:21), for Genesis says that God "credited" Abraham's faith to him for righteousness. In the same way righteousness is credited to the account of those who believe in Jesus today. This is possible because Jesus' death, the full payment for human sin, provides the basis on which God himself can be righteous and forgive sinners, pronouncing them righteous in the divine court. ▶ SACRIFICE, PROPITIATION, JUSTIFICA-TION, SUBSTITUTION

But Romans goes beyond this issue of a forensic, or legal, righteousness. God declares sinful human beings who believe in Jesus guiltless, righteous in his sight. But God goes on to make his promise a reality. God acts in sinners who believe in Jesus so that we actually *become* righteous.

The theme of Romans 6–8 is becoming righteous. Believers are united by faith to Jesus. In this union we share in both Jesus' death and his resurrection. Raised to new life in Jesus, we can now "offer [ourselves] to God ... and offer the parts of [our] body to him as instruments of righteousness" (Rom. 6:13). As Ephesians puts it, we are given a "new self, created to be like God in true righteousness and holiness" (Eph. 4:24).

Paul traces Christian experience in Romans 7. Even though we are renewed, we cannot receive righteousness by struggling to keep the law in our own strength. The solution is to recognize the presence and the power of the Holy Spirit (Rom. 8). As we rely on him and remain open to his leading (Rom. 8:9), we will be transformed from within. The Spirit changes us dramatically so that "the righteous requirements of the law might be fully met in us, who do not live according to the sinful nature but according to the Spirit" (Rom. 8:4).

The Christian is enabled to live a truly righteous life — one that conforms not only to the law's demands for behavior in accord with its standard but also to God's ultimate demand for behavior in accord with his own character. As the Holy Spirit reshapes our personalities, the standards that Old Testament law engraved on stone are written on our hearts, just as those standards are written on the heart of God (2 Cor. 3:3; Hebrews 8:10).

In each testament "righteous" and "righteousness" speak of conformity to a standard or norm. For Israel and the church that norm has always been the expressed will of God, which always reflects his own character as the standard and the measure of righteousness.

In the Old Testament a righteous person was one who feared God and who expressed that relationship with the Lord by keeping God's commands. No one fully lived up to God's standards. But righteous is seldom used in an absolute sense in the Old Testament; it describes the general pattern of a person's life and does not imply sinlessness.

Jesus shifted the focus of Israel's thinking about righteousness. He called on his hearers to achieve a new measure of righteousness, not by conformity to God's law but by an inner conformity to the personality of God himself. By this standard all people fall short (Rom. 3:23). But Jesus died to pay for the sins of humankind. On that basis God has promised to pronounce those who believe in Jesus righteous, even though they have fallen short. So Christians have, first of all, an imputed righteousness: a righteousness that is credited to our account despite our failures. ◗ IMPUTATION

But Christianity offers humanity far more than a legal decree. Because we who believe in Jesus are given new life in him and the Holy Spirit as our guide and enabler, we have the prospect of actually *being* righteous. This does not come from struggling to keep a law that at best regulates behavior. This comes from an inner transformation worked by the Spirit as we rely on him. As we become more like God in our inner selves, our actions conform to the behavior that the law demands.

For us Jesus is the key. We have forgiveness in him. We have obtained God's positive judgment in the divine court. Because of Jesus we are righteous in the judge's sight. And through our union with Jesus, we have the promise of inner transformation as well. As we grow in our Christian life, we will actually become righteous, because we will truly be like our Lord.

SABBATH

The seventh day of the week has a deep significance in the Old Testament. Its meaning is so deeply embedded in the history of God's people that many Christians feel its practices should find modern expression in Sunday, the Christian "Lord's Day," which is the first day of the week.

The Sabbath in the Old Testament. The Hebrew word *shabat* means "rest" or "ceasing or coming to the end of an activity." Only where this word is used of a day of rest does it seem to suggest peace or repose. Other Hebrew words for rest carry the sense of relaxation, enjoyment, peace, and tranquility.

The Sabbath day has great significance in Old Testament faith. First, Sabbath witnessed to God as Creator, for God rested after the six days during which he actively shaped the universe. Israel was not to work on that day, remembering that God "rested the seventh day. Therefore the LORD blessed the Sabbath day and made it holy" (Exod. 19:8-11). The Sabbath was also a sign of Israel's covenant relationship with the Lord, celebrating mutual commitment (Exod. 31:12-17). The Sabbath is also linked with deliverance from Egypt. Deuteronomy 5:15 tells Israel to "remember that you were slaves in Egypt and that the LORD your God brought you out of there . . . therefore the LORD your God commanded you to keep the Sabbath day." Each seventh day was thus linked with creation, covenant, and redemption. As Israel set aside all work on the seventh day, it recognized the whole foundation of Israel's identity and relationship with the Lord.

There was also a humanitarian and practical aspect to the Sabbath. Household slaves and animals were also given time to relax and restore strength. Even the land was to be given a Sabbath rest every seventh year to retain its nutrients, and during that year any produce borne naturally was to be available to the poor (Exod. 23:10-11). The people in Jesus' day disregarded the Sabbath's expression of God's concern for his creatures, and Jesus came in conflict with legalists who were outraged that he would heal on the Sabbath (Luke 6:1–9; 13:10–16; 14:1–4; John 5:9–18; 7:22–23).

Sabbath to Sunday. As significant as the Sabbath is in the Old Testament, it is not retained in the New Testament. Instead we see the early church meeting on the first day of the week, the day that Jesus rose from the dead (Matt. 28:1; Mark 16:2; Luke 24:1; John 20:1). Jesus appeared eight times to the disciples after his resurrection. Six of these were on the first day of the week. Many are convinced that the Day of Pentecost, when the Holy Spirit came upon Jesus' followers, was also the first day of the week. Thus the church's weekly celebration of God's work for us now apparently shifts to the first day. This first day became the Lord's Day, for Jesus' resurrection is the central reality of sacred history (Acts 20:7; 1 Cor. 16:2; Rev. 1:10). Writings from the second century reflect this view. Ignatius says that Christians "have come to the possession of a new hope, no longer observing the Sabbath, but living in observance of the Lord's Day, on which also our life has sprung up again by Him and by His death." Justin Martyr, in A.D. 250, describes the church's worship "on the day called Sunday." Clearly the resurrection of Jesus, so central in the Christian's faith, marks a great shift from Old Testament to New Testament times and practices.

The lasting significance of Sabbath. Christians have been divided about the significance of Sabbath for us. Sunday-keeping seems to have always involved rest and worship. As Christianity became progressively legalistic in medieval days (A.D. 600–1500), some applied the Old Testament Sabbath laws to the Lord's Day. Despite the objections of many significant Christian leaders, practices for Sunday-keeping were based on Old Testament Sabbath law. Among the Reformers Luther felt that all times were holy, so neither Sabbath nor Sunday were needed. But because workers needed a day of rest and time for worship, it was permissible to keep Sunday. Calvin saw the Sabbath as a symbol of Christian rest. While it was good to set aside one day in seven for Christian worship, he endorsed no strict rules for keeping it. Yet at times restrictions even greater than those imposed by Old Testament Sabbath law have shaped Christian ideas of how to honor the Lord's Day. In some communities in the past two hundred years, no work, play, or quiet walks have been permitted.

The Bible contains no command that we observe Sunday as a day for rest and worship. And no New Testament laws set limits of what one can or should do on the Lord's Day. Any precedent we see in the Old Testament Sabbath should focus on the significance of that earlier day rather than on the ways that it was observed. The Sabbath was a memorial recalling God's work for his people, and it was also established so that those who knew God might experience rest. For us the Lord's Day is also a memorial recalling God's work for us in Christ, powerfully confirmed in Jesus' resurrection. And for us it is a day of rest, one in seven set aside for our physical benefit as well as for our spiritual strengthening. How should you and I keep Sunday? Our answer is found not in the Old Testament law but in the purposes of the day.

We worship and we rest. Just how each of us chooses to worship and to rest, just how we intend to remember and honor our Lord, is something that God and most churches leave up to you and me.

SACRAMENTS

The word comes from the history of religions, not from the Bible. In the widest sense a sacrament is any religious sign possessing a hidden meaning.

Catholic doctrine holds that the sacraments are a means of conveying grace. They work objectively, not depending on the faith of the receiver as long as his or her attitude presents no obstacle. Catholics observe seven sacraments: baptism, confirmation, Eucharist (the Lord's Supper), penance, extreme unction, orders, and marriage.

Protestants in the Reformed and Lutheran traditions identify baptism and the Lord's Supper as sacraments. That is, they view these practices as means by which grace is given. ▶ **GRACE**

But the sacraments are simply a visible sign of the Word; their effectiveness depends on the faith of the believer, just as a faith response to God's Word is necessary for salvation. Both the Word and the sacraments witness to Christ and his promise of forgiveness of sins.

Other Protestants view baptism and the Lord's Supper as ordinances, not sacraments. That is, these practices were commanded by Christ and are testimonies to his work for us, but they are not means through which grace is given.

The differences will continue to exist. But for all of us the work of Christ reflected in baptism and in the Lord's Supper is the basis for all that grace we so freely receive. And faith in Jesus is the key to every blessing from God.

SACRIFICE

The idea of sacrifice isn't particularly popular with the critics of Christianity. Blood sacrifice is dismissed as primitive superstition. Self-sacrifice is dismissed as psychologically unhealthy. But for Christians both blood sacrifice and self-sacrifice are honored concepts.

Blood sacrifice. Jesus is history's ultimate blood sacrifice. But the first is found in Eden, just after the Fall, where God killed animals to provide skin coverings for sinful Adam and Eve (Gen. 3:21). The tradition of sacrifice is found in many ancient cultures that saw the sacrificial animal as food for the gods. But in the Old Testament the blood is central. "The life of the flesh is the blood," Leviticus 17:11 says, "and I have given it to you on the altar; it is the blood that makes atonement for your sins." The message of sacrifice in the Old Testament is that sin brings death, but God will accept another's life in substitution for the sinner. ◗ ATONEMENT

Noah, Abraham, and other ancient people of faith offered sacrifices. But it is not until the Mosaic law was established that a thoroughgoing sacrificial system existed among God's people. In the law violations called for making sin offerings, and the system's central sacrifice, made once a year on the Day of Atonement, was for all the sins of the people. This sacrificial system provided a way in which God's sinful people could approach the Lord.

But the Old Testament prophets often condemned their contemporaries for treating the sacrifices of their religion as mere ritual and offering them to God while continuing in sinful ways. Sacrifice in the Old Testament is to be the expression of a penitent heart, and offerings are to express the worship of a morally pure people (Amos 5:21–27; Mic. 6:6–8; Isa. 1:13–17).

Jesus, too, condemned a merely ritual faith, challenging his critics to "go and learn what this means: 'I desire mercy, not sacrifice'" (Matt. 9:13; 12:7). According to Jesus, love for God and neighbor is more important than all burnt offerings and sacrifices (Mark 12:33–34).

The criticism of Israel's ritualistic faith is no rejection of the principle of sacrifice. It is, instead, a rejection of Israel's misinterpretation of sacrifice. At heart, sacrifice is an expression of faith, not a ritual. It was to be offered by people who were not only aware of their sin but also confident that God was faithful to his Word and would accept them despite their failures. When Old Testament believers stood at the altar, watching a sacrificial animal about to die because of their sins, they acted out a reality ultimately expressed in Jesus' cross. Sin brings death. But

God will accept the life of a substitute and welcome the sinner into relationship with him.

The New Testament interprets Christ's death on the cross as history's culminating sacrifice. "God presented him as a sacrifice of atonement, through faith in his blood" (Rom. 3:25). Jesus died "for us" and justified us "by his blood" (Rom. 5:8–9). Three full chapters of Hebrews explore the meaning of blood sacrifice (Heb. 8–10). The Old Testament sanctuary and sacrifices were "a copy and shadow of what is in heaven" (Heb. 8:5), serving as illustrations for the present time (Heb. 9:1–9). Christ, with his own blood, entered no earthly temple but entered heaven itself "once for all by his own blood, having obtained eternal redemption" (Heb. 9:12). Jesus' one sacrifice dealt fully and finally with sin and was enough to "take away the sins of many people" (Heb. 9:23–28). So the sacrifices of history were illustrations, God's way of instructing humanity so that the meaning of Jesus' death would be understood. The repeated sacrifices of the Old Testament were "only a shadow of the good things that are coming — not the realities themselves" (Heb. 10:1). They are no longer necessary, because "we have been made holy through the sacrifice of the body of Jesus once for all" (Heb. 10:10).

Yes, Christians believe in blood sacrifice. We are convinced that only the blood of Christ — only his life exchanged for ours — could have won forgiveness for sinners. Blood sacrifice is not "primitive." It is basic to Christian faith.

Self-sacrifice. What is the role of self-denial and self-sacrifice in our faith? Perhaps surprisingly, Christianity teaches that self-sacrifice is a way to self-fulfillment.

For one thing, Paul in the New Testament adopts the language of sacrifice to speak of the Christian lifestyle. Christians are to present themselves to God as "living sacrifices," in wholehearted commitment to his will (Rom. 12:1). Most importantly, however, Jesus teaches us that we are to love one another "as I have loved you" (John 13:34). Jesus, in suffering for us, left us an example and calls us to "follow in his steps" (1 Peter 2:21). John puts it simply and clearly: "Jesus Christ laid down his life for us. And we ought to lay down our lives for our brothers" (1 John 3:16). We do not always live up to this ideal. But the ideal is embedded in our faith.

Ultimately, though, self-sacrifice is in our own self-interest. Paul picks up this theme in Philippians. Exhorting unity, Paul writes, "do nothing out of selfish ambition or vain conceit, but in humility consider others better than yourselves. Each of you should look not only to your own interests, but also to the interests of others" (Phil. 2:3–4). Then Paul turns to Christ, our example in humility, and points out that the path of his self-sacrifice led to glory. Jesus sacrificed himself for us, and "therefore God exalted him to the highest place and gave him the name that is above every name" (Phil. 2:9). Putting others first wins the approval of God. And the approval of God brings blessings we can't even imagine.

SAINTS

Saints aren't believers whose special holiness or closeness to God sets them apart from other Christians. The biblical term means simply a "holy one," one set apart to God. And the Bible applies the name to all Christians (Eph. 1:1; Col. 1:4, 12, 26). It is not the quality of our lives that sets us apart to God; it is what Jesus has done for us. Faith in Jesus brings us all into God's family and makes us his special, precious possessions. In Jesus all believers are, in the biblical sense of the word, God's saints.

How about the Catholic practice of making some people into saints and appealing to them for help when in trouble? This is a practice that has no foundation in Scripture. After all, when each of us can come boldly to God's very throne and are assured that we will "receive mercy and find grace to help us in our time of need" (Heb. 4:16), what use could we possibly have for intermediaries?

SALVATION

We believe in a salvation rooted in God's mercy and Jesus' death and resurrection; this salvation is granted to all who believe in him. Our answer to the question, "What must I do to be saved?" remains the same: "Believe on the Lord Jesus Christ, and you will be saved" (Acts 16:31).

But just what is this salvation we speak of? And what does it mean to be saved?

Salvation in the Old Testament. Three elements make up the Old Testament's concept of salvation, which is expressed primarily in the word *yasha'*. The first element is distress. Danger or suffering overwhelm people or nations unable to help themselves. The second element is a deliverer, a savior; one person acts on behalf of the sufferers to deliver them from their situation. The third element is a great release. The Savior's action culminates in peace or safety for the distressed.

In our Old Testament people are saved from danger or enemies, which threaten in this world. Only a few references seem to suggest deliverance from sin or from spiritual powers (Ps. 51:14; 79:9; Ezek. 37:23).

The Old Testament always pictures God as the deliverer. God is the savior of his people. The Lord might bring salvation through a human agency (Judg. 3:9; 6:14), but he is the source and cause of all saving action. "No king is saved by the size of his army; no warrior escapes by his great strength," the psalmist says (Ps. 33:16). God alone can bring deliverance. "I do not trust in my bow, my sword does not bring me victory; but you give us victory over our enemies, you put our adversaries to shame. In God we make our boast all day long, and we will praise your name forever" (Ps. 44:6–8).

What does the believer do in view of the conviction that salvation from danger or enemies must come from God? The psalmist sums up the thrust of our Old Testament: "We wait in hope for the Lord; he is our help and our shield. In him our hearts rejoice, for we trust his holy name" (Ps. 33:20–21).

Confident expectation — faith — is the believer's role. Ancient Israel would and should assemble its armies. David would stoop to pick up smooth stones for his sling as he moved toward Goliath and destiny. But the most important thing that a believer could do, the only thing that really could count, was to maintain a close relationship with the Lord. As Isaiah cries out to Israel, "In repentance and rest is your salvation, in quietness and trust is your strength" (Isa. 30:15).

Always eager to deliver his people, God calls to them: "Turn to me and be saved, all you ends of the earth, for I am God, and there is no other" (Isa. 45:22).

Salvation in the New Testament. The basic concept established so firmly in the Old Testament is the foundation of our New Testament's teaching about salvation. Salvation is from God, who acts to deliver the helpless who trust in him.

The primary Greek term for salvation is *sozo* (verb), *soteria* (noun). At times the term is used in the Old Testament sense of deliverance from some pressing physical danger (Matt. 24:13; Mark 13:13–20; Acts 27:20). Jesus' healing miracles saved the sick in the sense of restoring lost health and wholeness (Matt. 9:21–22; Mark 5:23, 28, 34; Luke 7:50). But in most contexts salvation focuses on what God has done in Christ to deliver human beings from the powers of death, sin, and Satan. In the New Testament the greatest enemies of humankind are spiritual, not physical; spiritual terrors threaten people with eternal loss.

New Testament salvation has three distinct aspects, reflected in our past, present, and future tenses. Historically Jesus died for us and accomplished all that was necessary for our salvation. When we trust Jesus, we are considered to have died with him and have been raised again (Rom. 6:3–5). Christians have been saved, for in God's sight the great transaction is complete. So the Bible says, "according to his mercy he saved us" (Titus 3:5), and he "has saved us and called us to a holy life" (2 Tim. 1:9). Because of what Jesus has done, we who believe are saved and have already passed from death to life.

But it is also true that Jesus is saving us. Salvation has great impact on our present experience. We who have been reconciled to God by Christ's death "are being saved" through Jesus' life (Rom. 5:10). As Romans 6:5–14 emphasizes, our union with Jesus in his death and resurrection brings release from our natural slavery to sin, freeing us to serve God and to live righteous lives. ♦ RIGHTEOUS

Finally, the Bible assures us that we will be saved. In the resurrection Christians will be fully delivered from the last taint of sin, perfected at last, completely pure and holy. This certain future is beautifully described in Romans 8:18–39 and 1 Corinthians 15:12–58.

The New Testament and Old Testament doctrines of salvation are the same. True, the Old Testament emphasizes deliverance from physical enemies in this life, while the New Testament emphasizes deliverance from sin and its impact. But in each testament human beings are seen to be helpless. In each testament God acts and becomes our Savior. And in each testament we human beings are simply asked to trust.

Just how helpless we are spiritually is expressed in a number of biblical themes. ♦ DEATH, SIN, HEAVEN AND HELL Just how God has acted is triumphantly announced in the gospel. Jesus, the eternal Son of God, entered our world to bring us salvation (John 3:17; 1 Tim. 1:15). His death won us forgiveness and new life, gifts guaranteed by his resurrection (2 Tim. 4:18; Heb. 7:25). Jesus saves us from wrath (Rom. 5:9), adopts us into God's family, and assures us of resurrection to an eternity to be spent in fellowship with him. ♦ WRATH OF GOD, RESURRECTION God *has* acted. Salvation has been won. Now all that remains for us is to trust God, relying completely on Jesus, counting on the salvation that he has already won. ♦ BELIEF

So what does it mean when we speak of salvation or of being saved? First, it means that we confess our helplessness to combat sin and the spiritual forces that hold humanity captive. Second, it means that we confess Jesus, who has acted in history to provide deliverance for us in his cross. Third, it means that we confess God's trustworthiness as we abandon ourselves to him and rely on him alone to bring us deliverance.

We have an exciting grasp of what Jesus' death means for us. Because Jesus died for us, we who are saved no longer live in the path of

God's wrath but have become his sons and daughters through faith (Gal. 3:26–29). Because Jesus died, we are being saved. We no longer are controlled by sin. Because of Jesus we can choose to do the will of God and can live truly righteous lives. And because Jesus died, we will be saved. When the resurrection comes, the last vestige of sin will be cleansed. Then, completely renewed, we will spend eternity with our Lord.

SANCTIFICATION

Christians all believe that faith in Christ produces a true change of life and character. This is what we mean by sanctification. But we are divided on several significant issues. Is sanctification "entire," in the sense that we can be free from sin in this life? And how does sanctification take place? Is it by a growing process, or does it involve a crisis experience and a "second work of grace"? Let's look first at what Christians hold in common and then at our differences.

Sanctification in the Old and New Testaments. The English word *sanctify* comes from the basic Hebrew word for holiness. In the Old Testament sanctification emphasizes ritual separation: Items or persons (priests, for example) are sanctified or set aside from common or ordinary use and wholly dedicated for use in worship. In the New Testament the word *sanctification* comes from a Greek word meaning "to make holy." However, there are striking differences in emphasis between the testaments. In the Old Testament the emphasis is on the sanctification of objects and places; in the New Testament, the emphasis is on sanctification of persons. Old Testament sanctification is essentially ritual; New Testament sanctification is not. Old Testament sanctification separates the holy from the common; New Testament sanctification infuses the common with the Spirit of God, transforming the ordinary. Christian sanctification is a call not only to inner cleansing but also to practical righteousness so that every aspect of our daily life can express the essential character and goodness of God. ♦ **HOLINESS**

This does not mean that the Old Testament is unconcerned with personal holiness. The psalmist expresses the desire of believers of every era: "Create in me a pure heart, O God, and renew a right spirit within me" (Ps. 51:10).

This work of God's Spirit restores joy (Ps. 51:11), turns the heart to God (Ps. 51:17), delivers from acts of sin (Ps. 51:14), and issues in praise (Ps. 51:15). The same expectation of transformation is seen in other Old Testament passages (Ps. 24:1–6; Amos 2:6–11).

In the New Testament we hear Jesus pray for the sanctification of his followers. In what has been called Christ's High Priestly Prayer (John 17), he appeals to the Father to sanctify us through his Word so that we might be sent into the world to glorify God by doing his will.

Various New Testament passages make it clear that we need to look at sanctification from two perspectives. In one sense every believer is sanctified, that is, set aside for God by virtue of what Jesus has done for us. This is sometimes called *positional* sanctification, and it reflects the fact that ultimately our holiness in God's sight rests entirely on Jesus' work for us. Thus Paul writes to believers in Corinth, saying, "You were washed, you were sanctified, you were justified in the name of the Lord Jesus Christ and by the Spirit of our God" (1 Cor. 6:11). In fact, the phrase, "those who are sanctified," is a phrase that means simply "the saved" (Acts 20:32; 26:18; Rom. 15:16; 1 Cor. 1:2). Sanctification in this positional sense is accomplished only by Jesus' blood (Heb. 10:13–29).

But there is also a *practical* sanctification. Christians are called not only to be holy in God's sight but also to be holy in all we say and do. The transformation of the Christian into the likeness of Jesus is no abstract concept. We who belong to Jesus are "being transformed into his [Jesus'] likeness with ever-increasing glory, which comes from the Lord, who is the Spirit" (2 Cor. 3:18). It is this practical dimension of sanctification that Paul writes about: "May God himself, the God of peace, sanctify you through and through. May your whole spirit, soul and body be kept blameless at the coming of our Lord Jesus Christ. The one who calls you is faithful and he will do it" (1 Thess. 5:23–24).

The Spirit and the Word (John 17:17) are agents God uses to sanctify us "through and through," that we may increasingly reflect the presence of Jesus in our lives.

Christians agree that through Jesus we have been made holy in God's sight and that sanctification makes both a change in our experience as well as a positional change in our relationship with God. But Christians also disagree on two very significant issues.

Is practical sanctification complete? When Paul asks God to sanctify the Thessalonians "through and through," does he imply full deliverance from all sin in this life? Christians in Wesleyan and other traditions are convinced he does. These "holiness" Christians believe that God's grace can eradicate the sin nature and release the believer to wholeheartedly desire and to always choose God's will. They base this belief on verses like Romans 6:1–23; 1 Thessalonians 5:23; 1 John 3:3, and on other passages that seem to imply full deliverance (Matt. 5:8; John 17:17;

Rom. 6:6–19; 2 Cor. 7:1; Eph. 4:24; 5:26; Phil. 2:15; Col. 1:22; 1 Thess. 3:13; 5:23; 1 Peter 1:16).

Christians in Lutheran, Calvinist, and other traditions reject the idea of a total cleansing in this life. Eradication of the sin nature must await resurrection. As Luther puts it, "On this side of eternity the Christian is *simul justus et peccator*, both righteous and a sinner, holy and profane, an enemy of God and yet a child of God."

There is a struggle going on within the believer as sin tugs against the Spirit of God. By relying on the Spirit, the Christian can choose to do right, and Christians can live holy lives. But we do not make this choice because our inner bent toward sin has been removed. We make our choices as God gives grace to overcome sin's power and as we trust the Lord fully.

Actually, no Christian tradition dismisses the sins of believers as irrelevant. No Christian tradition expects believers to go on living the same kind of life we led before salvation. We all believe that God's sanctifying grace brings a real transformation of character. Why, then, does one tradition call for an "entire" sanctification and the other deny it?

Part of the answer is found in each tradition's concept of sin. The Wesleyan/Arminian view sees sin only as conscious, willful disobedience to God's known will. As finite creatures all human beings fall short of God's perfection. In this sense there is no such thing as a "sinless perfection" until resurrection comes. But only deliberate sin is sin in the holiness tradition. So "entire sanctification" relates only to deliberate sin. The deliverance that those in the holiness tradition expect and claim is deliverance from the desire and the choice to sin deliberately.

The Calvinist and other traditions that reject entire sanctification see sin differently. Sin involves more than deliberate acts. There is a Greek word which suggests that falling short of full conformity to God's will is also sin. Since falling short as well as deliberate disobedience constitutes sin, no human being can live a completely sinless life in this world.

It would be wrong to dismiss the differences between traditions merely as arguments about definitions and words. But it would also be wrong for Calvinists to accuse their holiness brothers and sisters of pretending total purity. It would be just as wrong for holiness Christians to accuse the others of ignoring God's call to a holy life. It is clear that a key to our understanding each other is to grasp the differences in each group's view of sin.

How does sanctification happen? If Christians all expect faith to lead to a change in character and lifestyle, how will this happen? Again there is a solid foundation of agreement. We agree that Christ's death and resurrection bring us not only salvation but also sanctification. Both forgiveness and the power of new life come to us in Jesus. We also agree that God uses his Word to produce that true change in life and character. And we agree that the Holy Spirit is the agent who works sanctification within us. And there is another area of agreement that is sometimes overlooked. We all agree that sanctification involves a process, that transformation takes place over time as faith grows and matures.

The thing that sets the holiness movement apart is the conviction that there is a second moment, different from the moment of salvation, when God's grace operates to renew the Christian. This moment does not replace the process by which the Spirit of God works in us to perfect us, but it is crucial to the process. Wesley writes of the believer's growing awareness that a "desperate wickedness" exists deep in his or her heart. That awareness stimulates an earnest desire and hunger for righteousness. The believer longs to experience the renewal of God's image and his likeness within. This all leads to that sanctifying moment when the Holy Spirit graciously works in the believer, eradicating the sin nature and replacing our bent toward evil with a love that inclines us to God and to good. Wesley writes, "Entire sanctification, or Christian perfection, is neither more nor less than pure love — love expelling sin and governing both the heart and life of the child of God." This love which God alone can shed in our hearts, a love planted in a moment of sanctifying grace, must and will grow as the Holy Spirit nurtures the new thing he has planted in us and as the process of sanctification continues.

On the one hand, then, some Christians see sanctification as a gradual process by which believers grow more and more like Jesus. Other Christians see a process punctuated by a special working of the Holy Spirit, followed by a continuing process of deeper growth. But for all of us, every step depends on the working of the Holy Spirit in our lives. No growth, transformation, or goodness comes apart from our relationship with our Lord.

As is so often the case, a review of our differences tends to underline the convictions Christians hold in common. We may describe what happens within us in different terms. We may argue over the definition of sin. We may focus on gradual growth or emphasize a crisis experience. But we do believe that in Jesus Christ we are called to a holy life. We believe that the Holy Spirit is the resource we need to lift us beyond ourselves. God's love can overcome our passion for sin. His resurrection power can fill us, enabling us to do his will. We are convinced that Christians are called not just to approve of righteousness but to *be* righteous. Holiness is an ideal. In many ways we will all fall short. But as we grow in our relationship with Jesus Christ, we *do* become more and more like him.

How good it is to find our hearts desiring holiness. How good it is to sense God's Spirit at work within, leading us to choose those things that please Jesus and reflect his character in our world.

SATAN

Christians believe in an unseen spiritual universe. We also believe in the personal being of Satan, who is more than an impersonal force or evil influence.

Satan means "adversary" in Hebrew, while the common name of Satan, the Devil, means "one who slanders or abuses." Both testaments portray Satan as God's adversary, the committed enemy of humankind.

At times in history Christians have held exaggerated and superstitious ideas about Satan. The Bible's picture is simpler yet perhaps more grim.

Satan was created as a powerful angel called Lucifer, meaning "light bearer." But pride and a twisted desire to stand in God's own place warped Lucifer. It was Satan's fall that introduced sin and evil into the universe. He then led a rebellion among the angels in which perhaps a third of these beings chose to follow him (see Isa. 14:12–15; Ezek. 28:11–19; 1 Tim. 3:6). ◆ **ANGELS, DEMONS**

This all apparently took place before Adam's creation, for we first meet Satan in the Garden of Eden, influencing Eve to act against God's command (Gen. 3). ◆ **TEMPTATION** The New Testament describes Satan as the "ruler of the kingdom of the air" (Eph. 2:2), the "prince of this world" (John 12:31), still actively deceiving human beings and blinding them to truth about God. Satan's dark influence is primarily exercised in and through human cultures and social structures rather than directly. For one thing, Satan lacks the divine attribute of omnipresence. He cannot be all places at once, influencing every person. For another, Satan can deceive but cannot control the human will. Yet Satanic influence is expressed in structures of society that appeal to our sinful nature. As for the specific choices people make, we have no need to turn to Satan for our explanation. There's really no ground for the excuse, "The devil made me do it."

The Bible pictures Satan as a powerful and implacable enemy of God and his people. Yet Satan is now a defeated enemy. Christ's death destroyed Satan's most powerful hold on humanity. Jesus broke Satan's power, opened our eyes to God, and now reveals to believers the realities once masked by Satan's illusions.

Yet Satan has a grim role in earth's future. The Bible foretells a day when Satan will lead another rebellion, working through people to whom he gives supernatural powers (2 Thess. 2). There will be terrible suffering and worldwide upheaval in those days. But Satan's destiny is fixed. Ultimately Jesus will cast Satan into what the Bible calls a lake of burning sulfur, to be "tormented day and night for ever and ever" (Rev. 20:7–10).

What is the Christian's attitude toward Satan? Believers have tended to err in one of two directions. Some have overemphasized Satan's powers and involvement in human affairs and have seen the Devil in every situation. Others have dismissed Satan's existence or influence. It seems clear from Scripture that Christians are to recognize Satan as real. We need to respect his powers and be aware of how he works. Yet we need not be terrified by Satan or the demonic. Christ has defeated Satan. In Jesus' victory over death, Christ disarmed all evil supernatural powers of their greatest weapon and exposed their weakness in his resurrection's public triumph (Col. 2:15). Now Christ has given us the Spirit of God to be with us always. Because of this we need not fear Satan or the supernatural; the one who is with and in us is far greater than the evil one who lurks in the world (1 John 4:4).

SCIENCE

How do we react when noted scientists attack tenets of Christian faith? Or when other scientists testify for them? That probably depends on how well we understand "science" and claims of "scientific basis."

Essentially science is a methodology, a specific and limited approach to gaining knowledge. The scientist observes and gathers information and data from the material universe. Scientists study the data and develop theories (hypotheses) to explain what they have found. They plan experiments to test those hypotheses to indicate whether their theories are correct or if they need to be modified. Out of this process come the practical applications that have given us our present mastery of our environment and that have enabled us to step off this planet onto our moon.

Science has serious limitations, however. First, the scientific method can only be applied to gather data from the material universe. Science can make no valid statements about a spiritual universe, simply because its methods have no means of access to it. Second, data gathered by science can come only from the present. Scientists cannot move back in time to observe what happened at the Creation. All they can do is gather information from what exists today and then reason back to what may have been. The third limitation is most serious: Scientists must reason from incomplete data. The history of science has shown again and again that the most confidently held theories of scientists have had to be revised or discarded as more data comes to light.

Scientists, like others, are curious about questions of origin and of the nature of our universe. It is not surprising when they try to develop theories from the data their methods have gathered. They ask questions: How old is the earth? What can we tell from carbon-14 dating? What does the fact that the stars are exploding away from an imaginary center imply? Was there really a "big bang" some four billion years ago from which the material universe came? What does the discovery of a few bones in a cave in Africa suggest about the age and origin of the human race?

From data gathered in the scientists' here and now, some have made their guesses about a past they cannot observe. Unfortunately some theories about the past have been presented (and accepted) as "scientific" fact. Today a generation is taught as fact the theory that human beings came, with all animal life, from some primeval sea where life was spontaneously generated by the chance combination of chemicals.

Some Christians today shrug it all off. They believe in God and Scripture, and untroubled by any logical conflict, they believe in evolution, too. Others argue that the biblical portrait of the Creation not only rules out the scientific view, but that in fact there is clear scientific evidence that supports Scripture.

This last approach is fascinating. Christian scientists marshal the facts gathered by the scientific method and organize them to support the Bible's teaching and to cast doubt on the view of the scientific community. A number of books written by Christians present just such arguments. It is possible to say that the biblical view of the Creation, the Flood, etc., are also "scientific" — depending on how we use that slippery word.

By scientific, some people mean a view derived *only* by interpreting data gathered from the material universe. Such people resent the claim of Christians that the biblical picture is scientific, because they know that the biblical picture is ultimately founded on revelation. On the other hand, all that Christians who argue for the scientific character of their beliefs mean is that the biblical view is supported by evidence, just as the views proposed by some scientists are supported by evidence. In the first sense the biblical view is patently not scientific, for it rests on the conviction that God has revealed the origin of our universe, the origin of life, as well as the future toward which our universe hurtles. In the second sense both views are scientific. Each group draws on evidence gathered by the scientific method to support and to attack. But ultimately *neither* view is truly scientific.

Science, as noted earlier, is limited to dealing with the here and now. Scientists can develop theories about the ancient past. But no one can develop an experiment that duplicates the Creation. And no one can travel back in time to observe what happened. So any person's reconstruction of the past is theory alone: It is a person's best guess in view of both information held and presuppositions. The secular scientist presupposes that there is no God and thus organizes the data to develop an alternative explanation for the present. The Christian scientist presupposes that the God of the Bible is real and thus organizes the data. Both secularist and Christian, then, argue for or against their views, using the data the scientific method has gathered.

The real issue is simple. Do we rely for our beliefs on the teachings of the Bible, God's inspired Word, which, in view of the evidence presented by Christian scientists, is not at all unreasonable? Or do we rely on the notions of people who base their claim for authority on the mantle of science and who at best can show that their view also is not unreasonable, although it may be wrong? ◢ **EVOLUTION, CREATION**

SCRIPTURE

Christians are convinced that ours is a revealed religion: God has spoken to us. Our beliefs are truths unveiled by God, not the best guesses or highest thoughts of mere human beings. This conviction is expressed in a number of terms and concepts sketched in this book. ◢ **INSPIRATION, REVELATION, TRUTH, WORD OF GOD** Summing them all up, we believe that what God has communicated to us is recorded in our Scriptures, the Bible. We are confident that our Bible is both reliable and relevant, a clear and understandable message from the Lord, our authority in faith and morals. As theologian Emil Brunner affirms in *Faith and Reason*, "The church has always called the Scriptures of the Old and New Testaments the 'word of God.' In so doing, the church expresses the fundamental truth of the Christian faith, namely, that in these books the historical self-manifestation of God is offered to faith in an incomparable, decisive, and unique manner; this means that no Christian faith can either rise or be preserved which ignores the 'Holy Scripture.'"

By studying the writings of the early church fathers, we know that the same books of the Old Testament and New Testament that we accept as authoritative today were recognized as authoritative from the beginning. Christians have always relied on the Scriptures for our knowledge of God and his will. Only "by living according to your word" can we keep our way pure (Ps. 119:9). Only the Scriptures are "able to make you wise for salvation through faith in Christ Jesus." Only the Scriptures are God's primary means for "teaching, rebuking, correcting and training in righteousness" (2 Tim. 3:15–16).

Essentially the message and teachings of the Scripture are quite clear. Luther notes that "the Holy Spirit is the plainest writer and speaker in heaven and earth," and concludes that "therefore his words cannot have more than one, and that the simplest, sense, which we call the literal, ordinary, natural sense. That the things indicated by the simple sense of His simple words should signify something further and different, and therefore one thing should always signify another, is more than a question of words or of language."

While some Christians have looked for allegorical rather than literal meanings in Scripture, most Christians are generally agreed. God intended his Word to be understood and so communicated his thoughts in words that can and should be taken in their "literal, ordinary, natural, and simplest" sense.

How, then, do we interpret the Bible? For the most part what we read is very clear. But general principles for interpreting Scripture include the following:

Consider the literary form. Historical narrative is different from poetry in the way it uses words. The Bible contains both of these, plus prophecies, parables, and proverbs. The "plain sense" of words will always be affected by the literary form in which they are set.

Consider the historical context. We need to learn all we can about historical setting and the way words or phrases were used in the time they were written. For instance, Amos 2:6 refers to selling the needy for a pair of sandals. The phrase indicated a legal process by which the poor were sold into slavery for money to pay off a debt.

Consider the rest of Scripture. The Bible contains sixty-six books bound together in a single whole. Revelation unfolded gradually over many centuries, and many aspects of God's plan came to light over a thousand years after the first Scriptures were recorded. Yet the Bible does not contradict itself. We need to compare passage with passage, Scripture with Scripture. We need to interpret whatever we are studying in view of Scripture's whole.

Coming to understand Scripture's plain sense is the beginning in Bible study. But understanding alone is not the end. God has given us the Bible for a purpose. To fulfill his purpose, you and I need to go on to:

Consider what the passage reveals about God. Whether law or story, psalm or prophecy, saying or instruction, the Scriptures tell us who God is and what his plans and purposes are. As we study the Bible, we seek to know him and to trace his thoughts, willingly submitting our notions about reality to the reality which God's Word reveals.

Consider how God invites us to respond. God speaks to us in Scripture for our benefit and upbuilding. But we must respond to the Lord, trust what he says, and apply it to our own experience. Our focus in Bible study is sharpened as we pray for insight into how God wants us to live and as we commit ourselves to put his words into practice. It is the person who acknowledges Jesus, who "hears these words of mine and puts them into practice," whose life is built on a secure and sound foundation. ▶

OBEDIENCE

We not only believe in Scripture, we risk everything on its trustworthiness. Through the Bible we come to understand and to know God. Through the Bible we learn how to live godly lives. While there may be some passages and sections in Scripture which are difficult to understand, all the major teachings are undoubtedly clear. When we take the Bible seriously and take its words in their plain sense, we *do* know truth about God and we *do* know how to live to be pleasing to the Lord.

SECOND COMING

Christians look forward to Jesus' return. We count on the angels' promise given to Christ's disciples at his ascension: "This same Jesus, who has been taken from you into heaven, will come back in the same way you have seen him go into heaven" (Acts 1:11).

Even the Old Testament implies the second coming. It portrays Israel's Messiah both as a suffering Savior (Isa. 53) and as a mighty ruler, who establishes peace and justice on earth. ▶ MESSIAH, KINGDOM Many Christians are convinced that, just as prophecies about Christ's suffering were fulfilled when Jesus lived on earth, prophecies that focus on his power and rule will be fulfilled when Jesus comes back again. ▶ PROPHECY Such passages as Zechariah 14:4–5 seem to apply to this second coming of Jesus: "On that day his feet will stand on the Mount of Olives, east of Jerusalem, and the Mount of Olives will be split in two from east to west. . . . Then the LORD my God will come, and all the holy ones with him."

In Old Testament passages there is seldom a clear division of events that belong to the first coming and those that belong to the second (see Isa. 61:1–2 with Luke 4:17–19 in which Jesus stops reading at a place that divides features of his second coming from his first.

The second coming may only be implied in the Old Testament, but it is clearly and explicitly taught in the New Testament (Matt. 19:28; 23:39; 24; Mark 13:24–37; Luke 12:35–48; 17:22–37; 21:25–28; Rom. 11:25–27; 1 Cor. 11:26; 15:51–58; 1 Thess. 4:13–18; 2 Thess. 1:7–10; 2 Peter 3:10–12; Rev. 16:15; 19:11–21).

These passages associate a number of things with Jesus' second coming: a terrible tribulation; an angelic gathering of the saved; a divine judgment on ungodliness linked with war, famine, earthquakes, and persecution; an evil empire established; heaven and earth ending in consuming flames; and more. Yet, as is common in prophecy, there is no clear ordering of the events associated with Jesus' return. Nor is the time span over which they occur spelled out, unless we take Daniel's prophecy of a "seventieth week" (a seven-year period) to establish a time frame. What we do note is that Jesus' first coming spanned thirty years. We need not squeeze the events of Jesus' return into a moment of time.

But perhaps the question most Christians wonder about is: When will Jesus come again?

Jesus himself said, "No one knows about the day or hour, not even the angels in heaven, nor the Son, but only the Father" (Matt. 24:36). Jesus went on to note only that his return will be sudden and unexpected. "Therefore keep watch," Jesus told his followers, "because you do not know on what day your Lord will come. . . . So you also must be ready, because the Son of Man will come at an hour when you do not expect him" (Matt. 24:42–44).

Throughout the centuries Christians have taken these words to heart. We do not know when Jesus will come. We only know that God has fixed an hour and that you and I are to remain ready.

So Christians who pay attention to Jesus' words have expected an imminent return. He can come at any moment, and each generation can look forward happily to the possibility that Jesus may come back in their lifetime. Will he? We do not know. But he *can*. And when Jesus does come, the world will be set right, and you and I will be caught up to live forever with our Lord.

SECURITY

We Christians are comfortable in our relationship with Jesus. None of us believe that God will reject us in a moment of anger. After all, we have many promises: "Whoever hears my word and believes him who sent me has eternal life and will not be condemned; he has crossed over from death to life" (John 5:24). "I give them eternal life, and they shall never perish; no one can snatch them out of my hand" (John 10:28).

Paul calls a "trustworthy statement" this tenet of the early church's faith: "If we are faithless, he will remain faithful, for he cannot disown himself" (2 Tim. 2:13). And Hebrews quotes this promise from the divine word: "Never will I leave you; never will I forsake you" (Heb. 13:5).

These promises give us a sense of security in our relationship with God. We have been given life in Jesus; death is behind us. We may fail the Lord, but he will never fail us.

Still some Christian traditions are unwilling to suggest that this security implies a guarantee of perseverance. Peter warns against turning one's back on the way of righteousness and on the sacred commandments, having escaped the world's corruption by "knowing our Lord and Savior Jesus Christ" (2 Peter 2:20–21; Heb. 6:4–6; 10:26). Such verses suggest that, while God may never turn his back on us, we may turn our backs on him and fall from grace. After all, Hebrews 10:36 says that "you need to persevere."

Yet none of us view the Christian life as a tightrope along which we must totter fearfully lest we make a mistake and fall into condemnation. All of us are comfortable in the conviction that what Jesus has done for us has won us a full and complete salvation. We trust ourselves to Jesus and believe that he saves us to the uttermost (Heb. 7:25).

But some Christians are concerned that "once saved, always saved" misrepresents God's commitment to holiness. The best way, and the biblical way, to guard Christians against a careless lifestyle seems to them to emphasize the fact that God calls to holiness all who are united to Jesus. It is unthinkable that a person might believe, then wander carelessly in sin and still be saved.

But none of us really believe that. Those convinced that faith in Jesus secures an eternal life that can never be lost make a very different claim. A. A. Hodge puts it this way: The doctrine "does not affirm certainty of salvation because we have once truly believed, but (rather) the certainty of perseverance in holiness if we have truly believed" (*Outlines of Theology*, p. 544).

Paul sums it up in 2 Timothy 2:19: "God's solid foundation stands firm, sealed with this inscription: 'The Lord knows those who are his,' and 'Everyone who confesses the name of the Lord must turn away from wickedness.'" Faith in Jesus brings us dynamic new life within. God will work in us, guiding us along the path of holiness, helping us freely choose what is good in his sight.

What about those who claim to believe and then later turn away? John says, "They went out from us, but they did not really belong to us. For if they had belonged to us, they would have remained with us" (1 John 2:19). How can he be so sure? Because "no one who lives in him keeps on sinning." Jesus, the Son of God, appeared to destroy the Devil's work. "No one who is born of God will continue to sin, because God's seed remains in him; he cannot go on sinning because he has been born of God" (1 John 3:6–9).

The direction of the believer's life is toward holiness. We are secure in Jesus, not because our faith makes us one of the elect and not because our obedience maintains relationship with the Lord. We are secure in Jesus because God's seed has been planted in us, and the dynamic of Christ's own life in us is expressed in our growing commitment to good.
▸ SIN, RIGHTEOUSNESS

SEPARATION

Some Christians always seem to be too troubled by the sins of their age to live in it. In earlier ages monks and hermits left communities they found corrupt and looked for holiness by isolating themselves from temptation. In modern times some congregations have tried to isolate themselves from the corrupting influences of their society. The isolation may take the form of farming communes established by some religious groups or a simple withdrawal by members of other religious groups from social activities that seem to them too closely associated with sin. It is not unusual that those whose faith is threatened by the world will also withdraw from close contact with persons whose beliefs or lifestyle differ from their own.

In contrast, other Christians have chosen to identify closely with others in their society. Involvement, not withdrawal, seems to them to be the Christian approach. Granted that either separation from or involvement in one's society can be carried to extremes, what insights can we gain from the way the Bible uses the word *separate?*

Separation in the Old Testament. Of the several Hebrew words translated "separate" in our versions, two are important. The word *badal* means "to make a distinction between something and something else," and it is often used to describe Israel's separation from other nations. Separation (being distinct from) is also the reason for many of Israel's religious practices. Thus Leviticus 20:24–25 says, "I am the LORD your God, who has set you apart from the nations. You must therefore make a distinction between clean and unclean animals and between clean and unclean birds." The religion of Israel constantly reminded God's people that they were different from others because of their relationship with the Lord.

The word *nazar* means to separate and is often used with a

preposition that means "to abstain from" or "to keep away from." Thus in Leviticus 15:31, we have: "You must keep the Israelites separate from things which make them unclean, so they will not die in their uncleanness for defiling my dwelling place, which is among them."

In the Old Testament, separation does involve a call to live apart from unbelievers and to abstain from practices that are not taught by the law.

Separation in the New Testament. The critical Greek word here is *aphorizo*. It means "to set apart" or "to separate." Paul used this word when he confronted Peter about wrongfully separating himself from Gentile believers when Jewish believers from Jerusalem visited Antioch (Gal. 2:12). It is also used in 2 Corinthians 6:17, in which Paul quotes Isaiah 52:11, arguing that Christians are not to be "yoked together" with unbelievers.

But there is a significant difference between Old Testament and New Testament ages. In Old Testament times Israel existed as a separate nation as well as a faith community. In New Testament times the church exists as smaller communities of faith scattered in every society and culture. While Christians clearly are to be separate from sin, we must still keep contact with unbelievers in our neighborhoods.

In 1 Corinthians 5, Paul taught that the church should purify itself by expelling any immoral person. ♦ DISCIPLINE Then he added, "I have written you in my letter not to associate with sexually immoral people — not at all meaning the people of this world who are greedy and swindlers, or idolaters. In that case you would have to leave this world" (1 Cor. 5:9–10). And he adds, "What business is it of mine to judge those outside the church?" (1 Cor. 5:12). Paul counsels the believers to live nonjudgmentally with those outside the church, not withdrawing, but expecting the purity of our lives to witness to them of the beauty of Jesus (John 17:15–18). Christians are to be separated from sin. ♦ SANCTIFI-CATION, HOLINESS We are to be different from others, but we are not to isolate ourselves from those who need to hear the gospel and sense in our lives the prospect of hope (1 Peter 4:15).

SERVANTHOOD

The seed of servanthood is found in the Old Testament. Isaiah describes the coming Messiah as God's servant, formed to bring his salvation to the ends of the earth (Isa. 49:1–7). In his obedience the servant knows "the word that sustains the weary," and because of his deep faith in the sovereign Lord, he commits himself to an obedience that brings him great suffering (Isa. 50:4–7). Ultimately the servant spoken of in Isaiah suffers and dies for our transgressions to bring us peace and healing (Isa. 53:4–6).

These powerful passages in Isaiah are applied to Jesus (Matt. 12:15–21), who taught that the "Son of Man did not come to be served, but to serve, and to give his life as a ransom for many" (Matt. 20:28). Jesus is the ideal servant. He is committed fully to do God's will. And clearly God's will for Jesus was the sacrifice of himself for the benefit of others.

In an extended passage in Matthew's gospel, Jesus calls us to servanthood. He looks at greatness and teaches that it can be found only by living humbly with others (Matt. 18:1–9). Remembering that our brothers and sisters are sheep, we seek to restore those who go astray (Matt. 18:10–14). Remembering that in a family hurts come, we are quick to forgive (Matt. 18:15–20). Remembering how much we have been forgiven by God, we eagerly forgive each other (Matt. 18:21–35). The attitude of humility, which our actions reveal, contrasts with the ways others go about seeking spiritual achievement: by zeal for the law (Matt. 19:1–15), by benevolences they can well afford (Matt. 19:16–30), or by working harder than others and expecting a greater reward (Matt. 20:1–16). In contrast, Jesus teaches his disciples, who are eager to be first, that "whoever wants to become great among you must be your servant, and whoever wants to be first must be your slave — just as the Son of Man did not come to be served, but to serve, and to give his life as a ransom for many" (Matt. 20:24–28).

What does Christian servanthood involve? First of all, it is a Christlike attitude, doing "nothing out of selfish ambition or vain conceit, but in humility consider[ing] others better than yourselves. Each of you should look not only to your own interests, but also to the interests of others" (Phil. 2:3–4). Servanthood involves a commitment to do the will of God and in the doing, to give ourselves for others as Jesus did.

SIN

We are all too familiar with sin. We see evidences of sin in our daily newspapers. We sense it in our own lives: in the choices we make, in the ways we react to others. Everywhere, in history past and in the flow of current events, we see clear evidence that something terribly wrong has been introduced into our world and is working itself out in individuals, societies, and nations.

While secular idealists dream of some Utopia that might exist if only the environment were changed or if only behavior were modified scientifically, Christians speak of the existence of sin and evil. ◗ EVIL Christians attribute the cause of personal and social failure to an inner warping of human nature itself, a nature that is alienated from God. Only the Christian doctrine of sin can explain the flaws we see in individuals and society. And only the Christian doctrine of sin can show us the remedy: a restoration of relationship with God through Jesus Christ.

Many cultures and religions share a high moral vision. We are able to see how things ought to be. But a great gap always exists between humanity's vision and reality, between what the individual should do and what he or she actually does, between what society should be and what it is. One popular explanation for this universal experience is mankind's supposed animal ancestry. Moral failures are simply evidence that we haven't yet evolved enough to leave our "brute origins" behind. But Christians have a different explanation. The morality gap is a result of sin. Sin, far from an indication that we haven't yet come far enough, is evidence that we human beings have left our true origin far, far behind us. Created pure, Adam and Eve made a single tragic choice that echoes and re-echoes throughout all time like a cry of hostile despair.

What is sin? Where did it come from, and how does it affect human experience? The true explanation is found in Christianity alone, just as the one remedy for sin is found in personal relationship with Jesus Christ.

To understand what Christians believe about sin, we need to examine both Old and New Testaments for sin's description, impact, and remedy. We also need to see how different theological traditions have understood the Bible's teachings.

What is sin? Although there are different emphases within our traditions, Christians generally agree about sin. Some of us tend to see sin inclusively. That is, we take sin as "any and every want of conformity with the moral law of God, whether of excess or defect, whether of omission or commission. Sin is any want of conformity of the moral states or habits as well as actions of the human soul with the Law of God" (A. A. Hodge, *Outlines of Theology*, p. 316). Others of us tend to define sin exclusively. Our moral faculties have been distorted in the Fall, but "nothing is sin, strictly speaking, but a voluntary transgression of the known will of God" (John Wesley).

Whether Christians see sin as "every defect" or only as "a voluntary transgression of the known will of God," we agree that "all have sinned, and fallen short of the glory of God" (Rom. 6:23). Christians also agree that the effects of sin are felt in every person and in the fabric of society.

As Orton Wiley, a contemporary Wesleyan theologian, says, "We believe that original sin, or depravity, is the corruption of the nature of all the offspring of Adam, by reason of which everyone is very far gone from original righteousness or the pure state of our first parents at the time of their creation, is averse to God, is without spiritual life, and is inclined to evil, and that continually" (*Christian Theology*, Vol. 2, p. 121).

A look at the biblical vocabulary helps us understand what sin is. The principle Hebrew word for sin is *hata'*, meaning "to miss the mark," or "to fall short of the standard" that God has set for mankind. The other Hebrew words for sin also imply the existence of a divine standard. *Pesha'*, rendered "rebellion," means "a revolt against the standard." *'Awon*, rendered "iniquity" or "guilt," means "twisting the standard." The concept of sin suggested by these terms is inclusive: God's character and his law express a standard against which all human action is to be measured. Whether one rebels against the standard, twists it, or simply falls short of it, he or she is guilty of sin.

A similar picture is seen when we examine the New Testament words. Two major word groups portray sin. *Adikia* and other words in that family mean "wrongdoing," "unrighteousness," "injustice." The emphasis here is on conscious human action, on a willful violation that causes visible harm to other persons. *Hamartia*, usually translated "sin" in English versions, includes the meanings of all three Hebrew words. It also assumes a divine standard and sees human beings as falling short of the norm God has established.

At the same time, *hamartia* goes beyond the Old Testament meaning. In the New Testament *hamartia* describes humanity: It affirms that human nature itself has been so warped that we cannot match up to what God must expect. And it affirms that sin is expressed as an alien, malignant power that locks each person in its own unbreakable grip.

What is the origin of sin? We find our answer in Genesis 1–3. Adam and Eve were created sinless. Each had a truly free will. No inner twistedness distorted their vision of right and wrong, and no raging inner desires overwhelmed their judgment. Yet God told them not to eat from one tree that was planted in the Garden of Eden. The tree was necessary. Adam and Eve were created in the image and likeness of God. If Adam and Eve were to reflect him, they, too, must have the opportunity of moral choice.

We have no way of knowing how long Adam and Eve lived in their garden before they sinned. We have no way of knowing how often they gladly bypassed the forbidden fruit, remembering the command of the Lord. But we know that one day Satan crept into the garden, and finding

Eve alone, he confused her with his lies. Eve took the fruit and offered it to a clear-eyed Adam, who understood fully what he was doing when he, too, ate.

That choice warped the very nature of Adam and Eve. That warped nature has since been transmitted to every human being ever born into our world except Jesus, the sinless Son of God. Romans 5 looks back and says that "sin entered the world through one man, and death through sin, and in this way death came to all men, because all sinned." And so "death reigned" in human experience. Although the falling short, the rebellion, and the twisted behavior of human beings was not labeled "sin" until law was given and a standard thus established, still "sin was in the world." Sin gripped all mankind in its power, distorting experiences on earth and bringing every person under the condemnation of God (Rom. 5:12–17).

What are the consequences of sin? Sin is a complex biblical concept. It touches human beings at every level of our experience. Sin finds expression in our alienation from God and in the intuitive hostility and fear that human beings feel when confronted by God's self-revelation. Sin finds expression in interpersonal disharmony and strife. Pride, competitiveness, and selfishness all distort our relationships with others — even with those we love the most. Sin finds expression in society, where all too often injustice is supported by "the system" and where personal or political expediency overwhelm issues of right and wrong. Sin finds expression in war and crime. And sin finds expression within each of us, as Paul so graphically describes in Ephesians 2. The condition of a humanity dead in trespasses and sins is seen in that human beings follow "the ways of this world and of the ruler of the kingdom of the air, the spirit who is now at work in those who are disobedient. All of us also lived among them at one time, gratifying the cravings of our sinful nature and following its desires and thoughts. Like the rest, we were by nature objects of wrath" (Eph. 2:2–3).

Scripture speaks of sin as behavior that violates known standards. John's first letter notes, "everyone who sins breaks the law; in fact, sin is lawlessness" (1 John 3:4). What may not be known is that even those without scriptural revelation of "the law, do by nature the things required by the law" and thus show that "the requirements of the law are written on their hearts" (Rom. 2:14–15). Paul's point is that a moral sense is as much a part of human nature as is the capacity to think or to appreciate beauty. The specific content of God's standards may not be understood by all people, but all human beings who come into our world are moral beings. Human beings recognize the fact that moral standards must exist, and in fact they set up their own standards if God's are not known. All people sin when they violate God's revealed standards or the standards that their moral capacity has generated. Wrong behavior, behavior that violates the standards a person recognizes, is sin in the classic sense of a "willful violation of known standards."

The consequences of specific personal acts of sin are varied. Often there are natural (or cause/effect) consequences. The drunken man crashes his vehicle; the thief goes to jail; the homosexual develops AIDS. The person who lies is caught and loses the promotion. The adulterer is divorced. And of course each sin carries with it real guilt, making the person liable to punishment.

But the consequences of sin go far beyond the results of a person's willful acts. God suggested the basic consequences when he warned Adam and Eve that the day they ate of the forbidden fruit they would "surely die." They ate. And though the process that led to physical death was only initiated then, the more dreadful pall of spiritual death settled over them at once.

Genesis 3 and 4 illustrate this. Immediately after their sin, Adam and Eve felt guilt and shame. When God called, they ran and hid from him, fearing the Creator to whom they had been so close. Their own interpersonal harmony was shattered as Adam began to blame Eve. The deeper meanings of spiritual death are illustrated again as an angry Cain kills his brother Abel. Marriage is distorted as Lamech marries two women and then justifies murder by saying that the "young man" involved "injured" him. The nature and impact of the death God warned of is graphically illustrated in Genesis. Alienated from God, human beings are also alienated from one another, afflicted with hostility which continues to express itself in wars, crime, conflict, hatred, thought-lessness, and in hurting and being hurt. Death, and the meaning of its grip on humanity, is also a consequence of sin. ◆ **DEATH**

In Romans 7, the Bible explores another consequence of sin. The death that passed from Adam and Eve to all their offspring actually inclines the human personality toward evil. Law, which reveals God's standards, is related to our inner bent in a peculiar way. When God's law is known and his standards clearly stated, God's very "do not" produces in us "every kind of covetous desire" (Rom. 7:8).

Paul notes that while he acknowledges God's standards are good and right and while he wants to live by them, sin is in some sense "living" in him (Rom. 7:17). Sin is a dynamic force, a power, a principle at work within his personality. Sin is so powerful that "what I do is not the good I want to do; no, the evil I do not want to do — this I keep on doing" (Rom. 7:19). So sin is more than a willful act. It is more than spiritual death, with its power to alienate us from God and others. Sin is also a power that takes us captive, a bent toward evil, which the law cannot restrain. Sin actually energizes to move us toward evil. Adam and Eve were originally free from this inner bent. But when they chose to sin, they became twisted and bent within, with all the energy of their personalities channeled toward evil.

There is, of course, another consequence of sin. This consequence is eternal. Unless the inner personality is renewed and unless death is overcome by an infusion of spiritual life, the person will exist eternally as a lost soul. Human beings, shaped in God's image, are too precious to simply be blotted out as if they never existed. Each person will exist forever. The only issue is how we will exist, still twisted by sin and in its powerful grip or bright and fresh through God's spiritual renewal. ▶ HEAVEN AND HELL

Sin, then, is a complex and terrible force. Measured against the divine standard, sin is any falling short of, rebellion against, or twisting of God's will. Examined in its essential character, sin has several faces. Sin is a personal, willful choice to disobey God's known will. Sin is spiritual death, an alienation that finds expression in all the evil infecting our relationships and society. Sin is a power, an inner warping of the human personality; sin is a power that channels our energies and choices toward evil. And sin is terminal: Those in its grip have no way to escape unaided, and they have no hope of changing their condition or personalities.

The remedy for sin. The picture that Scripture paints of sin and its consequences is a good word from God. It is good because it turns our eyes away from ourselves and our own futile efforts to be sinless, and it challenges us to search for a remedy. It is good because it teaches us that we can have hope only if we surrender all hope in ourselves and instead, place our hope in God. It is good because the biblical revelation of sin is matched by a revelation of forgiveness. ▶ FORGIVENESS

When we look to Christ, whom the Bible sets forth as God's answer to the tragedy of sin, we discover that at every point Jesus counters the effects of sin. In his death he laid the foundation for forgiveness so that guilt no longer is an issue in our relationship with God. ▶ GUILT In his resurrection Jesus released the transforming power of God to remake and renew us.

Sin channeled our personality toward evil. When we accept Jesus into our lives as Savior, he invades our heart and begins to rechannel our choices toward righteousness. Sin existed as a living, overpowering force within us, but the Holy Spirit, whom Jesus gives us, is an even greater power. We can rely on the Spirit to energize us to actually do righteousness. Sin was death, an alienation from God and others. In

Jesus relationship is restored, and we can live in harmony with the Lord and others. We, who once willingly chose to sin, now can choose not to sin; instead we can do the will of God with joy and enthusiasm.

One day, when Jesus comes and we experience our own resurrection, every remnant of sin's consequences and every last shred of sin's presence will be removed. Until then we are vulnerable to the sin within us and to the sins others commit. But we are also able to draw on the power of Jesus, who forgives us when we do sin and who is constantly at work within us to enable us to choose and to do what is good.

SOCIAL CONCERN ◆ JUSTICE

SOUL AND SPIRIT

Sometimes people corrupt biblical concepts, and the words come to mean something different from what they mean in Scripture. At times the distorted meanings are generally accepted and become part of the average person's faith. This has certainly happened with the word *soul* and to some extent with the word *spirit*. Contrary to what many people seem to believe, the word *soul* in Scripture does not mean "that everlasting part of a human being, the part that separates from the body at death." What is the soul and what is its relationship to the spirit of a human being? And how do these important biblical concepts affect our understanding of our Christian faith?

The human soul. The Hebrew word translated "soul" is *nepesh*, which is also translated (correctly) as "life," "person," "self," "being," and "I." Essentially the word indicates personal existence: the life or self of a person, encompassing all the vital drives and desires, the emotions and will. The Hebrew Bible uses *nepesh* some seven hundred fifty times, and only one hundred nineteen of them are translated "soul" in the New International Version. It is best to take most of these occurrences as oblique ways of referring to a person himself or herself or to personal powers. Thus, for instance, when Ezekiel warns that "the soul that sins will die" (Ezek. 18:4, 20), the threat is not of eternal condemnation, but in context, it is a threat that the person will die in the coming war of judgment on the nation. So, too, the psalmist's praise for delivering "my soul" simply means "saved my life" from some present danger.

While "soul" in the Old Testament does not indicate some immaterial part of a person that continues after death, there is abundant teaching that each person does exist forever and that physical death is not the end for any of us. ◆ **RESURRECTION**

In the New Testament the word translated "soul" is *psuche*. The meaning is the same here as in the Old Testament, and though the Greek word occurs one hundred one times in the New Testament, it is translated "soul" only twenty-five times in the New International Version.

The human spirit. The Old Testament word is *ruah*, meaning "wind," "breath," or "spirit." While some take the symbolism to suggest the vitalizing principle of life rooted in God, the "spirit of man" seems to focus on individual character and attitude toward the Lord. While "spirit" is also ascribed to God and angels, "soul" is used uniquely in reference to human beings.

The New Testament word *pneuma* is used primarily in reference to the Holy Spirit. But a number of New Testament passages make it clear that it is the human spirit that has the potential to be aware of and responsive to God.

There is considerable overlap between soul and spirit in the Bible. Each indicates personal life itself, life after death, emotions, purpose, and commitment: the self. Yet *psuche* alone is used of physical life and of spiritual growth, and *pneuma* is associated with worship, understanding, attitude or disposition, and spiritual power.

Essentially soul and spirit are terms used to focus on the specialness of human beings and individuals. Rather than dividing up a person into separate elements, each seems to look at the same person as a whole, but from a slightly different perspective.

The spiritual and "soulish" person. The New Testament makes one special use of these terms that is significant. It speaks of the "soulish" person, who is either unconverted or who, though converted, lives like the rest of humankind, insensitive to the Lord. But it also speaks of the "spiritual" person, who both possesses the Holy Spirit and lives in responsive relationship to him. When we live "in the Spirit," our relationship with God lifts us beyond our limitations. We can discern and do God's will, and we can live holy lives that please God. ♦ HOLY SPIRIT

Christians believe that human beings are unique in all creation. The word *soul* suggests that all living beings are important, with a personal existence and life force given them by God. The word *spirit* lifts human beings above the rest of life on earth and links us with God, who has given us emotions, will, and the capacity to be aware of realities beyond this universe. No human being can be treated lightly or dismissed as unimportant, for each of us is a living soul, created by God that we might in Christ have fellowship with him.

SOVEREIGNTY

What Christians mean by the sovereignty of God is quite simple: God has the absolute right and freedom to govern everything as he chooses. Because God is truly sovereign, nothing that any human being can do and no circumstance can limit God's freedom to act as he wills.

Some people have reacted against the concept of God's absolute freedom of action. If that is true, they argue, how can there be evil in the universe? For if God is both good and free, he must have put an end to it. ◗ EVIL Others have reacted because they fear that total sovereignty implies the loss of free will for human beings. ◗ FREEDOM, FREE WILL, PREDESTINATION

But God *is* sovereign. He "works out everything in conformity with the purpose of his will" (Eph. 1:11). This doesn't need to concern us if we remember one thing: The way power is exercised always depends on the character of the person holding it. The God who is sovereign in our universe is the God of love, justice, grace, and goodness. God will never do anything that violates his own character; thus he alone can be trusted with the freedom of action he does have.

Two lines of scriptural teaching help us appreciate the way God has chosen to exercise his freedom of action. First, God has chosen to provide salvation. In this we see clearly that his sovereignty is no threat to us but is, instead, the basis of our hope. Second, God superintends the results of our choices. Peter discusses the case in which a believer does right but suffering follows. In 1 Peter 3:10–22, the apostle points out that Jesus found himself in exactly this situation. He did only good, but it was he who suffered instead of the unrighteous people who deserved a cross. But, Peter says, look at the result. It was through Jesus' suffering that he brought us to God. Looking at the cross in this way, we realize that God's sovereignty is great comfort, for it assures us that when we, too, suffer for doing right, God can and will bring good from the injustice.

Christians worship a sovereign God. He is totally free, able to do anything that he wills. Our wonder and our joy flow from the realization that what God has chosen to will is our blessing and our good.

SPIRIT ◗ HOLY SPIRIT

SPIRITUAL GIFTS

Christians these days are aware of spiritual gifts. But Christians don't all agree about them. Still the theme of spiritual giftedness is basic to the Christian's understanding of how and why each of us is truly important.

Spiritual gifts in the Old Testament. Although the reality of spiritual gifts is present in the Old Testament, the words *spiritual gifts* are not mentioned there. We see that reality in God's words to Moses about a man named Bezalel: "I have filled him with the Spirit of God, with skill, ability and knowledge in all kinds of crafts" to shape articles for the tabernacle where God's Old Testament people worshiped (Exod. 31:3). And God adds, "I have given skill to all the craftsmen to make everything I have commanded you" (Exod. 31:6). In the same way, the Spirit of God enabled Othniel to judge Israel (Judg. 3:10) and gave Samson strength (Judg. 14:6). Throughout the Old Testament, God is seen as the source of the gifts and abilities that enabled people to serve him and the community of Israel.

Foundational New Testament principles. The Greek word for spiritual gifts is *charisma,* or "grace gift." Essentially a spiritual gift is a special enablement or endowment that equips a believer to serve others in the community of faith. At times Christians use "spiritual gift" in the sense of any divine enablement for any kind of ministry.

Four passages in the New Testament focus on spiritual gifts; the two major passages are Romans 12 and 1 Corinthians 12. In each passage we are called on to see ourselves as members of Christ's body, a living organism. In the organism each of us has a special role, a special way that we contribute to the well-being of the whole. There are different gifts (1 Cor. 12:4), which God distributes sovereignly as he chooses (1 Cor. 12:6), with each believer having at least one gift (1 Cor. 12:7). These gifts are exercised when Christians live together in love, seeking to serve and help each other. As Peter says, "Each one should use whatever gift he has received to serve others, faithfully administering God's grace in its various forms" (1 Peter 4:10).

In the New Testament passages on gifts, the focus is always on the Christian community. Gifts are used for the common good (1 Cor. 12:7) and function to build up the body of Christ, helping individuals and the congregation become spiritually mature (Eph. 4:12–16).

Questions about spiritual gifts. Though Christians agree on the foundational issues about spiritual gifts, we do have questions that we tend to answer differently. Here are a few:

Are all the spiritual gifts listed in the Bible? Those who believe that they are draw up their lists from Romans 12, 1 Corinthians 12, and Ephesians 4. Others believe that the lists in these passages are simply representative, and that any way in which we can contribute to others should be considered a *charisma.*

Where do spiritual gifts operate? Some of us have associated spiritual gifts with church offices or institutional roles. Others note that the New Testament speaks always of interpersonal relationships and believe that the gifts function any time and place that Christians gather to share their faith and lives.

Can a person have more than one spiritual gift? Certainly Paul did (2 Cor. 1:1; 14:18). What may be most important is to realize that each of us has at least one.

Are the clearly supernatural gifts (speaking in tongues and healing, for example) intended to operate in the church today? This question has caused deep division. Some Christians think that 1 Corinthians 13:8 ("where there are prophecies, they will cease; where there are tongues, they will be stilled") indicates that when the last New Testament letter was written, these spectacular gifts no longer were given. Other Christians are convinced that the obviously supernatural gifts are intended for today — and that they have them! This debate has led to a tragic separation between Christian brothers and sisters as well as a rift in the church. The differences will probably persist, although today there is a new acceptance and growing appreciation by each side for the other. The very fact that the differences do exist, with truly committed believers on each side, warns us not to take sides hastily. Perhaps what is best is for each side to admit its lack of complete knowledge and for each side to admit also that God is free to work as he chooses in this age as in any other, despite interpretations of ours, which seem to limit his freedom.

How does a person tell what his or her spiritual gift is? It is seldom helpful to seek our gift by studying the biblical lists of gifts. Remembering that gifts operate in an interpersonal context, it is best to build close and caring relationships with other believers. As you and I seek to serve others, we discover our gift. We see how God uses us to strengthen others, and those others recognize our contribution. It is in the context of ministering that a person's spiritual gift is used and recognized.

The significance of spiritual gifts. It is all too easy for us to spend our time discussing our points of difference. What is more important is to note the significance of the things we agree on.

We agree that spiritual gifts are from God the Spirit, who alone is able to transform our efforts into effective ministry. How vital, then, that we rely on him and live close to Jesus. As Christ taught, "I am the vine; you are the branches" (John 15:5). It is only as we remain close to him that we have any spiritual power at all, for "apart from me you can do nothing" (John 15:5).

We agree that each Christian is spiritually significant. Each of us has a vital place in the body of Christ; each of us has the potential of contributing to others. Because God's Spirit enables us to serve others, every one of us is truly important; no one is insignificant in Christ's church.

As we live together, united by love, God will use each of us to enrich the others. In the fellowship of Christ's church and in service, each of us finds his or her gift.

SPIRITUALITY

Different religions have different notions of spirituality. In some Eastern religions the spiritual person is the one who abandons all earthly ambition, takes up the begging bowl, and sits meditating in silence. Christians have had no one dominant view, although in some eras the withdrawn monk has seemed the ideal. Probably for most of us, spirituality has some connotation of withdrawal from the world, of devotion to God expressed in prayer or in study. But in its deepest roots our Judeo-Christian heritage offers another image entirely.

For God's Old Testament people, the goal of religion was holiness. And holiness was expressed by living in this world by the law of God. In pure religion the rabbi was a man who supported himself by a trade, just as the apostle Paul worked as a tentmaker while he traveled and preached the gospel. The rabbi lived by the Word he studied, but he applied his religion in ordinary life. He studied the Word of God, not as an end in itself, but that it might be a light to his path.

Jesus himself is undoubtedly the one we look to as our model. How did Jesus live? He was unaffected by materialism, committed to prayer, and yet unceasingly active in doing God's will. He freely enjoyed the wedding feast, was comfortable in the company of known sinners, and was ready to confront hypocrisy and evil. No one looking at Jesus could imagine him isolating himself from other persons. No, Jesus was deeply involved, deeply compassionate, reaching out to touch the lives of others by his teaching and his healing. If we wonder what true spirituality is, we need only follow Jesus on his journeying in Galilee or Judea.

Even so, Christians have often tended to wander off on tangents. In Colosse too many believers were attracted by a common teaching. They accepted the idea that the material world somehow must be evil, while the immaterial universe is good and thus spiritual. These deceived believers tried to become spiritual by withdrawing from the world, by the worship of "spiritual" angelic beings, and by harsh treatment of their bodies. Paul confronts this false notion of spirituality bluntly:

Is the material essentially evil and unspiritual? No, Paul says to the Colossians, for God himself took on a real body, and "by Christ's physical body through death" acted to reconcile us to God (Col. 1:22). So in Christ "all the fullness of the Deity lives in bodily form" (Col. 2:9). Clearly there is no basic conflict between spirituality and life in the material universe.

What, then, is spirituality? Spirituality is to draw on our relationship with Jesus and as God's chosen people, to clothe ourselves "with compassion, kindness, humility, gentleness, and patience." Spirituality is to bear with and forgive each other. Spirituality is to love. Spirituality is to do, in word and deed, "all in the name of the Lord Jesus, giving thanks to God the Father through him" (Col. 3:12–17).

The apostle James puts it this way: "Religion that God our Father accepts as pure and faultless is this: to look after orphans and widows in their distress and to keep oneself from being polluted by the world" (Col. 1:27).

For us Christians, then, spirituality is no mystic withdrawal. To isolate oneself from this world of struggling human beings is neither right or good, much less "spiritual." Instead the spiritual person is one who draws from his or her personal relationship with Jesus the strength and wisdom to live Christ's kind of life in our world. When you and I live compassionately, kindly, in humility, gentleness, and patience, with believer and unbeliever alike, we approach the Christian ideal. Our goal, like Jesus' own, is to bring glory to God by completing the work he gives us to do (John 17:4; cf. John 15–19). ▶ **SANCTIFY**

STEWARDSHIP

Simply put, stewardship involves the recognition that God is the true possessor of all things. In loaning his possessions to us, God holds us responsible for what we do. This concept of Christian stewardship calls us to look at everything — our time, our money, our priorities — and to relate them to God's purposes.

Several of Jesus' parables are about stewardship. The parable of the shrewd manager, so often misunderstood (Luke 16:1–16), simply points out that money is not to be loved for itself but rather is to be used wisely to prepare for the future. Christians, whose focus is on eternity rather than this world, will wisely choose to lay up treasures in heaven rather than on earth (Matt. 6:19–21).

Jesus also told parables about servants whose master gave them resources to invest. The servants who used the resources and multiplied them by honest effort were rewarded with additional responsibility (Luke 19:11–26).

What do Christians see as matters of stewardship? Certainly our income and possessions. Certainly, too, the earth itself, whose ecology is now our responsibility. ♦ DOMINION The very hours of our life are also God's gift to us to be spent with due regard to our own needs and enjoyment and the needs of others. Perhaps, however, the most important thing that we have been entrusted with is the gospel. Christians are ambassadors for Christ (2 Cor. 5:20). We are his representatives in an alien world, called to give witness to our Lord by our life and words.

Stewardship is a serious issue to Christians. But, surprisingly, it isn't burdensome. Living for Jesus is a source of great joy. Representing Jesus is a privilege indeed. And making our choices in view of God's priorities points our way to a fulfilling life now and to glory beyond. ♦ REWARDS

SUBSTITUTION

From the very beginning of our era, Christians have talked the language of substitution. We have affirmed, with the writers of Scripture, that Christ died for us. Perhaps no passage makes it more clear than Romans 5: "At just the right time, when we were still powerless, Christ died for the ungodly. Very rarely will anyone die for a righteous man, though for a good man someone might possibly dare to die. But God demonstrates his own love for us in this: While we were still sinners, Christ died for us" (Rom. 5:6–8).

Many themes in Scripture help us understand the reason why Christ died a substitutionary death. We see the principle in Old Testament sacrifices and hear it in basic doctrines such as redemption, propitiation, and atonement. We see substitution in the Bible's teaching on sin and righteousness and in the exciting prospect of sanctification. By studying such basic doctrines and themes, we realize that true Christianity never has lost the sense of awe that comes when we realize that Jesus died for us. He hung on the cross in our place. And in his resurrection, we will take our new place in him. ♦ ATONEMENT, SACRIFICE, RIGHTEOUS-NESS, SIN, SALVATION, PROPITIATION, REDEMPTION, SANCTIFICATION

TEN COMMANDMENTS

We live in a moral universe. The God who ordained the laws of nature has also ordained moral laws. These moral laws are expressions of his own moral character and, as such, reveal much about who he is. They also warn us, for like natural law, moral law implies consequences. One who jumps from a window falls down, following the law of gravity. One who chooses to act against God's moral laws will also suffer consequences. Thus, the Ten Commandments, those brief injunctions that crystallize the moral principles by which we are all to live, are a great gift. Guided by them, we can make choices that lead away from what will harm us to what will do us good.

The Ten Commandments were originally written on two portable slabs of stone and are recorded for us in Exodus 20 and Deuteronomy 5. The Ten Commandments are regarded as special because God himself inscribed them on those stones and gave them to Moses on Mount Sinai.

Each of the commandments deals with relationships: relationship with God and relationships with others. While they are given specifically to Israel as a covenant community, the Ten Commandments have universal application to all human beings. The Ten, as listed by Protestant Christians, are:

THE COMMAND	ITS IMPLICATIONS
1. You shall have no other gods before me (Exod. 20:3).	Jahweh alone is to be recognized as God. ◗ JAHWEH
2. You shall not make for yourself an idol in the form of anything (Exod. 20:4).	No idol is to be made, either to represent Jahweh or any supernatural power.
3. You shall not misuse the name of the Lord your God (Exod. 20:7).	The name of Jahweh is not to be considered an empty symbol, as if God were not real and powerful.
4. Remember the Sabbath day by keeping it holy (Exod. 20:8).	God is to be honored as Creator by a day of rest, which patterns Israel's seven-day week.
5. Honor your father and your mother (Exod. 20:12).	Parents are to be honored and obeyed so that children will learn to submit to the Lord.
6. You shall not murder (Exod. 20:13).	Human life is sacred and is to be protected and guarded.

THE COMMAND	ITS IMPLICATIONS
7. You shall not commit adultery. (Exod. 20:14).	Covenant commitments are to be faithfully maintained.
8. You shall not steal (Exod. 20:15).	Others' property rights are to be respected.
9. You shall not give false testimony against your neighbor (Exod. 20:16).	Others' reputations are to be guarded.
10. You shall not covet (Exod. 20:17).	Others' possessions are not to be envied.

Each of these ten, with the exception of keeping the Sabbath, is restated as a New Testament principle for Christians. Christians have set Sunday apart as a special day to remember Jesus' resurrection. ♦ SABBATH

Many people believe that most other Old Testament commands are implicit in the Ten Commandments and are intended as illustrations to help Israel plumb the fullest meaning of the basic principles they establish.

Yet in Leviticus 19, we find two statements that Jesus said sum up the Law and the Prophets (Matt. 22:37–40). "Fear the LORD your God," Leviticus 19:14 says, calling for that reverential awe that views God with loving respect, and "love your neighbor as yourself" (Lev. 19:18). And this is what Christians believe the Ten Commandments and all other commands call for. The person who fears and loves God will cling to him only, will honor him as real and powerful, and will submit to him as a child does to its parents. The person who loves others will hold their lives precious, will be faithful to commitments, will guard their property and reputation, and will care about them as persons rather than envy their possessions.

Humanity has had God's Ten Commandments for millenniums now. Why do we still have crime and war, poverty and injustice? Christians believe it is because commandments written in stone, standing outside us, provide us with knowledge of our failures, but the commandments lack the power to change our character and our actions. This is why Jesus (and the Old Testament itself) focuses on love for God and others as the key to real morality. And this is why both testaments speak of a new covenant under which God promises to write his laws on our hearts, not in stone (2 Cor. 3:1–3; Jer. 31:31–34; Heb. 8:10–13). ♦ COVENANT

This new covenant was established by Jesus' death on Calvary. It commits God to work in the hearts and lives of Jesus' people to make us truly moral. And this, of course, is the real issue. The commandments can teach us what morality is, but only God, working in our lives through faith in Jesus, can make us truly good. ◆ **RIGHTEOUSNESS**

TONGUES

In the past hundred years the issue of speaking in tongues has been a divisive one. But most Christians today are reaffirming our unity in Christ, and speaking in tongues has found a place not only in traditional Pentecostal groups but also in most mainline denominations. ◆ **PENTE-COST** What are "tongues," and what is their role in Christian faith?

Tongues in the Bible. In the Old Testament the word *tongue* is used to indicate the physical organ and languages. It is also used symbolically, as the organ that expresses character by revealing the heart of the speaker. At times our New Testament uses the word *tongue* in all the Old Testament ways. For instance, when Acts indicates that the Spirit-filled disciples spoke in other tongues, the context makes clear that all the bystanders (Parthians, Medes, Elamites, Egyptians, Libyans, etc.) heard the message in their own native languages (Acts 2:4–12).

In 1 Corinthians 12 and 14, however, where speaking in tongues is identified as a spiritual gift, something unusual is in view. A tongue is not an understandable language, and it calls for a person gifted with "interpretation of tongues" to make any message intelligible (1 Cor. 12:10). Paul himself claims the gift of tongues (1 Cor. 14:18) and speaks of it as "praying with my spirit" (1 Cor. 14:14–17). He does, however, warn against a misuse of this gift when the church has gathered. To guard against misuse, tongues are to be used in public worship only when the person speaking (or another person) can interpret so that the church will be edified (1 Cor. 14:6–17). Paul is particularly concerned that unbelievers might come in, for they will misunderstand what they hear as mere babbling and will "say that you are out of your mind" (1 Cor. 14:23–24). In contrast, Paul urges that church gatherings concentrate on prophecy, that is, on clear teaching in the congregation's own language of what God has revealed to his people. In this case the stranger "will be convinced by all that he is a sinner" and so "he will fall down and worship God" (1 Cor. 14:24–25).

It is certainly clear from these chapters that speaking in tongues is a spiritual gift, that it edifies or builds up the person who speaks in tongues, and that when there is an interpreter present, speaking in tongues can also edify or build up the gathered congregation. It is just as clear that this gift is not to become central in our gathered experience as the people of God, for clear, intelligible instruction is more important then.

How Christians disagree. Christians acknowledge the gift of tongues as described in the Bible. But the nature and role of that gift is disputed.

To some, speaking in tongues is the definitive evidence that the Holy Spirit has come into one's life. Those without the gift lack the Spirit — if not the Spirit itself, at least that special link to the Spirit of which tongues is the sign. For them the possession of the gift of tongues is foundational to deeper spiritual experience and spiritual power. Often those of this persuasion believe that the tongues of Acts 2 and 1 Corinthians 12 are the same.

On the other hand, many Christians believe that the gift of tongues was temporary, limited to the age before the New Testament was complete. This and other extraordinary gifts were intended as signs, which were no longer needed when the whole Bible became available to the church. Typically, 1 Corinthians 13:8, which contrasts unfailing love with tongues that will be stilled, is quoted as proof of this view. A stronger theological argument rests on pneumatology: This camp is sure the Bible indicates that the Holy Spirit enters all Christians on conversion. ◆ HOLY SPIRIT Thus, speaking in tongues was never intended as a unique sign of the Spirit's presence in the Christian's life.

These theological distinctions reflect deep emotional commitments. Those who speak in tongues testify to a deeper life in Christ than they had known before. They understandably resent others who deride their experience as either hysteria and self-delusion or as something demonic. On the other hand, the traditionalist has often felt threatened by Pentecostal teaching, which has caused dispute and division in many congregations.

Today emotions are not as high as they have been, and mediating positions have developed. Those who speak in tongues recognize the reality of the Spirit's working in those who do not, and tongues is taking its place as one among many spiritual gifts, not the premier gift. ◆ SPIRITUAL GIFTS Those who have not spoken in tongues are less ready to rule out the experience of brothers and sisters who have. This moderating of attitudes increasingly permits us all not only to hold our own convictions on what has been a sensitive issue but also to affirm our unity with those Christians who differ from us.

When we look at the many books written on the issue, it is clear that Christians are not likely to come to a single, common conviction. So we must agree to disagree in this area. It is more striking to realize that in the

Epistles, only 1 Corinthians 12–14 deals with the question at all, and then it primarily tries to regulate the public misuse of the gift. The rest of the New Testament is silent about tongues but rich with instruction on love. Admittedly many issues find their focus in the debates about tongues, but there is no debate at all about the fact that we owe one another love. We do not owe each other agreement, but we are obligated to accept and love each other. Whatever our convictions about tongues, we remain the children of God together through faith in Jesus Christ (Gal. 3:26).

TRADITION

All of us have our traditions. We sometimes call them roots, our heritage from those who have gone on before us. Most of us honor our heritage and respect our traditions, looking back for guidance and insight. All this is right and good. Tradition becomes a problem only if it becomes a substitute for personal responsibility or if it replaces the authority of Scripture and vital, living guidance from God's Spirit.

Jesus condemned the religious leaders of his time for this very thing: "You nullify the word of God for the sake of your traditions" (Matt. 15:6). Their teachings were "but rules taught by men" (Matt. 15:9).

TRANSFORMATION

God points Christians toward a total transformation. This transformation is more than a possibility. It is a promise.

The Bible speaks of transformation in two contexts. The first is future: When resurrection comes, believers will be transformed into Jesus' image. Romans 8:29 tells us that "those God foreknew he also predestined to be conformed to the likeness of his Son." In 1 Corinthians 15:51–52, Paul picks up the theme: "We will all be changed — in a flash, in the twinkling of an eye." The perishable in us will become imperishable, the mortal immortal. John tells us that while we have no clear image of what that transformation truly involves, still, "when he appears, we shall be like him, for we shall see him as he is" (1 John 3:2).

While the full transformation that awaits us will transform us physically, the promise of moral transformation is even more exciting. To be like Jesus means to love as he loves, to value what he values, to desire what he desires. We look forward to that day when the last dark trace of sin in our personalities will be gone at last and we will be clean and pure.

But there is a present context for transformation as well. The Bible speaks of a work of God by which the Holy Spirit inscribes God's laws on our hearts (2 Cor. 3:1–3). By that work we "are being transformed into his [Jesus'] likeness with ever-increasing glory, which comes from the Lord, who is the Spirit" (2 Cor. 3:18). The same exciting theme is found in other passages. We who were once "dead in your transgressions and sins" have been "made alive with Christ" (Eph. 2:1, 5). This fresh life renews us within, so that Paul can write of putting on "the new self, created to be like God in true righteousness and holiness" (Eph. 4:24). The total renewal of personality and body awaits us at our resurrection. But right now we can experience an inner change, which makes possible a true righteousness and true holiness. ◗ **RIGHTEOUSNESS, HOLINESS, SANCTIFICATION**

For Christians who truly want to be godly, the promise of transformation is good news indeed!

TRIBULATION

Usually people who use the word *tribulation* are talking about Bible prophecy. This isn't the only thing the Bible talks about, though. Distress and troubles are spoken of often in Old Testament and New Testament alike. As Jesus said to his disciples, "In this world you will have trouble. But take heart! I have overcome the world" (John 16:33). There's no escape from the pressures that bring us distress.

Even so, the Bible talks about a period of special distress. The New International Version speaks of it as the "great tribulation" only in Revelation 7:14. Other versions tell of a "tribulation" in those prophetic New Testament passages that echo Old Testament prophetic themes. For instance, in Matthew, Jesus refers to a prophecy of Daniel yet to be fulfilled and warns, "for then there will be great distress unequaled from the beginning of the world until now — and never to be equaled again" (Matt. 24:21). Both testaments give clear biblical evidence. At history's end there will be a period of overwhelming disaster and suffering.

As with other prophesied events, what is not clear is just when this period will begin and just how it fits in with other future events. ◗ **PROPHECY** As to that, Christians will continue to disagree until Jesus comes, when we'll all learn more about God's plan. Until then we will have to wait.

Most Christians who like the study of prophecy will probably remain convinced that their view of the tribulation is right and that others are wrong. But we can all agree on one thing. In our tomorrows as well as in the tribulation period, we live in a world that brings pressures and distress. But knowing Jesus, we take heart. Jesus has overcome the world, and Jesus brings us inner peace (John 16:33).

TRINITY

Christians have never been able to explain the trinity or even understand how one God exists as three persons. When we've tried to explain the trinity, we've usually worked with analogy. We've noted that one egg is composed of three substances: shell, white, and yoke. Augustine used a tree's root, trunk, and branches. The shamrock, with its three petals, and a triangle have been used. At times some people have pointed to water to explain the trinity, for water can be ice, liquid, or a vapor. But somehow none of these analogies have satisfied Christians, much less outsiders. We are driven back to a simple position. The Bible clearly teaches that God the Father, God the Son, and God the Holy Spirit are each divine, each distinct, and yet there is just one God. Augustine, writing in the fifth century, sums up our Christian conviction: "The Father and the Son and the Holy Spirit, and each of these by Himself, is God, and at the same time they are all one God; and each of them by Himself is a complete substance, and yet they are all one substance."

While we soon become confused when we try to conceptualize the trinity and while our analogies break down, we really aren't troubled by so-called logical contradictions. After all, human beings don't understand many things in the material universe. Why should we expect to be able to comprehend God? But the real reason we aren't troubled by our failure to understand the trinity is that God's threeness and oneness are taught in Scripture.

God is three. Plural language is found even in the Old Testament. The name of God used in Genesis 1:1, *Elohim*, is plural, and in making human beings, God uses plural language: "Let *us* make man in *our* image" (Gen. 1:26, italics added). Even the Hebrew word in Israel's great affirmation, "the LORD our God is *one* LORD" (Deut. 6:4, italics added), uses a Hebrew term that emphasizes plurality in unity. Beyond this, we look back and see an Old Testament filled with references to God's Spirit, and we suspect that in many instances the "angel of the Lord" was a pre-incarnate Jesus.

We see these hints of plurality in the Old Testament because we look back with the perspective given by the New Testament revelation where we find bold statements. We see Jesus presented as one who was with God and was God from eternity (John 1:1–3). We hear Jesus speak of the Father as "the only true God" and yet affirm that "I and the Father are one" (John 10:30; 17:5). In towering statements, the Bible speaks of Jesus as God incarnate, one with and yet distinct from the Father (Phil. 2:5–11; Col. 1:15–20). In the same way Jesus identifies the Holy Spirit as one like himself (John 14:15–17). He is given divine attributes (1 Cor. 2:1–11; Heb. 9:14) and is identified with God in his acts (1 Cor. 12:4–6). In Ephesians 1, we see the role of Father, Son, and Spirit spelled out for us, with each acknowledged as God. We may not understand how it can be, but we are comfortable in the knowledge that the Bible presents one God who exists eternally as three: Father, Son, and Holy Spirit. ◗ **JESUS CHRIST, HOLY SPIRIT**

God is one. While the New Testament calls for us to acknowledge Father, Son, and Holy Spirit as God, the Old Testament undergirds the conviction that there remains only one God. Of course the New Testament teaches it too in words like "I and the Father are one" (John 10:30). The unity of God was especially important in Old Testament times, for ancient cultures multiplied gods and goddesses. Against this background Israel's Jahweh stands out unique, author of creation, life, and redemption. Only Israel, among all the ancient cultures, never differentiated deity sexually and so protected the people against the moral abuses of surrounding nations. Not only is the substance of God in the Old Testament one substance, but he is one in the total unity of his character and purpose. The Old Testament's call to Israel, "The Lord our God, the Lord is one" is followed by an exhortation to love the Lord completely, with all one's heart and soul and strength. The God Israel was to love is one God, even as the God we love and worship in Father, Son, and Spirit remains one.

Thus we are convinced. We do not really understand the trinity, and no analogies seem capable of symbolizing the three-in-oneness of God. We do not really understand. But we hear the testimony of Scripture and we believe. We believe and we worship. We worship the Father. We worship the Son. And we worship the Spirit. For these three are God, and these three are one.

TRUTH

When Christians claim to know "the truth," they tend to arouse hostility. Absolutes aren't popular in pluralistic societies, especially when the absolutes call for moral commitments that aren't popular either. In New Testament times people in the dominant Greek culture had long ago given up a search for absolutes, convinced by centuries of philosophic speculation that if there were truth, it must be as unknowable as the gods. In our day people prefer to think of things as being "true for you." They don't like to consider whether something might be right or wrong for everyone and true or false in itself. But the Christian concept of truth directly confronts us with absolutes that have strong moral implications.

At times, Christian thinkers have struggled with philosophical/theological definitions of truth. Augustine turned to logic and mathematics to show that universal truths do exist (2 plus 2 is always 4) and from that to argue that a God of truth must exist. Anselm defined truth in terms of what actually exists as it should and so conforms to the ideal that exists in the mind of God. Aquinas thought of truth as adequate definition, linking truth with knowledge. Others throughout history have rested their notions of truth on contemporary philosophical systems. Some moderns contrast truth with knowledge, suggesting that truth is what has been revealed to us by God, while knowledge is what human beings have discovered through senses and reason. But to grasp the real meaning of truth and to see truth's implication for our lives, we return to the Bible to see the ways this powerful word is used.

Truth in the Old Testament. The Hebrew word translated "truth" has two major connotations. The first of these is "faithful," "reliable." To say that God is true or that his Word is true means that God is a totally trustworthy person and that his spoken Word is reliable. The second sense is closely related: Truth is that which is in full harmony with reality. God's Word is true not only because the one who spoke it is trustworthy but also because what God reveals is in complete harmony with reality as God alone knows reality.

In the Old Testament, truth relates not only to the factual (for example, God created the universe and gave all creatures life) but also to the moral. What God has shown us about how human beings are to live provides a completely reliable guide. His words are a trustworthy expression of righteous ways, ways that maintain harmony with God and between human beings.

The Old Testament assumes that both factual and moral truth are revealed by God. Apart from revelation, which is God's disclosure of what otherwise is simply unavailable to human beings, truth could not be known. How wonderful that God has spoken. Because he has, we have his completely trustworthy Word, one that is in fullest harmony with reality, one on which we can and do rely.

Truth in the New Testament. The Greek word translated "truth" picks up both Old Testament themes, but it tends to emphasize harmony with reality. Such harmony is both factual and moral. So Paul speaks of "the truth" in some places and means all that God has revealed about himself in his creation (Rom. 1:18–20) and in the gospel (Eph. 1:13; Col. 1:5; 1 Tim. 2:4). God's revelation of truth has stripped away our illusions and put speculation to rest. He has shown us reality in his Word and has shown us his true self most fully in Jesus, who is *the* Truth (John 14:6).

But truth is to be obeyed and lived as well as recognized (Gal. 5:7). So the New Testament uses truth in a distinctive, experiential way. John, whose writings contain over half of the New Testament's uses of "truth" words, reminds us that truth is God's agent for cleansing and sanctifying his people (John 17:17). He quotes Jesus' call to his disciples to keep (obey, follow) his words so that they could "know the truth." Jesus added this promise: "The truth will set you free" (John 8:31–32). Jesus' point is that scriptural realities show us how to live: Reality is to be experienced as well as mentally acknowledged. As we commit ourselves to God's Word as a revelation of the way things really are and act on what Scripture teaches, we will know by experience the truth that Scripture portrays for us in words, and we will find freedom.

In this sense, then, truth cannot simply be accepted or learned or even believed. Truth requires commitment, for we are to put truth into practice.

We see the implications of this concept in many places. In Romans, Paul exhorts a transformation that comes by renewing our outlook, letting God's truth provide us with a new perspective on life. With this new perspective, "you will be able to test and approve of what God's will is — his good, pleasing and perfect will" (Rom. 12:2). We are to put God's will to the test by acting on it, and when we do, we will fully approve of it, for that will is good, pleasing, and perfect.

Jesus condemned Satan as a liar, "not holding to the truth, for there is no truth in him" (John 8:44). Satan, who had direct knowledge of God, refused to submit to God and would not live in accordance with God's will. He chose the lie rather than the truth, and everything the Devil stands for distorts that moral reality (truth), which is rooted in the nature of God, just as every choice that Satan makes is a rejection of truth.

In his first letter John shows us another implication of living by truth. He writes of those who claim to have fellowship with God but who also claim to be without sin. This, says John, is walking in darkness. It is a lie, and such persons "do not live by the truth" (1 John 1:6). How does a Christian live by the truth and so continue in fellowship with God? Rather than pretend sinlessness, "we confess our sins." God then "is faithful and just and will forgive us our sins and [continue to] purify us from all unrighteousness" (1 John 1:5–10). The truth is that you and I continue to fall short; we continue to sin. Denial of that reality means we are not living by the truth. God does not demand sinlessness in us, for he knows our weaknesses. He does call on us to acknowledge our sins and claim the forgiveness Jesus has won for us. God's way to maintain fellowship with him rests on the availability of continuing forgiveness rather than on our supposed perfections. Acknowledging and living by this truth frees us to experience fellowship with God.

Perhaps this is the most important aspect of truth for us Christians. We believe in absolute truth. We have a Bible, which is fully trustworthy and reliable. Our faith rests on that reality, not on mere human guesses or speculations. But Christians do not see truth as something to be primarily defended, argued, or toyed with by philosophers. Truth has been unveiled in the Scripture so that you and I can experience reality as God knows it. We are to take hold of the truth of the gospel, trusting ourselves fully to Jesus, and so pass from death to life. We are to take hold of the Scriptures in the same way, trusting ourselves to Jesus' words, and so begin to experience now the freeing power of a truth that can be practiced in our daily life. As we know the truth in this wonderful experiential sense, we are set free and fulfilled.

UNBELIEF

At first, unbelief seems more a lack than anything else. The word in the New Testament literally means "without faith"; and the unbeliever is simply one who has not responded to God with faith. But on a deeper level unbelief exhibits a sinful heart "that turns away from the living God" (Heb. 3:12). As Paul shows in Romans 1, everyone has clear evidence of God's existence through the "things that are made." God has made himself plain to humanity, so that those who pull back from him are "without excuse" (Rom. 1:18–20). ◆ **REVELATION**

Even so, Christians aren't primarily concerned with blaming unbelievers. Instead, throughout the centuries, Christians have reached out to share the good news of Jesus with others. Through foreign missions and friendships with neighbors, we share the promise that because of Jesus, God will accept any who turn from unbelief to faith. Like God himself, we are unready to condemn unbelief until others have had every opportunity to hear about and to respond to God's great love.

◆ **EVANGELISM, FAITH**

UNFORGIVABLE SIN

The very mention of the unforgivable sin strikes fear into some of us. Have we committed an unforgivable sin? Is it possible that God will reject us for some sin we don't even understand? Yet, as counselors and pastors have pointed out to many an anxious caller, a person who is worried about the unforgivable sin could hardly commit it. Why? Because the unforgivable sin that Jesus speaks of in our Gospels reveals a unique hardness toward Jesus and toward God.

What is the unforgivable sin? Jesus had been healing and teaching among his people for a long time. The religious leaders, who saw this upstart prophet as a threat to their hold on the people, had hardened against him and were firm in their opposition. Yet Jesus did notable miracles, demonstrating to all his power and his position as God's spokesperson. ◆ PROPHET Finally the frustrated enemies began to circulate a rumor. Jesus' miracles were evidence of demonic, not divine, power. Satan and not God was the source of this man's wonders.

In Matthew 12:22–32, Jesus confronts his accusers. At first he simply reasons with them. If Satan drives out Satan, he is fighting himself, and that brings ruin to any kingdom. Only if Jesus had power to bind Satan (to make him helpless), could he treat Satan's demons with such contempt. But then Jesus warns the accusers. In fact, Jesus' miracles are performed in the power of the Holy Spirit. To call the Spirit of God at work through Jesus Satan is a terrible blasphemy and will not be forgiven.

But why won't it be forgiven? Note that Jesus does not say it is unforgivable, but that it will not be forgiven. Those who made this terrible accusation were so hardened against Jesus that even the clearest proof of his position as God's spokesperson was rejected. When miracles that compel belief were twisted into something dark and evil, it was completely clear that nothing could ever touch the heart and mind of the accuser. It was this total commitment against Christ, evidenced in their blasphemy against the Spirit, that led Jesus to tell these men that they were beyond forgiveness.

But can we commit the unforgivable sin today? Nearly all say, "No." Why? Well, Jesus is not physically present in our world. He has not been performing miracles openly among us. And no one today is accusing Jesus of acting in demonic power rather than in the power of God's Holy Spirit. The conditions that led Jesus to speak of a sin that will not be forgiven have never existed since Christ walked on our earth.

Why are some people worried that they may have committed this terrible sin and be beyond hope? Partly because some human beings are in the grip of anxiety and have focused on this biblical incident to explain their fears. But partly, too, because some have never grasped the wonder of the gospel, which offers a full and complete salvation to anyone who believes.

The people who wonder if God will save *them* are often those who *already believe* that Jesus saves. A person who denied Jesus as fully as the religious leaders of his own time would never consider the possibility that Jesus is God or that he or she needs to be saved.

Will Jesus save the anxious person who fears he or she is beyond the reach of Christ's love? For all such there is Jesus' own promise: "Whoever comes to me I will never drive away" (John 6:37). Do you believe Jesus *can* save? Now you have his promise. Come to him. He will never cast you out. Salvation truly is yours, and you can be at peace.

UNION WITH CHRIST

Some people believe that religious language is made up of words without meaning. This notion has philosophical roots: Only words that denote things that can be verified by the senses (as one can touch or see the solid reality of a tree) have meaning. Words about abstract concepts, like God, have no real meaning, and one cannot even apply notions like "true" or "false" to them. Undoubtedly the Christian's belief in a union between believers and Jesus Christ would seem like meaningless jargon to such people.

Of course, the phrase "union with Christ" isn't meaningless. It is no more meaningless than words like *love* or *hope*. You may not be able to touch or hear or see or taste or measure hope, but it is just such unmeasurable things that have the greatest impact on human experience.

So it is with our union with Jesus. Materialists, whose idea of reality locks them into those things that have physical existence, may never acknowledge the possibility. But we have seen our lives and the lives of others transformed by union with Jesus. We experience daily the benefits that flow to us because we are in fact and in reality intimately linked to Jesus Christ, who is the source of our salvation and of all that is good in our present life.

Union in Christ's death and resurrection. Romans 6 teaches that the baptizing work of the Holy Spirit has united us to Jesus in his death: "We were therefore buried with him through baptism into death in order that just as Christ was raised from the dead through the glory of the Father, we too may live a new life" (Rom. 6:4). ◆ **BAPTISM** In this union we died, and in this union we live. God considers this union so real that Christ could carry our sins to the cross and his resurrection life can flow into us.

Romans 7 suggests an imperfect but clear analogy. A couple who marry also form a union, and under the law, they are one. Both their assets and liabilities are shared as long as they live. Should a pauper marry a millionaire, the millionaire's wealth becomes the wealth of the spouse as if both participated in gaining it. Our union with Jesus is even more a union than is marriage. Faith in Jesus makes us one with him. In this relationship all he has done is credited to us, and that resurrection life he possesses is a resource on which you and I can freely draw.

Romans 6 goes on to challenge us to live in the light of our union with Jesus. Believing that we died with Christ and that we live in him, we count ourselves dead to sin. Because our union is real, we can choose to reject sin and instead, offer ourselves to God "as those who have been brought from death to life" (Rom. 6:13), committing every part of our body to him in the service of righteousness.

The power and impact of union with Jesus is reflected in Paul's confession in Galatians 2:20: "I have been crucified with Christ and I no longer live, but Christ lives in me. The life I live in the body, I live by faith in the Son of God, who loved me and gave himself for me."

Union with Christ's body. The New Testament teaches that all believers are linked with Jesus and each other in an organic union. The only image adequate to express this reality is that of a living body, an organism. In this one body Jesus is the head, and each of us is a vital contributing part (see Rom. 12; 1 Cor. 12; Eph. 4).

There are many implications of this aspect of our union. Each of us draws our life from the head, who is the source of our vitality. Each of us receives guidance and direction. ▶ BODY OF CHRIST, HEAD

Because the body is real and we are united to Jesus in it, we are also united to other Christians. At last we can know what it means not to be alone. As Christians live together in growing love, we experience a belonging and acceptance that only Jesus' people can know.

Living in union with Jesus. Because talk of union with Jesus is not a meaningless jumble of empty words, we can experience an inner transformation that changes us and every relationship. In beautiful imagery Jesus spoke of himself as a vine and of believers as branches. Because of the vital principle of life that flows through the vine, its branches can bear fruit. Jesus speaks passionately of God's desire that we bear fruit, and he tells us the secret: "Abide [remain] in me" (John 15:5-7). Our union with Jesus is real, and we live experientially in that union as trusting obedience keeps us in the center of God's love (John 15:9-14).

And what is the fruit of our union with Jesus? The fruit of our union, fruit produced by the Holy Spirit sent by Jesus to live within us, is the love, joy, peace, patience, goodness, gentleness, and other traits that show the transformation of sinners into righteous women and men. ♦ RIGHTEOUS

Is our union with Jesus only meaningless words? Never! It is in our union with Jesus that we find our hope, and through our union with Jesus we find the power to truly love.

UNITY

People ask, Why are there so many denominations? Why do you have different beliefs? Why are some Christians political, while others draw back from involvement? For many people such differences are inconsistencies that raise questions about the validity of Christianity itself.

At the same time such people never seem to ask about their country, Why do we have different political parties? Why are some people conservative and others liberal? How can some be for capital punishment and others against it? How can some want a stronger federal government and others want to shift responsibilities to the states?

Should such questions be asked, the reaction might be, What do you mean? We may differ, but we are all Americans.

Perhaps it is fair to give the same answer to those questions about Christianity. Why even ask? We may differ, but we are all Christians! Neither Christian faith nor American citizenship demands that persons give up their differences and become cookie-cutter copies of each other. Both faith and citizenship allow for a wide range of individual differences and preferences.

Still some Christians have missed this rather obvious point. They see in Jesus' High Priestly Prayer our Lord's desire that "they be brought to complete unity to let the world know that you sent me and have loved them even as you have loved me" (John 17:23). And they conclude that this unity does not exist in Christianity. To them, unity must be marked by a single denomination, a single doctrinal statement, a single organized superchurch. But is this kind of unity even implied in our New Testament?

The verse in John 17 asks that Jesus' followers be brought "to one." In Romans 15:5, the "spirit of unity" spoken of is literally "give you the same mind. . . ." In context Paul is speaking of unity in worship, with "one heart and mouth . . . glorify God" (Rom. 15:6). Ephesians 4:3 and

4:13 speak of "unity," and Colossians 3:14 identifies love as that which binds other virtues together in unity. There are few clues in these passages to suggest the massive organizational unity that some claim we must desire.

Another New Testament word expresses the unanimity and concerted action that, at its best, marked the early church. The word is *homothumadon* (found in Acts 1:14; 2:1, 46; 4:24; 5:12; 7:57; 8:6; 12:20; 15:25; 18:12; 19:29 and Rom. 15:6). In looking through these passages, we see the church praying, worshiping, and reaching decisions together. Here, and in the term itself, we have a fascinating image of shared lives. For *homothumadon* pictures, not a thousand trumpets blowing the same note, but a great orchestra. As the different instruments are tuned, we can imagine discords. But under the baton of a great conductor, we hear those same instruments blend, each pouring out its distinctive sounds in what becomes one great, complex symphony.

Perhaps this is the unity for which Christ prays, not a unity in uniformity but a unity in a diversity that blends together as each tradition and person recognizes the lordship of Jesus and responds to his direction, pouring out its contribution to a complex, beautiful whole.

What seems so striking to us is not what makes us different from each other, but that underneath it all we are bound together by what we hold in common. In fact, Paul reminds us that there "is one body and one Spirit — just as you were called to one hope when you were called — one Lord, one faith, one baptism, one God and Father of us all" (Eph. 4:4–6). There is a single body of Christ, to which all of us are joined when we trust the Lord (1 Cor. 12:13). These realities exist and remind us that despite our differences, we who trust Jesus Christ are brothers and sisters in a single family. On this mystical but very real level, Christian unity does exist and is a basic fact of Christian faith.

What Paul urges in both Ephesians and 1 Corinthians is that we live in the context of our unity. Ephesians 4 urges us to "make every effort to keep the unity of the Spirit through the bond of peace." The same passage begins, "Be completely humble and gentle; be patient, bearing with one another in love" (Eph. 4:2–3). In 1 Corinthians 12, Paul calls on us to be open to each other's gifts, to honor each other, and to be ready to weep with those who weep and rejoice with those who rejoice. A similar thought is seen in Philippians where Paul calls for like-mindedness, being "one in spirit and purpose" (Phil. 2:2). The apostle prescribes, "Do nothing out of selfish ambition or vain conceit, but in humility consider others better than yourselves. Each of you should not look only to your own interests, but also to the interests of others" (Phil. 2:3–4).

Adding up this testimony, it seems that Christians are to maintain a unity that already exists, not by organizational conformity but by an attitude of openness and love. It is this attitude that permits us to accept each other despite our differences.

So it is best to look at Christian unity with a distinct perspective shaped by Scripture. First, we affirm that there is one Christian faith to which we all subscribe. Our basic unity in belief and conviction rests on Scripture's revelation of reality and on personal relationship with God through Jesus Christ. That oneness exists today as it has through the ages, for the core of Christian faith is held in common by all believers. Second, we acknowledge our differences. We differ in traditions, practices, worship, as well as in the way we look at and formulate our common beliefs. But these differences do not destroy unity. Instead they blend as an orchestra blends, for no single instrument is capable of expressing the full range of beauty that exists in a symphony. Third, we realize that Christians are charged with the task of maintaining a spiritual unity that already exists. This unity is expressed not in organizational mergers but in the love, acceptance, and humility that we are to adopt in our dealings with each other. What better way could we show the world the unity for which Christ prayed? We affirm before all people the fact that we differ, but we still love each other as members of the one family of our God.

WILL OF GOD

Christians speak of the "will of God" in two senses. One is deeply personal. We believe that God cares about the choices each person makes and that he wants to guide us in the choices that shape our lives. The other is majestic and awesome. We believe that God has made choices of his own, and those choices that express his will — his purposes and plans — will stand firm through time and into eternity.

God's plans and purposes. We scan the Old Testament and constantly meet a God who announces ahead of time what he will do. ♦ COVENANT, PROPHECY, PREDESTINATION As the Lord says through the prophet, "Surely, as I have planned, so it will be, and as I have purposed, so it will stand" (Isa. 14:24).

The New Testament shows the same conviction. God's will often indicates his purposes, which in view of who he is stand as absolutely determined. ♦ SOVEREIGNTY In this sense it is clear that God's will has determined many things that affect you and me.

The new birth we enjoy is not rooted in the human will but in God's will (John 1:13; 1 Peter 1:21). God has absolutely determined that everyone who looks to the Son and believes in him will have eternal life (John 6:38–40). Jesus died according to the fixed purposes and determined will of God (Acts 4:28). Jesus has rescued us from this present evil world according to God's will (Gal. 1:4), and a whole series of divine choices characterize his plan of salvation (Eph. 1:5–11). It is awesome to realize that God's will is the controlling reality in our universe. But it is stunning to realize that the focus of God's purpose is our salvation. The passages that emphasize God's determined will are passages that emphasize God's determination to bring us to himself in Jesus Christ.

The idea of a sovereign God, whose will controls, is hardly frightening to Christians. We know him too well to fear him; we know him as our God of love.

God's guiding will. Colossians 1:9–14 looks at the relationship of "that which God has willed" to our personal growth and goodness. Here and in other passages (see Acts 18:21; Rom. 2:18; 1 Peter 2:15) the phrase indicates what God has revealed to us in the Scriptures. This is the first principle on which we operate in seeking to live according to God's will. We are convinced that God has expressed what he plans to do and what he wants us to do. We "do the will" of the Father by responding to his revealed standards and desires (Matt. 7:21; Mark 3:35). Practicing that "good and pleasing and perfect" will of God is a key to our personal transformation (Rom. 12:2).

But Christians believe there is an even more personal will of God for each person. We sense it in Jesus' prayer in the Garden of Gethsemane, where he asks that if possible, the cup of his suffering might be removed. But Jesus' prayer concludes, "yet not as I will, but as you will" (Matt. 26:39). Like Jesus, Christians choose to submit, seeking what God wants for us. Like Paul we may often be uncertain about the future (Acts 18:21; Rom. 1:10). But we are also sure that plans made without dependence on God and a willingness to submit to him display an evil attitude (James 4:15).

The passages that speak of God's will for us do not explain how we can be sure a particular choice is in God's will. For some Christians this is a mystical, subjective thing; for others it is simply a matter of planning with prayer. But we do know that as we live close to the Lord, he will show us step by step what his will for us is (John 7:17; 1 John 5:14). God has given us his Holy Spirit to be with us always. As we step out in faith, committed to do God's will, we trust the Spirit to guide us in the choices that will keep our lives on his intended path. ◆ **HOLY SPIRIT**

WITNESS OF THE SPIRIT

People may ask us, How do you *know* that you belong to God? It sometimes bothers outsiders that we exude an assurance about our relationship with God. But there really is an assurance that comes to us with faith in Jesus. We know that we know God. We know that Christ has saved us and that heaven is assured. We know that Jesus is present with us now, walking with us in our life on earth.

So how can we claim to know? We have two bases for our assurance. The first basis is objective. We have the clear testimony of Scripture, the recorded promise that all who believe in Jesus Christ pass from death to life. We believe that Word from God and base our claim of assurance on it.

The second basis of Christian assurance is subjective. We have an inner testimony that matches the objective, external testimony of Scripture. Deep within us our own spirit and the Holy Spirit unite, and the conviction that salvation has come pervades us. Our assurance is not just an intellectual thing. It is emotional certainty as well as cognitive conviction. This certainty is so great that our attitudes, perspective, and choices are affected. We know that we are God's own now, and all of life becomes different as that assurance grows.

Christians understand this subjective, transforming certainty as the "witness of the Spirit" spoken of in Romans 8:15–16: "You did not receive a spirit that makes you a slave again to fear, but you received the Spirit of sonship. And by him we cry, '*Abba*, Father.' The Spirit himself testifies with our spirit that we are God's children."

We are not being presumptuous when we claim to know that we belong to God; not at all. We are simply declaring our confidence that God keeps the promises he makes to us in his Word. And we are simply testifying that when we believed, an inner certainty gripped us, a certainty that we recognize as the whispered witness of the Holy Spirit of God.

WORD OF GOD

This phrase is probably one of the most familiar of Christian phrases. It occurs hundreds of times in the Scripture. And there the "word of God" means more than "the Bible." The phrase focuses on communication. God has spoken, revealing both truth and himself to us. ◗ REVELATION, SCRIPTURE His every revelation, recorded for us in the words of Scripture, is "right and true," and we rely on that revelation completely.

But the "word of God" is also a powerful image of God's vital presence in human affairs. God's word was the creative force that brought our universe into existence. As Psalm 33:6 says, "By the word of the LORD were the heavens made, their starry host by the breath of his mouth." God's words of covenant promise initiated relationship with his people. His "ten words" (his commandments, see Deut. 4:31) established the moral order. His words coming through the prophets proclaim both judgment and salvation. In words so powerful that they give shape to history before it happens, God announces, "I make known the end from the beginning, from ancient times, what is still to come" (Isa. 46:10). More than the book in which they are recorded, God's words give existence, shape, and form to the universe and to our lives.

In the New Testament the Greek term that picks up the deepest meaning of "word" is *logos*. It, too, expresses the active presence of God, communicated in event as well as through spoken words. The words uttered by Jesus make the sick and maimed whole and drive demons away (Matt. 8:8–16; Luke 7:7). The words spoken by Jesus are so powerful that they bring life to the dead and reverse spiritual decay (John 5:24; 17:17; 1 Peter 1:23). Jesus' words call for response, and our response is not to some dead page of print but to God himself. As we take Jesus' words to heart, keeping and obeying them, we are drawn ever deeper into a vital love relationship with the Lord (John 8:31–32; 14:15–24).

At times in our New Testament, the *logos* is the gospel itself, expressing all that Jesus is for humanity. And even today the Holy Spirit is active in the Word, speaking within believers to give Scripture's recorded terms their deepest and truest meanings.

John's gospel opens with the revelation that Jesus is himself the pre-existent *logos*, the Word that existed forever as and with God. In his incarnation Jesus so fully expresses who God is that he could say, "No one has ever seen God, but God the only Son, who is at the Father's side, has made him known" (John 1:1–18).

And so the Word expresses God's vital self-expression in the totality of his involvement in his universe and in our lives. He creates and recreates, commands, judges, and saves. He steps into our world in person, invites us to relationship with him, and continues to guide us along life's way.

When we speak of the "Word of God," we also mean the Bible. We believe that God has expressed himself in words and has given us a true account of his acts and intentions. In the written Word we have trustworthy knowledge, and in the written Word we come face to face with God. We take his written Word to heart and act on what he has revealed, for such expression of faith in him is his desire.

But when we say "the Word of God," we affirm more than the book. We confess our faith that God has expressed himself in all his acts in history and in Jesus Christ, showing us who he is and who he wants to be for you and me.

WORLD

A number of words in the Greek New Testament are translated "world." One simply means "earth," usually as ground rather than water or air. Another carries the popular meaning of "the inhabited earth." It is the third word, *kosmos*, that has given shape to the suspicious attitude of many Christians toward this world and toward the time and society in which they live.

The word *kosmos* basically means "order" or "arrangement." It can mean the whole order of created things or simply the world as that place where human beings live out their brief life span. But *kosmos* is also a theological term, and many Christians tend to use the word *world* in a theological sense. In this sense the word *world* suggests a human society and system that are warped and twisted by sin, surging with the blind beliefs and passions of a spiritually deadened humankind. The New Testament calls this world a dark system (Eph. 6:12), energized by principles that are not from God (Col. 2:20; 1 John 2:16). The entire system lies under Satan (1 John 5:19) and constitutes that kingdom of his from which we have been delivered by Christ (Col. 1:13–14). The world system is hostile to God (1 Cor. 2:12; 3:19; 11:32; Eph. 2:2; James 1:27; 4:4; 1 John 2:15–17). It expresses and encompasses everything from which Christians want to draw back.

But the warped society of the world is our society, too. It is the environment in which Christians must live. Thus we have an ambivalent attitude toward it. This ambivalence is reflected in Scripture, too. Christians have been sent by Jesus to live "in the world" but are to resist being "of" the world (John 17:14–18). We are to love the human beings caught in the world's webs; we are not to withdraw from them or to judge them (1 Cor. 5:9–13). We are to establish bridges of relationship and caring with unbelievers, but we are not to be unequally yoked to them (2 Cor. 6:14–18).

Living in the world is also dangerous. We may be drawn into the world's ways of thinking and acting. Paul urges Christians not to be squeezed into the world's mold, but to be transformed by God's renewal of our minds (Rom. 12:1). We are to live our earthly lives not for "evil human desires" but rather by the will of God (1 Peter 4:2). John defines what in this world is distinctively "not from the Father." He speaks of the "cravings of sinful man" and the "lust of his eyes" and the "boasting of what he has and does" (1 John 2:15–17). It is not that we possess "worldly" things; it is that "worldly" ideas and attitudes possess us.

When we hold the values of society instead of God's values, when we desire what others desire rather than what God desires, when our pride is rooted in what we have and do rather than in God, then in John's words we "love the world" and the "love of the Father" is not in us.

It has been all too easy for Christians to miss the meaning of the Bible's teaching about the world. Some of us have ignored it and identified ourselves completely with our time and our society. God's kingdom and America (or Britain or Peru) have seemed one and the same, and Christian faith is merely a means to social reform. Others of us have overemphasized the wickedness of the world and made it an excuse for some monastic withdrawal. Still others have missed the point entirely and have identified worldliness with such things as dancing, movie going, and smoking. These distortions have led many Christians to wonder just what the "world" is. They use the word with mild distaste but without understanding.

What the Bible teaches about the world is simple. Scripture says we are called to love God and to judge ourselves. Love for God demands that we look at our desires and see if they are in harmony with his own or if they reflect the passions of the unsaved. Love for the Father demands that we look at our attitudes and see if they have been shaped by a growing understanding of God's Word or if they mirror distorted attitudes expressed in our society. Love for the Father demands that we examine our ways to see if they copy the lives of the lost around us or if they imitate the life of Jesus. The world outside is no danger to Christians. It is the world inside that is our peril.

So we live in our warped societies, and we try to be good citizens. We try to be loving friends to all around us. We try to do good. Above all, we try to be different, moved not by the cravings of sinful people but by the love of God.

WORSHIP

The Book of Revelation draws back the curtains and invites us to peer into heaven itself. We are shown a throne, encircled by an emerald rainbow, ablaze with flashing lightning, aquiver with rumbling thunder. Surrounding the throne are living creatures and elders of our race, giving glory, honor, and thanks to the one who sits on the throne, worshiping him who lives forever and ever. Bowing before him, all cry out their praise: "You are worthy, our Lord and God, to receive glory and honor and power, for you created all things, and by your will they were created and have their being" (Rev. 4:11). This, in a single image, captures the Christian concept of worship.

The key words translated "worship" in the Old Testament and New Testament have a common meaning. The central pair of words means simply "to bow down," or "to prostrate oneself in respect." The secondary pair of words (associated in the Old Testament with ritual practices and in the New Testament with heart attitude and lifestyle) indicates worshipfully serving the Lord.

Bowing down is significant because it portrays a recognition of our creaturehood. We bow down: He is lifted up. Worship is lifting up the Lord, focusing our attention on who he is and what he has done, and voicing praise. Worship has God as its object. Worship is giving him glory, honor, and thanks. ♦ **PRAISE**

Worship is also expressed in a heart attitude and lifestyle that likewise give God the central place. Romans 12:1 calls on us, "in view of God's mercy, to offer your bodies as living sacrifices, holy and pleasing to God — which is your spiritual worship." To live always with a sense of who God is, to "love God with all your heart and with all your soul and with all your mind," is worship indeed.

From the beginning Christians have shared in public worship, even as Israel's relationship to God was celebrated at worship festivals in which all of the people were involved. Christian worship services, as we trace them in church history, have commonly involved hearing the Word of God, prayers, hymns, confession, doxologies, benedictions, as well as celebration of the Lord's Supper. While patterns and forms have changed throughout the centuries, the primary elements of our public worship have remained the same.

Not every Christian tradition has maintained a strong stance on public worship. At times, our church services focus so much on teaching or on evangelistic preaching that the Godward lift of the heart is lost. At times Christian music celebrates the feelings of believers more than the wonderful works and attributes of God. While instruction is important and while our experiences are important to share, it is vital that worship focuses our thoughts and hearts on God so that we can give him glory together.

Why is worship important to Christians? Simply because God is who he is, and worship is his desire (John 4:23) and his due.

Great is the LORD and most worthy of praise;
    his greatness no one can fathom.
One generation will commend your works to another;
    they will tell of your mighty acts.
They will speak of the glorious splendor of your majesty,
    and I will meditate on your wonderful works.
They will tell of the power of your awesome works,
    and I will proclaim your great deeds.
They will celebrate your abundant goodness
    and joyfully sing of your righteousness.
My mouth will speak in praise of the LORD.
    Let every creature praise his holy name
    for ever and ever.

(Ps. 145:3–7; 21)

WRATH OF GOD

It seems like a grim item with which to close a book on the vocabulary of Christian faith. But the wrath of God is, in more than one sense, a message of hope.

It seems strange, because Scripture warns us against anger. Although anger may be justified, it too easily leads us to sin. The Old Testament calls it a cause of strife (Prov. 30:33) and something cruel (Prov. 22:24) to be avoided (Prov. 29:8). The New Testament bluntly commands us to "get rid of all bitterness, rage and anger" and replace them with kindness and compassion (Eph. 4:31–32).

Some people have argued that it is inconsistent for God to tell us to forego revenge and be compassionate and yet be angry himself. But both testaments speak of the wrath of God, and they use the same Hebrew and Greek terms that are used to identify human anger. But there are vast differences between God's anger and our own.

In the first place, God's anger is never capricious and is never expressed in uncontrollable tantrums. God's anger is a righteous anger, provoked only by sin. What God becomes angry about is injustice. Exodus 22:22–24 says, "Do not take advantage of a widow or an orphan. If you do and they cry out to me, I will certainly hear their cry. My anger will be aroused." This and other violations of relationship are pictured in the Old Testament as the cause of divine wrath (Deut. 4:23–26; 29:23–28). God's anger is kindled when he is not trusted (Exod. 4:14), when he is disobeyed (Numbers 21:6), and when he is spurned for false deities (Exod. 32:10–12).

It would be totally wrong to see God as some unemotional,

uninvolved force who is unaffected by the doings of humanity. The God we worship cares intensely. That caring is expressed both in the anger that moves him to punish and in the compassion that leads him to forgive. But always God's wrath is tempered, and while his anger is momentary, his favor lasts a lifetime (Ps. 30:5).

The stereotype of an angry Old Testament God is inaccurate, for it suggests an uncontrollable wrath aroused by trifles. On the contrary, the Old Testament pictures a loving God who is moved by righteous anger, whose wrath is exercised in necessary punishment of sin. Even then God's wrath is ultimately for our good. Disciplinary punishments may bring reform, and the destruction of the evil may free us to enjoy a life of peace.

However angry God becomes, his wrath is never the controlling factor in his choices. We human beings, falling so short of perfection, can never know a truly righteous anger. Only the Lord is "the compassionate and gracious God, slow to anger, abounding in love and faithfulness, maintaining love to thousands, and forgiving wickedness, rebellion and sin. Yet he does not leave the guilty unpunished" (Exod. 34:6).

So Christians do not apologize for the Old Testament's angry God. We see justice in the Flood as he judged a wicked world (Gen. 6:1–7). We honor God's anger at Egypt's persecution of his people as he punished Egypt with plagues (Exod. 15:7). We respect his right to use the pagan armies with which he punished his idolatrous people, Israel (Isa. 10:5). God's anger and God's acts of judgment are both justified, and the anger of God, aroused by sin, is rightly to be feared by people and nations who stray from righteousness.

The New Testament emphasizes the love of God, but even Jesus continues to warn us against God's anger. Wrath in the New Testament is focused on those who refuse to respond to the offer of a salvation purchased by the death of God's own Son (John 3:36; Rom. 3:5; Eph. 2:3). That wrath is never directed at us because Jesus has paid fully for the sins of all who believe in him. Everything that arouses God's anger is forgiven for Jesus' sake. But the unsaved, who still bear the guilt of their own sins, remain in the court of a God who must and who will judge sin.

But there is another striking feature of the New Testament's teaching on the wrath of God. God's wrath is not treated as something that people need to fear now, except as it might be exercised indirectly through government or natural consequences. When the New Testament speaks of God's wrath, it speaks of history's end, when Christ will return and "in blazing fire with his powerful angels, he will punish those who do not know God and do not obey the gospel of our Lord Jesus" (2 Thess. 1:7–8). Only at history's end, but surely then, God's wrath will be unleashed (Luke 21:23; Rom. 2:5–8; 9:22; 1 Thess. 1:10; 2:16).

Why this delay? Romans 2:4 tells us that it is because God is rich in kindness, tolerance, and patience. God is holding back in order to provide people with an opportunity to repent. The withholding of God's wrath is one hallmark of this day of forgiveness and grace. Those who stubbornly resist and reject his grace store up "wrath against yourself for the day of God's wrath, when his righteous judgment will be revealed" (Rom. 2:5).

Our God is no stranger to anger. His wrath is not to be dismissed lightly as if love rules out righteous anger and compassion drains sin of its evil. God remains God, and human sin arouses his wrath and merits his punishment.

Christians see the fullest expression of God's wrath in his greatest act of love. On Calvary Jesus died because of sins, bearing the punishment that we deserve. And yet that terrible act of judgment opens the door to forgiveness for all who accept it as Christ's gift. Only the punishment of sin by our righteous God could clear the way for him to welcome us in love.

So how does word of the wrath of God become a message of hope? In many ways. In God's wrath we see God as a person who cares deeply and is fully involved. A force or thing could never heed our cries, but a person with the emotional capacity to care deeply may.

Word of the wrath of God is a message of hope for another reason, too. We see the things that arouse God's anger, and we sense his commitment to the good and right. We take hope from the fact that there is morality rooted in the universe, that mere might does not make right, and the strong will not overcome the weak.

Word of the wrath of God is a message of hope because it helps us understand the death of Jesus. God unleashed wrath's destroying bolt, crushing the one who hung there on the cross. And then the good word comes: It was the punishment for our sins he suffered, for he had none of his own. The cross exhausted the wrath of God as sin's full penalty was paid, and from that same cross there now flows forgiving love.

Word of the wrath of God is a message of hope for us who believe, because we know that Jesus died to deliver us from the wrath to come (1 Thess. 5:9).

Finally, word of God's wrath is a message of hope even for the unsaved. It is a word of wrath withheld, a promise of a day of grace when salvation can still be found. And it is also a warning most stern. If the Son of God, who died for sinners, seems unworthy of your trust, then wrath will surely come when he returns.

Wrath has its honored place in the vocabulary of our faith. Even the wrath of God reminds us of his love. And even fear of punishment to come is intended to turn our eyes to Jesus and his forgiving love.

Index

(NOTE: Numbers in italics indicate beginning page of major entries in text)